THE AMERICAN ARCHAEOLOGIST

With much gratitude and great affection,
this book is dedicated to
Dale Child.

The American Archaeologist

A Profile

MELINDA A. ZEDER

ALTAMIRA
PRESS

A Division of Sage Publications, Inc.
Walnut Creek ▪ *London* ▪ *New Delhi*

PUBLISHED IN COOPERATION WITH
THE SOCIETY FOR AMERICAN ARCHAEOLOGY

For information contact:

AltaMira Press
A Division of Sage Publications, Inc.
1630 North Main Street, Suite 367
Walnut Creek, California 94596
U.S.A.
explore@altamira.sagepub.com

Sage Publications Ltd.
6 Bonhill Street
London EC2A 4PU
United Kingdom

Sage Publications India Pvt. Ltd.
M-32 Market
Greater Kailash 1
New Delhi 110 04S
India

PRINTED IN THE UNITED STATES OF AMERICA

Library of Congress Cataloging-in-Publication Data

Zeder, Melinda A.
 The American Archaeologist : a profile / Melinda A.
    Zeder
   p. cm.
 Includes bibliographic references.
 ISBN 0-7619-9192-1 (cloth). — ISBN 0-7619-9194-8 (pbk.)
 1. Archaeologists—Employment—United States.
    2. Archaeologists—Education—United States.
    3. Archaeology—Research—United States.
    I. Title.
 CC107.Z43   1997
 331.7′619301′0973—dc21   97-33753
                                  CIP

97 98 99 00 01 02 03 10 9 8 7 6 5 4 3 2 1

Cover Design by Joanna Ebenstein
Production by Labrecque Publishing Services

Contents

List of Illustrations

FIGURES

Foreword

Patty Jo Watson
Washington University

Archaeologists in the Americas have become increasingly reflective in light of the Society for American Archaeology's 50th anniversary (1985), the 500th year after Columbus's arrival in the Western Hemisphere (1992), and the approaching turn of the millennium (2000). A series of special publications—such as *American Antiquity*'s 50th anniversary issue; Meltzer, Fowler, and Sabloff 1986; D. Thomas 1989–1991; and articles in *Archaeology* magazine's futurist issue—have summed up present processes and events in Americanist archaeology and looked to the future. In this summing-up mode, and to secure an empirical grip on the archaeological personnel in one major international organization, the governance group of the SAA launched a detailed questionnaire study in 1994 of its membership (approximately 5,000) and of some 1,000 nonmembers. Melinda A. Zeder agreed to coordinate the study and write up the results, which she has done with characteristic efficiency and élan, resulting in this landmark volume on the American archaeologist.

Most readers will find many of the results surprising and—in some instances—alarming. For example, in Chapter 4 we learn that a large number of private sector respondents judge their graduate training to have been seriously inadequate in preparing them for the sociopolitical reality of the current job market in archaeology. This is a clear indication that many archaeological curricula require substantial revision *now* if they are not to become entirely obsolete. Related findings indicate that archaeologists in the private sector, as a group, express higher job satisfaction than do archaeologists in other settings, such as academia. Zeder also points out, however, that the level of job satisfaction of archaeologists employed in various archaeological work settings seems at times to run counter both to employment preferences and to the actual conditions of employment in these various settings.

Another series of critical data in Chapter 4 center on the relative situations of women and men in archaeology. Gross gender inequity is no longer commonly present, but there are some disturbing new tendencies: as examples, more men than women leave academia at the MA level, apparently for rewarding private positions, while more women than men end up in short-term, marginal, and dead-end academic positions. Some of the gender-differentiated data—especially those on publishing (women publish less than men) and on personal lives (significantly more men are able to combine marriage and children with demanding careers than is possible for women, who continue to bear the major burdens of child-rearing)—are similar to those recently elicited by the American Anthropological Association's Committee to Study the Academic Employment of Women in Anthropology (Bradley and Dahl 1993; Hammel 1993; Webster and Burton 1992). Like the AAA's and other studies published over the past few years, the strong implication is that women and men were—and, to an unfortunate extent, still are—socialized quite differently (Brush 1991; Ogilvie 1986; Rossiter 1982, 1995; Sonnert and Holton 1995a, 1995b, 1996. See also the "Women in Science" series in *Science* March 13, 1992; April 16, 1993; March 11, 1994; and "How Much Money is Your Ph.D. Worth?" *Science* September 24, 1993: 1810–1813). That is, girls, as a social class, are not being taught how to compete and succeed in the way that boys are, from preschool on into college and through graduate school. Moreover, those differential socialization processes are apparently quite effective. Similar patterns in all the natural science fields (with the possible exception of biology) are now the focus of concern and attempts at remediation by the National Academy of Sciences (Davidson and Skidmore eds. 1993) and National Academy of Engineering (Matyas and Dix eds. 1992). Designers of archaeological curricula and of public-outreach initiatives must also address this issue explicitly, and soon, or the discipline of archaeology will be much the worse for it.

Rather than revealing any more of the punchlines in this book, I urge the reader to start reading; and I commend the SAA, the Questionnaire Committee, and Melinda Zeder for a monumental task well done. The self-study of Americanist archaeology they have designed and implemented will stand as a benchmark well into the 21st century.

About the Author

Melinda Zeder received her PhD from the University of Michigan in the 1980s award decade, 10.4 years after the receipt of her BA, and 7.4 years after receipt of an ongoing MA from the same institution. After completing her degree, she entered the private sector, directing a small firm that specialized in zooarchaeological analysis. In the early 1990s she assumed a position in a government museum setting as Deputy Chair of the Department of Anthropology at the Smithsonian Institution's National Museum of Natural History, where her work effort was directed primarily toward administration, repatriation, and collections management. She assumed her present position as Associate Curator of Old World Archaeology and Zooarchaeology in the Smithsonian's Center for Archaeobiological Research in 1992, and now devotes most of her effort to field and laboratory work and writing for publication (Figure 1). Her primary research interests focus on the archaeology of the Near East, although she maintains a secondary regional research interest in the southeastern United States. She has con- ducted field research in Iran, Turkey, Israel, and Syria. Her topical interests center on the origin and impact of food producing economies in the Near East, as well as on the role of animal economy in emergent complexity in both the Old and New Worlds. She uses zooarchaeological analysis as her primary research tool. She has published widely on these subjects, and is the author of *Feeding Cities: Specialized Animal Economy in the Ancient Near East*, and the co-editor, with Richard I. Meadow, of *Approaches to the Analysis of Animal Bones from the Middle East*. She was recently awarded the Gordon R. Willey Prize by the American Anthropological Association. She currently serves as Chair of the Senate of Scientists of the National Museum of Natural History. Married to another archaeologist, she has two dependent teenage daughters—one of whom recently spent a month with her counting goat bones in her field laboratory in the home of a bedouin family in northeastern Syria. She is highly satisfied with all aspects of her current employment, career trajectory, and with the training she received for her current position.

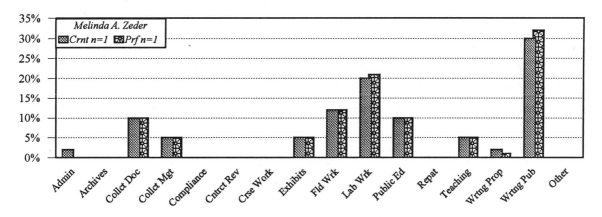

Fig. 1 *Current and Preferred Work Effort of the Author in a Government Museum Setting*

Note the correspondence between the percentage of work effort currently devoted to different activities and the profile of preferred activities, a correlation that is largely responsible for the high levels of career satisfaction expressed by the author.

Acknowledgments

This book, which presents a comprehensive analysis of the results of the 1994 SAA Census, is the culmination of a lengthy and complex project. It is a project that could not have been accomplished without the help and encouragement of a great many people whose contributions are gratefully acknowledged here. The SAA Census grew out of a long-felt need for a better understanding of the nature, interests, and needs of the membership of the Society for American Archaeology, the largest organization of professional archaeologists in the world. The Census project was given official sanction by the SAA Executive Board in late 1992 when I was asked, as Chair of the SAA Membership Committee, to undertake the task of designing and implementing a survey of SAA members. I was aided in the initial design phase by the members of the Membership Committee, who provided their varied and diverse insights into what questions we should ask, and how we should go about asking these questions. The members of the committee were Jeffery Hantman, Rosemary Joyce, Mark Lynott, Elizabeth Moore, and Joseph Sculdenrine.

It is through the input of these committee members, and a number of other interested groups and individuals, that the project grew from a more narrowly focused membership survey of a single professional society to a robust census aimed at achieving an empirically based perspective on the status and health of archaeology in America today. In particular, I would like to acknowledge the input of individuals who participated in two panel workshops for government and private sector archaeologists held at the SAA annual meeting in St. Louis in 1993: Adrienne Anderson, Judy Bense, Dennis Blanton, Jon Czaplicki, William Doelle, Jeff Hantman, John Jameson, Shereen Lerner, Mark Lynott, Virgil Noble, Larry Nordby, Joe Schuldenrein, and Don Weir. I would also like to recognize the input of SAA Executive Board members who received various drafts of the Census and provided useful comments on its content.

A particularly active voice in the framing of the Census instrument that deserves special recognition is the SAA's Committee for the Status of Women in Archaeology (COSWA), which provided lengthy comments and suggestions for collecting the information on gender equity in archaeology that is one of the major themes of this book. In particular I would like to acknowledge the efforts of Barbara Stark, Miriam Stark, and Peggy Nelson, who deserve a great deal of credit for making sure that information needed to monitor the status of women in archaeology was captured by the Census.

I am also grateful to both the Society for Historical Archaeology (SHA) and the Society for Professional Archaeology (SOPA) for making available the instruments and summaries of the results of surveys they had conducted of their memberships. And I would like to thank the people who agreed to serve as test-marketing guinea pigs by filling out an early draft of the Census and providing their comments on both the format and the substance of the census instrument.

Many of these same groups and individuals participated in framing an exhaustive query protocol used to process the volume of data provided by the large response to the SAA Census. Here again, COSWA members were particularly active in providing an extensive list of questions to be asked of this remarkable data set. I would also like to thank John Yellen and Bonnie Magness-Gardiner for providing data on archaeological funding from NSF and NEH databases to compare with Census data on funding from these agencies.

Another aspect of the project was identifying the population to be included in the Census. Here the efforts of Veletta Canouts were especially helpful in providing extensive lists of names of federal, state, and avocational archaeologists from the National Park Service's Archaeology and Ethnography Program mailing list. This database was key to forming the population of non-SAA members who were asked to fill out the Census.

Bob Henrickson, who was enlisted to help in the implementation part of the project, helped select the nonmember sample by painstakingly cross-checking the large NPS database and the membership lists of SHA, SOPA, and the Southeastern Archaeological Conference (SEAC) against the SAA membership rolls. In particular, I would like to acknowledge Bob's tireless efforts in performing all the data entry and initial editing of entered data. This was a monumental task, and a task well done.

And of course the SAA Executive Office devoted considerable staff and financial resources to this project. I would like to especially acknowledge their extraordinary efforts in the design of the Census, in compiling lists of current and former SAA members and nonmember contract archaeologists, and in the massive project of producing, mailing, and collating the returned forms. Special thanks are due to Brighid Brady-de Lambert, David Whitlock, and Jim Young for assistance in composing the mailing list and mailing the Census; Janet Walker (as well as Karen Doehner and Mark Aldenderfer) for helping edit the summary articles of Census results published in the April and September 1997 issues of the *SAA Bulletin* (Zeder 1997a and b); and Tobi Brimsek, current SAA Executive Director, who assisted in the final write-up and review of Census results. Above all I would like to thank Ralph Johnson, former SAA Executive Director, whose upbeat, can-do attitude and shared passion for compulsive attention to detail played a major role in taking this project from its initial "neat idea!" phase to its realization as a book-length manuscript.

I would also like to recognize the patience and fortitude of Mitch Allen, Publisher of AltaMira Press, who, early on, saw a book in the project, and who stuck with me through the sometimes prickly processes of realizing this vision. I would also like to thank Production Manager Rachel Fudge and the staff of Labrecque Publishing for their considerable efforts in the copy editing and production phase of the publication of this book.

The support of the Smithsonian Institution was also critical in accomplishing this project. Recognizing this as a significant scholarly research endeavor with important implications for the discipline, I was able to devote large portions of my time over the past five years, and essentially all of my research time this past year, to the design, implementation, and analysis of Census results. In addition, the Smithsonian supplied significant financial support in the purchase of computer hardware and software needed to process and present these results. I am particularly grateful for the purchase of Harvard Graphics 3.0, which was used to produce the graphs that figure so prominently in this book. After this project I think I can rightfully fashion myself as something of a Harvard Graphics Poster Child.

A central figure in this effort has been Bruce Smith. Indeed, this whole thing was his idea. It was Bruce who, as President-elect of the SAA in 1992, proposed that a survey be conducted and that I direct the project. As President of the SAA from 1993 to 1995, he headed the SAA Executive Board, which sanctioned and supported the design, mailing, and initial data processing of the Census. As a Smithsonian colleague, he has given me invaluable advice, counsel, and support throughout the process of analyzing and presenting Census results.

My family is also due both thanks and apologies for having to put up with my single-minded attention to this project over the past several years, especially for having to listen to countless factoids about American archaeologists over the dinner table. My daughter, Katie Blackman, also helped collate and label data reports into the eight fat volumes of Census output that now line my shelves.

I especially want to recognize the efforts of Dale Child. A former senior programmer for the federal government, Dale has worked as a Smithsonian volunteer for the past 15 years, assisting with computer problems and projects. In particular, she has designed—and redesigned—all the data storage and processing packages I use in my research and curation activities. In 1995 Dale agreed to take on the thorny problem of producing reports on the large and unruly SAA Census database. Since then she has donated countless hours to transforming the raw Census data into a robust and accessible database, and generating the nearly 1,000 data reports used to write this book. She, for the most part without complaint, endured my seemingly endless requests to look at the data in a slightly different way—designing, running, and rerunning reports that added and eliminated students from the tabulations, focused on the research interests of retired males, compared the salaries of private sector women living in the Northeast to those in the Southwest—almost to the extent of tabulating the publications of left-handed lapsed Catholics in their 50s living in Walla Walla. She was the heart of this project, as she has been in much of my research over the past 15 years, and it is in grateful acknowledgment of all of her efforts that I dedicate this book to her.

Finally, I want to thank the 1,677 individuals who took time from their busy schedules to fill out and return the Census form. Not only did these people candidly respond to eight pages of sometimes intrusive questions about their education, employment, interests, and aspirations, many also provided lengthy, if at times testy, commentary on the health and future directions of our profession. These people are the backbone of this project. For it is the information they provided that has built this profile of American archaeology on the cusp of the 21st century.

Taking the Pulse

Introduction

Drawing a Profile of the American Archaeologist

If you were to ask the man on the street for his image of an archaeologist, he would probably draw a profile taken directly from grade-B movies of the 1940s. An archaeologist is a short, rumpled male in his early 60s with a slightly crazed, faraway look in his eyes and a penchant for mummies and curses that will inevitably lead to his demise. Or else the person you've buttonholed would draw from a modern movie version of an archaeologist and paint a picture of a swashbuckling adventurer more at home in his action-packed, exotic field setting than in the ivy-covered university halls where between archaeological exploits he lectures to adoring coeds. In both cases the archaeologist would be male, white, university or museum based, and specializing in remote regions of the ancient world. If you were to remind your interviewee that some archaeologists are women, he would probably respond with a profile of the dishy daughter of the rumpled and doomed archaeologist, or that of a dowdy spinster in support hose and orthopedic shoes who has dedicated her matronly life to the study of some dead language or ancient fertility goddess.

Ask an archaeologist for such a profile and you are likely to get a less colorful yet somewhat more accurate portrayal. It would, however, be a profile drawn principally from his or her own singular context. The university archaeologist is likely to base his idealized portrait on the 50ish males who occupy the majority of tenured, full-professor positions these days and who devote, or would like to devote, most of their time to field research, writing, and an occasional graduate-level seminar. The government archaeologist might paint a picture of the public servant working for the preservation of archaeological resources for the public good. The private consultant will draw from his experience on the "front lines" of archaeology, struggling to conduct large-scale projects on time and on budget in a disciplinary environment that undervalues his contribution to the study of the human past. If the archaeologist is female, she might cast today's archaeologist in the image of a woman striving to make it in a male-dominated discipline in which the employment climate is slowly, perhaps reluctantly, turning from glacially resistant to only uncomfortably chilly. And while each of these portraits has a certain salience in today's archaeology, none capture the full range

of experience of the American archaeologist as we approach the year 2000. Moreover, none of these perspectives would give you an idea of the dynamic forces that are reshaping American archaeology today.

In the early 1990s the Society for American Archaeology (SAA) initiated a project designed to "take the pulse of archaeology in the Americas." The largest professional archaeological organization in the Americas, the SAA has a membership of more than 5,000 student, professional, and avocational archaeologists, representing virtually every archaeological work setting and every major disciplinary interest group in American archaeology today. Yet at the time the SAA had only a limited and largely impressionistic picture of its members. Who are they? Where do they work? What are they interested in? How do they spend their time? There were no reliable answers to these basic questions. In late 1992 I was asked by the SAA Executive Board to design and implement a survey that would help the Society draw a more empirically grounded profile of its members. In undertaking this task I brought together a group of archaeologists representing major constituencies of the archaeological community, university- and museum-based professional and student archaeologists, government archaeologists, private sector archaeologists, and archaeologists interested in the status of women in the discipline. Together we designed a rather more ambitious survey instrument than had first been envisioned—an eight-page Census that sought to build a detailed and comprehensive picture not just of the SAA membership, but of our profession as a whole. The Census was mailed to the more than 5,000 SAA members, as well as a sample of 1,000 non-member archaeologists. The nearly 1,700 Census forms returned to us represent a quite respectable response rate of about 30 percent. These responses tell a compelling story of a discipline in the midst of significant change.

Tracing Primary Themes

Broadly speaking, Census results illuminate two major overarching and related themes in American archaeology. One concerns the changing face of the archaeological workforce, focusing in particular on the status of women and men in the discipline. The other involves the changing nature of the workplace, principally caused by the growth of private and public sector archaeology. In many areas there have been significant strides toward gender equity in American archaeology. Women are increasingly better represented in the archaeological workforce, especially in academic work settings. There is greater gender equity in the proportion of females with advanced degrees and in the amount of time it takes them to receive these degrees. The substantial difference between the salaries of men and women performing similar jobs with similar amounts of training and experience is narrowing among younger archaeologists. Yet there are also areas where long-standing inequities remain, and even where new ones may be emerging. For though a higher proportion of younger women than men are going into academia overall, there is a persistent, if not increasing, tendency for women in academia to occupy nontenure-track positions with more limited potential for advancement and job security. Although salary imbalances between men and women who have more recently entered the archaeological workforce are smaller than they are among more senior archaeologists, salary differences still persist between the younger men and women in similar positions, especially in academic and museum settings. While there is parity between men and women in both the submission and the ultimate success of applications for funding to support archaeological research, almost all sources of archaeological funding show major disparities in the levels of funding allocated to men and women. Moreover, women continue to make greater personal sacrifices in their family lives to pursue careers in archaeology. They both marry less frequently and are more likely to delay, or forgo, having children than are men.

A second major theme that emerges from the SAA Census is the growth of public and private sector archaeology, and the widening schism between archaeology as a business and archaeology as an academic pursuit. Federal and state legislation that mandates assessment of the cultural resources put at risk by both civil and private construction projects has spurred the development of multimillion-dollar archaeological businesses. The private firms and independent consultants that participate in this work represent the fastest-growing sector of the archaeological workforce. Not only do private sector archaeologists have greater earning potential than archaeologists in other work settings, the private sector also has one of the largest proportions of people who are highly satisfied with their current positions, and the smallest proportion who claim to be unsatisfied with their careers in archaeology. The increased awareness of the importance of preserving the nation's cultural heritage has also resulted in a parallel, though perhaps not as dramatic, growth in the proportion of the archaeological workforce employed in government settings (federal, state, and local). And though the salary potential of government archaeologists is not as great as it is for private sector or academic archaeologists, in government archaeology there is greater gender equity in salaries,

fewer employees are pegged to the lowest salary brackets, and archaeologists enjoy wider access to more comprehensive benefits than in any other employment setting. Moreover, while fewer government archaeologists claim to be highly satisfied with their jobs, there are also fewer people in government archaeology who are unsatisfied with their careers than in either academic or museum settings. Yet a significant number of people in these two growing sectors of archaeological employment believe the academic training they received failed to provide them with either realistic expectations for their current careers or the training necessary to succeed in these careers. Moreover, there is a growing sense that the theoretical underpinnings and methodological strategies of the archaeology practiced in universities and museums are seriously out of touch with the realities of archaeology in the private sector. The disaffection of private and public sector archaeologists from academic archaeology is already having an impact on the educational trajectories of younger archaeologists just embarking on their careers in archaeology, and may well be the most significant challenge facing American archaeology in the new millennium.

A variety of subplots and crosscutting themes also emerge from the SAA Census. The Census captures important trends in research interests: regional, theoretical, methodological, and topical. It allows us to compare the nature of archaeology practiced in different archaeological work settings, highlights how archaeologists spend their time, and offers insights into how and where archaeologists would prefer to practice their profession. It gives us a measure of the productivity of today's archaeologists and the avenues by which they present the results of their work. It lets us contrast the sources and volume of funding available by work setting, gender, and type of archaeological endeavor.

In short, the Census gives us the most comprehensive and complete picture of this profession ever drawn—one that, perhaps paradoxically for a field that looks to the past, is alive with change, potential, and new challenges. In some ways this picture is emblematic of current trends in many of the behavioral sciences that are also experiencing important sea changes in the demographics of their practitioners and in the nature of their practices. This is, then, a story for the professional archaeologist concerned about the health and future directions of the field, for the student charting a career in archaeology, and for the non-archaeologist interested in the sociology of the behavioral sciences in the later part of the 20th century.

Telling the Story

The story is told in eight parts. The remainder of this first chapter goes into more detail about the framing of the Census and the nature of the response. It also gives some practical guidelines for following the text, as well as the tabular and graphical presentation of Census results in the chapters that follow. Chapter 2, entitled "Profiling the American Archaeologist," examines demographic factors such as age and gender composition of American archaeologists, ethnic heritage and socioeconomic backgrounds, and marriage and family lives. Chapter 3, "Educating the American Archaeologist," examines current trends in the pursuit of higher academic degrees that prepare one for a career in archaeology. The archaeological employment setting is discussed in Chapter 4, "Archaeological Employment in the Americas." This more lengthy chapter looks at several aspects of archaeological positions, including employment trends in different archaeological work settings, rates of compensation both in terms of salaries and benefits and in terms of potential for promotion and salary growth over time, levels of career satisfaction, and employment preferences. The chapter also includes a more focused examination of positions in two major archaeological work settings—academia and the private sector. Chapter 5, "Archaeological Research in the Americas," examines current research trends, including regional research interests, research topics, schools of archaeological theory followed, and research tools used in the pursuit of archaeological questions. Chapter 6, "Publication and Professional Activities," traces trends in the publication and oral presentation of archaeology today, as well as the involvement of archaeologists in professional organizations that represent and promote American archaeology. This chapter is followed by a consideration of archaeological funding—Chapter 7, "Paying for American Archaeology?"—which examines both sources for more traditional research-oriented archaeology and those that fund the cultural resource management projects forming the core of private sector archaeology. Chapter 8, "What's Next?" presents a synthesis of the results of the Census, emphasizing, in particular, open questions and ongoing trends in American archaeology. This final chapter draws together the major crosscutting themes captured in the Census and developed throughout the book to form an overview of a profession undergoing a period of profound change in its composition, its goals, and its future directions.

The SAA Census

The Instrument

Designing the SAA Census instrument was an organic process that began in the fall of 1992 with the initial single goal of capturing basic demographic information about the SAA membership (that is, age, gender, work setting, and the like). Such information would not only help the Society better meet the needs of its current membership, it would also enhance its efforts to recruit new members. As chair of the Membership Committee charged with collecting this information, I wanted to make sure that the questionnaire we distributed addressed all sectors of the

archaeological community. So I asked five individuals to join me on the Membership Committee, knowing that they could add the perspectives of different archaeological constituencies to my own background as a museum-based research archaeologist. These individuals are Jeffery Hantman (University of Virginia), Rosemary Joyce (Phoebe Hearst Museum of Anthropology, former chair of the Committee for the Status of Women in Archaeology), Mark Lynott (National Park Service Midwest Archaeological Center), Elizabeth Moore (Virginia Museum of Natural History, then a graduate student at American University), and Joseph Sculdenrine (Geo-Archaeology Research Associates).

Since the mid to late 1980s there had been a number of other survey efforts directed at profiling American archaeology. In 1987, as part of an effort to chart the future of the SAA as it ended its management agreement with the American Anthropological Association, the SAA distributed a small survey that sampled demographic data and solicited opinions from about 700 SAA members (Evans 1988). In 1990–91 the Society of Professional Archaeologists (SOPA, an organization that certifies the credentials of member archaeologists and binds them to observe an established code of professional standards) sponsored a membership survey that collected information from just under 350 professional archaeologists (Lees 1991; Noble 1992). Perhaps the most ambitious of these earlier efforts was the 1991 membership survey sponsored by the Society for Historical Archaeology (SHA) that captured information about the careers, research interests, and workplace conditions of a little more than 800 historical archaeologists (Wall and Rothschild 1995). In addition, over the years the Committee for the Status of Women in Archaeology (COSWA), as well as individual scholars interested in issues of gender equity in archaeology, has conducted a number of small, formal, and more ad hoc survey efforts asking specific questions about the status of women in archaeology (see Nelson et al. 1994; Claassen 1994).

These efforts signaled a widespread recognition that American archaeology was entering a period of profound change and that there was a pressing need to gain an informed overview of the nature and scope of the changes that were taking place. Each of these efforts succeeded in providing important information about the membership of these different organizations or about specific issues that affected a certain sector of the archaeological workforce. However, the scope of these survey efforts was necessarily limited, both by the focused nature of the questions asked and by the size and composition of their respondent pools. As the largest professional archaeological society in the Americas, SAA has a membership that is not delimited by any specific research topic, time period, or even region (though an Americanist emphasis is clearly evident in its history and current membership). Moreover, SAA membership represents all archaeological work settings—academia and museums, government and the private sector—and includes as well a considerable number of avocational archaeologists. The SAA Census thus had the potential of reaching the broadest and most representative sample of archaeologists ever surveyed. As the Census team recognized the full scale of the challenge, we expanded our goals and ambitiously (even perhaps somewhat naively) decided to try to capture the most comprehensive picture possible of American archaeology in the late 20th century.

We made liberal use of earlier surveys in designing the SAA Census. Committee members also made extensive suggestions about the kinds of information that should be collected and how to most effectively frame the questions needed to solicit that information. To better represent the interests of government and private sector archaeologists, we hosted two roundtable discussions at the 1992 SAA meetings in St. Louis, and asked those who attended for comments on a draft version of the Census. Various drafts of the Census were also circulated for comment to other groups as well, including the SAA Executive Board, COSWA, and a "test market" group of about 20 individuals who filled out the questionnaire and gave us feedback about content, style, clarity, and length of time needed to complete it. Response to our appeals for assistance in designing the Census was enthusiastic and extremely helpful. COSWA was particularly active in helping frame the instrument and develop the data-processing protocol that we later used to help us tease out meaningful patterns from the Census responses. By the time we were ready to mail the Census in late January 1994, the instrument had grown to a hefty eight pages (Appendix) and included questions about family life, ethnic and socioeconomic origins; a means to look at degree status and years it takes to complete degrees; a grid monitoring percentage of effort spent in various different work settings performing a broad range of activities; questions about job and training satisfaction, salary levels and career trajectories, research interests, and publication; and an extensive section on funding.

The Sample

Since this was the first large-scale attempt to capture baseline information about the status of SAA members, rather than information from a selected sample of its members, we decided to distribute the questionnaire to the entire 5,000-plus membership. This full-coverage approach also avoided the problems associated with designing a representative sampling strategy. Lacking even basic information on the gender and age of members, let alone their work setting or research interests, there was in fact no way to implement a more selective sampling strategy.

As the project expanded from a simple membership survey to an attempt at painting a profile of American archaeology as a whole, it also became clear that we needed to solicit information from non–SAA members. Even though the SAA is the largest and most inclusive professional archaeological organization in the Americas, we believed it essential to also collect information from archaeologists who had chosen not to belong to the Society. To do this we included 1,000 non–SAA members, embracing former SAA members; contract archaeologists selected from a list compiled by the SAA; federal, state, and avocational archaeologists drawn from the National Park Service's Archaeology and Ethnography Program mailing list; and archaeologists taken from membership lists of the Society for Historical Archaeology (SHA) and the Southeastern Archaeological Conference (SEAC).

The Response

Although the ice storms of the winter of 1994 delayed delivery of the Census forms for up to six weeks in some cases, well after the March 15 return deadline, we still received nearly 1,700 completed Census forms out of 6,071 forms mailed—a 28 percent response rate (Figure 1.1a). The response rate for SAA members was even higher: 31 percent of the 5,071 members polled. Within the membership, the response rate of SAA nonstudent members was better than that of students; 35 percent (1,300) of nonstudent SAA members returned completed Census forms, compared to 19 percent (253) of student members. The strong representation of nonstudent, "professional" members in the Census responses is clearly seen in Figure 1.1b, which compares the distribution of the Census forms mailed to the returned responses by membership type. While "professional" SAA members comprised 61 percent of the total sample of Census forms mailed, this category of member was responsible for 78 percent of all Census forms completed and returned to us.

We can also examine the Census responses by region. For our purposes the sample is broken into 10 distinct regions: 6 regions in the United States (Figure 1.2), the U.S. Trust Territories, Canada, Latin America (Mexico, Central and South America), and responses from countries outside the Western Hemisphere (labeled "International" responses). When the SAA member response is broken down by region (Figure 1.3a), we see a fairly even response across all regions. Most regions registered a roughly 30 to 33 percent response rate, with a low of 27 percent in the Northeastern and Western United States and in the Trust Territories, and a high of 39 percent in the Southwestern United States. Given the mailing delays we experienced, the response rate of international members located outside of the Western Hemisphere (18 percent) was surprisingly high. While the regional distribution of Census responses resembles the actual regional distribution of SAA members (Figure 1.3b), the Midwest and Southwestern United

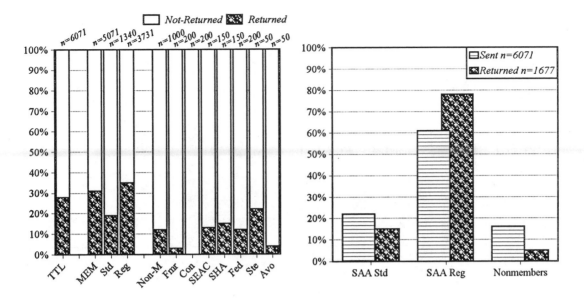

Fig. 1.1 *Response to the SAA Census by Membership Type*

a Proportion of Census forms returned

b Distribution of Census forms mailed and returned

Note the higher response of SAA members (especially "professional" members) when compared to nonmembers.

States are somewhat better represented in the Census responses than they are in the membership itself. Archaeologists from the Northeastern and Western states are somewhat underrepresented in our sample of returned Census forms, compared to their representation in the SAA membership rolls. And while the difference between the regional distribution of the SAA membership rolls and the Census responses is statistically significant (χ^2=50.35, df=9, p<.001), in no region is this difference greater than 4 percent.

The response of non–SAA members was, perhaps predictably, less robust (Figure 1.1a and b). Only 12 percent of the nonmembers polled responded to the Census, ranging from a puzzling 0 percent of the 200 contract archaeologists sampled, to a stronger 22 percent of the state archaeologists. The reason for this lower response rate from nonmembers may be attributable, at least in part, to some level of disaffection from the SAA. However, the fact that the nonmember Census forms were mailed about a week later than the forms mailed to members, likely

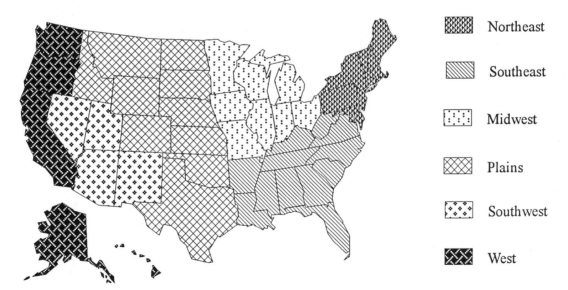

Fig 1.2 *Regions in the United States*

Northeast

Southeast

Midwest

Plains

Southwest

West

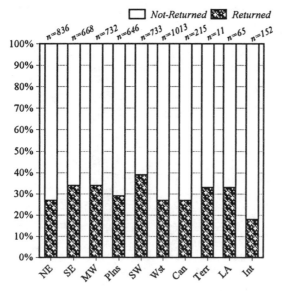

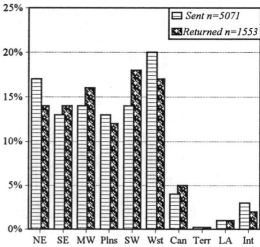

Fig. 1.3 *Response to the SAA Census by Region*

a Proportions of Census forms returned

b Distribution of Census forms mailed and returned

Note the generally even response in all regions.

arriving well after the stated return deadline, probably also contributed to the lack of response from these individuals.

Thus when interpreting the results of the SAA Census it is necessary to keep in mind that the response primarily reflects the situation of nonstudent "professional" members of the Society for American Archaeology who felt committed enough to the SAA and the mission of the Census to take the hour or so needed to fill out and return the somewhat daunting eight-page questionnaire they received. Even so, the nearly 30 percent response rate we achieved certainly surpassed the somewhat gloomy 5–10 percent return rate projected by an expert in association surveys consulted during the design phase of the project. What we obtained, then, was data from the largest sample of archaeologists ever polled for such a purpose—a sample comprised of student and professional archaeologists from all major sectors of the archaeological workforce distributed throughout the Americas, including all 50 United States and the District of Columbia; 2 U.S. Trust Territories (Puerto Rico and Guam); 6 Canadian provinces; Mexico and 6 other Caribbean and Central and South American countries; as well as 7 countries outside of the Western Hemisphere. Moreover, the vast majority of respondents filled out all sections of the Census, including those that addressed such sensitive topics as salary and job satisfaction, as well as those that demanded considerable thought and time to complete, such as the work setting and activity grids and the funding-history table. Many appended lengthy comments to the final section, which

solicited feedback. We even received several manuscripts on the health and status of American archaeology!

Suggestions for Using This Volume

Data Tables and Graphs

In preparing for the data-processing stage of the project, we developed a lengthy query protocol, once again with extensive consultation with the SAA Executive Board, COSWA, and other interested groups and individuals. As Dale Child (who implemented this part of the project) ruefully remarked, by the time we were finished, the query protocol basically called for cross-tabulating "everything by everything else." Actually, we were a bit more restrained in our approach, but still the query protocol called for examining almost all aspects of the Census data by age, gender, region, work setting, membership status, and in some cases by year of entry into the archaeological workforce and by highest degree achieved. We also subdivided categories, examining, for instance, region and work setting by both age and gender. The results of this query phase, which was conducted from June 1995 to February 1996, now fill eight thick binders.

There is no way to present all of the data recovered by the SAA Census in this book. Nor are all of the data generated pertinent to its underlying goals. Instead, I will concentrate on the most striking and meaningful trends in the data as they relate to the broad topics of archaeological demographics, training, employment, research interests, publication and professional service, and funding. Although I will present some data in a tabular format, I will rely more heavily on graphical presentation of the data as the most effective way to convey the nature and strength of the trends I want to highlight. I will also consistently use the same graphic formats throughout the text, the most common of which have already been presented in Figures 1.1 and 1.3. Figures 1.1a and 1.3a present information on mailed and returned Census forms as *proportions,* with each bar adding up to 100 percent. In the following chapters, proportional graphs may take this stacked 100 percent or cumulative format, or they may show only the proportion of one category of information contrasted to the proportion achieved by a component of a separate population. For example, the proportion of women in academia within the total sample of female respondents may be compared to the proportion of men in academia within the total sample of male respondents. Proportional graphs may sometimes be shown in point/line format to highlight trends over time. In all cases the size of the sample from which the proportion is computed is shown either above or below the bar or point.

Alternatively, data may be shown in *distributional* histograms in which a number of bars arrayed either from left to right, or sometimes top to bottom, represent a single population and add up to 100 percent. Figures 1.1b and 1.3b are distribution graphs that show the distribution of Census forms mailed by membership status and region, compared with the distribution of returned Census forms segregated in this way. In this case the sample size of each population examined is shown in a box, usually located in the upper right-hand corner of the graph.

Even though the presentation of sample sizes on the graphs may in some cases detract a bit from the visual clarity of the graphs, I have decided to keep with this convention, for two reasons. First, it allows the reader to instantly judge the strength of the comparison being made. Comparisons based on large samples obviously carry more weight than those based on smaller samples, and the reader should not have to wade through lots of text or turn to an appendix to ferret out such basic information. Second, the presentation of information on sample size allows the reader interested in doing additional work with the Census data to easily extract the raw data on which the graphical presentations are based.

Those interested in working with the data on which these graphs are based can obtain a copy of the raw counts of aggregate data by writing to Melinda Zeder, Census Data, Department of Anthropology, MRC 112, National Museum of Natural History, Smithsonian Institution, Washington, D.C. 20560.

Statistics

Statistical treatment of the data is restricted to simple Pearsons chi-square comparisons. A nonparametric statistic, chi square is useful in cases where populations compared may not be normally distributed or where sample sizes are small (Thomas 1986: 262). It is also a statistic familiar to most social scientists. Results of chi-square comparisons are presented, either in the text usually following the convention used above (which lists the chi-square value, the degrees of freedom, and the probability that the result of the test is statistically significant; for example, χ^2=3.271, df=1, p=.071), or in the figure or figure heading itself. As a general rule, the cutoff for statistical significance adopted here is the 95 percent confidence interval. Results that are significant at better than the .001 level of probability (better than the 99.9 percent confidence interval) are held to be highly significant, while results significant at the .001 through .050 level of probability (95–99 percent) are labeled significant. Chi-square values that are significant at the .060 through .090 level of probability (94–90 percent) are held to be only weakly significant at best.

Text

The story that lies within the responses to the 1994 SAA Census is complex, rich, nuanced, and, I believe, compelling. Telling this story required a comprehensive and thorough exploration of Census data and the patterns that can be teased from them. This is what I have endeavored to do here. However, I have also tried to help the reader follow this complex story line by occasionally stepping back from the detailed examination of Census data and presenting a more synthetic discussion of the general trends emerging from the data. In particular, each chapter begins with a summary of the primary findings discussed in the body of the chapter. In addition, summary statements of emerging patterns are woven into the ongoing discussion of Census data and are set off with a bullet (•) at the beginning and the end of the summary. For those who bought this book for the pictures, figure headings include a brief statement of the most salient patterns illustrated in the figures, which are designed to help the reader quickly grasp the broader significance of the data displayed and link these data more directly to the ongoing discussion in the text. Finally, readers who wish to look up information on specific topics of interest should use the detailed table of contents, which includes a listing of all 167 figures, which together provide an exhaustive guide to information presented in this book.

2 Profiling the American Archaeologist

Introduction

Chapter Summary

This chapter builds a basic profile of the profession and introduces themes that will run throughout the rest of this book. Data presented here reveal important shifts in the age and gender composition of American archaeology, from a strong male bias among older professional archaeologists toward a virtually even representation of men and women among archaeologists in their 20s and 30s. It is this group of younger archaeologists who are setting the trends in training, employment, research, and productivity that are shaping the future of American archaeology. Regional trends in the distribution of male and female student and professional archaeologists are also examined here. In addition, this chapter provides unequivocal empirical support for the impression one gets when attending any major gathering of archaeologists in North America—that American archaeologists are a remarkably homogenous group composed almost exclusively of people of European ancestry. There is also a trend toward increasingly higher representation of individuals from middle to upper socioeconomic backgrounds among the ranks of younger archaeologists, especially among women.

Finally, an examination of the family life of the American archaeologist demonstrates long-standing, persistent imbalances in the personal choices men and women, especially women with doctoral degrees, make in their pursuit of a career in archaeology. Men in the profession are more likely to marry and to stay married, or to remarry if divorced or widowed. And while women eventually have children at the same rate as their male counterparts, they are much more likely to delay parenthood longer than men, and are more likely to be left with dependent children after divorce.

General Demographic Trends

Gender Distribution in Student and Professional Archaeologists

When considering information on the gender and age of American archaeologists, we need to distinguish between two different populations: students and professionals. Both populations have distinctive gender- and age-related patterns that are key to understanding general trends in archaeology today. Looking at the aggregate gender composition of students and professionals (Figure 2.1), we see a dramatic difference in the proportions of men and women in each of these two populations. Of the 250 students who noted their gender, 127 were female and 123 were male, a 51 percent to 49 percent split between females and males. In contrast, women make up only 36 percent (621 individuals), while men make up 64 percent (1,013) of the professional nonstudent respondents. The difference between the gender composition of student and professional archaeologists is highly significant (χ^2=20.930, df=1, p<.001), and has been noted in earlier studies where it is often interpreted as a sign of gender-based discrimination preventing women from pursuing professional careers in archaeology (Kramer and Stark 1994: 21; Kelley and Hill 1994: 49; Wylie 1994: 66). However, perhaps due to their more limited samples, none of these earlier studies have looked at age-based variation in student and professional gender composition. Doing this allows us to identify significant trends that call for a reevaluation of earlier conclusions based on aggregate data.

Age and Gender Trends Among Students

Turning first to the students, when we look at the distribution of student respondents by age (Figure 2.2a), it is clear that the respondent pool does not reflect the actual universe of graduate students in archaeology. Only 7 percent of the student respondents are in their 20s, and yet these younger students almost certainly predominate among student archaeologists. The poor representation of students in their 20s probably comes about because these individuals are not members of the Society for American Archaeology and were therefore underrepresented in the sample of archaeologists on our mailing list. There are a couple of possible reasons for the underenrollment of younger students in the SAA. First, even at reduced student rates, SAA membership fees may be out of reach of these individuals. Moreover, since students in their 20s may not be far enough along in their studies to present papers at annual meetings or begin the search for jobs, there may be few compelling reasons for them to join the SAA. Remember too that the response rate of SAA student members to the Census was relatively low when compared to nonstudents. Perhaps younger student members were less likely than older students to take the

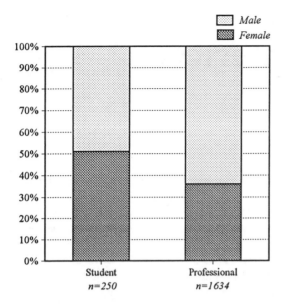

Fig. 2.1 *Proportions of Men and Women Among Student and Professional Archaeologists*

Note the essentially even representation of men and women among students, and the predominance of men among professional archaeologists.

time to fill out and return the Census. Thus, rather than typifying the "student body" of future archaeologists as a whole, the pool of student respondents likely represents upper-level graduate students on the threshold of becoming professional archaeologists.

When we examine age data for these upper-level graduate students by gender, we see that female students tend

to be older than male students. The average age of the female student respondent is 35.7, while the average age of the male student is 33.6. Looking at the distribution of students across different age cohorts (Figure 2.2a), there is a clear, though not statistically significant (χ^2=7.445, df=5, p=0.190), tendency for women to be better represented in the older age groups. Male students are more highly concentrated in the 30–39-year-old age cohort; female students are more widely dispersed across the full age spectrum. Proportionately, women are especially well represented in the older age cohorts where they contribute 60 percent or more to the population of older students (Figure 2.2b).

This pattern is also evident in Figure 2.3, which compares student and professional archaeologists by age and gender. Students make up 34 percent of both the female and male respondents in their 30s (Figure 2.3a and b). In males, student representation falls to 8 percent of the men in their 40s, and less than 5 percent of the older male archaeologists are students (Figure 2.3b). In contrast, students make up 14 percent of the female respondents in their 40s, 12 percent of the females in their 50s, and 20 percent of the small sample of older women respondents (Figure 2.3a). The difference between the proportions of students in the older age cohorts of men and women is highly significant (χ^2=31.499, df=5, p<.001).

Age and Gender Trends Among Professionals

Age data for the professional population assumes a highly normal distribution, concentrated sharply on the 40–49 year age cohort (Figure 2.4a). Clearly, aging baby boomers

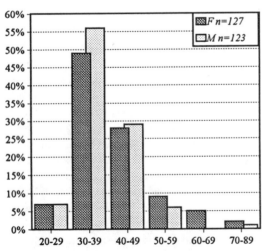

Fig. 2.2 *Student Archaeologists by Age and Gender*

a Distribution of male and female students over six age cohorts

b Proportions of male and female students in each age cohort

Note the tendency for women students to be older than men, and the generally even representation of men and women in most age cohorts.

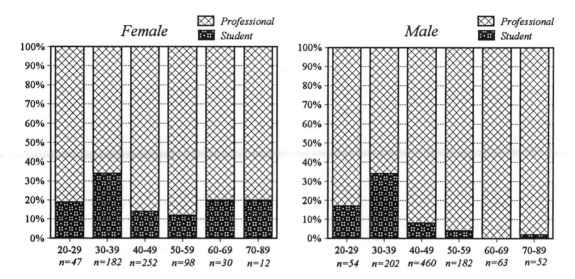

Fig. 2.3 *Proportions of Student and Professional Archaeologists Within Each Age Cohort*

a Females   **b** Males

Note the tendency for female students to be better represented in the older age cohorts, and the concentration of male students in the younger age cohorts.

dominate the ranks of professional archaeology. However, as was the case with the students, I suspect that the younger age cohorts are underrepresented in our sample when compared to the actual universe of professional archaeologists. Once again, younger archaeologists who either have recently graduated or are not pursuing higher graduate degrees may elect not to join the SAA. We will look at this question more closely in Chapter 4 when we examine employment settings. In particular we will see that our

sample of private sector archaeologists comes primarily from the ranks of mid- to upper-level management. Strikingly absent are crew members, crew chiefs, and field directors, despite the likelihood that these people outnumber higher-level managers. It is further likely that crew positions are filled by younger people (both students and nonstudents) just starting out in their careers in archaeology. Apparently these people tend not to join the SAA. The disenfranchisement of this possibly quite sizable

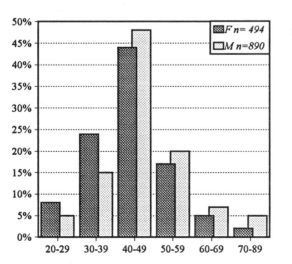

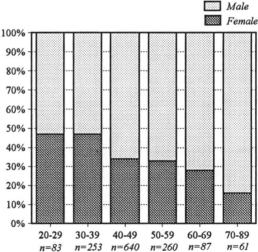

Fig. 2.4 *Professional Archaeologists by Age and Gender*

a Distribution of male and female professionals over six age cohorts

b Proportions of male and female professionals in each age cohort

Note the tendency for women professionals to be younger than men, and the increasingly even representation of women in the younger age cohorts.

group of archaeologists from the major professional organization of the discipline is an important topic that we will return to repeatedly.

When we look at these data by both age and gender, we see that while female students tend to be older than male students, the reverse is true among professional archaeologists. Women in the archaeological workforce tend to be quite a bit younger than men. The average age of the female nonstudent respondent is 43, while the average male is nearly 5 years older at 47.9. When the age distributions of male and female professional archaeologists are compared (Figure 2.4a), there is a clear, and highly significant (χ^2=39.392, df=6, p<.001), tendency for women to be better represented in the younger age cohorts.

Perhaps the most dramatic demographic pattern in age and gender composition is the increasingly greater proportional representation of professional women in each younger age cadre (Figure 2.4b). Women make up only 16 percent of the professional archaeologists over 70, 28 percent of those in their 60s, 33 percent of the 50–59 year olds, 34 percent of those in their 40s, and 47 percent of professional archaeologists in their 30s and 20s. In both these younger age cohorts, the male–female distribution is statistically indistinguishable from a 50–50 split (for 30–39 year olds χ^2=0.334, df=1, p=0.564; for 20–29 year olds χ^2=0.150, df=1, p=0.699).

• Thus, when the ranks of professional archaeologists are partitioned by age, we see a clear trend toward gender parity in younger professional archaeologists. The apparent imbalance between the proportions of men and women in

the aggregate data may not then be a sign of ongoing discrimination against women in the archaeological workforce, but rather a remnant of earlier forces that discouraged women from pursuing professional careers in archaeology. It is also possible, however, that the gender imbalance among archaeologists in their 40s and 50s is the result of women leaving archaeology, possibly to pursue a family life, or because they have reached the archaeological equivalent of the corporate glass ceiling. A definitive answer to the question of whether these demographic patterns represent past or persistent gender-based inequities in professional archaeology may have to await the results of another broad-based census in 10 years or so. However, there are trends in the current data that can, and will, be used to revisit this question throughout the course of this book. •

Trends in Regional Distribution

Regional distributions of males and females in both the student and professional populations are generally quite similar to one another (Figures 2.5 and 2.6). In fact when the regional distribution data for men and women are compared over the six separate regions in the United States, there is no statistical difference between either the male and female students or the male and female professionals (for students: χ^2=3.710, df=5, p=0.592; for professionals: χ^2=8.243, df=5, p=0.143). However, a closer examination of the distributional data reveals some subtle differences that are worth noting. In both the professional and, especially, the student populations there is an apparent tendency for men to be better represented in

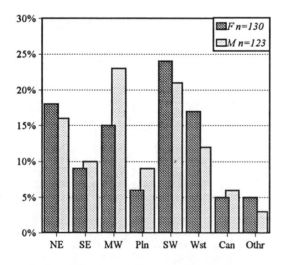

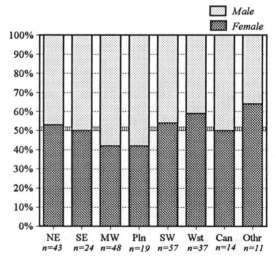

Fig. 2.5 *Student Archaeologists by Region and Gender*

a Distribution of male and female students

b Proportions of male and female students in each region (hatched line = proportion of women among student respondents)

Note the tendency for women to be better represented in the Northeast, Southwest, and West, and the tendency for men to be better represented in the Southeast, Plains, and, especially, in the Midwest.

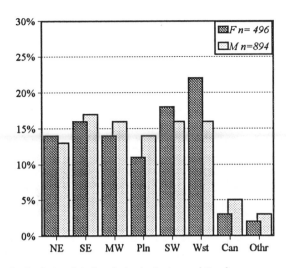

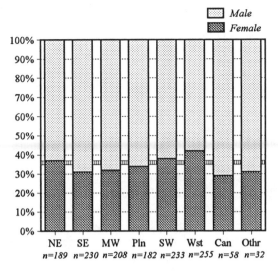

Fig. 2.6 *Professional Archaeologists by Region and Gender*

a Distribution of male and female professionals by region

b Proportions of male and female professionals in each region (hatched line = proportion of women among professional respondents)

Note the tendency for women to be better represented in the Northeast, Southwest, and especially the West, and the tendency for men to be better represented in the Southeast, Midwest, and the Plains.

the Midwest, Plains, and, to a lesser extent, the Southeast when compared to women. On the other hand, women students and professionals both appear to be differentially well represented in the Northeast, Southwest, and West when compared to men. Women professionals are especially well represented in the West (Figure 2.6). When these distributional data are grouped into these two broader regional zones (the Northeast, Southwest, and West versus the Southeast, Midwest, and Plains) the differential representation of professional men and women is statistically significant (χ^2=6.318, df=1, p=.012), while that difference between the smaller sample of male and female students is only weakly significant (χ^2=12.588, df=1, p=.083).

Ethnic Heritage

For a discipline dedicated to the study of human diversity over the ages, American archaeology is starkly homogeneous in its own ethnic make-up (Figure 2.7). Of the 1,644 individuals who responded to this part of the Census, 1,470 (89 percent) reported that they were of European ancestry, 2 were African American, 4 were of Asian heritage, 15 were Hispanic (with 5 coming from Latin American countries), and 10 people classified themselves as Native Americans. One hundred and forty-two individuals (9 percent) classified their ethnic heritage as "Other," and most of these were Canadians who objected, reasonably, to being classified as "European *American*," or others who expressed a general objection to being so

classified. The majority of people who classified themselves as "Other" are then likely to be of European descent. Eliminating this "Other" group from our sample, we see then that a full 98 percent of the respondents claim European heritage. There is no difference between men and women in ethnic diversity. While it is possible that minority groups may be better represented in the actual universe of American archaeology than they are on the

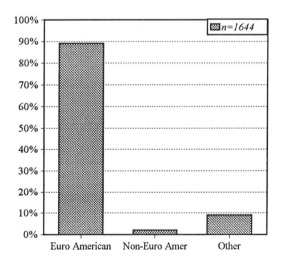

Fig. 2.7 *Ethnic Heritage of American Archaeologists*

Note the dominance of individuals of European American heritage.

rolls of the SAA, it is likely that the overwhelming predominance of European Americans in the Census respondent pool is typical of American archaeologists as a whole.

Socioeconomic Background

When asked to specify their socioeconomic background, women were more likely than men to report that they came from upper-middle and upper class backgrounds, while men were more likely to report that they came from lower-middle and lower class backgrounds (Table 2.1; χ^2=12.082, df=2, p=.002). Moreover, the tendency for women to come from higher socioeconomic brackets is found in almost every age cohort. A longitudinal look at socioeconomic data also reveals a general trend for archaeologists to come from increasingly higher socioeconomic backgrounds. For females there is a steady increase in the proportion of women from upper-middle and upper class backgrounds in each younger age cohort. Among males, with the exception of the 20–29 year olds, there is a steady increase in the representation of those from middle class backgrounds and a corresponding decrease in men who come from lower-middle and lower class brackets.

Family Life

Some of the most clear-cut differences between men and women in American archaeology come in the area of family life. It would seem that very different considerations shape the personal choices men and women archaeologists make about whether to marry, whom to marry, and whether and when to have children. It would also seem that there are clear and consistent differences between the trajectories of the family lives of women who hold doctoral degrees when compared to men, as well as the lives of women holding less advanced degrees.

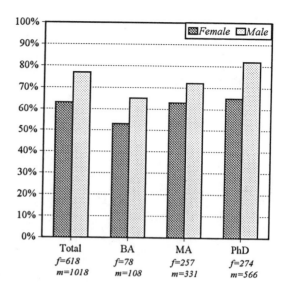

Fig. 2.8 *Marriage Rates by Gender and Highest Degree*

Note the generally greater proportion of married men, and the increasing disparities between marriage rates of men and women, in each higher degree category.

Marriage

Looking first at marriage rates (Figure 2.8), for the population of Census respondents as a whole, there is a sizable and significant difference between the proportions of men and women who are married or in long-term relationships. Seventy-seven percent of the male respondents reported that they were married, while 63 percent of the women were married (Figure 2.8; χ^2=40.679, df=1, p<.001).

Marriage rates of men and women in archaeology also show considerable variation when examined by age of respondent (Figure 2.9). In the younger age cohorts, one can trace a steady increase in the proportions of married

	20–29 %	30–39 %	40–49 %	50–59 %	60–69 %	70–79 %	80–89 %	Total %
Female								
Upper	31	26	27	24	27	12	50	27
Middle	58	55	56	44	60	63	50	54
Lower	11	19	17	32	13	25	0	19
Total Number	48	182	249	95	30	8	2	614
Male								
Upper	19	18	18	18	28	20	53	20
Middle	52	61	59	51	41	68	38	56
Lower	29	21	23	31	31	12	8	24
Total Number	52	201	459	180	64	41	13	1010

Table 2.1 *Proportion of Women and Men from Different Socioeconomic Backgrounds in Each Age Cohort*

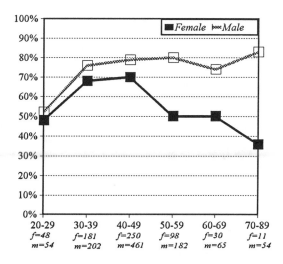

Fig. 2.9 *Marriage Rates by Age and Gender*

Note the sharp drop in the proportion of married women in the 50–59 age cohort.

individuals in both the male and female respondent pools. Moreover, up to this point it would seem that there is little difference between the marriage rates of men and women, apart from a slight tendency (which increases with age) for the marriage rate of women to lag behind that of men. For respondents in their 20s, the proportion of married women (46 percent) is statistically indistinguishable from the proportion of men who are married (52 percent; $\chi^2=0.368$, df=1, p=0.544). There is a larger, but only weakly significant difference between the proportions of married women (68 percent) and men (76 percent) in their 30s ($\chi^2=3.271$, df=1, p=.071). By the 40s there is a 9 percent difference between the marriage rates of women and men, which is significant at the .005 level of probability ($\chi^2=7.711$, df=1).

In the 50–59 age cohort, however, there is a startling 30 percent difference between marriage rates in men and women. Men continue the steady increase in the proportion of married individuals, which rises to 80 percent for men in their 50s and remains fairly constant for men in their 60s through their 80s. But for women, the marriage rate plummets from 70 percent for 40–49 year olds to 50 percent for women in their 50s. The proportion of married women remains at 50 percent for women in their 60s, falling to 36 percent among women in their 70s and 80s.

With the benefit of hindsight it would have been useful to ask respondents to specify whether they are widowed or divorced, rather than to lump these two categories in with the status of "single." As a result, we cannot definitively determine whether unmarried women in their 50s chose never to marry, or whether there is an especially high rate of divorce or widowhood in these older age cohorts. Thus

it is impossible to say for certain whether the low proportions of married women in older cohorts stem from past conditions (no longer as keenly felt by women in younger cohorts) that discouraged these women from marrying when they were starting out in their careers, or from ongoing conditions that result in a high divorce/widowhood rate among older women. Judging from the steepness of the drop between the marriage rates of women in their 40s and those in their 50s, however, I would suspect that the latter possibility probably plays a substantial role in shaping this pattern. Moreover, for women in their 50s it would seem more likely that it is divorce rather than widowhood that is the major factor in the precipitous drop in the proportion of married individuals. Given the generally greater longevity of women, widowhood may well play a role in the low marriage rates in women in their 60s, 70s, and 80s.

On the other hand, it might be tempting to relate the decline in the proportion of married women in the older age cohorts to the overall decline in the representation of women among the ranks of older professional archaeologists discussed earlier. Specifically, one wonders, could these two patterns both stem from a departure of women from the archaeological workforce when they marry? While this may be a contributing factor to the decline in the representation of older women among professional archaeologists, the data do not support the conclusion that this is the primary factor influencing this pattern. If this were the case, one would expect the decline in the proportion of women among professional archaeologists to coincide with the decline in the female marriage rates. Instead, changes in the representation of women within different age cohorts show little correlation with female marriage rate. Specifically, while the overall representation of women in the profession declines between the 30–39 and the 40–49 age cohorts, the proportion of married women shows some increase over this time. Moreover, the overall representation of women in archaeology is steady between the 40–49 and the 50–59 cohorts, despite the dramatic decline in marriage rates between women in their 40s and 50s.

When the data are segregated by highest academic degree earned, we see that these differences in the family lives of men and women archaeologists are particularly pronounced among those archaeologists who hold PhD degrees (Figure 2.8). For both men and women, there is a steady increase in the marriage rate in each progressively higher degree category. This is, in part, an artifact of the higher proportion of younger individuals in the BA and MA populations who may still be working toward their PhD (student respondents were included in these populations). In each degree category, however, we also see a growing and increasingly significant disparity between the marriage rates of men and women. In the smaller BA population the difference between the 53 percent marriage

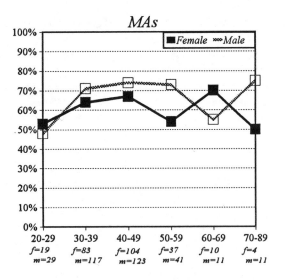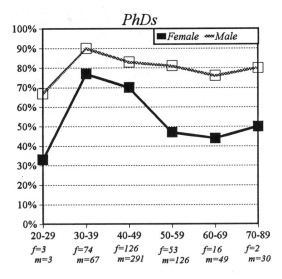

Figure 2.10 *Marriage Rates by Highest Degree, Age, and Gender*

a MA respondents

b PhD respondents

Note the similarity between the marriage rates of the MA population, and the disparity between men and women with doctoral degrees.

rate for women and the 65 percent marriage rate for men is only weakly significant (χ^2=2.825, df=1, p=.093). For the larger MA pool, the 9 percent difference between the marriage rates of women (63 percent) and men (72 percent) is more significant (χ^2=2.825, df=1, p=.027). In the PhD population, the marriage rate for women is virtually the same as it is for MA women (65 percent), but the proportion of male PhDs who are married is now 82 percent, a full 17 percent greater than the proportion of married PhD women (χ^2=29.946, df=1, p<.001).

And yet the difference in the marriage rates of men and women by degree is not entirely an artifact of the higher proportion of younger individuals in the BA and MA populations. This becomes clear when we look at marriage rates both by highest degree and by age. Unfortunately, the BA population is not large enough to reliably compare marriage rates for men and women by age. However, both the MA and the PhD populations *are* large enough to partition in this way, and when we do this we find a dramatic difference between the two populations (Figure 2.10). In the MA population there is some tendency for women's marriage rates to be slightly lower than men in many of the age cohorts (Figure 2.10a). Overall, however, the marriage rates for MA women in every age group closely echo those of MA men. The differences between the proportions of married men and women in the different age groups is never significant at the .05 level of probability, and most are statistically indistinguishable from one another. MA women do experience a 13 percentage point decline in marriage rate between the 40–49 and the 50–59 age cohorts. Given the smaller sample size of

the 50–59 cohort, however, it is difficult to judge just how significant this decline is.

Instead, it is the PhD population that seems to have been primarily responsible for the patterns observed in the general respondent population (Figure 2.10b). The marriage rate of PhD men jumps to 90 percent for men in their 30s, drops slightly to 83 percent for men in their 40s, and remains fairly constant at 75–80 percent in the older age cohorts. In contrast, the marriage rate rises only to 77 percent for PhD women in their 30s, dips slightly to 71 percent in the 40–49 year olds, and then tumbles to 47 percent in the PhD women over 50.

• It would seem that men in all degree categories tend to marry at higher rates than women and to stay married, or possibly to remarry if divorced or widowed, more frequently than women. Of the various degree categories, men with PhDs have the highest marriage rates across all age cohorts. In contrast, women in archaeology are generally less likely to marry then men. But this pattern varies, depending on the highest degree held. In both the BA and the MA pool, marriage rates for women are only slightly lower than they are for men. Rather, it is the women with PhDs who are most likely either never to marry or not to remarry after divorce or widowhood. It is, then, the women with the highest professional degrees who are most keenly affected by forces that mitigate against being able to successfully juggle a career in archaeology with a marriage. Moreover, while the impact of these forces is most strongly felt by women over 50, the significant disparity in marriage rates between both PhD women and men in the

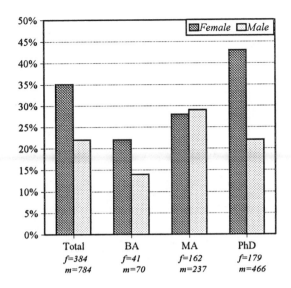

Fig. 2.11 *Archaeologist Spouses by Gender and Highest Degree*

Note the greater tendency of women to marry within the profession, especially women with doctoral degrees.

40s *and* in their 30s indicates that even younger female PhDs find it harder than their male counterparts to balance the demands of a professional and a private life. •

Spouse's Profession

But whom are these archaeologists marrying? Are they marrying within the profession, or do they tend to marry individuals from other walks of life? And is there any difference in the spousal preferences of men and women archaeologists? Judging by the data presented in Figure 2.11, it appears that all archaeologists, whether men or women, in all degree categories are more likely to marry individuals outside the profession than to marry fellow archaeologists. However, as with marriage rates, there are clear differences in the spousal choices of men and women in different degree categories.

Archaeologists with BAs as their highest degree are the least likely to marry within the profession. Among BA archaeologists women tend to marry archaeologists more than men. Given the smaller size of the BA population, however, it is difficult to evaluate the statistical significance of the 14 percentage point difference between men and women in the proportions of archaeologist spouses. Among the larger pool of MA archaeologists, men and women tend to marry archaeologists at essentially the same rate; around 30 percent of both MA men and women are married to archaeologists. The proportion of women who marry within the profession jumps to 43 percent among women with PhDs, an increase that is significant at the .005 level of probability (χ^2=7.884, df=1). At the same time, the proportion of PhD men with archaeologist spouses shows a significant decline; 29 percent of the

men with MAs were married to archaeologists compared to 21 percent of the men with PhDs (χ^2=4.653, df=1, p=.031). To some extent the decline in the proportion of PhD men who are married to archaeologists is attributable to the higher proportion of older men in the PhD population and the propensity of older men in all degree categories to marry nonarchaeologists. However, when we segregate the MA and PhD populations by age, this would not seem to be the only factor operating here.

When spousal data are broken down by highest degree, gender, *and* age, the difference between the MA and the PhD populations becomes even clearer (Figure 2.12). For individuals whose highest degree is an MA, the patterns for male and female spousal choices are essentially identical to one another. Even the apparent variation in the proportion of archaeologist spouses among MA men and women in their 30s is not statistically significant (Figure 2.12a; χ^2=.001, df=1, p=.978). Moreover, both men and women with MAs show the same steep decline in the proportion of archaeologist spouses with age.

In contrast, PhD women in their 30s and 40s are each almost two times as likely to marry another archaeologist as PhD men (Figure 2.12b). In both age cohorts, essentially half of the married women are married to archaeologists, while less than a quarter of the married men in their 30s and 40s have archaeologist spouses. This pattern changes abruptly in the 50–59 age cohort where we see a strong, and significant, 30 percent drop in the proportion of women with spouses in archaeology when compared to PhD women in their 40s (χ^2=7.404, df=1, p=.007). The proportion of archaeologist spouses among women in their 50s (20 percent) is statistically identical to the proportion of men in their 50s with archaeologist spouses (14 percent).

• It would seem that once again women with doctoral degrees stand out from both PhD men and from men and women with less advanced degrees. When married, women with PhDs are much more likely to be married to another archaeologist than are men. However, as with the data on marriage rates, there is a marked difference in the spousal choices of PhD women aged 50 and older when compared to younger women with doctoral degrees. Some future survey effort might want to see if there is any connection between the sharp declines in both the marriage rate and the proportion of archaeologist spouses among older PhD women. If divorce is a major factor in the decline of marriage rates among these older women, are those women married to archaeologists more likely to divorce than those who marry outside the profession? •

Dependents

Because of some ambiguity in the phrasing of Census questions, information on dependents is a little more difficult to sort out than information on marriage rates or

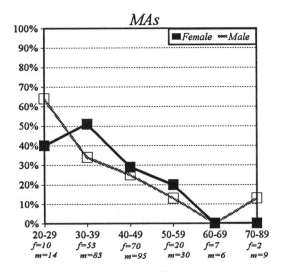

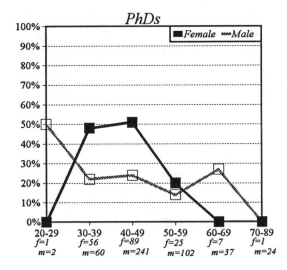

Fig. 2.12 *Archaeologists' Spouses by Highest Degree, Age, and Gender*

a MA respondents

b PhD respondents

Note the similarity between the proportion of individuals with archaeologist spouses of the MA population, the disparity between younger men and women with doctoral degrees who marry within the profession, and the sharp drop in the proportion of archaeologist spouses for PhD women in the 50–59 age cohort.

spousal choices. First, since we asked for information on the number of "dependents" a respondent had, rather than the number of "children," it is difficult to say whether a reported lack of dependents means that a respondent never had any children, or that they were no longer supporting any children. It is also difficult to tell whether older individuals with dependents were counting children they had when they were younger, or whether they were currently supporting a dependent spouse. Also, rather than asking for a simple "yes" or "no" response to the question of whether a respondent had any dependents, we asked for the number of dependents. Thus it is impossible to tell if the sizable number of individuals who failed to answer this question did so because they had no dependents or because they felt the question too intrusive. As a result, only respondents that recorded "0" in the response box for dependents are counted as having no dependents, while those who responded with "1" or more are counted as having dependents. Even with these caveats in mind, however, the information collected on dependents serves to both reinforce and enrich our understanding of the choices that men and women in archaeology make in their family lives.

Once again, when we look at the aggregate data for the population as a whole, as well as by highest degree, there is a marked difference between male and female archaeologists. In all cases men are significantly more likely to have dependents than women (Figure 2.13). The proportion of men with dependents is quite high, at about 70 percent for both men with BAs and men with MAs and increasing to 80 percent of the men with PhDs. In contrast, only 38

percent of the women with BAs have dependents, leveling off at 56 percent of the women with MAs and PhDs.

When we break these data down by age as well as by highest degree and gender, once again the patterns for men and women with MAs are quite similar to one another (Figure 2.14a), while PhD men and women vary substantially from one another (Figure 2.14b). The proportions of individuals with dependents are almost identical for MA men and women in their 20s, 30s, and 40s. It is difficult to interpret the drop in the proportion of MA women

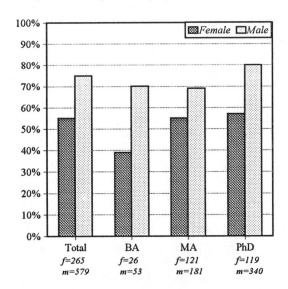

Fig. 2.13 *Dependents by Gender and Highest Degree*

Note the generally greater proportion of men with dependents.

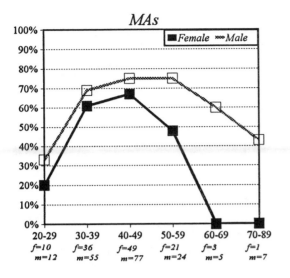

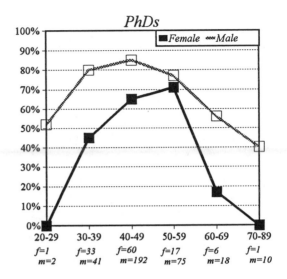

Fig. 2.14 *Dependents by Highest Degree, Age, and Gender*

a MA respondents

b PhD respondents

Note the similarity between the proportion of MAs with dependents, and the tendency for PhD women to have children later than PhD males.

with dependents in the 50–59 age cohort, though it may well be related to decline in the marriage rate of these individuals, noted earlier. The dramatic difference between the proportions of males and females with dependents in the older cohorts is likely the result of older men claiming wives as dependents.

In the PhD population around 80 percent of men in their 30s, 40s, and 50s have dependents (Figure 2.14b). In contrast, only 45 percent of PhD women in their 30s have dependents, increasing to 65 percent among women in

their 40s, and peaking at 71 percent among women in their 50s, a rate that is statistically indistinguishable from that of PhD men in their 50s. It would seem, then, that while PhD women eventually achieve the same dependent rate as PhD men, they are substantially more likely to delay having children than men.

This pattern becomes clearer when we compare the proportion of married men and women to the proportion of men and women with dependents by highest degree (Figures 2.15 and 2.16). For archaeologists whose highest

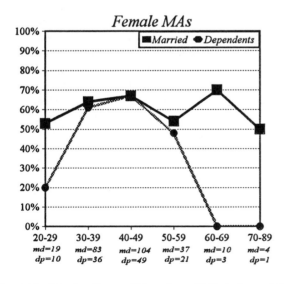

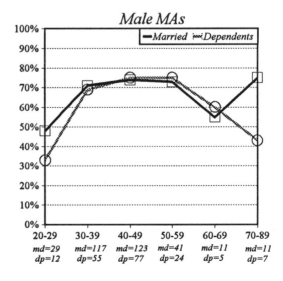

Fig. 2.15 *Marriage Rates and Dependents of MAs by Age and Gender*

a Females

b Males

Note the similarity between the proportions of married individuals and individuals with dependents for both females and males with MAs as their highest degree.

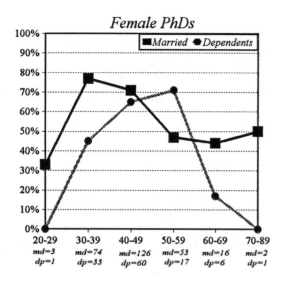

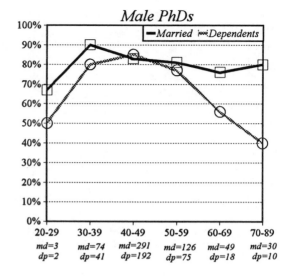

Fig. 2.16 *Marriage Rates and Dependents of PhDs by Age and Gender*

a Females   **b** Males

Note the similarity between the proportions of married individuals and individuals with dependents among PhD men, and the substantial delay in parenthood of PhD women. Note also that the proportion of women in the 50–59 cohort who have dependents is higher than the proportion of those who are married, possibly indicating women left with dependents after divorce.

degree is an MA, the marriage and dependent rates of men and women are practically identical to one another in the key age cohorts, from the 30s through the 50s (Figure 2.15a and b). Essentially all married men and women in these age cohorts have dependents.

Among men with doctoral degrees, there seems to be a slight, though not significant, lag between marriage and fatherhood among 30–39 year olds (Figure 2.16b; $\chi^2=1.747$, df=1, p=0.186). However, by the time males with PhDs reach their 40s the proportion of married men is the same as the proportion of men with dependents. For women with doctoral degrees the delay in parenthood is very pronounced (Figure 2.16a). While 77 percent of PhD women in their 30s are married, only 45 percent of these women have dependents, a difference that is significant at the .002 level of probability ($\chi^2=9.337$, df=1). The proportion of PhD women in their 40s who are married is equal to the proportion of these women with dependents, indicating that by this time almost all married women archaeologists have children. In the 50–59 age cohort of

PhD women, however, the proportion of women with dependents is 22 percent *higher* than the proportion of married PhD women, a difference that is significant at the .009 level of probability ($\chi^2=2.833$, df=1). If indeed the decline in marriage rates in PhD women in their 50s is related to divorce, the higher proportions of women with dependents in this age group may then point to a fairly substantial number of single women with dependent children.

●   Thus, as with the data on marriage rates and spousal choices, it would seem that women with PhDs make different personal choices when it comes to questions of whether and when to have children. Specifically, while they eventually have children at the same rate as their male counterparts, women with doctoral degrees in archaeology are much more likely to delay parenthood longer than either male archaeologists or women with less advanced degrees, and they may be more likely to be left with dependent children after divorce.   ●

3 Educating the American Archaeologist

Introduction

Chapter Summary

The majority of American archaeologists hold advanced degrees from institutions of higher education. As a result, analysis of patterns of postgraduate education not only provides "leading indicators" of future change in archaeology, it also gives us a clear look at a number of dramatic trends in recent years that have already reshaped the profession. Consideration of the degree status of all Census respondents by age cohort and by decade in which degrees were conferred illuminates long-term trends in the education of American archaeologists, and provides a longitudinal baseline of comparison against which recent trends clearly stand out. One of the most striking of these trends is a movement toward greater gender parity in the proportion of men and women receiving advanced degrees. There is also a surprising drop in the proportion of males going on for doctoral degrees, especially among younger men, that may signal an important change in the types of careers younger male archaeologists are pursuing. Tracking the length of time professional archaeologists spend on their education reveals a startling increase in the number of years it takes to obtain advanced degrees in archaeology, as well as a significant increase in the average age of degree recipients. A closer look at degree-granting institutions highlights a dramatic proliferation of universities and colleges with PhD programs—a development that would seem to run counter to the apparent decline in the proportions of people with PhDs among younger archaeologists. It also reveals significant changes over time in the institutions that produce the majority of archaeologists with higher degrees.

Defining Degree Status

To examine Census data on degree status, it was necessary to first partition Census respondents not only by the highest degree they had earned to date, but by the highest *final* degree in their academic career. Individuals who had completed their education needed to be distinguished from those still pursuing more advanced degrees. The convention adopted was to count as the final academic degree the highest degree earned by those with nonstudent memberships in the SAA. Thus, respondents identified as having either BAs or MAs as final degrees are those whose highest degree was either a bachelor's or master's *and* who held nonstudent memberships in the SAA. Although one cannot be certain that these individuals (especially those in their 20s and 30s) will not return to graduate school to pursue more advanced degrees, the fact that most are professional members of the SAA, paying full membership dues, would seem to indicate that they are fully launched into the profession. It is also useful, however, to look at trends among those who acquire MA degrees as part of their doctoral studies. This population of "ongoing" MAs is comprised of both nonstudent respondents who earned MAs before moving on to obtain doctoral degrees, as well as students who have earned master's degrees and are still enrolled in graduate school.

As for the PhDs, for the most part it is safe to assume that those with doctoral degrees will not pursue additional degrees, at least not in archaeology. However, there were a number of respondents with doctoral degrees who also claimed student membership status. Most received their doctorates in 1993 or 1994, in which case their student status probably legitimately dates to when they were still enrolled in graduate school. Others with PhDs dating to the early 1990s and even as long ago as the late 1980s may have been fudging a bit on their membership status. All of these "student" PhDs were left in the PhD pool, to make sure that the sample included the most recent degree recipients.

Degree Status by Gender and Age

Aggregate Patterns in Degree Status

Aggregate data on final degrees reveal a profession rich in PhDs; 60 percent of Census respondents hold doctoral degrees (Figure 3.1a). And while the degree profiles of men and women are roughly similar, there are significant differences in degree status of male and female professional archaeologists (χ^2=11.090, df=3, p=.004). The proportion of men and women with BAs as their final degree is equally low at only 9 percent. However, 42 percent of the professional female respondents hold MAs as their final degree, compared to 33 percent of the men. In contrast, 63 percent of the men have PhDs, compared to 55 percent of the women. The differential representation of women in the MA and PhD populations is also seen in Figure 3.1b,

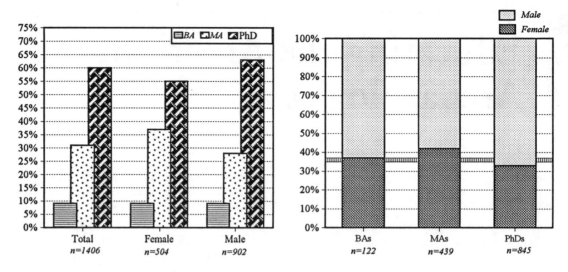

Fig. 3.1 *Highest Final Degrees in Archaeology*

a Distribution of final degrees for total population, females, and males

b Proportion of males and females in each final degree category (hatched line = proportion of women among professional respondents)

Note the higher proportions of females with final MAs, and the higher proportion of males with PhDs.

which compares the representation of males and females in each degree category to their representation within the pool of professional respondents as a whole (indicated by the hatched bar running across the graph). The representation of women among MAs, at 41 percent, is significantly greater than the representation of women within the total population of professional respondents (36 percent; χ^2=5.520, df=1, p=.019). In contrast, women make up only 33 percent of the respondents with PhDs. The disparity between the degree status of males and females in the aggregate body of today's archaeologists has been noted in earlier survey efforts (Gifford-Gonzalez 1994: 162–163; Wall and Rothschild 1995: 25). When contrasted to data that shows an even split between male and female students in graduate programs, the lower proportion of PhD women is sometimes taken as an indication that women face more difficulties in finishing their degrees than men (Kelley and Hill 1994: 50; Kramer and Stark 1994: 17).

Methods of Tracking Temporal Trends in Degree Status

Once again the comparatively large size of this survey population allows it to be segregated by age, and by so doing we are able to isolate important trends that both enhance and alter the view built solely on aggregate data. There are two ways to examine temporal trends in training. The first is simply to segregate the sample by age cohort, as was done in Chapter 2. However, unlike high school (or even, to some extent, undergraduate college programs) where

the majority of graduating seniors belong to a single age cohort, each year's graduating class of master's and doctoral students is likely to contain a fairly wide spread of ages. Looking at highest degree by age cohort *only*, then, might obscure patterns specific to the decade in which individuals received their degrees.

This point is made graphically clear in Figure 3.2, which compares the current ages of men and women who received final MAs and PhDs in the 1970s, 1980s, and 1990s. In some cases a single age cohort dominates the graduates of certain decades, for instance 40–49 year olds in the final MAs of the 1970s (Figure 3.2a) and in the PhDs of the 1980s (Figure 3.2d). In most cases, however, two and sometimes three age cohorts are well represented in a single award decade. There are also decades in which the age distributions of men and women receiving degrees vary significantly from one another. Among MAs of the 1990s, for example (Figure 3.2e), there is a significantly greater proportion of men under 40 when compared to women (χ^2=4.367, df=1, p=.037). Women who received their PhDs in the 1980s tend to be younger than the men who received their PhDs during this decade (Figure 3.2d), though the difference is only weakly significant (χ^2=7.026, df=1, p=.071). Perhaps the most marked difference in age distribution of men and women is seen in the PhDs awarded in the first half of the 1990s (Figure 3.2f). Two-thirds of the women receiving PhDs in the early 1990s were under 40, while more than half of the men were over 40, a difference that is significant at the .001 level of probability (χ^2=10.300, df=1).

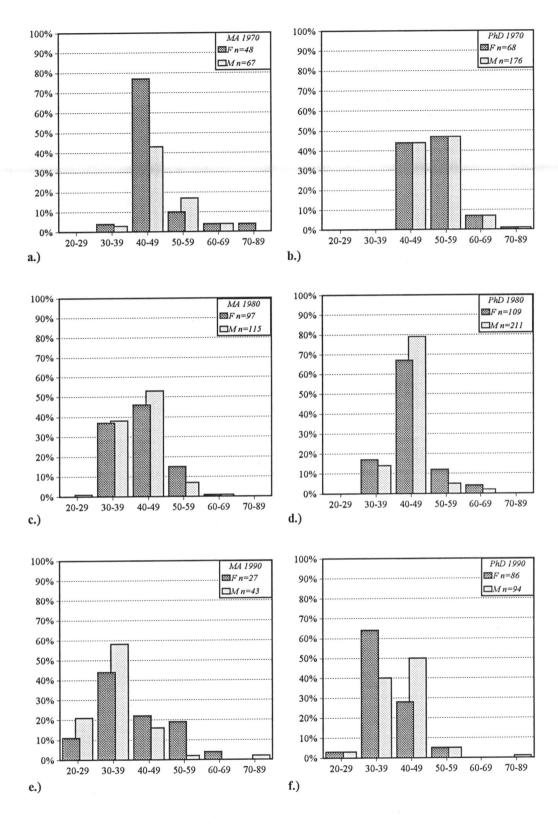

Fig. 3.2 *Age Distributions Within Award Decade*

a Final MAs awarded in the 1970s   **b** PhDs awarded in the 1970s
c Final MAs awarded in the 1980s   **d** PhDs awarded in the 1980s
e Final MAs awarded in the 1990s   **f** PhDs awarded in the 1990s

Note the wide spread of ages in each award decade.

At the same time, however, individuals within a single age cohort may in fact represent as many as four separate award decades. Figure 3.3 looks at the decade in which men and women received their degrees within the three best-represented age cohorts (30–39, 40–49, and 50–59). Individuals in their 30s with final MAs (Figure 3.3a) received these degrees in either the 1990s, the 1980s, or even, in the case of a few people, in the 1970s. The 50–59 age cohort received their MAs (Figure 3.3e) and their PhDs (Figure 3.3f) over four different decades, from the 1960s to the 1990s. Here too there are some important differences between men and women. In particular, more than 70 percent of the PhD women in their 30s received their degrees in the 1990s (Figure 3.3b), while 43 percent of the PhD men in their 30s received their doctorates in the 1980s, a difference that is significant at the .02 level of probability (χ^2=5.333, df=1). Proportionately more men in their 30s received their MAs in the 1990s when compared to women (Figure 3.3a), though the difference is not statistically significant. Finally, 65 percent of the women in their 50s with final MAs (Figure 3.3e) received these degrees relatively recently, in the 1980s and 1990s. In contrast, 78 percent of the MA men in their 50s received their MAs in the 1970s and 1960s (χ^2=14.082, df=3, p=.003).

Data on degrees earned by age cohort are not without value, however. As long as the age distributions with award decade are kept in mind, degree data for individual age cohorts refine and help focus our understanding of past and future trends in archaeological training. In particular, the younger cohorts allow us to forecast future patterns in degree distribution. Just as the recipients of doctoral degrees awarded in the 1990s are primarily in their 30s and 40s, the future graduates of the 2000 award decade are currently in their 20s and 30s. An examination of the degree status of these individuals allows us to forecast educational trends of archaeologists who will enter the profession in the early 21st century.

Gender Trends in Degree Status over Time

With these caveats in mind we can turn to an examination of the Census data of highest degree earned over time. Figure 3.4 presents the distribution of BAs, MAs, and PhDs by decade for women (Figure 3.4a) and men (Figure 3.4b). Several trends are readily apparent. First, there is a steady progressive decline in the proportion of women with BAs as their final degree in each more recent decade. The proportion of BA women falls steadily over time, from one-third of the small pool of women who earned their degrees in the 1950s to only 4 percent of the women earning degrees in the 1990s (χ^2=14.607, df=1, p<.001). In contrast, the proportion of male BAs remains at about 15 percent from the 1950s through the 1970s and then drops precipitously to 4 percent in the 1980s (χ^2=24.413, df=1, p<.001).

Second, among both men and women there is a steady increase in the proportion of those who earn MAs as their final degree in each decade from the 1950s up to the 1980s. In the 1990s the proportion of males with MAs relative to other degrees drops slightly. Among women earning degrees in the 1990s, on the other hand, there is a marked decline in the proportion who earned final MAs and a corresponding jump in PhDs. This sharp increase in the proportion of women earning PhDs during this most recent award decade is preceded by a more gradual but nonetheless steady increase in female PhDs from the 1950s through the 1980s. Male PhDs show a steady decrease over the decades from the 1950s through the 1980s with only a slight, though not significant, increase in the proportion of men earning doctoral degrees in the 1990s.

Arraying the degree data for men and women by age cohort (Figure 3.5) shows some of the same trends, but also contradicts other patterns evident when degree data are displayed by award decade. Once again, among men and, to a lesser extent, women, there is an increase in the proportion of those who earn MAs as their final degree in each younger age cohort. This trend is especially strongly manifested among younger males (Figure 3.5b), both in the smaller 20–29 cohort and the larger, more representative 30–39 cohort. However, the increase of MAs among younger men and the corresponding decline in PhDs is much more marked than when the data are arrayed by award decade. Moreover, in strong contrast to the pattern of increasing proportions of PhDs among women graduating in more recent award decades, when these data are displayed by age we see a gradual decrease and then a flattening in the proportion of women who graduate with PhDs in each younger age cohort (Figure 3.5a).

Figures 3.6 and 3.7 allow us to examine these patterns more closely by eliminating BAs from the computations and directly comparing proportions of men and women who hold MA and PhD degrees as their final degrees, both by award decade and by age cohort. Looking first at MAs among older age cohorts and less recent award decades (Figure 3.6), there is a substantial increase in the proportion of men who end their studies with an MA degree relative to those who earn PhDs. This is especially marked when degree data are presented by award decade (Figure 3.6a), where there is a 27 percentage point increase in the proportion of men with MAs from the 1950s to the 1980s (χ^2=8.353, df=1, p=.002). An increase in the proportion of males earning final MAs is evident but less pronounced in the older age cohorts from the 60s to the 40s (Figure 3.6b). The proportion of older MA women is more stable, with some indication of a slight but insignificant increase in the proportion who earned MAs as their final degrees from the 1960s to the 1980s and from the 60–69 age cohort to the 40–49 cohort. In both the older age cohorts and the less recent award decades, a substantially, and in most cases significantly, higher proportion of women end their studies

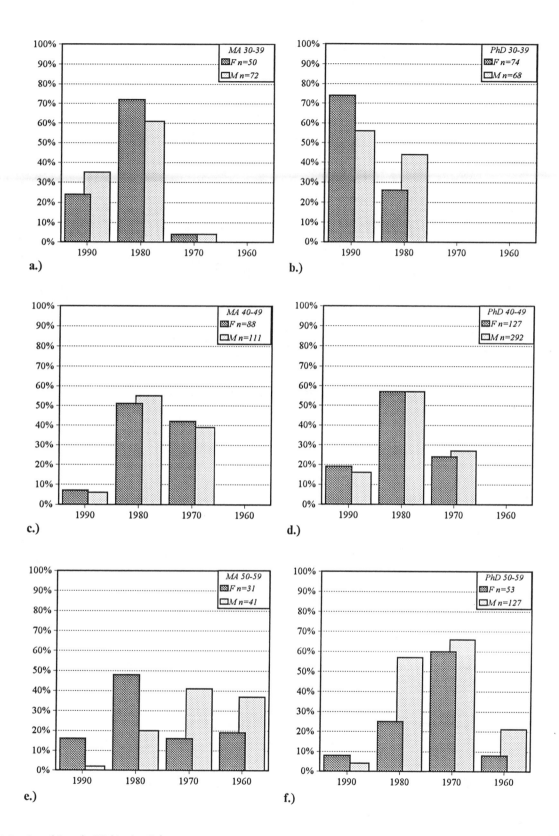

Fig. 3.3 *Award Decades Within Age Cohort*

a Final MAs in the 30–39 age cohort

c Final MAs in the 40–49 age cohort

e Final MAs in the 50–59 age cohort

b PhDs in the 30–39 age cohort

d PhDs in the 40–49 age cohort

f PhDs in the 50–59 age cohort

Note the diversity of award decades represented in each age cohort.

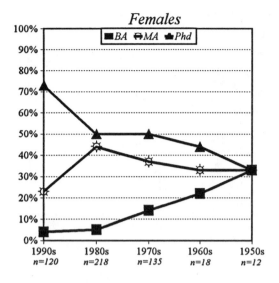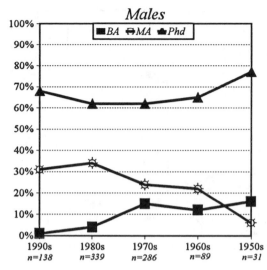

Fig. 3.4 *Final Degrees by Award Decade*

a Proportions of different final degrees among women by award decade

b Proportions of different final degrees among men by award decade

Note the decline in the proportions of final BAs and the increase in the proportion of final MAs in both men and women. Note also the increase in the proportion of PhDs among women, and the decline in PhDs among men.

with MAs when compared to men. This pattern reverses in the 30–39 age cohort and in the degrees awarded in the 1990s, when for the first time there are proportionately more men than women whose final degree is an MA. This reversal in the proportions of male and female MAs is especially strong when the degree data are examined by age cohort (Figure 3.6b), but is more muted when the data are displayed by award decade (Figure 3.6a).

Figure 3.7 looks at these same patterns from the vantage point of the PhD recipients. Mirroring the increase in male MAs, among men there is a fairly strong decline in the proportion of PhDs over time, especially when the data are examined by award decade (Figure 3.7a). The proportion of females who earn PhDs is fairly steady, though there is some indication of a slight decline in PhDs among those in their 40s when compared to those in their

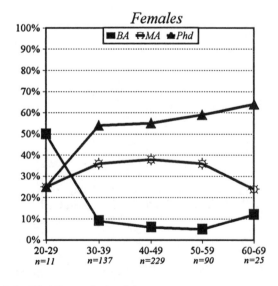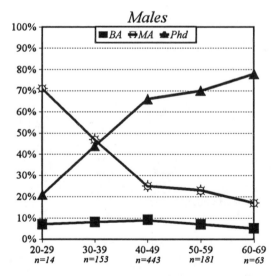

Fig. 3.5 *Final Degrees by Age Cohort*

a Proportions of different final degrees among women by age cohort

b Proportions of different final degrees among men by age cohort

Note the increase in the proportions of final MAs in both genders, and the decrease in the proportions of PhDs.

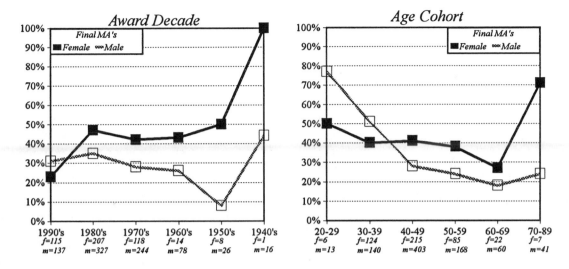

Fig. 3.6 *Final MAs Relative to PhDs*

a Final MAs by award decade

b Final MAs by age cohort

Note the higher proportion of final MAs among women in less recent decades and in older age cohorts when compared to men, and the reversal of this pattern in the 1990s and among younger archaeologists.

50s (Figure 3.7b), as well as between degree recipients of the 1980s when compared to the 1970s (Figure 3.7a). In all of the older age cohorts and less recent award decades, proportionately more males hold PhDs than women, a pattern that reverses in the 30–39 year cohort and in the 1990 award decade. The large and highly significant jump in female PhDs among 1990s graduates (Figure 3.7a; χ^2=17.068, df=1, p<.001) is the looking-glass image of the decline in the proportion of women who graduated during the decade with a final MA. There is no indication, how-

ever, of such a sharp increase in the proportion of female PhDs in the 30–39 age cohort (Figure 3.7b). Likewise, the steep decline in male PhDs seen in the 30–39 age cohort is not reflected in the proportion of males who received their PhDs in the 1990s, which seems to increase slightly relative to the preceding decade.

The lack of correspondence between degree status of men and women when data are arrayed in these two different ways is an artifact of the above-mentioned blending of age cohorts within award decades, and award decades

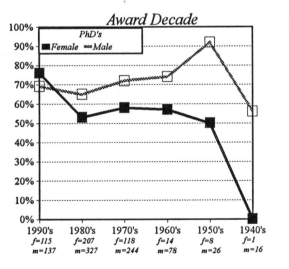

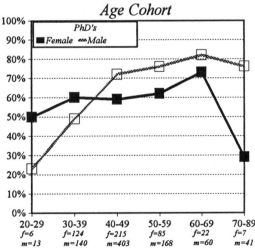

Fig. 3.7 *PhDs Relative to Final MAs*

a PhDs by award decade

b PhDs by age cohort

Note the higher proportion of PhDs among men in less recent decades and in older age cohorts when compared to women, and the reversal of this pattern in the 1990s and among younger archaeologists.

within age cohorts. For the men the mixture of several different age cohorts within the 1990 award decade dampens the patterns seen so clearly in younger male age cohorts. Half of the doctorates awarded to men in the 1990s were received by men who are currently in their 40s (Figure 3.2f). In contrast, almost 80 percent of the men receiving final MAs in the 1990s are under 40 (Figure 3.2e). Thus the apparent increase in the proportion of male PhDs in the 1990s is mostly an artifact of older men completing their doctoral studies, while the high proportion of men in the 1990s who end their studies with MA degrees may be a better reflection of more recent trends in degree status of male archaeologists.

For women the inclusion of a number of award decades within single age cohorts is primarily responsible for obscuring recent trends in female degree status. Roughly three-quarters of the female PhDs currently in their 30s earned their doctorates in the 1990s (Figure 3.3b). However, when examining the degree status of women in the 30–39 cohort, the high proportion of women in their 30s who earned final MAs in the 1980s (Figure 3.3a) masks the jump in recent female PhDs that is so evident when the data are displayed by award decade. In fact, the jump in the proportion of women earning PhDs in the 1990s would be even higher were it not for the number of older women, in their 40s, 50s, and even 60s, who received final MA degrees during this decade (Figure 3.2e).

What is needed to control for this blending effect is to segregate the population by both award decade and by age. Figure 3.8 segregates the sample by gender, age, and degree decade, contrasting the proportions of MAs to PhDs within each age cohort of people who obtained their final academic degrees during that decade. Data for women are displayed in the graphs on the left side of the figure; men are on the right. And while segregating the population into such small subgroups makes it difficult to statistically test patterns in certain cases, it does give a clear perspective on the most recent trends in degree status. For the most part, proportions of PhDs and final MAs for men and women in both the 1970s (Figure 3.8a and b) and 1980s (Figure 3.8c and d) are quite similar to one another. While proportionally more males hold PhDs than MAs as their final degrees than is the case for women, this difference is significant only in the 40–49 age cohorts (for the 1970s: χ^2=7.071, df=1, p=.008; for the 1980s: χ^2=3.853, df=1, p=.050). This is not the case among graduates of the 1990s, specifically among the younger graduates (Figure 3.8e and f). Eighty-two percent of the women in their 30s who graduated in the 1990s hold doctoral degrees, compared to only 60 percent of the men (χ^2=7.559, df=1, p=.006). In the smaller 20–29 year old cohort, half of the 6 women who graduated in the 1990s hold PhDs, while three-quarters of the 12 males in their 20s who hold nonstudent memberships in the SAA appear to have com-

pleted their academic careers with master's degrees. Thus it would seem that though there is a marked and ongoing increase in the proportion of PhDs among the youngest and most recent female graduates, there is an opposite but similarly strong tendency among younger males to terminate their studies at the master's degree level.

This conclusion is bolstered when we make a similar comparison of the proportions of final and ongoing MA degrees among men and women graduates in the 1990s (Figure 3.9). Although the proportions of final and ongoing MAs among men and women 1990s graduates in their 40s are essentially identical at about 50 percent each, women in their 30s appear much more likely to obtain ongoing MAs than men. Nearly 70 percent of the women in their 30s earning master's degrees in the 1990s are still pursuing their studies or have gone on to obtain doctoral degrees. In contrast, only 48 percent of the men in their 30s have continued their studies past the MA level. There is an apparent jump in the proportion of ongoing MAs in both the men and women 1990s graduates in their 20s. However, this increase is probably an artifact of the types of 20 year olds who are likely to join the SAA and to fill out this Census (upper-level graduate students and a handful of recent PhDs), rather than being representative of the universe of 20 year old archaeologists as a whole. Yet the fact that only 12 percent of the women in their 20s have final MAs compared to 31 percent of the men is likely reflective of an overall tendency for younger men to end their training at the master's degree level.

These changes in male and female degree status are apparent not only when one contrasts the proportions of different degrees within each gender, but also when the actual numbers of males and females are directly compared. Figure 3.10 presents the proportions of men and women in each award decade and age cohort for ongoing MAs (Figure 3.10a and b), for PhDs (Figure 3.10c and d), and for final MAs (Figure 3.10e and f). Graphs that display these data by age cohort also include a representation of the proportion of women in the overall population of respondents in that age cohort, which is shown as an asterisk (*) in the bar for each age cohort. In both the ongoing MAs and in the PhDs there is a strong, steady increase in the numbers of women relative to men in each more recent award decade and in each younger age cohort. Women represent 50 percent of the ongoing MAs in their 30s and 60 percent of the ongoing MAs in their 20s. Women PhDs make up a little more than half of the PhDs in their 30s and exactly 50 percent of the PhDs graduating in the 1990s. The increase in the representation of women closely matches the overall increase in the representation of women in younger cohorts, and indeed only in one instance is the proportion of women in a degree pool significantly less than the proportion of women in the cohort as a whole (ongoing MAs in their 40s: χ^2=11.958, df=1, p=.001). However, it is interesting to note that the

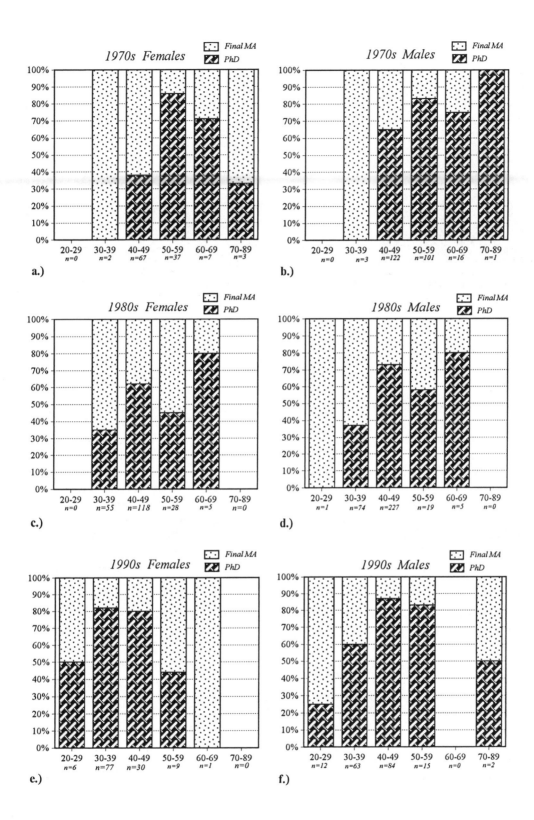

Fig. 3.8 *Final MAs and PhDs by Age Cohort and Award Decade*

a Females in the 1970s
c Females in the 1980s
e Females in the 1990s

b Males in the 1970s
d Males in the 1980s
f Males in the 1990s

Note the higher proportion of PhDs among younger women in the 1990s, and the higher proportion of final MAs among younger men in the 1990s.

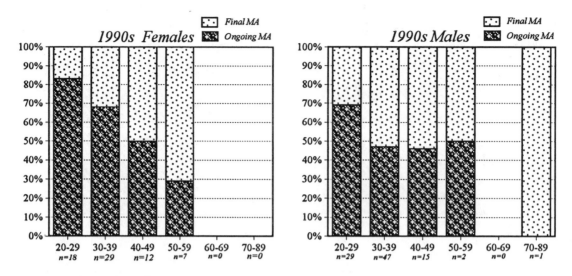

Fig. 3.9 *Final MAs and Ongoing MAs by Age Cohort for the 1990 Award Decade*

a Females in the 1990s   **b** Males in the 1990s

Note the higher proportion of ongoing MAs among younger women graduating in the 1990s, and the higher proportion of final MAs among younger men.

proportion of older women who obtained ongoing MAs and PhDs is less in all cases than the proportion of these women in the cohort as a whole, while the proportion of younger women in their 20s and 30s who have obtained these degrees is somewhat *higher* than the proportion of women in these younger cohorts.

This pattern is not seen among those who earn MAs as their final degree. Women are relatively better represented among the ranks of older final MAs than they are among older ongoing MAs and PhDs, making up a little over 40 percent of both the 40–49 and the 50–59 cohorts of final MAs (Figure 3.10f), compared to 30 percent of both ongoing MAs and PhDs in their 40s and 50s (Figure 3.10b and d). Moreover, the proportion of women among those who hold a master's as a final degree is significantly greater than the proportion of women in these cohorts (for the 40–49 cohort: χ^2=7.431, df=1, p=.006; for the 50–59 cohort: χ^2=2.884, df=1, p=.084). However, unlike the ongoing MAs and the PhDs, which show a strong increase in the representation of women relative to men in the younger cohorts, among final MAs the representation of women falls very slightly to 40 percent of the 30–39 cohort and more steeply to only 22 percent of the 20–29 year cohort. Instead, it is the number of men who end their studies with MAs that appears to be on the increase in the younger and most recent graduates. In both cohorts of archaeologists in their 20s and 30s, the male-to-female ratio among those with final MA degrees is *greater* than it is in the cohort as a whole.

• To summarize, over the years there has been a gradual but steady decline in the proportion of men earning doctoral degrees. The rate of this decline has accelerated

sharply among the males in their 20s and 30s. Close to 80 percent of the males in their 60s who received their final degrees in the 1950s and 1960s hold doctoral degrees. Among the younger males graduating with final degrees in the 1990s, less than 50 percent have PhDs. We see the opposite pattern among women, where the proportion of women with PhDs has shown a steady increase over the years. Once again, the pace of this change has accelerated among younger women just beginning their careers. While only about half of the older women who received their degrees in the 1950s through the 1980s hold doctoral degrees, a little more than 80 percent of the women in their 30s who entered the job market in the 1990s have PhDs. Moreover, PhDs are not just relatively better represented among these younger women when compared to men; women actually outnumber younger male PhDs. Finally, judging from the steady increase in the proportion of ongoing MAs among younger women, this trend appears not only likely to continue but perhaps even to intensify in graduates of the early 21st century. •

Length of Time Spent Obtaining Degrees

Measuring Time Between Degrees

Since we asked Census respondents to list the years in which they received their various degrees, we can compute both the number of years it took an individual to obtain a graduate degree, as well as his or her age on receipt of that degree. When these data are grouped by award decade, we can follow trends in the length of time taken to obtain degrees in archaeology across the last six decades. One word of caution should be kept in mind. While it is possible to calculate the number of years between the receipt

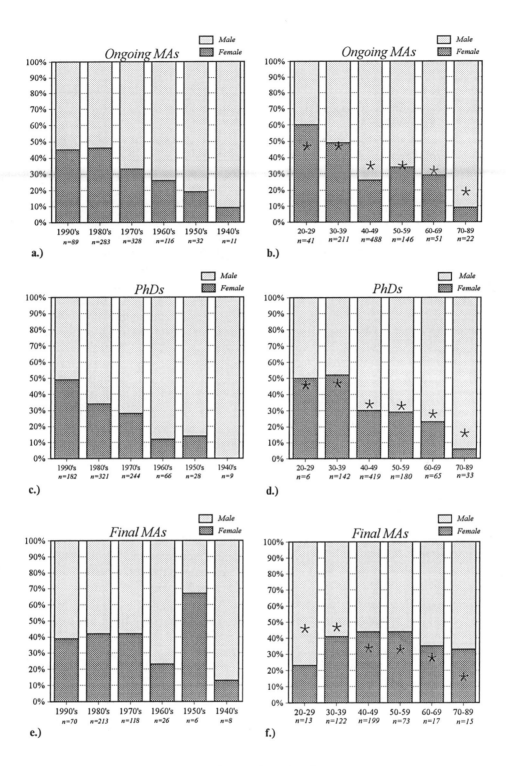

Fig. 3.10 *Gender Representation Within Graduate Degrees by Award Decade and Age*

a Ongoing MAs by award decade

c PhDs by award decade

e Final MAs by award decade

b Ongoing MAs by age cohort (* = proportion of women within age cohort, including professionals and students)

d PhDs by age cohort (* = proportion of women within overall age cohort, professionals only)

f Final MAs by age cohort (* = proportion of women within overall age cohort, professionals only)

Note the increasingly even representation of women and men among ongoing MAs and PhDs, and the increasingly greater representation of men among final MAs.

of an individual's bachelors degree and his or her MA or PhD degree, this is not necessarily a measure of the number of years spent in graduate school actively pursuing that degree. Using only degree award dates we cannot tell whether respondents were continuously engaged in graduate studies during the years between degrees, or whether they left school for a while to pursue other activities before returning to finish a degree. This possibility becomes more real in the case of older recipients of degrees, and needs to be taken into account in evaluating trends in length of time spent in graduate programs.

Longitudinal Trends in Obtaining Different Graduate Degrees

Figures 3.11 and 3.12 present summary data for doctoral and master's degrees on the years spent obtaining degrees and the age on receipt of degrees by award decade. Looking first at the entire population of PhDs (Figure 3.11a), there has been a staggering increase over the past six decades in the length of time taken to obtain a doctoral degree. The PhD recipient in the 1990s now takes an average of 13.6 years after receipt of a BA to obtain a doctoral degree. The average age of the 1990s PhD recipient is 36.5 years old. In comparison, the average PhD degree recipient in the 1960s took only 7.8 years beyond the BA to finish the degree and was 31.4 years old on graduation. Thus, the length of time it takes to obtain a PhD has nearly doubled since 1960.

Not all PhD training trajectories are the same, however. In some graduate programs students do not acquire master's degrees as part of their training, in some the MA is automatically awarded when course work is finished, and in still others the master's degree carries special examination and thesis requirements of its own. If students change graduate programs after receiving their master's degree, they may have to meet overlapping course and examination requirements of both the MA- and the PhD-granting institution. All of these various possibilities should make a difference in the speed with which students progress through their graduate studies. When we break the PhD data down into groups of PhDs who did not receive MAs along the way (Figure 3.11b), and those who hold both MAs and PhDs (Figure 3.11c), we can clearly see that it takes longer to complete a PhD when one also earns a master's degree as part of one's graduate training. In almost every decade, those with MAs have taken substantially longer to finish their doctorates than those without MA degrees. Over the years there has been a considerable increase in the proportion of PhDs with master's degrees (from 69 percent in the 1960s to 95 percent in the 1990s), and it is possible that the higher proportion of PhDs with MAs has helped boost the time spent obtaining a doctoral degree, as seen in the population of PhDs as a whole. However, an increase in the proportion of PhDs

with intermediate master's degrees in the pool of PhD recipients would not seem to be the only factor operating here. Both subgroups of doctoral recipients, those with and those without master's degrees, show similar increases in the number of years between the BA and PhD and in the average age of the PhD recipient.

In the case of PhDs who earn master's degrees as part of their doctoral studies, we can look more closely at the training process by comparing the two different phases of obtaining a doctoral degree, the years leading up to the receipt of an ongoing MA (Figure 3.12a) and the years between the receipt of the MA and the PhD (Figure 3.12b). Clearly, the balance of the time spent pursuing a PhD comes after the receipt of the MA. In each award decade it takes from one to three years longer to progress from an MA to a PhD than it does to progress from a BA to an ongoing MA. Over the decades, moreover, we also see increases in the number of years devoted to both phases of the pursuit of a doctoral degree. Since the 1960s the average number of years taken to obtain an ongoing MA has increased by a little more than 2 years, from 4.1 years in the 1960s to 6.4 years in the 1990s. It is the post-MA period, however, that has increased most substantially. In the 1960s the average PhD recipient took 5.3 years after the MA to receive a doctorate. In the 1990s the period between the MA and the PhD has increased by 3 years to 8.3 years. While changing institutions during one's doctoral studies can lengthen the duration of one's doctoral studies, the increase seen here in the two phases of the doctoral studies cannot be attributed to higher number of individuals switching graduate programs between the MA and the PhD. In fact, over time there has been a *decrease* in the proportion of individuals who receive MAs and PhDs from different institutions, from 44 percent in the 1960s to 36 percent in the 1990s.

Comparing data for ongoing MAs (Figure 3.12a) to MAs earned as a final degree (Figure 3.12c), it is plain that a final MA takes longer to complete than a master's degree earned as a step toward a PhD. In each of the decades examined, the final MA takes one to three years longer to complete than the ongoing MA. As with the PhDs, final MAs now take substantially longer to receive and recipients are quite a bit older than they were in earlier decades. In the 1960s it took an average of 5.1 years to obtain a final MA degree and the recipient was 27.9 years old when he or she graduated. Today the average recipient of a final MA receives the degree 9.6 years after being awarded a bachelor's degree, and is 35.1 years old on graduation.

To some extent the time taken to obtain master's and doctoral degrees in recent decades may be elevated by the presence of older individuals in the sample of degree recipients. For example, the pool of PhD recipients in the 1980s contains 7 individuals currently in their 60s who took an average of 26.3 years to finish their degrees; the 1990s sample of final MAs includes 12 individuals in their 40s who

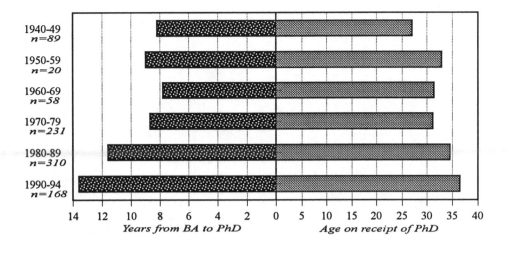

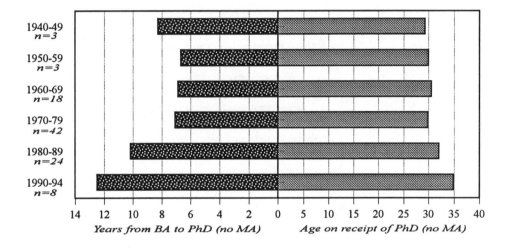

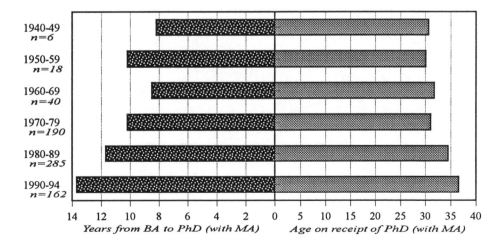

Fig. 3.11 *Length of Time to Obtain a PhD by Award Decade*

a BA to PhD, total sample of PhDs

b BA to PhD, without an MA

c BA to PhD, with an MA

Note the increase in time taken to obtain a PhD in more recent award decades. Note also that it takes longer to complete a PhD if an MA is also earned than a PhD without an MA.

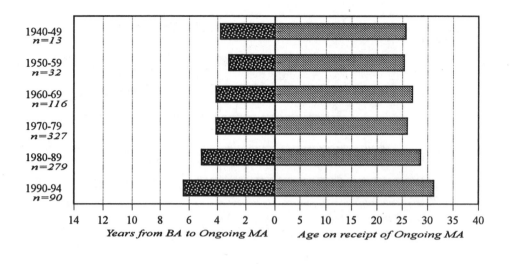

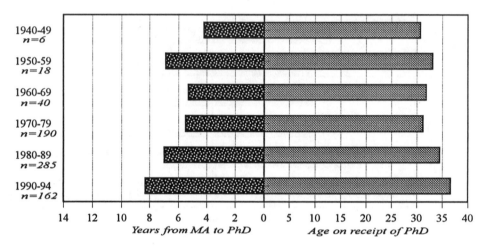

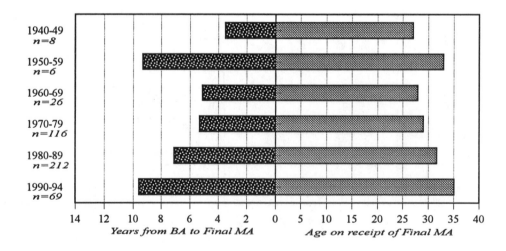

Fig. 3.12 *Length of Time to Obtain Ongoing and Final MAs and to Move from an MA to a PhD*

a BA to ongoing MA
b MA to PhD
c BA to final MA

Note the increase in time taken to obtain MAs and to move from an MA to a PhD in more recent award decades. Note also that it takes longer to complete a final MA than an ongoing MA.

took an average of 13.2 years to finish their degrees. These older degree recipients were probably not continuously enrolled in full-time graduate school over these years. Instead they are more likely people who either returned to school to pursue advanced degrees after some hiatus in their studies, or who were enrolled part time. While older students probably also returned to school to finish their degrees in earlier decades, they are not as likely to be represented in our sample of degree recipients. The majority of 1940s, 1950s, and 1960s graduates are currently in their mid-50s, 60s, and 70s. These people were in their 20s and early 30s when they received their degrees and probably proceeded without interruption from their bachelor's degrees to their master's degrees and on to their PhDs. Individuals who took a less direct route to their graduate studies in these earlier decades and received their degrees later in life are now probably making quite a different kind of contribution to the archaeological record than they

did during their active careers. In contrast, older degree recipients are increasingly well represented in the 1970s, 1980s, and 1990s. The presence of older degree recipients in the more recent decades and their absence in earlier decades could, then, make the increase in the number of years between degrees and in the average age of graduates noted in more recent years seem greater than it really is. For the most part, the samples of degree recipients in more recent decades are large enough to compensate for the presence of older returning students. But it is also possible to try to correct for this bias by looking only at the data for youngest age cohorts in each degree decade. For the 1940s this is the 70 and 80 year olds, for the 1950s it is the 60 and 70 year olds, for the 1960s it is the 50 and 60 year olds, for the 1970s it is the 40 and 50 year olds, and so on.

When older returning students are removed from the sample (Figure 3.13), we do indeed see some drop in the length of time it takes to obtain various degrees. The

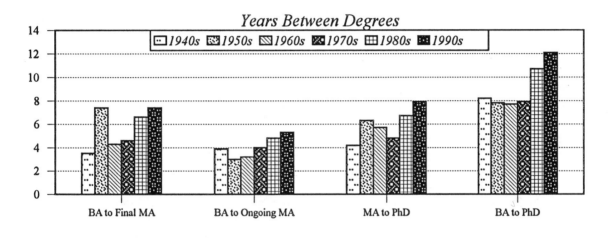

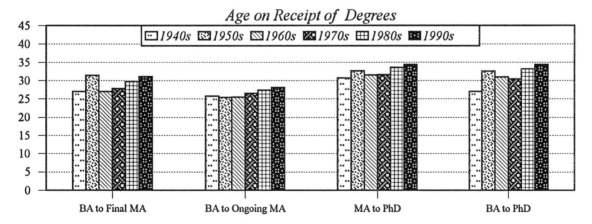

Fig. 3.13 *Length of Time to Obtain Degrees in Archaeology, Excluding Older Degree Recipients*

a Average number of years to obtain degrees in archaeology by award decade

b Average age on receipt of degree by award decade

Note the decrease in the number of years taken to complete degrees and average ages on receipt of degrees when older degree receipients are removed from the sample. Note, however, the persistent trend toward longer graduate studies, which accelerates in the 1980s and 1990s.

number of years between the BA and PhD for 1990s graduates drops from 13.2 years to 12.1; the length of time it takes to obtain a final MA in the 1990s drops from 9.6 years to 7.4 years (Figure 3.13a). The average age of the 1990s final MA recipient drops from 35.1 to 31.1; the average age of the 1990s PhD recipient drops from 36.5 to 34.4 (Figure 3.13b). However, even these corrected data show a marked increase in the length of time taken to obtain advanced degrees in archaeology and in the average age of the degree recipient. The 1980s and 1990s show the greatest increase. This is especially true for the final MAs, where between the 1970s and the 1980s there is a jump of two years in the time taken to obtain a final MA and an additional one-year increase between the 1980s and 1990s. Perhaps this trend is reflective of enhanced requirements for completion of an MA in these more recent decades.

The largest jump, however, is seen in the PhDs. Even these corrected data show a three-year increase from the 1970s to the 1980s in the average number of years between the BA and PhD, and an additional two-year increase from the 1980s to the 1990s. Figure 3.13a also clearly demonstrates that the majority of the increase in the number of years between the BA and the PhD comes in the post-MA phase of the PhD studies. While the length of time taken to obtain an ongoing MA has risen only a little more than a year between the 1970s and the 1990s, during this same time there has been a greater than three-year increase in the average post-MA period.

• It would seem an inescapable conclusion that the time taken to obtain advanced degrees in archaeology has seen a quantum leap over the last few decades. Even students who are more or less continuously enrolled in graduate programs are taking as much as twice as long to complete graduate degrees as they were 20 years ago. Today's entry-level master's graduate is well into his or her 30s, and the newly minted PhD is likely to be pushing 40. •

Gender Trends in Obtaining Graduate Degrees

One might ask whether both men and women are equally affected by increases in the length of graduate studies, or whether changes in the gender composition of the degree recipients in more recent decades (as noted above) could *also* be influencing trends in the length of time taken to receive degrees. Census data indicate that this is not the case. Figures 3.14 and 3.15 break down the data on years spent obtaining various degrees and the average age of degree recipients by gender. All age cohorts are included here, both the younger continuously enrolled graduates and the older graduates returning to their studies. Figure 3.14 presents data for ongoing MAs (Figure 3.14a and b), for the MA to PhD years (Figure 3.14c and d), and for final MAs (Figure 3.14e and f). In Figure 3.15 data are presented for the PhD population as a whole (Figure 3.15a

and b), for PhDs without MAs (Figure 3.15c and d), and for PhDs with MAs (Figure 3.15e and f). It is immediately apparent that both men and women have experienced essentially identical trends in the length of time taken to complete graduate degrees. It is also clear that across the decades, and in all degree categories, there is little difference in the time men and women take to complete their degrees. Men and women seldom vary by more than one year either in the average number of years taken to obtain a degree or in their age on receipt of a degree. In those instances where there is greater variation, the difference is more likely attributable to a smaller sample size (as in the case of ongoing MAs in the 1940s and 1950s, Figure 3.14a and b), or the presence of older returning students in the sample. The influence of this second factor is especially keenly felt in two of the most striking cases in which men and women differ in the length of time they take to receive graduate degrees, the 1990s final MAs (Figure 3.14e and f) and the doctoral graduates of the 1990s (Figure 3.15). In the first case, women obtaining final MAs in the 1990s (Figure 3.15e) take an average of 11.7 years to complete these degrees and are almost 39 years old when they graduate (Figure 3.15f). In contrast, men receiving final MAs in the 1990s take an average of 8.3 years to complete the degree and are a little under 34 years old when they receive their MA degree. However, this difference is primarily an artifact of the number of older women in the pool of 1990s final MAs (Figure 3.2e) and the fact that so many younger men are ending their studies at the MA level. In the case of the disparity between male and female PhD recipients in the 1990s (Figure 3.15), the increase in the time men take to finish their doctorate and their relatively advanced average age on graduation (almost 38 years old compared to average for females at 35) is due to the high proportion of older men among the 1990s doctoral recipients (Figure 3.2f) and the large increase in the proportion of younger women going on for doctoral degrees. When older degree recipients are eliminated from the sample, there is no difference between the length of time younger, continuously enrolled men and women take to complete PhDs in the 1990s. Both receive their degrees a little less than 10.5 years after the BA and are 32 years old on graduation.

• Thus, it would seem that there is no current, and little past, disparity in the time men and women take to complete graduate degrees when they are continuously enrolled in graduate programs. Any disparity in these data is most likely attributable to older students returning to complete their degrees after some hiatus in their studies. In earlier decades, this phenomenon was more common among women than for men, and it still seems to be affecting women who are ending their academic careers with master's degrees in the 1990s. For the recent PhDs, however, it is the men who seem to have a larger number of

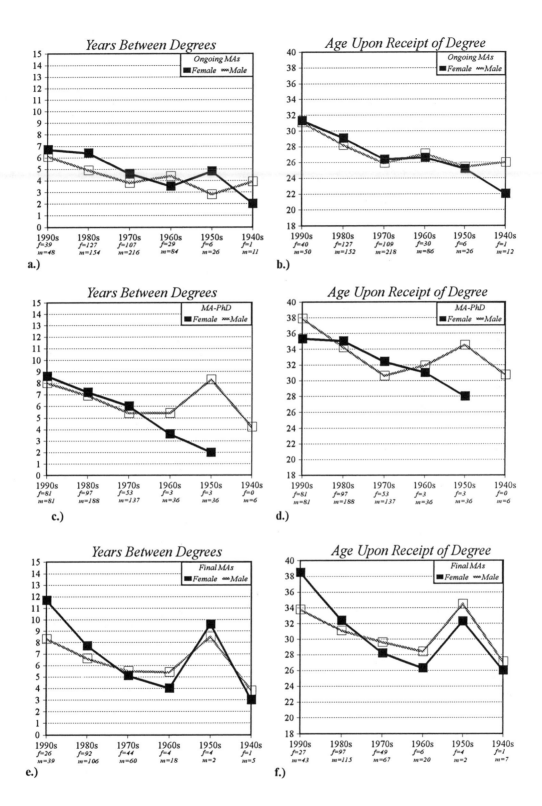

Fig. 3.14 *Length of Time to Obtain MA Degrees and to Move from an MA to a PhD by Gender and Award Decade*

a Average years between BA and ongoing MA
b Average age on receipt of an ongoing MA
c Average years between MA and PhD
d Average age on receipt of PhD with an MA
e Average years between BA and final MA
f Average age on receipt of final MA

Note the similarity in the length of time men and women have taken in almost all cohorts to receive ongoing and final MAs, and to progress from an ongoing MA to a PhD. Note, however, the exception of women graduating in the 1990s with final MAs.

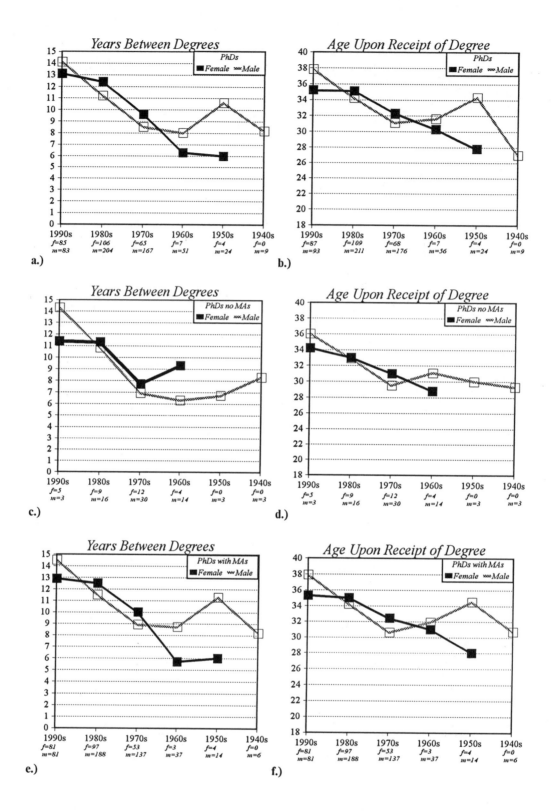

Fig. 3.15 *Length of Time to Obtain a PhD by Gender and Award Decade*

a Average years between BA and PhD

c Average years between BA and PhD without an MA

d Average years between BA and PhD with an MA

b Average age on receipt of PhD

d Average age on receipt of PhD without an MA

f Average age on receipt of PhD with an MA

Note the similarity in the length of time men and women have taken in almost all cohorts to receive PhDs with and without ongoing MAs. Also note, however, the exception of men graduating in the 1990s with PhDs.

older returning graduates and a relatively depressed number of younger, continuously enrolled students. •

Degree-Granting Institutions

Productivity of Institutions Granting Graduate Degrees

The SAA Census also asked individuals to list the institutions from which they received their degrees, allowing us to look more closely at trends in education by the actual institutions granting graduate degrees in archaeology. While it is important to keep in mind that these data represent only the institutions attended by Census respondents, not the actual universe of degree-granting institutions, patterns seen in these data provide a useful perspective on the trends discussed earlier in this chapter. Table 3.1 presents the 10 institutions that have the greatest number of final MA, ongoing MA, and PhD graduates in our sample. At first glance the most striking feature of this table is the dominance of the University of Arizona. Arizona tops the list of degree-granting institutions for all graduate degrees examined here. To a certain extent, the somewhat higher representation of respondents from the Southwest in the Census population discussed in Chapter 1 may have helped boost the number of graduates from the University of Arizona, as well as contributed to the strong showing of other Southwestern institutions. But it is important to remember that regional attributions were based on current residence. Graduates of schools in a particular region are not all necessarily still living there.

A bit more subtle, but ultimately more important, pattern is the degree of overlap between the lists of the top 10 institutions awarding these different graduate degrees. Seven of the 10 PhD-granting institutions with the most graduates are also found on the list of the 10 institutions that have granted the most ongoing MA degrees. Given the increasingly high proportion of people who remain at the same institution throughout their graduate studies mentioned earlier, this overlap is not surprising. In contrast, the list of institutions that have granted the greatest

number of final MA degrees shares only 4 institutions with the list of top 10 PhD-granting institutions and only 3 with the top 10 ongoing MA-granting ones. It would seem that those who end their studies with an MA degree are not simply graduate students who choose, for whatever reason, not to go on for the PhD. Rather, many of these individuals attend a different set of institutions than students enrolled in PhD programs. A number of these institutions do not offer PhDs, but instead have graduate programs aimed specifically at the MA as the final professional degree.

It would also seem that the separation between final and ongoing MA-granting institutions has become particularly acute in the 1980s and 1990s. In the case of 5 of the top 10 final MA-granting institutions, the balance of the degrees were awarded in the last 5 to 15 years (Arizona State, Northern Arizona University, University of Wisconsin at Milwaukee, Southern Illinois University at Carbondale, and University of Tennessee at Knoxville). Moreover, just below the top 10 final MA-granting institutions on the list presented in Table 3.1 (but not shown in this table) is a group of universities that granted final MAs to 6 Census respondents apiece (California State University at Fullerton, California State University at Sacramento, Sonoma State University, Eastern New Mexico University, University of Kansas, and Southern Florida University). Almost all of these degrees were awarded in the 1980s and 1990s. Moreover, these institutions either are absent from the list of ongoing MA institutions or are very poorly represented there. Looking at the overall list of final MA-granting institutions, of the 96 institutions that awarded final MAs from the 1940s through the 1970s, three-quarters are also represented on the list of 144 institutions that granted ongoing MAs over that period of time. In contrast, there are 135 institutions represented by Census respondents who received final MAs in the 1980s and 1990s, compared to 121 institutions that have granted ongoing MAs during the last two decades. Moreover, only a little more than half of the institutions granting final

Final MA		Ongoing MA		PhD	
Name	**Number**	**Name**	**Number**	**Name**	**Number**
Arizona (Tucson)	23	Arizona (Tucson)	52	Arizona (Tucson)	59
Arizona State (Tempe)	15	Michigan (Ann Arbor)	37	Michigan (Ann Arbor)	42
Colorado (Boulder)	13	California (Los Angeles)	24	Harvard	41
Washington State (Pullman)	13	New Mexico (Albuquerque)	22	Arizona State (Tempe)	30
Northern Arizona (Flagstaff)	11	SUNY (Binghamton)	22	California (Berkeley)	27
New Mexico (Albuquerque)	11	Harvard	21	Chicago	26
Texas (Austin)	10	Colorado (Boulder)	19	California (Los Angeles)	26
S. Illinois (Carbondale)	9	Chicago	19	Washington State (Pullman)	26
Wisconsin (Milwaukee)	9	California (Berkeley)	19	Pennsylvania	25
Tennessee (Knoxville)	8	Wisconsin (Madison)	19	New Mexico (Albuquerque)	24

Table 3.1 *Top 10 Degree-Granting Institutions*

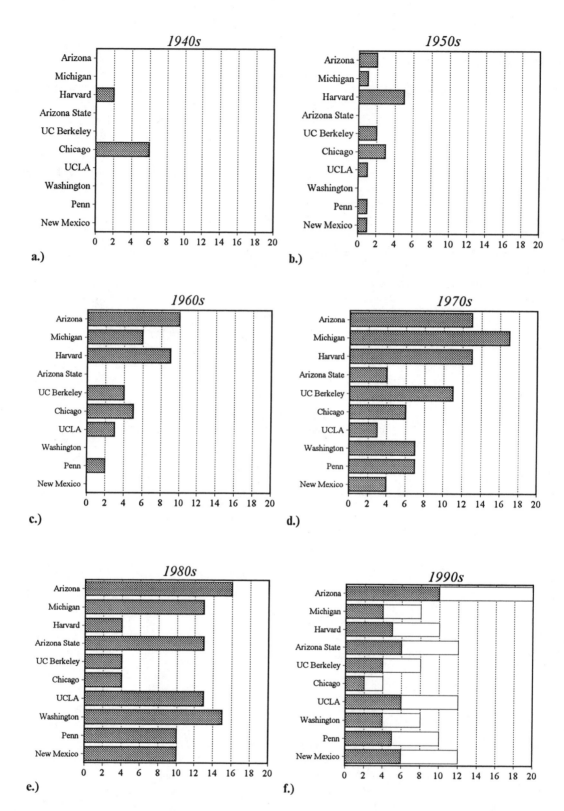

Fig. 3.16 *Number of Graduates of the 10 Best-Represented PhD-Granting Institutions by Award Decade*

a 1940s   **b** 1950s
c 1960s   **d** 1970s
e 1980s   **f** 1990s

Note the decline in the number of graduates from East Coast and Midwestern institutions in recent decades, and the increase in the number of graduates from institutions in the Southwest and West.

MAs during this time also granted MAs to people who either have received their doctorates or are still engaged in graduate studies. The growing distinction between final and ongoing MA institutions in the 1980s and 1990s, and the corresponding development of graduate programs specifically aimed at producing master's degrees, may well have contributed to the marked increase in the length of time it takes to obtain final MAs in the 1980s and 1990s, noted above.

Longitudinal Trends in Productivity of PhD-Granting Institutions

With the larger size of our sample of PhD recipients, we can look more closely at changing patterns over time in PhD-granting institutions. Figure 3.16 presents the number of PhD graduates from each of the 10 PhD-granting institutions that are best represented in our sample, arranged by award decade. Again it is important to remember here that these data represent only Census respondents, and are thus only proxy evidence of actual trends over time. However, given the size and breadth of our sample, patterns seen here probably are generally representative of ongoing trends. Representation of these top 10 institutions over time is not steady. Particular schools, such as Harvard University and especially the University of Chicago, dominate earlier decades, but contribute a much smaller proportion to the graduate pool of later decades. The University of Michigan, which is the best-represented school among graduates of the 1970s, has a much smaller share of the graduates of the early 1990s. The progressive ascendancy of the University of Arizona among PhD-granting institutions is particularly striking, and is part of a general trend showing a gradual decline in the number of graduates produced by traditional powerhouses on the

East Coast and in the Midwest, and an increase in the number of graduates from universities in the Southwest and on the West Coast.

Gender Trends in PhD-Granting Institutions

When we look at the gender breakdown of the top five PhD-granting institutions over the last three decades (Figure 3.17), the proportion of women among the graduating doctoral students shows increases in all instances. In the 1970s women made up less than 30 percent of the graduating PhDs from all five schools, yet by the 1990s they constitute 50 percent or more of the graduates of these top PhD-producing universities. The proportion of women among the 1990s PhD graduates of the University of Arizona and Arizona State, at about 70 percent, is particularly impressive. This trend corresponds to an earlier pattern discussed in Chapter 2 that identified a strong representation of women among students in the Southwest (see Figure 2.5).

It is also interesting to note that the increase in the proportion of women PhD graduates in recent decades seems to have been felt first in these top 10 PhD-granting institutions. Figure 3.18 compares the proportion of female and male PhD graduates in each award decade in the top 10 PhD-granting institutions (Figure 3.18a) to that in the other institutions represented in our sample (Figure 3.18b). While women seemed at least marginally, though not significantly, better represented in the other degree-granting institutions in earlier decades, by the 1970s the representation of women both in the top 10 and in the other PhD-granting institutions was about the same, at slightly less than 30 percent. In the 1980s, however, women comprised 50 percent of the graduates of the top 10 institutions, while they made up less than 30

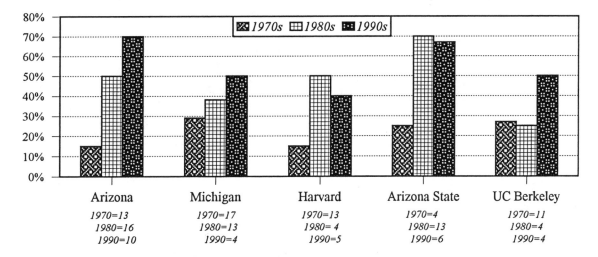

Fig. 3.17 *Representation of Women Among Graduates of the Top Five PhD-Granting Institutions over the Last Three Award Decades*

Note the increase in the proportion of women PhDs in all five institutions between the 1970s and 1980s, and the particularly high proportion of women among the more recent graduates of University of Arizona and Arizona State University.

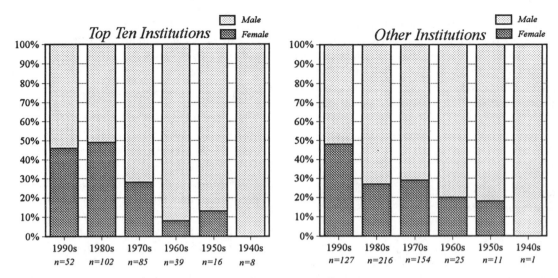

Fig. 3.18 *Representation of Men and Women Among Graduates of PhD-Granting Institutions by Award Decade*

a Top 10 PhD-granting institutions   **b** Other PhD-granting institutions

Note that the proportion of women PhDs increases first in the 1980s in the top 10 institutions.

percent of the graduates of the other universities (χ^2= 3.036, df=1, p=.08). By the 1990s both the leading PhD-granting institutions and the other institutions represented in our sample are producing essentially equal numbers of male and female doctoral graduates. Since the schools identified here as the top 10 PhD-granting institutions in terms of numbers of graduates also appear on other lists of the schools with the highest-caliber doctoral programs (Plog and Rice 1993), it would appear that the trend toward better representation of women among graduating doctoral students happened first in the leading PhD programs, with other institutions catching up to this trend only in the following decade.

Proliferation of PhD-Granting Institutions

Comparing the proportions of graduates from these top 10 schools to those from other institutions over the decades (Figure 3.19), signals a steady decrease in the share of graduates these 10 universities contribute to the overall pool of doctoral graduates in each decade. This trend is tied not so much to the decline in the productivity of these 10 schools (which are still among the most productive of PhD-granting institutions) as it is to the overall increase in the number of PhD-granting programs. This pattern is made graphically clear in Figure 3.20, which presents the number of PhD-granting institutions represented in our sample and the number of degrees awarded by decade. The number of PhD-granting institutions has grown exponen-

tially from only 3 in the 1940s to more than 70 in the 1980s. Doctoral recipients from the first half of the 1990s come from 60 different institutions. And while it is true that the proliferation in the number of PhD-granting institutions is directly proportional to the number of graduates, the fact that the ratio of graduates to institutions remains constant at about three to one over the decades is an indication of a remarkable proliferation of PhD-granting institutions.

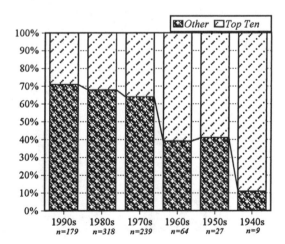

Fig. 3.19 *PhDs Awarded by the Top 10 Institutions Compared to Other Institutions by Award Decade*

Note the increase in the proportion of graduates from other institutions.

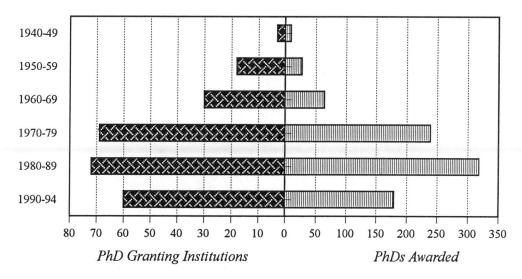

Fig. 3.20 *Number of PhD-Granting Institutions and PhDs Granted by Award Decade*

Note the proliferation in the number of PhD-granting institutions in more recent award decades.

• Thus, we have two trends in our data that appear to be on a collision course. While the number of PhD-granting institutions has been increasing over the years, the number of males pursuing PhDs has been steadily decreasing. It may be that until now the decline in the number of men seeking doctoral degrees has been compensated for by a marked increase in the number of women in PhD programs. At some point, however, there may be a net decrease in the number of students interested in attending these many different doctoral programs. Since final MAs seem to come from a different set of institutions than those that produce the majority of ongoing MAs and PhDs, the increase in the number of these younger men seeking an MA as their final degree would not compensate for this potential decrease in enrollment in doctoral programs. Thus if these trends continue and there is no fresh infusion of students interested in pursuing doctoral degrees in archaeology (a boomlet from the offspring of the baby boomer generation, for example) or a change in PhD programs that would make them more attractive to those students now electing to end their graduate studies at the master's degree level, then there is a real—and perhaps even *pressing*—potential of having too many PhD programs and too few PhD students. •

4 Archaeological Employment in the Americas

Introduction

Chapter Summary

This chapter presents a comprehensive examination of employment in American archaeology. Up to this point our discussion has focused on trends in basic demographics and educational trajectories. Here these trends are placed within the larger context of a discipline undergoing a period of profound transformation. At the heart of this transformation is a major restructuring in archaeological employment caused by the growth of public, and, especially, private sector archaeology that is challenging the long-standing status quo of archaeological practice in academia and museums, as well as reshaping almost every aspect of American archaeology. This chapter takes an in-depth look at these fundamental changes through an examination of where American archaeologists work, what they do there, what they would prefer to be doing, how much they earn, and how they view their careers in archaeology. In so doing, patterns in demographics and training noted earlier are themselves seen as part of these broader changes and shifts in where and how American archaeologists practice their trade. This understanding of the context and conditions of archaeological employment provides, in turn, a necessary context for a consideration of trends in research, publications, and funding in the chapters that follow.

Data presented in this chapter show that the marked increase in the proportion of women in archaeology, identified in Chapters 2 and 3, is accompanied by a significant shift among younger women away from jobs that straddle two or more major work settings, or in which archaeology is only a minor component, and toward more full-time employment in the four primary sectors of archaeological employment: academia, government, museums, and the private sector. And while the representation of women in these primary employment sectors has risen sharply, there has, in fact, been little change over the past 30 years in the distribution of women across these sectors. The increased representation of women in academia relative to men is not attributable to growth in the proportion of the female workforce who are employed in academia. Indeed, there has been some decline in academic employment among women. Instead this growth is largely an artifact of a significant movement of younger men away from these traditional sectors of archaeological employment, especially

from academia. The decline of men in academia is accompanied by a marked increase in the proportion of males pursuing careers in private sector and, to a lesser extent, in government-based archaeology. Both of these growth sectors tend to employ large numbers of individuals with master's degrees, a factor that probably explains the increasing number of younger men who are ending their studies with master's degrees. Moreover, people with master's degrees in government and the private sector have quite similar earning potentials as those with PhDs, especially when compared to those in academic and museum settings. The generally higher and faster-growing salaries in the private sector may also be a factor in the growth of private sector employment among younger men.

Data on income in archaeology also reveal that the substantial salary gap between older men and women is narrowing among cohorts of younger archaeologists who have entered the workforce more recently. And yet while there is greater equity in the salaries paid to younger men and women employed in similar jobs with similar training and experience, women are still more likely to earn salaries at the lower end of the salary scale and men on the upper end. This is especially true in museum work settings, but it is also seen in academic settings as well. There appears to be a somewhat greater gender equity in salaries in the private sector and, especially, in government work settings. It is difficult to tell from the SAA Census data whether the apparent trend toward greater gender equity in salaries is a correction of earlier imbalances that will follow these young archaeologists throughout their careers, or whether these women will face similar barriers to salary growth as those encountered by earlier generations.

A closer examination of jobs in the academic employment sector reveals persistent imbalances in the potential for advancement between men and women. In particular, there is an increasing proportion of women hired in non-tenure-track jobs (for example, visiting or adjunct professor positions). Even though fewer men are pursuing careers in academia, it would seem that those who do are more likely to secure one of the decreasing number of tenure-track positions. In contrast, while proportionately fewer women go into careers in the private sector than men, the women who are employed there tend to have more equal access to higher-level positions. Moreover, with the exception of CEOs of larger firms, who seem to be primarily male, salaries of higher-level managers in the private sector show greater gender parity than that seen in academia. A direct comparison of the salaries earned by people in different jobs in academia and the private sector indicates that the earning potential of private-sector positions is at least competitive with positions at comparable levels within academia, if not greater.

Quite at odds with current employment trends, employment preferences and career expectations among archaeologists still clearly favor more traditional academic and museum jobs. Not only is there a general preference for employment in museums, there are also relatively high levels of job satisfaction among both men and women in museum positions, despite the generally lower salaries of archaeologists in such jobs. Job satisfaction among academics, however, is not as high as might be predicted from the stated preferences of most respondents for employment in academic settings. This is especially true of women in academia. In contrast, people employed in the public and private sectors are generally quite satisfied with their careers in archaeology, and with their levels of financial compensation. There is, however, a strong tendency for government and private sector archaeologists to feel that the training they received ill prepared them for their current careers and that these careers are not consistent with their original expectations. These latter trends signal a failure among many academic institutions training future archaeologists to recognize and adapt to the changing nature of the archaeological workforce—a factor that has no doubt contributed to the changes in educational trajectories noted in the previous chapter.

Defining Employment Setting

Before turning to a discussion of trends in archaeological employment, it is important to define how the SAA Census data were used to determine respondent employment setting. The Census provided a list of 13 possible work settings that fell into four major general employment sectors: academic (community college, undergraduate university, graduate university, and academic-based cultural resource management operations), government (federal, state, local), museum (government, university, and private museums), and private (independent consultant, private firm, and private foundation). Retired and "other" categories were also listed (see Appendix). At any one time in their careers archaeologists may divide their efforts between one or more different settings. To capture this aspect of archaeological employment, instead of asking respondents to note their primary work setting, we decided to ask them to record the percentage of time spent in any of these settings. Respondents were also asked to use this same method for indicating their employment preferences. A similar grid was provided for activities conducted in the course of their archaeological endeavors. In this way

we thought we could capture a fairly fine-grained image both of the settings in which archaeologists practice their discipline as well as what they do there.

To be more generally useful in examining trends in archaeological employment, however, this information also needed to be aggregated into broader, more encompassing categories. Eight employment categories were devised. The first four include the major employment sectors (academic, government, museum, and private). A respondent spending a minimum of 50 percent or more of his or her time in work settings that fall within one of the four major employment sectors was assigned to that sector. Using this criterion, a surprisingly large 83 percent of the respondent population could be assigned to one of the primary employment categories. Most of these individuals had full-time employment in archaeology with more than 60 percent of their time spent in a single work setting.

The remaining four categories were devised for individuals who did not fit into one of the major settings. Those who spend less than 50 percent of their time in a single employment sector but more than 50 percent of their total work effort in archaeology were assigned to the "mixed" employment category (5 percent of the respondent pool). Most of these individuals were employed at least part time in academia and part time in either the private sector or in a museum. There was also a separate "underemployed" category for those who spend less than 50 percent of their work effort engaged in archaeology (3 percent). Those who responded that 100 percent of their time was spent outside of an archaeological work setting were assigned to an "other" category (4 percent). Employment settings listed by respondents under "other" were mostly either jobs in related fields, or jobs outside the profession altogether. Those who indicated that they were 100 percent retired and listed no other work setting were assigned to the "retired" category (5 percent).

Once again, one needs to be cognizant of the fact that the sample of Census respondents is dominated by SAA members already well launched into professional careers in archaeology. The high proportion of respondents with full-time employment in single work settings is probably a reflection of the nature of the sample rather than the actual employment environment in archaeology. The proportion of part-time and underemployed archaeologists in the general universe of American archaeology is likely to be larger than is apparent here. Trends examined will, then, focus primarily on those within the primary employment sectors, though some effort will be made to examine aspects of these other smaller employment categories.

Trends in Archaeological Employment

Aggregate Patterns in Employment

Looking first at the professional nonstudent respondents to the Census (Figure 4.1), over one-third (35 percent) of

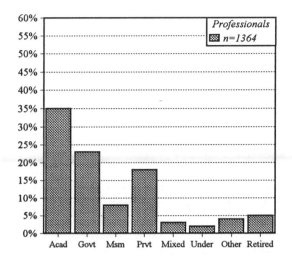

Fig 4.1 *Professional Archaeologists by Employment Sector*

Note the high proportions of respondents in the four primary employment sectors, and the low proportion in the four smaller employment categories.

the nonstudent respondents spend the majority of their time in an academic work setting. Archaeologists working in the government employment sector are the next most commonly represented group at 23 percent, followed by private-sector archaeologists at 18 percent of the professional respondent pool. Archaeologists working primarily in museum settings represent 8 percent of the sample. As noted above, archaeologists who fall into the four additional employment categories generally make up a little less than 5 percent of the respondent pool each, a figure that is likely to underrepresent their number in the actual universe of American archaeologists.

This employment profile is notably different from profiles based on earlier survey efforts conducted by the Society for Historical Archaeology (SHA) (Wall and Rothschild 1995), and the Society for Professional Archaeology (SOPA) (Lees 1991: 2). Figure 4.2 compares the distribution of SAA Census respondents in the four primary employment settings to the employment profiles drawn by the SHA and SOPA surveys. The SHA survey reports a higher representation of government and private sector archaeologists and a smaller proportion of academic archaeologists than found in the SAA Census. The SOPA survey respondent pool was dominated by private sector archaeologists. In each of these three survey efforts, however, the employment complexion of the respondent pool is perhaps a better reflection of the appeal of these organizations to different archaeological constituencies than of the actual universe of archaeologists in the Americas. The SHA draws a major portion of its membership from government-based historic-preservation offices and from private firms conducting archaeological reconnaissance of

threatened historic sites. And because SOPA is an organization that holds as its central mission the certification of professional archaeologists, it comes as no surprise that the majority of *its* members come from the private sector. In contrast, the SAA grew out of the older tradition of academic and museum-based archaeology that dominated the field in the early 1930s when the Society was formed. This strong academic constituency continues to be a major force in the SAA to this day. The growth of public and private sector archaeology, however, has been keenly felt by the SAA, both changing the nature of its membership and shaping many of its central goals and initiatives. We get some impression of these changes when we compare the employment profile drawn by the SAA Census to those profiles generated by a more limited survey of SAA members conducted in the late 1980s (Evans 1988) (Figure 4.2). While the representation of museum and private sector archaeologists in the SAA membership has remained relatively constant over the seven years that separate these two survey efforts, there has been a considerable increase in the representation of government archaeologists among SAA members and a relative decline in representation of academics. Even so, academic archaeology is still likely to be overrepresented in the 1994 SAA Census at the expense of government and, especially, private sector archaeology. And yet, both the SHA and SOPA surveys are perhaps even *more* likely to overrepresent government and private sector archaeologists, at the expense of academics. Given the larger membership pool of the SAA and the broader

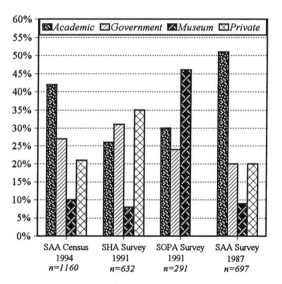

Fig. 4.2 *Representation of Employment Sectors in Various Survey Efforts*

Note the higher proportion of academic archaeologists in the SAA Census population when compared to the SHA and SOPA survey populations, but the decrease in the proportion of academics in the 1994 SAA Census when compared to the 1987 SAA Survey.

scope of its mission compared to these other organizations, it is more likely that the employment profile presented here is at least generally a closer fit to the actual make-up of American archaeology.

Gender and Employment

Looking at the aggregate data for professional archaeologists broken down by gender (Figure 4.3a), we see little difference in the distribution of men and women across the four major employment sectors (χ^2=2.698, df=3, p=0.441). In fact the proportions of men and women in government and private sector work settings are identical. And while proportionately more of the male respondents are employed in the academic sector than are women, this 5 percent difference is not statistically significant. The difference between the distribution of men and women in the four additional categories devised here *is* significant (χ^2=16.991, df=3, p=.001), with a greater proportion of women in the mixed, underemployed, and other categories and a much higher proportion of men in the retired category.

When we look at the relative numbers of men and women within different work settings (Figure 4.3b), we see that the proportion of women in each of the four major work settings is close to the 36 percent representation of women in the overall population of nonstudent respondents, indicated here as the hatched bar running across the graph. Women in academia, who make up 33 percent of the pool of professional academics, are slightly, but not significantly, underrepresented compared to the total

population, while women in museums at 41 percent are slightly, but again not significantly, overrepresented. In contrast, the nearly 60 percent representation of women within the category of respondents classified as "underemployed" is significantly different from their representation within the total population of nonstudent respondents (χ^2=6.876, df=1, p=.009). At nearly 80 percent, the proportion of men among retired respondents is significantly greater than the overall 64 percent representation of men in the total nonstudent population (χ^2=6.759, df=1, p=.009)—an artifact, no doubt, of the generally older profile of the male population noted in Chapter 2.

When we break down the work settings of the student population, once again we see a close correspondence between men and women (Figure 4.4a). Male students show a slightly, though not significantly, greater tendency than female students to spend the balance of their work effort in academic settings. Male students are also somewhat more likely than females to list the private sector as their dominant work setting, while women students are more likely to spend time in more than one employment sector, usually mixing academic employment with employment in the private sector and museums. There is also a slightly greater, though not significant, tendency for proportionately more female students to work in government settings. Numerically female students outnumber male students in the government and mixed work setting categories (Figure 4.4b), where their 60 percent share of the student populations within these work settings is nearly 10 percent greater than their proportional representation within the student population as a whole

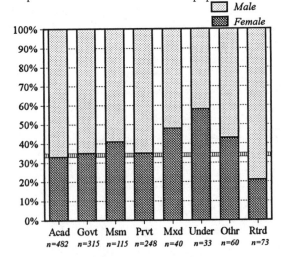

Fig. 4.3 *Professional Archaeologists by Employment Sector and Gender*

a Distribution of employment sectors among male and female professionals

b Proportional representation of professional men and women within each employment sector (hatched bar = proportion of women in professional population)

Note the generally even distribution of employment sectors among men and women. Note also the higher proportion of professional women in mixed, underemployed, and other settings, and the high proportion of men among retirees.

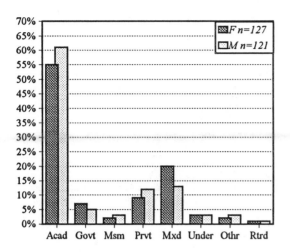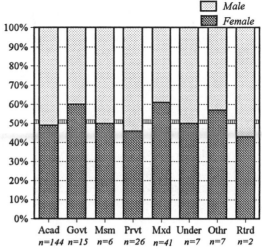

Fig. 4.4 *Student Archaeologists by Employment Sector and Gender*

a Distribution of employment sectors among male and female students

b Proportional representation of men and women students within each employment sector (hatched bar = proportion of women in student population)

Note the slightly higher proportion of male students who spend the balance of their time in academic and private sector settings, and the higher proportion of female students in mixed and government work settings.

(at 51 percent). In all other instances the representation of men and women students is essentially even.

Trends in Employment by Gender and Age

As has been the case in earlier chapters, the picture of the profession portrayed in the aggregate data fails to capture the dynamic changes that are currently reshaping the nature of American archaeology. Breaking down the data for the professional nonstudent population by age reveals significant movement in employment trends (Figure 4.5). And while the same trends seem to affect both women and men in archaeology, they do so in quite different ways. The most dramatic changes are seen in academic employment. In the 50–59 year old cohort, the oldest cohort without a sizable portion of retired individuals, academics clearly dominate, both in women and, especially, in men (Figure 4.5d). Almost half of the male archaeologists in their 50s are employed in academic settings. Although still the major employment sector for women, only a little over a third of the women in their 50s (36 percent) work in academic settings. The proportion of women in their 40s who are employed in academia is essentially the same as it is among women in their 50s. However, the proportion of academics among males in their 40s is a full 10 percent lower than it is among men in their 50s, a drop from 48 percent to 38 percent (Figure 4.5c). There is another 10 percent decrease in the proportion of males in academia among archaeologists in their 30s (Figure 4.5b). Almost as many men in their 30s are employed in government settings as there are in academia. In contrast, the proportion

of women in their 30s employed in academia is only slightly less than among women in their 40s, and for the first time proportionately more of the women in this cohort work in academia than men. The private sector dominates among professional archaeologists in their 20s, both male and female (Figure 4.5a). Employment patterns in this small group of young professional archaeologists cannot be taken as a presage of the archaeological workforce of the future, however, since, as we saw in Chapter 3, most of the academicians of the 21st century are still in school.

With the exception of a marked jump in the proportion of women in museums among women in their 30s, the museum employment sector has for the most part remained fairly constant for both men and women. Instead, it is the public and private sectors of archaeological employment that seem to be drawing an increasingly larger share of the archaeological workforce. Over time we see the government employment sector increase for both men and women equally from 20 percent of the 50–59 age cohort to 27 percent of the 40–49 cohort. Among respondents in their 30s the proportion of women employed in government work decreases slightly to 23 percent, while the proportion of men rises slightly to 28 percent.

The private sector shows a steady and even steeper climb in its share of the archaeological workforce, especially among men. In the 50–59 age cohort private sector archaeologists comprise about 15 percent of the workforce, with proportionately slightly more of the women in archaeology employed in this sector than the men. In the 40–49 cohort this figure has risen to 20 percent, with men

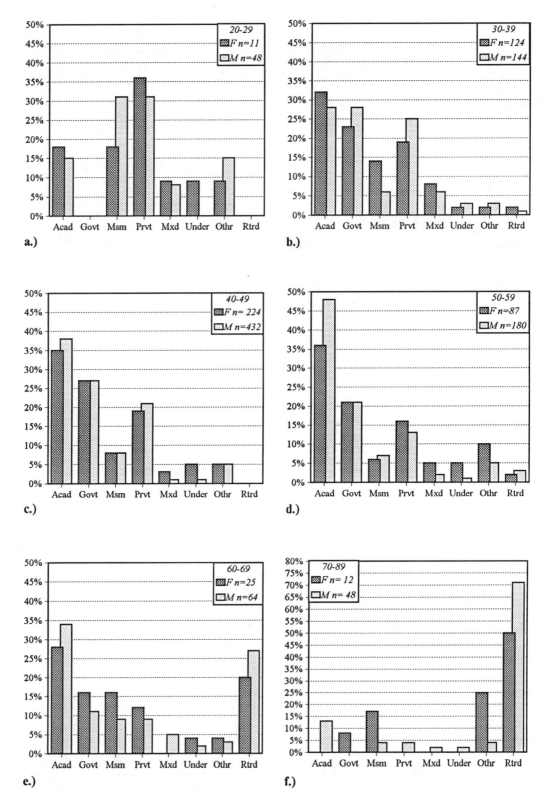

Fig. 4.5 *Employment Sectors of Professional Archaeologists by Gender and Age*

a 20–29 age cohort   b 30–39 age cohort

c 40–49 age cohort   d 50–59 age cohort

e 60–69 age cohort   f 70–89 age cohort

Note the decline in the proportions of academic men and women in progressively younger cohorts, and the corresponding increase in the private and public sectors.

a little better represented than women. The representation of private sector archaeologists among females in their 30s is constant, at 19 percent, while the proportion of male archaeologists employed here has continued to rise from 21 percent to 25 percent of the total male workforce.

There is also movement in the smaller mixed, underemployed, and other employment categories. These three categories combined account for a full 20 percent of the female archaeologists in their 50s, compared to only 8 percent of the male workforce. This figure falls to 13 percent among women in their 40s, remaining essentially constant at 7 percent in the men. Among archaeologists in their 30s these employment categories account for 12 percent of both the female and male professional archaeologists. The proportion of people employed in multiple work settings (usually academia and private sector archaeology) has risen to over 5 percent in both men and women. The proportion of underemployed women has fallen from 5 percent to 2 percent, as has the proportion of women employed in other settings outside of archaeology. And though the difference is slight, for the first time proportionately more men fall into these more marginal employment sectors than women. Finally, looking at the retired category in archaeologists over 60 years old (Figure 4.5e and f), it would seem that males tend to retire earlier than women, with women tending to continue active employment in archaeology into their 60s and even 70s. Twenty-seven percent of the men in their 60s are retired compared to 20 percent of the women. In their 70s and 80s more than 70 percent of the men are retired, compared to only 50 percent of the women.

In Chapter 2 we saw that, relative to men, the representation of women in archaeology has grown steadily in each successively younger age cohort, climbing from about a fifth of the oldest 70–89 cohort to just under half of the professional archaeologists in their 20s and 30s. But has this infusion of women into the field been distributed equally across all employment sectors, or have certain sectors felt the impact of the increased representation of women in archaeology more strongly than others? In Figure 4.6 the proportion of men and women in each work setting is compared to the overall representation of men and women within each age cohort, again displayed as the hatched line running across each graph. Perhaps the most visually striking aspect of these graphs is the steady decrease in the proportional representation of women in the mixed, underemployed, and other categories in the younger cohorts. The representation of women in these categories among archaeologist in their 50s is substantially greater than the proportional representation of women in the cohort as a whole (Figure 4.6d). At 62 percent the proportional share of women in the underemployed category of archaeologists in their 40s is significantly greater than the 34 percent representation of women in the overall cohort (Figure 4.6c; χ^2=5.532, df=1, p=.019). Among archaeolo-

gists in their 30s, however, the proportional representation of women in these secondary employment categories is essentially the same as it is in the overall population of archaeologists in this age group, while the proportion of men in the underemployed and other categories is for the first time greater (though not significantly so) than the overall proportion of men in this age group (Figure 4.5b).

Patterns within the four major work settings are visually a bit more subtle, but are ultimately more important for understanding the forces reshaping the nature of the professional workforce. Among 60–69 year olds the proportion of women in the government, museum, and private sector workforces is greater than their overall representation in the pool of archaeologists in this cohort (Figure 4.6e). In contrast, at 24 percent, the proportion of women in the academic workforce is somewhat, though not significantly, less than their 28 percent representation within the 60–69 age cohort as a whole. The impact of the apparent tendency of men to retire earlier than women is difficult to evaluate here. If men in all employment sectors tend to retire early, then the proportional representation of women in these settings would be equally affected by the removal of men from active employment. Thus the actual representation of women in government, museums, and the private sector before retirement began to remove a large number of men from the workforce may have been generally the same as their overall representation within this age group, while the proportion of women in academia would have been even lower than is currently the case, probably around 20 percent. If, on the other hand, men in academia tend to retire later than men in other work settings, then the current proportions of men and women in academia may be more reflective of the preretirement profile, and the representation of women in the other primary work settings may have originally been more similar to that now seen in the academic sector.

Examination of the relative numbers of men and women in the 50–59 year old cohort supports the first scenario (Figure 4.6d). Here we see that the representation of women in the government and private sectors is about the same as the 33 percent representation of women in the overall age cohort, if not slightly higher, while the proportion of women in museums is only slightly lower. In contrast, at 27 percent the proportion of women in academia is quite a bit depressed relative to their overall representation among archaeologists in this cohort. This picture changes dramatically among archaeologists in their 40s, where the proportion of women in all four primary settings is virtually identical to their overall representation in this age group (Figure 4.6c). Among professional archaeologists in their 30s, there are 40 women who work primarily in academia, compared to 41 men. The 49 percent share of women in the academic workforce is, for the first time, greater than the overall proportion of women in the age cohort, at 46 percent (Figure 4.6b). The representation

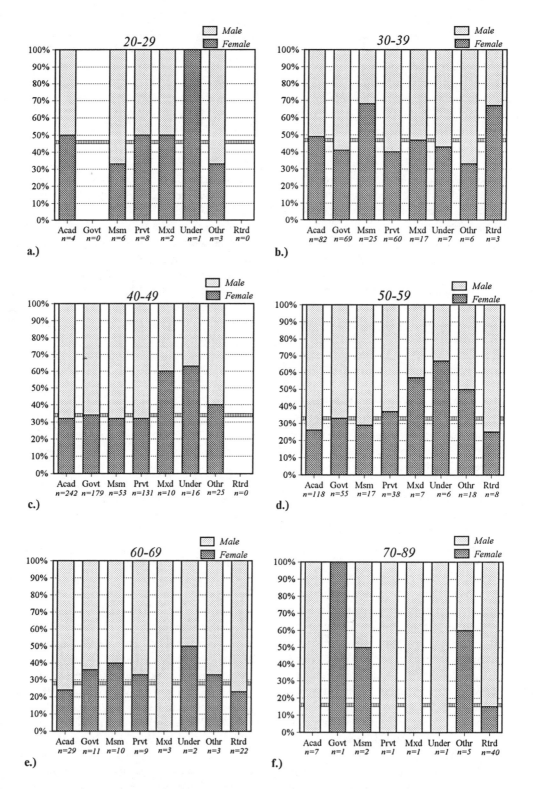

Fig. 4.6 *Representation of Professional Men and Women Within Each Employment Sector by Age (hatched bar = proportion of women in the age cohort)*

a 20–29 age cohort

b 30–39 age cohort

c 40–49 age cohort

d 50–59 age cohort

e 60–69 age cohort

f 70–89 age cohort

Note the decline in the proportion of women in the mixed, underemployed, and other categories in each younger cohort, and the increase in the proportion of women employed in the four primary employment sectors.

of women in museum settings, at 68 percent, is significantly greater than the overall representation of women among archaeologists in their 30s (χ^2=4.326, df=1, p=.038). Given the relatively small museum population, however, this sudden jump in female employment is difficult to evaluate. This cohort is also remarkable for the change in the proportional representation of men in government and private sector archaeology. For the first time the proportion of men among archaeologists employed in these two sectors is greater than the representation of men in the age cohort as a whole.

These data would seem to signal a fundamental shift in the archaeological employment environment. They suggest that 20 years ago males were likely favored in the academic and museum settings, and females in the government and private sectors. For archaeologists in their 40s, while the overall number of women in the workforce is still only half that of men, there seems to have been no differential preference for hiring one gender over another in any of the four primary work sectors. Finally, the current employment climate stands as a direct reversal of the pattern seen among archaeologists in their 50s, seeming to favor the employment of women in the academic and museum sectors and men in the public and private sectors of archaeological employment.

However, as has repeatedly been the case with the Census data, initial impressions are not always accurate, and the real story is a bit more complex and much more subtle than it seems. If there had been a major reversal in the employment climate from one that favored men in the academic and museum settings and women in the public and private sectors, to one that favored women in academia and museums and men in government and private consulting, then we should see a corresponding realignment in the representation of different work settings within each gender. Specifically, with each younger cohort, we should see an increase in the proportion of women who are employed in academic and museum settings, and a decrease in the proportion of the male workforce entering these two employment sectors. Likewise there should be a decrease in the segment of the female workforce employed in the government and private sectors, and an increase in the segment of the male workforce entering these two archaeological employment arenas.

Figure 4.7 takes the distributional data for the four major employment sectors displayed in three of the graphs included in Figure 4.6 (b, c, and d) and presents them by gender and then by age cohort within gender. Arranging these data in this way brings into sharper focus patterns that were evident but somewhat harder to see in earlier discussion, which was aimed at directly comparing male and female distributional data across all eight employment categories. In terms of male employment (Figure 4.7b), there is strong evidence of major restructuring in archaeological employment. There is a steep and highly significant 20 percentage point decrease between the 50–59 and the 30–39 age cohorts in the proportion of the male workforce employed in academia (χ^2=13.204, df=1, p.001). This decrease is offset by a strong and significant 12 point increase in the proportion of males employed in the private sector, (χ^2=7.216, df=1, p=.007). There is also a somewhat less marked 7 point net increase in public sector

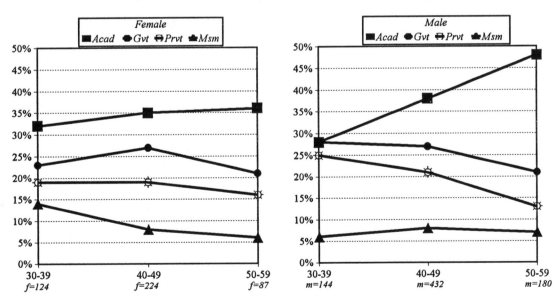

Fig. 4.7 *Representation of Professional Men and Women Within Primary Employment Sectors for Selected Age Cohorts*

a Females   **b** Males

Note the steep decline in the proportion of younger men employed in academia, and the increase in the proportion employed in private sector and government jobs. Note also the relative lack of significant change in the female employment profile over the three age cohorts displayed here.

employment (χ^2=2.743, df=1, p=.098). The museum employment sector shows a slight decline. Clearly the composition of the male workforce has changed over the last two decades.

But has this change been met by a corresponding reordering of the employment profile among women? Examination of Figure 4.7a would indicate that it has not. Rather than increasing, the proportion of the female workforce employed in academia has instead seen a slight, albeit not significant, *decrease* over the last two decades. The government employment sector has seen some small net gain over the last three decades; and the private sector has risen slightly, though again not statistically significantly, over this time. Only the museum sector has seen a substantial increase over these past 20 years, which is significant only at the .062 level of probability (χ^2=3.471, df=1). Most of this growth has occurred in the last 10 years and, as mentioned earlier, is difficult to interpret, given the small size of the museum population. Thus it would seem that, in contrast to men in archaeology, the profile of female employment has remained fairly constant over the past 20 years. If there have been any changes in the female employment profile, they are similar in direction, though not in degree, to those seen among men. The academic employment sector for both men and women is shrinking relative to the public, and particularly the private sector, shares of the archaeological workforce.

These patterns are reminiscent of those evident in the data generated by the SHA survey (Wall and Rothschild 1995: Table 2). While the relative representation of different employment sectors was different in the earlier survey from those reported here, the SHA survey data also captured patterns indicative of increasing equity in the ratio of females to males in all major sectors of archaeological employment. Moreover, decreases in the proportion of both women and men (but especially men) employed in academia are also evident in the SHA survey, as are the parallel increases in private and public sector archaeology.

• In sum, there are multiple overlapping factors shaping the recent profile of employment in American archaeology. Younger women are now more likely to work full time in the major sectors of archaeological employment. Moreover, from less than a quarter of the archaeologists in their 60s, women now comprise roughly half the archaeological workforce. And yet, with the possible exception of museums, the increase in the number of women within mainstream work settings has not been channeled to any one employment sector. There may be proportionately more women in the workforce, but the employment patterns for women are little changed from those of 20 to 30 years ago. Paradoxically, the observed increase in the representation of women in academia relative to men is, in fact, paralleled by an overall small *decline* in the number of

women employed in academia when compared to their employment in other work settings. At the same time, the observed increase in female employment in government and private sector settings contrasts with the decreased representation of women in these arenas relative to men. Yet, as this in-depth examination of Census data shows, it is not a significant restructuring of the female workforce that is responsible for the dramatic shifts in the overall employment profile of younger archaeologists. Instead, it is the male workforce that is the most volatile element in recent archaeological employment trends. It is the dramatic decrease in the proportion of males in academia over the past 20 years that is responsible for the apparent growth in the representation of women in academia relative to men. Likewise, it is the increase in the proportion of younger male archaeologists entering the public and private sectors that is principally responsible for the apparent depression in the representation of women in these areas relative to men. For both men and women, academic employment seems to be shrinking in favor of government and, especially, private sector archaeology. Yet, the impact of this change seems to be relatively muted among women, while a major restructuring in male employment trends has resulted in a profound and ongoing transformation in the profile of archaeological employment. •

Employment and Degree Status

In Chapter 3 we saw that men and women are following somewhat different educational trajectories from one another. The proportion of younger women going on for PhDs has increased, so that female PhDs in their 30s now slightly outnumber males. Among males, however, there has been a sharp decrease in the number of younger men going on for PhDs and a corresponding increase in the proportion of MAs among younger men. It is useful, then, to examine the degree status of individuals in different work sectors to explore the connections between these trends in education and employment.

Figure 4.8 presents a breakdown of individuals employed in the four major archaeological work settings by highest degree. The markedly different pattern of degree composition within these settings is immediately apparent. PhDs clearly dominate in academia. To a slightly lesser extent, they are also dominant in museum settings. In contrast, over half of those employed in government hold MAs, while MAs and PhDs are approximately evenly represented in the private sector. When the degree profiles of these four employment sectors are contrasted, in each case the differences between them are significant at better than a .05 level of probability.

These same patterns generally hold true when the data on degree status in the workplace are broken down by gender (Figure 4.9), though there are some notable

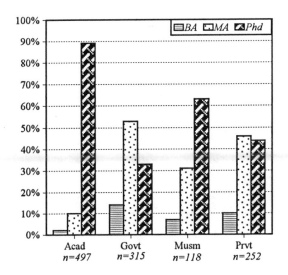

Fig. 4.8 *Degrees by Employment Sector*

Note the high proportions of PhDs among academic and museum professionals, and MAs among government and private sector archaeologists.

variations. Over 90 percent of the males employed in academia hold PhDs, compared to slightly less than 80 percent of the women, a difference that is significant at the .053 level of probability (χ^2=5.875, df=2). Men working in museum settings are also somewhat more likely to hold PhDs than are women, though, given the smaller sample of museum workers, this difference is not statistically significant. While those with MAs dominate among both men and women employed in government settings, there are proportionately more males in government archaeology with PhDs than females. The degree profiles of men

and women in the private sector are the most similar, though even here there is a slight tendency for proportionally more men to hold PhDs.

Breaking down these patterns by age helps further clarify some of the age-related trends in both employment and degree status (Figure 4.10). In all four employment sectors there has been a marked increase in the proportion of MAs among men in their 30s compared to men in their 40s (Figure 4.10b). This increase is statistically significant in the three larger employment sectors (academia: χ^2=24.135, df=1, p.001; government: χ^2=7.594, df=1, p=.022; private sector: χ^2=6.397, df=1, p=.041). In contrast, the degree profile of women within these different employment sectors has been steadier. While there have been some increases in the proportions of women with MAs, they have been less marked and are in no instance statistically significant. Moreover, the increase in MAs among women in government and the private sector seems to have occurred between the 50–59 and the 40–49 age cohorts, with the proportion of MAs holding steady among younger women in government, and dropping somewhat in 30–39 year old women in the private sector. In academia the proportion of women with MAs has decreased somewhat, and there has been a small corresponding increase in the proportion of female PhDs.

• It would seem that changes in the degree profile of younger archaeologists are linked to changes in archaeological employment. Proportionately more male archaeologists are ending their education with master's degrees to pursue careers in work settings that employ higher proportions of non-PhD archaeologists. It is important to point out that the MAs in our sample are not necessarily people

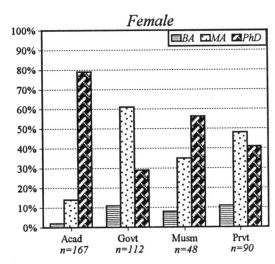

Fig. 4.9 *Degrees by Employment Sector and Gender*

a Females   b Males

Note the higher proportion of PhDs among males in all work settings, especially in academia.

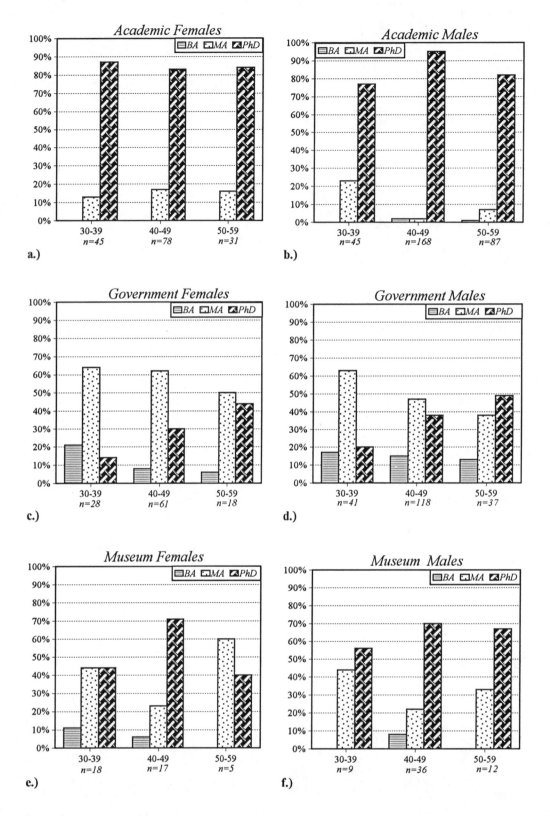

Fig. 4.10 *Degrees by Employment Sector, Gender, and Age*

a Academic females

c Government females

e Museum females

b Academic males

d Government males

f Museum males

Note the increase in the proportion of MAs between males in their 30s and 40s in all employment sectors.

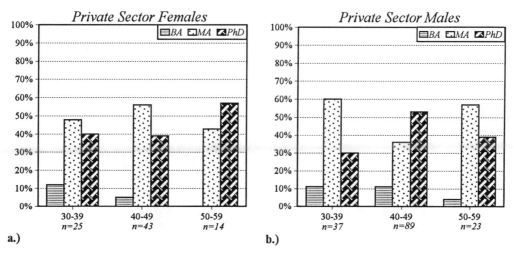

Fig 4.10 *Degrees by Employment Sector, Gender, and Age (continued)*
g Private sector females   **h** Private sector males

who left graduate school partway through a PhD program. Nor are the archaeologists entering the private sector doing so as a last resort after having failed to obtain a position in academia. Both the time it takes to obtain MAs and the changes in the institutions conferring these degrees suggest that many of the younger MAs in our sample have attended programs specifically aimed at producing MAs in archaeology, and are consciously structuring their education to accommodate the realities of the current archaeological job market.

In contrast, the dramatic changes seen in the educational trajectories of younger women seem somewhat out of step with female employment trends that have shown little real change over the past 20 years. More than three-quarters of the younger women receiving their degrees in the 1990s obtain PhDs, but less than one-third of them secure positions in job sectors where this degree will give them the most advantage. In some ways women seem to be following educational trajectories that are more in sync with the career opportunities open to men in earlier decades, when over half of the males in archaeology held positions in academia. In reality, even for women the growth sectors in archaeological employment lie in work settings where a PhD is not a critical requirement for employment. And yet these current realities in archaeological employment may be offset by other factors that make going on for a PhD a more desirable option for women. The substantially smaller decline in the proportion of women employed in academia, the increase in the numbers of women in academia relative to men, and a possible expansion in job opportunities open to women in academia and museums may all create at least the perception that women have a better chance of securing a job in these employment sectors. These factors may also, therefore, make it worth the substantial investment of time (and money) needed to obtain the credentials required for careers in these more traditional, and as we will see below, generally preferred arenas of archaeological employment. ●

Regional Distribution of Archaeological Employment

When we look at the distribution of employment sectors by region, we see some very clear and highly significant differences (Figure 4.11). Academic archaeologists plainly dominate in the Northeast and Midwest (Figure 4.11a and c), and the employment profiles of these two areas, though statistically indistinguishable from each other, are significantly different from the profiles of all other regions in the United States at better than the .001 level of probability. The Southeast and the Plains stand out from other regions in the high proportion of government-based archaeologists (Figure 4.12b and d). The concentration of government archaeologists in the Southeast is probably due to the inclusion of the District of Columbia and Virginia within this region (Figure 1.2). Had Maryland, with its Washington metropolitan suburbs, been included with the Southeastern states, the proportion of government archaeologists in the Southeast would have been higher still. The strong representation of government archaeologists in the Plains can be linked to a good response rate from archaeologists working at the National Park Service Midwest Archaeological Center in Nebraska. Private sector archaeologists are also well represented in the Plains. The Southwest and West are significantly different from other regions in the high proportions of private sector and government archaeologists and a relatively depressed representation of the academic employment sector, especially when compared to the Northeast and the Midwest. In fact, in the Southwest, academics are less well represented than either government or private sector archaeologists.

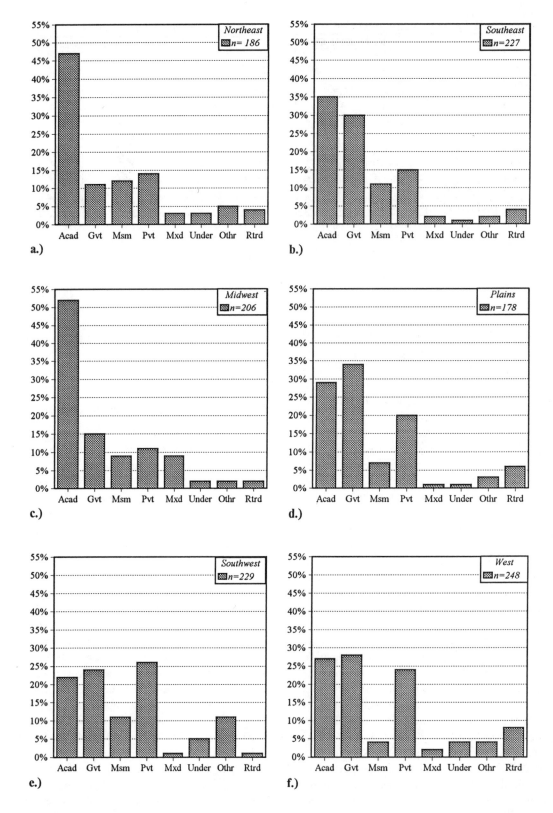

Fig. 4.11 *Employment Sector by Region*

a Northeast
c Midwest
e Southwest

b Southeast
d Plains
f West

Note the distinctive profile of employment sectors within each region.

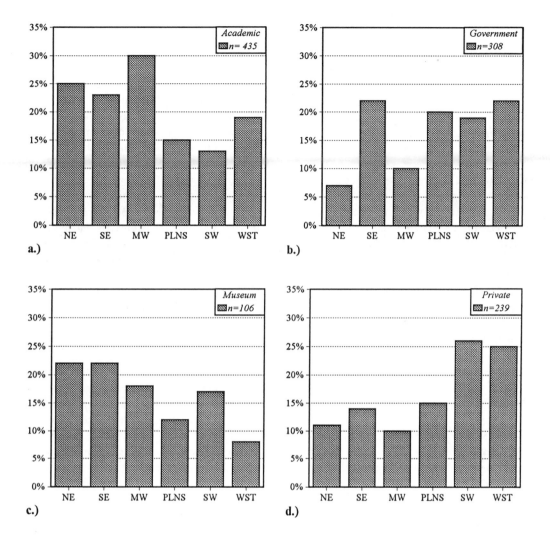

Fig. 4.12 *Region by Employment Sector*

a Academia   b Government
c Museums   d Private sector

Note the concentration of academics and museum professionals in the East and Midwest, and of private and public sector archaeologists in the Plains and West.

Displaying these regional data by employment sector (Figure 4.12) reveals distinctive regional profiles for each sector. With the exception of the profiles of academics and museum professionals, which are statistically indistinguishable from one another, the regional distributions of archaeologists in all other employment sectors are significantly different from one another, at better than the .005 level of probability. Academics are concentrated primarily in the Eastern United States and Midwest (Figure 4.12a). Museum professionals are also commonly found in the East, though the Midwest and Southwest are fairly well represented here as well (Figure 4.12b). Even with the large spike in the proportion of government archaeologists from the Southeast, the majority of archaeologists working in government settings can be found in states west of the Mississippi (Figure 4.12b). Finally, more than 50 percent of the

private sector archaeologists who responded to the Census are located in the West and Southwest (Figure 4.12d).

• It would seem, then, that jobs in the more traditional sectors of archaeological employment (universities and museums) are more heavily concentrated in the eastern and Midwestern parts of the country, while the government and private sector jobs are better represented in the western United States. A regional shift in the proportion of advanced degrees awarded in archaeology was noted in Chapter 3. Through the 1970s, universities located in the East and the Midwest had produced the majority of PhDs in archaeology; in the 1980s and 1990s, schools in the West and Southwest have been producing the majority of PhDs, as well as the majority of the growing number of MAs. Perhaps, like the linked shifts in degree profile and employment trends, there is also a connection here between the region in which archaeological training is sought and the regional location of the growth sectors of archaeological employment. •

Current and Preferred Employment and Activities

Employment

Measuring Current and Preferred Employment

Census respondents were asked to specify not only their current work settings and the activities they perform there, but also their preferred employment settings and activities. Comparing respondents' current employment circumstances with their preferences provides a means of monitoring how closely the realities of archaeological employment mesh with expectations of where and how respondents would like to practice archaeology.

Figure 4.13 presents the current and preferred work settings of men and women professional archaeologists. Figure 4.13a contrasts the current (as of 1993) work setting of professional men and women, while Figure 4.13b compares their preferred work settings. These same data are rearranged in Figure 4.13c and d, allowing us to compare the current and preferred work settings of each gender separately. Percentages displayed in these graphs show the proportion of the respondents who either currently spend some portion of their work effort in a particular work setting or would prefer to do so. They do not reflect the proportional representation of each work setting among all the possible settings in which respondents might be employed. For example, when looking at the current work settings for professional men presented in Figure 4.13a, the bar for graduate university settings should be read as meaning that 27 percent of the professional male respondents spend at least some portion of their work effort in a graduate university, *not* that graduate universities comprise 27 percent of the work settings in which professional males spend some time. Since respondents usually work in more than one setting at a time, the total percentage distribution for any group shown here will add up to more than 100 percent.

Gender Trends in Current and Preferred Employment

As we saw when these data were aggregated into broader employment categories (Figure 4.3), the current employment profiles of professional men and women are in general quite similar (Figure 4.13a). It appears that a slightly higher proportion of professional males spend time in graduate universities, in state and local governments, and in private firms; while women tend to be more frequently found in government and university museums, as independent consultants, and in work settings listed under "other." However, the differences between the current employment of men and women pro-

fessionals are only marginally significant at best (χ^2=21.246, df=14, p=.095).

The stated employment preferences of men and women (Figure 4.13b) are significantly different from one another (χ^2=25.540, df=14, p=.030), with the primary differences in respondent preferences being for employment in graduate university and museum settings. While the majority of both men and women said that they would like to spend at least some of their productive effort in a graduate university (over 40 percent for both), this preference is apparently stronger among men. In contrast, professional women show a stronger preference for museum settings, especially university museums. When the preferences of men and women for employment in graduate universities is contrasted with their preferences for employment in museum settings, the difference is highly significant at the .004 level of probability (χ^2=8.198, df=1).

For both men and women, employment preferences are significantly different from their current employment profiles (Figure 4.13c and d) (for women, χ^2=71.286, df=14, p.001; for men, χ^2=97.463, df=14, p.001). The gap between current and preferred employment levels in graduate universities is particularly large, at about 20 percent for each gender. There is also a substantial difference between current and preferred employment levels in all three museum settings. In the case of university museums, the preference of women for this work setting is nearly 20 percent higher than current employment levels; among men this difference is less than 10 percent.

The proportion of people who would prefer employment in government and private sector work settings is either roughly the same as, or slightly less than, the proportion currently employed there. This is especially true among men, particularly those in government settings. These patterns seem somewhat paradoxical, considering recent trends that indicate an increase in the number of younger men entering the government and private employment sectors. Breaking these aggregate data down by age reveals a growing preference among younger men for employment in private firms. Only 10 percent of males in their 50s expressed a preference for employment in a private firm, compared to 22 percent of the males in their 30s. Preferences for employment in government settings among men has remained relatively constant at about 14 percent. The stated preferences of males for employment in graduate universities is, however, consistently quite high at about 50 percent of every age cohort.

Current and Preferred Student Employment We can also get some perspective on the employment preferences of younger archaeologists by looking at the preferred work settings of student respondents (Figure 4.14). Despite recent trends in employment, and perhaps contrary to the stated preferences of younger professional archaeologists, there is still an overwhelming preference among student

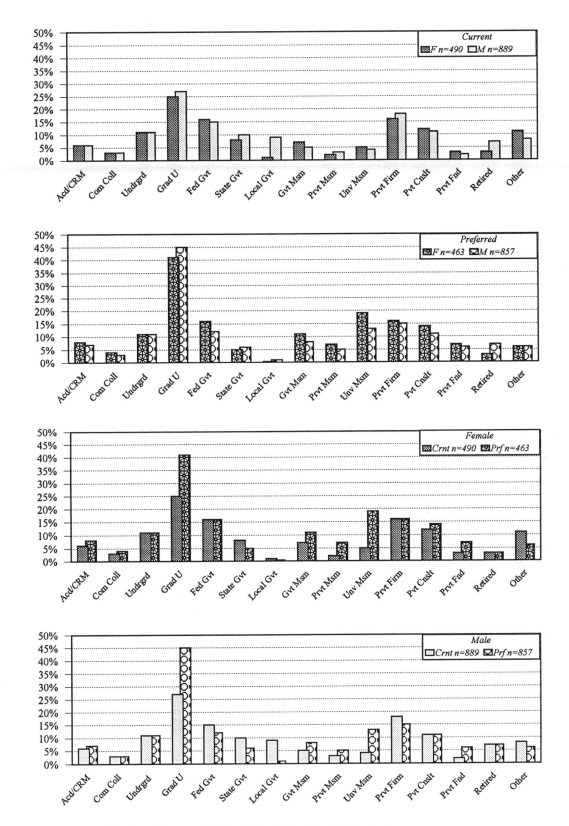

Fig. 4.13 *Current and Preferred Work Settings of Male and Female Professional Archaeologists*

a Current work settings of men and women

b Preferred work settings of men and women

c Current and preferred work settings of women

d Current and preferred work settings of men

Note the similarities in current employment profiles of men and women. Note also the generally higher preference among males for employment in graduate universities, and of females for employment in museum settings.

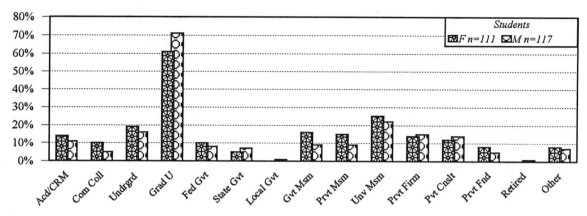

Fig. 4.14 *Preferred Work Settings of Male and Female Students*

Note the strong preference for employment in graduate universities of both men and women students, and the low preference for employment in government work settings. Note also the slightly higher preference of male students for employment in graduate universities, and of female students for employment in museum settings.

archaeologists for employment in academia. Moreover, as in the nonstudent professional population, the preference for work in this setting is higher among men. Employment in a university museum setting is the next highest student employment preference, but here the preference of women for this work setting is slightly higher than it is for male students. Among women students, private and government museums are the next most preferred future work settings. For males, however, private sector work settings—both in private firms and work as an independent consultant—are preferred over employment in either of the other two museum settings. Government work settings seem to be the least preferred among students.

Current and Preferred Employment by Employment Setting It is also instructive to compare current and preferred employment profiles within the four major employment sectors (Figure 4.15). When the data are displayed this way we see that by and large, respondents show the highest preference for the general sector in which they are currently employed. Those in academia show a strong preference for working in one of the four academic settings. Similarly, individuals in each of the three other employment sectors state a general preference for the sector in which they are currently employed. Yet in each case the profile of preferred work settings of respondents working in one of the four major employment sectors is significantly different from their current employment circumstances within that sector (for academics: χ^2=71.487, df=13, p.001; for government: χ^2=192.637, df=14, p.001; for museums: χ^2=31.565, df=12, p=.002; for the private sector: χ^2=85.808, df=14, p.001). For academics the primary differences between current and preferred employment profile lie within the academic settings themselves (Figure 4.15a). Fewer archaeologists would prefer working in community colleges, in undergraduate universities, and in academic consulting businesses than are currently

employed in these settings, while more academics would prefer employment in a graduate university. Proportionally more academics, especially women, would also prefer to spend at least some of their time in a university museum. The difference between current and preferred employment profiles of museum-based archaeologists (Figure 4.15c) also lies primarily within museum settings. Fewer respondents state a preference for employment in government museums than currently work there, while there is a greater preference for work in a university museum. The only work setting outside of a museum that shows a fairly strong preference level among museum professionals is a graduate university.

Private firms seem to be the most preferred work setting among private sector archaeologists (Figure 4.15d). However, the proportion of individuals who would prefer working for a private firm is quite a bit less than the proportion of individuals currently working in such firms. In contrast, slightly more private sector archaeologists would prefer working as independent consultants than is currently the case. Once again, employment in a graduate university stands out among the employment preferences of private sector archaeologists, as does, to a lesser degree, employment within a university museum. In each of the three government work settings, the proportion of individuals who would prefer employment in these settings is less than the proportion of individuals currently working there (Figure 4.15b). In fact, more government archaeologists would prefer to work in a graduate university than would prefer employment in either a state or a local governmental agency.

It is interesting to note the similarity between the range of current employment settings in which people in the mixed and underemployed categories work (Figure 4.15e and f). Both groups tend to conduct their archaeological activities in a similar mix of academic and private sector settings. The prime differences between the two

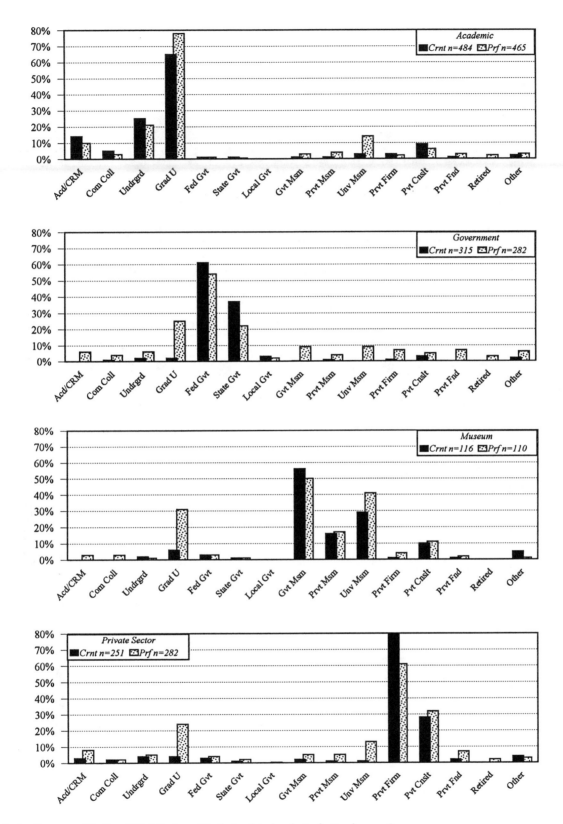

Fig. 4.15 *Current and Preferred Work Settings of Professional Archaeologists by Employment Sector*

a Academia

b Government

c Museums

d Private sector

Note the general correspondence between current and preferred work settings within each employment sector. Note also the preference for employment in graduate universities and university museums in all employment sectors.

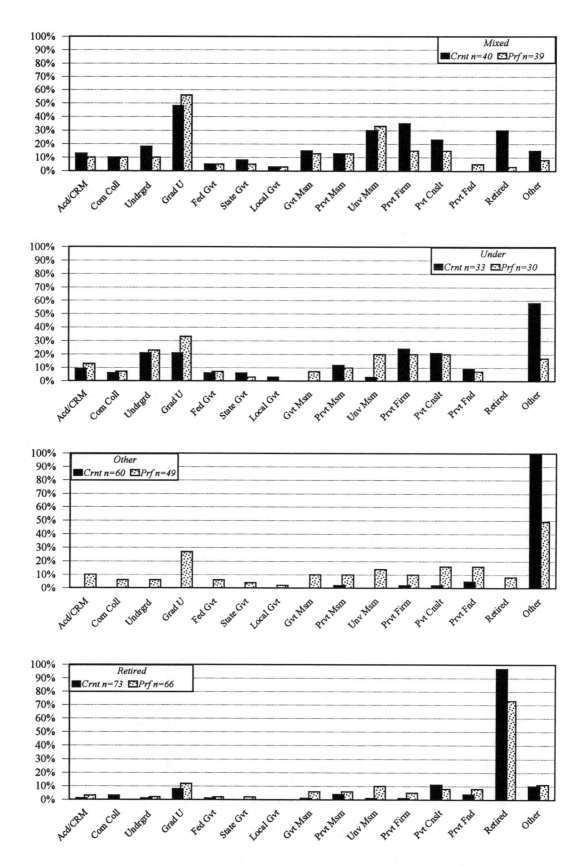

Fig. 4.15 *Current and Preferred Work Settings of Professional Archaeologists by Employment Sector (continued)*

e Mixed settings

f Underemployed

g Other nonarchaeological employment

h Retired

employment categories lie in the reduced proportion of work effort devoted to work in archaeology by those in the underemployed category (usually less than 20 percent of their work effort is spent in any one setting) and the higher proportion of underemployed individuals employed in "other" work settings. People employed outside of archaeology and those respondents who say they are retired are concentrated, by definition, in the other and retired employment settings (Figure 4.15g and h). All of those in these smaller employment categories, however, show the strongest preference for employment in a graduate university setting, followed in most cases by a preference for employment in a university museum. Private sector settings also fared well among the preferred employment settings of underemployed individuals, as well as, to a lesser extent, those employed in mixed settings or outside of archaeology.

Activities

Measuring Current and Preferred Activities Respondents were also asked to report the proportion of their work effort spent conducting various activities. The list provided in the Census included 15 separate types of activities in which archaeologists are most likely to engage, as well as an "other" category to cover activities that might not be included on this list. Once again these data are displayed in the form of percentages of respondents who conduct these various activities, not as the percentage share of a particular activity among all activities conducted by respondents. It is also important to keep in mind that the data presented in the graphs included in this section do not reflect the *amount* of time respondents spend conducting these various activities. Instead, they indicate only that respondents spend at least *some* time engaged in a certain activity, or that they would prefer to do so. Data were collected on the amount of time respondents spend performing these various activities, however, and will be cited when relevant.

Gender Trends in Current and Preferred Activities As was done for work setting profiles, current and preferred activities of professional men and women are compared in four related graphs (Figure 4.16). In the profiles in Figure 4.16a we see that the activities currently conducted by men and women are generally quite similar to one another, with the same activities predominating among both men and women. More archaeologists are engaged in writing publications than any other activity listed here. Fieldwork is the second most common activity, followed by administration, teaching, and laboratory analysis. Despite the general similarities, the activity profiles of male and female archaeologists are significantly different from one another (χ^2=37.247, df=15, p=.001). Proportionally more men than women spend at least some portion of their time engaged in administration, teaching, writing publications,

and fieldwork. In contrast, there are very few activities that more women engage in than men, and in no case is the difference greater than 5 percent.

Some recent discussions of gender differences in the practice of archaeology have focused on a proposed dichotomy between fieldwork and lab work. In particular Gero (1985, 1994) has proposed that fieldwork (meaning the active and adventurous pursuit of archaeological information) has been the prerogative of *men,* while lab work (the passive, safe processing of information once acquired) is the domain of *women.* If Gero's model matched current realities in archaeological practice, we would expect to find proportionally more men engaged in fieldwork than lab work. Women, on the other hand, should be found more frequently in the lab than in the field. From the data presented in Figure 4.16a, it *does* appear that proportionately more men spend time in the field than women; 57 percent of the male professional archaeologists polled conduct fieldwork, compared to 43 percent of the women. Yet, while proportionally fewer women are engaged in fieldwork than men, those women who do go into the field devote essentially the same amount time to fieldwork as men. On average, men who conduct fieldwork spend 23 percent of their time in the field, while women spend 21 percent of their total work effort engaged in fieldwork.

There are no data, however, to support the notion that laboratory analysis is primarily women's work, or, for that matter, that women work primarily in the lab. While proportionally fewer women are engaged in fieldwork than men, women who work in the field still outnumber women who work in a laboratory setting. Further, instead of proportionately more women being engaged in laboratory-based research than men, the actual proportions of men and women in the lab are about the same. In fact, proportionately slightly more men do lab work than women. Those women who perform laboratory analysis, however, tend to devote more time to this activity than men. Women spend an average of 26 percent of their time engaged in lab work, compared to men, who devote 16 percent of their time to laboratory analysis.

When we look at the preferred activities of men and women (Figure 4.16b), we see that while proportionately more men conduct fieldwork than women, more men also expressed a preference for such work. Seventy-one percent of the men polled expressed a preference for conducting fieldwork compared to 62 percent of the women. Also, far from being a marginal refuge for those denied access to a preferred archaeological activity, relatively high proportions of both men and women expressed a fairly strong preference for laboratory-based work, a preference that is held, in fact, by proportionately more men than women. Thus it may be that proportionately fewer women engage in fieldwork simply because they prefer this activity less than men, rather than because they face active discrimination against their participation in fieldwork. Of course the

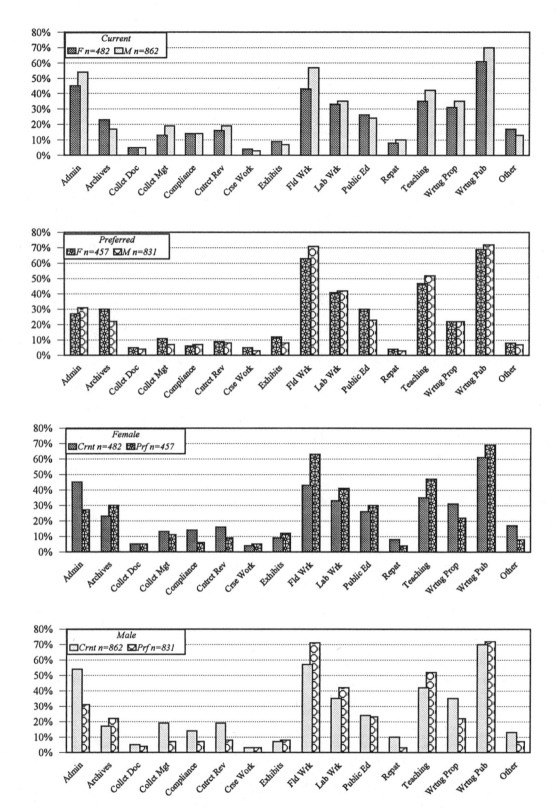

Fig. 4.16 *Current and Preferred Activities of Male and Female Professional Archaeologists*

a Current activities of men and women   **c** Current and preferred activities of women

b Preferred activities of men and women   **d** Current and preferred activities of men

Note the generally higher preference for writing, teaching, field and lab work, and the low preference for administration, compliance and contract review, and repatriation. Also note the higher proportion of men engaged in fieldwork and the higher male preference for fieldwork.

weaker preference of women for fieldwork may in itself be shaped by circumstances that make women less able to leave home for protracted periods of time, though this scenario is hard to reconcile with the fact that women in archaeology are less likely marry and have children than men. Moreover, whatever forces shape the likelihood of women's engaging in field research, there are no data to support the supposition that women's work in archaeology is disproportionately restricted to a much less desirable, more marginal laboratory setting.

When we compare current and preferred activity profiles by gender (Figure 4.16c and d), we see that in general those activities that are performed by the most archaeologists are also the most preferred activities. In fact in most cases, more people would prefer to be engaged in these commonly conducted activities than currently are. This is especially true for fieldwork, teaching, writing publications, and lab work. The only commonly practiced activities that have fairly low preference levels are administration and writing proposals. Those activities practiced by the fewest number of archaeologists are also among the least preferred: collections management, compliance and contract review, and repatriation, for example. Exceptions are archival research and, to a lesser extent, work on exhibits where the preference levels are higher than current practice.

It is interesting to note that despite the decided preference for fieldwork over administration among archaeologists, age-related trends indicate a strong inverse relationship in the practice of these two activities (Figure 4.17). With each progressively older age cohort, both the number of individuals engaged in fieldwork and the pro-

portion of time they spend there decrease, while the number of people engaged in administration and the time devoted to administrative activities both increase.

Current and Preferred Student Activities Like the profiles of preferred work settings among students, an examination of student activity preferences gives us some perspective on the hopes and expectations of younger archaeologists on the threshold of entering the archaeological job market (Figure 4.18). Student preferences, for both men and women, are strongly focused on four basic activities: fieldwork, teaching, writing publications, and lab work. In most cases the degree of preference of male and female students for these activities is essentially the same. However, even though fieldwork is the preferred activity of more female students than any other activity listed—as was the case among professional archaeologists—the proportion of women students who would prefer to engage in fieldwork is still about 10 percent less than the proportion of male students who would like to work in the field. Since these younger women are even less likely to be married and have children than older professional women, this pattern bolsters the argument that factors other than an imbalance in personal family commitments shape male and female preferences for fieldwork. Another interesting difference in student preferences is the stronger preference of women for archival research and public education. Activities that seem the least preferred among students are administration, collections documentation, collections management, compliance and contract review, exhibits preparation, and repatriation.

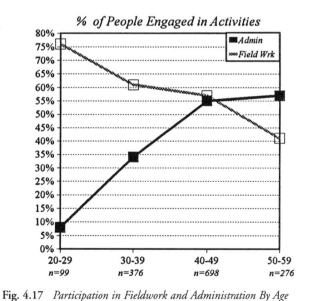

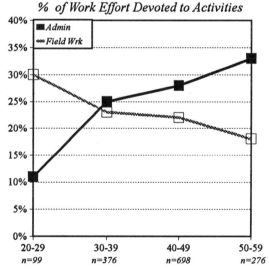

Fig. 4.17 *Participation in Fieldwork and Administration By Age*

a Percentage of respondents (including students) engaged in fieldwork and administration

b Percentage of total work effort devoted to fieldwork and administration

Note the decline in the proportion of older people engaged in fieldwork and the time devoted to fieldwork. Note also the corresponding increase in both the proportion of people and time devoted to administration in older cohorts.

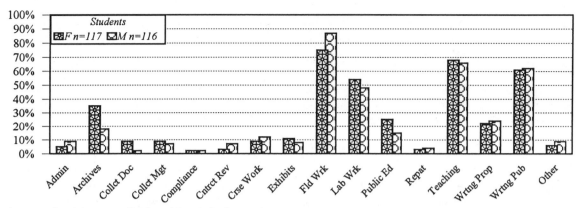

Fig. 4.18 *Preferred Activities of Male and Female Students*

Note the strong preference for fieldwork, teaching, writing for publication, and lab work among students, and the similarity of the preferred activities of students to the current activity profile of academics. Note also the higher preference of male students for fieldwork.

Current and Preferred Activities by Employment Setting How well do the activity preferences of tomorrow's professional archaeologists mesh with various employment sectors open to them? Comparing the expectations of students about to enter the archaeological job market with the activities currently conducted by professional archaeologists working in the four major sectors of archaeological employment (Figure 4.19), we see a close match between the student preferences and the activities profile of academics (Figure 4.19a). Based on the strong preference of students for employment in a graduate university discussed above, this should come as no surprise. All four of the primary preferences listed by students figure prominently among the most commonly practiced activities of archaeologists employed in academia, though not perhaps in the order of preference expressed by students. It is teaching, not fieldwork, that is practiced by more academicians than any other activity listed, followed by writing publications and then by fieldwork. Administration comes next as the activity performed by the most academic archaeologists, followed by proposal writing and then by lab work.

In general, the activity preferences of academic archaeologists resemble the activities commonly conducted by academics. Fieldwork, lab work, teaching, and writing publications are the activities preferred by the most archaeologists employed in academia. Teaching is preferred by more academic archaeologists than any other activity. Yet the number of people who prefer teaching is essentially the same as the number of academics who currently teach. Substantially more academics would like to conduct fieldwork and lab work than are currently engaged in these activities, and a few more would like to be engaged in writing books and articles than is currently the case. In contrast, while 45 percent of all academic archaeologists are engaged in administration, only 21 percent listed administration as a preferred activity. Substantially fewer academicians would prefer writing proposals for funding than currently do so.

The activity profile of archaeologists in academia is markedly different from the profiles of archaeologists in the other three employment sectors. In fact, each employment sector has a profile of activities that is significantly different from the other employment sectors at better than the .001 level of probability. Perhaps the most distinctive feature of the three nonacademic employment sectors is the comparatively higher proportion of archaeologists engaged in administrative activities. Well over half of the archaeologists employed in government, museums, and the private sector perform at least some administrative activities, compared to only 45 percent of the academic archaeologists. The proportion of individuals engaged in administrative activities is particularly high among government archaeologists, where close to 70 percent devote an average of more than one-third of their total work effort to administrative activities. In contrast, museum professionals engaged in administration spend about 30 percent of their time on these activities; private sector archaeologists spend 23 percent of their time on administration, while academics devote an average of only 19 percent of their total work effort to administration.

Government archaeology is further distinguished by the high proportions of individuals involved in compliance and contract review and in public education (Figure 4.19b). Proportionately more government archaeologists conduct fieldwork than academic archaeologists, and the proportion of government archaeologists who write publications and conduct laboratory analysis is about the same as in academia. The fact that so few government archaeologists spend time writing proposals for funding is not unexpected. As we will see in Chapter 7, most of the funds awarded for archaeology come from government agencies. It would seem that government archaeologists devote more time to reviewing proposals and monitoring funds allocated

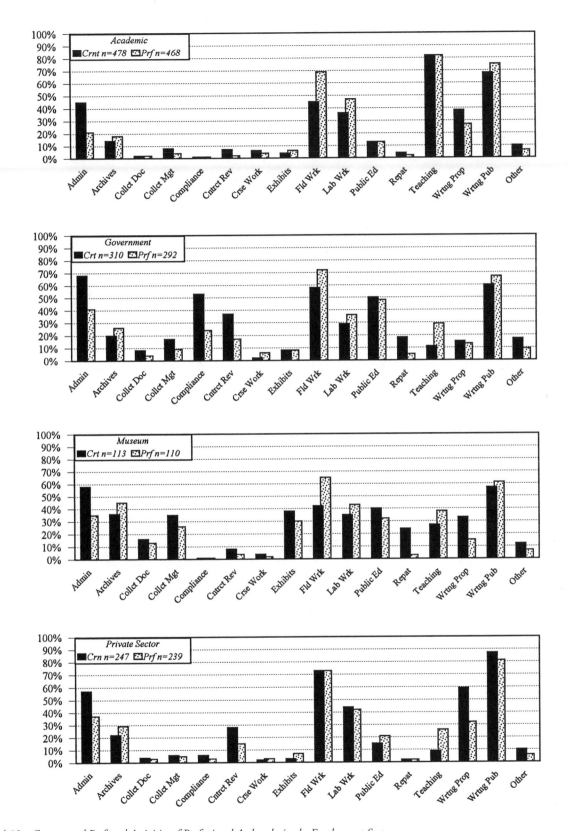

Fig. 4.19 *Current and Preferred Activities of Professional Archaeologists by Employment Sector*

a Academia

b Government

c Museums

d Private sector

Note the distinctive activity profiles of archaeologists employed in different sectors. Note also the common preference for fieldwork, lab work, and writing for publication in all sectors, and the common lack of preference for administration.

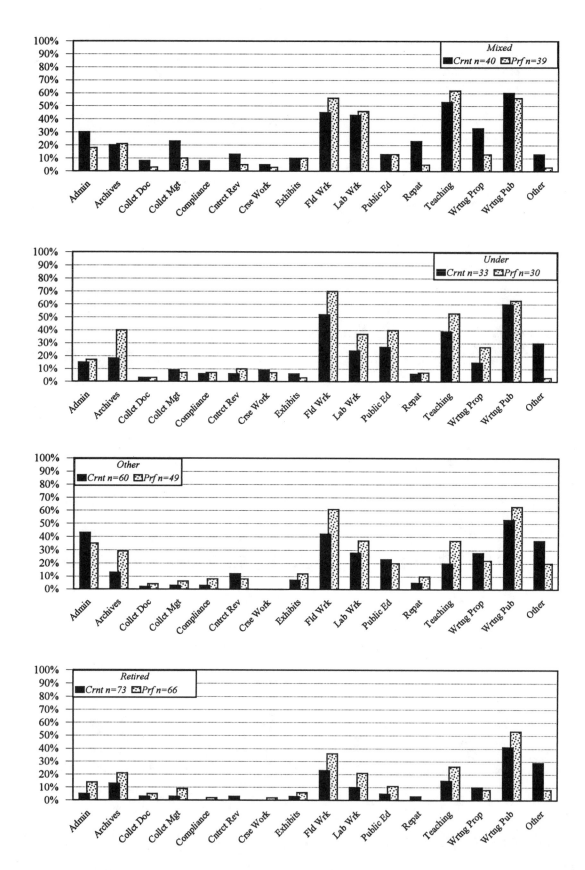

Fig. 4.19 *Current and Preferred Activities of Professional Archaeologists by Employment Sector (continued)*

e Mixed settings   g Other nonarchaeological employment

f Underemployed   h Retired

to archaeologists employed in different sectors, however, than to writing proposals to fund their own work.

In many ways, the activity profile of museum-based archaeologists is more similar to that of academic archaeologists than to any other employment sector. The proportions of museum professionals engaged in writing for publication, conducting field and lab work, and writing proposals are quite similar to those in academia. And while the proportion of museum archaeologists who teach is quite a bit less than that found among academics, teaching is much more commonly represented here than in the government or private sectors. Museum archaeologists are distinguished from archaeologists in other employment sectors by their greater involvement in exhibits, collections management, archival research, and repatriation.

Private sector archaeology differs from other archaeological employment sectors in the proportion of individuals engaged in writing publications and conducting fieldwork, which at 81 percent and 73 percent respectively are higher than in any other employment sector. Since private sector archaeology is largely funded on a contractual basis awarded through a competitive bidding process, it is not surprising that more people are also engaged in writing proposals in the private sector than in any other sector of archaeological employment. It is also no surprise that contract review is practiced by a relatively high proportion of private sector archaeologists.

Current activity profiles of those in the four smaller employment categories (Figure 4.19e, f, g, and h) are generally quite similar to one another, with writing for publication and fieldwork the activities performed by the highest numbers of individuals in each group. Not unexpectedly, a relatively large number of people in mixed and underemployed categories are engaged in teaching. It is also not surprising to find a higher proportion of people performing administrative and other activities among those working outside of archaeology.

The profile of actual activities conducted by archaeologists in all employment categories is significantly different from the profile of preferred activities. Moreover, the preferences of archaeologists of each employment sector are also distinctively different from those of archaeologists in other employment sectors. And yet each sector shares certain basic similarities. As was the case for academic archaeologists, archaeologists in the other nonacademic employment sectors share a preference for fieldwork and writing publications. In most instances, the proportion of people who would prefer to be engaged in these activities exceeds the actual proportion of individuals who are currently conducting fieldwork and writing books or articles. In the private sector, however, where large proportions of the workforce are engaged in fieldwork and writing publications, the preference for these activities is equal to, or in the case of writing, a bit less than the proportions of individuals currently conducting them. This is also the case for

individuals working in mixed settings, one of which is often within the domain of private sector archaeology. Laboratory research is also a preferred activity among archaeologists in all sectors, as is archival research.

Archaeologists in different employment categories also share certain least-preferred activities. In almost all cases, the proportion of people who list administration as a preferred activity is much lower than the proportion of people currently engaged in administrative activities. The only exception to this pattern is found among retired archaeologists, who may miss their days as department chair or museum director. Writing proposals and preparing compliance and contract reviews also have generally low preference levels, even in work sectors where they are prominently represented among the list of currently performed activities. More individuals employed less than half-time in archaeology, however, would prefer to be writing proposals for funding than currently are. Almost no archaeologists in any employment category expressed a preference for repatriation-related activities.

- Thus there is a close correlation between the kinds of activities commonly conducted in these different employment settings and the degree of preference for employment in that setting. Preferred activities of teaching, writing for publication, fieldwork, and lab work are well represented in academia, while academics are less likely to engage in less preferred activities, such as compliance and contract review and repatriation. Moreover, proportionately fewer academics are engaged in administrative activities than archaeologists in any other work setting, and they usually spend less time on administration than other archaeologists. This close correspondence between the kinds of work academic archaeologists do and the kinds of work archaeologists most prefer is likely a major factor in the generally high preference levels for employment in academia. Despite the higher proportion of museum professionals engaged in less preferred activities like administration and repatriation, museum-based archaeology also commonly involves more highly preferred activities, such as writing, field and lab work, and archival research, all of which probably contribute to the overall higher preference for employment in museum settings seen among both men and, especially, women.

In contrast, a large number of people in government archaeology spend a great deal of time engaged in administrative activities. Moreover, many government archaeologists also perform less preferred activities like compliance and contract review and repatriation, undoubtedly contributing to the generally lower number of people who expressed a preference for employment in government settings.

Judging from the large numbers of consulting archaeologists engaged in highly preferred activities like fieldwork, writing for publication, and lab work, preference levels for employment in the private sector might be expected to have been significantly higher than they were. Here, however, we are probably dealing with differences in the nature of these activities that were not captured in the SAA Census. In the private sector, the kinds of field and laboratory analyses conducted and the form of the final publication of this work are not fully determined by the individual archaeologist's interests or initiative. Rather, they are dictated to a greater degree by both law and contractual arrangements, and must be carried out in highly structured ways according to strictly maintained schedules. The archaeology performed by government archaeologists is also likely to be subject to similar constraints. It would also seem that government archaeologists are more likely to monitor the work of other archaeologists in different work settings than they are to be actively pursuing their own research. In contrast, academic and museum-based archaeologists are usually granted much more freedom to follow their own research interests, as well as greater flexibility in structuring the methods and schedule of their research. It is this greater degree of research independence that probably plays a major role in boosting the preference level for these employment sectors over employment in either the private or public sectors. •

Compensation

A major section of the SAA Census dealt with the compensation archaeologists receive for their labors. Respondents were asked to specify current salary levels, report information on the sources as well as the proportion of their yearly earning garnered from different sources, list the kinds of employee benefits they received, and indicate whether their current salaries met their financial needs. Now it is undoubtedly true that "Nobody goes into archaeology for the money," as one respondent commented, complaining about the number and scope of the questions asked in this section. Nevertheless, issues of compensation are in fact quite central to a profile of American archaeology. Data on salaries and other forms of financial compensation give us a firm empirical foundation for examining the relative status of different groups of archaeologists: men and women, young and old, archaeologists with different graduate degrees and those working in different employment sectors. They also provide important insights into the factors that shape educational and career trajectories. However, of all the other topics addressed in this profile of American archaeology, the subject of compensation must be approached with the most care. A superficial examination of these data could result in seriously distorted, misleading, and perhaps even unnecessarily incendiary conclusions about the current condition of the profession. It is not enough to simply compare the salaries of men and women, or of academic and private sector archaeologists. Instead, to properly

examine trends in compensation, we need to try to control for a number of crosscutting factors that influence levels of compensation. Factors such as age, education, seniority, and similarity in the nature of job responsibilities must all be taken into account in drawing these comparisons.

This discussion is broken into three parts. The first focuses on the yearly earnings of archaeologists, comparing salaries of men and women in progressively more narrowly defined groups, and looking at relative salaries and potentials for salary growth of different employment sectors. The second part examines sources of compensation, as well as the level of work effort in archaeology that receives no compensation. The final section takes a look at the benefits available to archaeologists working in different employment sectors.

Salaries

Measuring Salary Levels For a number of reasons it would have been optimal to have respondents record actual dollar amounts when reporting their earnings. However, in designing the Census instrument we worried that respondents might feel this level of specificity was too intrusive into their private financial lives. Instead, we believed that we would get a better response to this sensitive question if respondents were asked to denote their earnings by checking one of 11 salary levels, beginning with $0–$10,000, and increasing in $10,000 increments up to a final category for those who earn over $100,000 per year (Appendix). Respondents were also asked to report their total yearly earnings from all sources, not just those gained for their efforts in archaeology. Since another part of the Census asked respondents to specify the proportions of their yearly earnings received from sources both inside and outside of archaeology, we hoped to get a good picture of the total income of archaeologists today, regardless of the source of this income, as well as a sense of the level of compensation received for archaeological endeavors alone. The response to these questions was gratifying. Of the 1,677 individuals who returned the Census, 1,603 (96 percent) completed the section on salaries.

The following graphs group the 11 salary categories into 5 broader categories: 0–$20,000, $20,000–$40,000, $40,000–$60,000, and $80,000–$100,000+. After experimenting with several different ways of lumping and splitting these complex data, I decided that this five-part grouping yielded the clearest visual presentation that still captured the subtle trends evident in finer-scale but more cluttered graphs.

As in other aspects of this study, the significance of salary differences was tested with the chi-square (χ^2) statistic. These tests were performed using the 11 original salary levels, as well as the 5 more-inclusive groups defined above. In some cases statistics were run comparing the proportions of individuals making more or less than a certain amount. Even though the chi-square statistic is recommended in cases where sample sizes are small, it is still very much dependent on the size of the groups compared. If the groups are relatively large (men and women with PhDs, for example), a very slight difference in the salary distributions of the groups may prove highly significant. In contrast, when groups were fairly small (such as men and women in academia who have PhDs and entered the job market in the 1970s), only very major differences in salaries were statistically significant. Thus, a difference that is highly significant, when comparing fairly large populations, may have no statistical significance when the groups are relatively small. As a general rule, once one of the populations contained 50 or fewer members, patterns that had proven highly significant in larger populations (that is, with a probability level of better than .001) were no longer statistically significant even at the most generous .09 level of probability. The chi-square statistic's loss of resolution in smaller populations proved especially troublesome when dealing with salary data, because to provide a truly accurate view of these data it was necessary to partition them into small, narrowly defined groups. Since the statistic requires that at least 80 percent of all cells contain five or more individuals, this problem was particularly acute when comparing the distribution of salaries across all 11 salary levels. Although lumping the data into five or even two salary categories was helpful, it was still difficult to evaluate the statistical significance of apparent differences between small groups. Thus, it is important to strike a balance when evaluating these kinds of fine-scale comparisons. On the one hand we cannot rigidly dismiss all but the grossest disparities between the salaries of tightly defined groups. Nor, however, can we afford to make more than is warranted of slight salary differences between small groups.

In the following presentation, the chi-square statistic for the populations compared in each graph is provided in the figure heading. In each case the chi-square was computed using the five larger salary categories. Additional statistical results are cited in the text when relevant. Salary distributions will be examined first by comparing fairly broadly defined large groups, that is, gender and age. Then these groups are partitioned into progressively smaller but more directly comparable groups on the basis of factors of seniority, education, and employment. In evaluating the significance of differences noted between these smaller groups, reference will be made to tests of similar patterns in larger and more statistically reliable populations.

Salaries by Gender and Age Viewed in the aggregate, there is a marked and highly significant difference between the salary distributions of professional men and women in archaeology (Figure 4.20). Sixty-three percent of professional female archaeologists make under $40,000 per year, while 61 percent of the males make over $40,000. How-

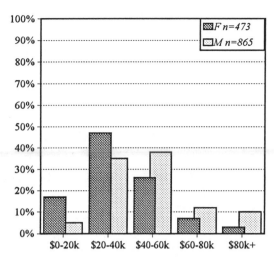

Fig. 4.20 *Salaries of Male and Female Professional Archaeologists ($\chi^2=91.429$, df=4, p<.001)*

Note the large differential between salaries of men and women.

ever, since professional men in archaeology tend to be older than professional women, much of this salary differential could be attributed to seniority alone. Comparing the salaries of men and women in the same age cohorts (Figure 4.21) shows that even though the difference between salary distributions narrows in the younger cohorts, there are clear and statistically significant differences between the salary distribution of men and women in all age cohorts. The difference among the oldest archaeologists, in their 70s and 80s (Figure 4.21f), is quite stark. It is more subtle in the 60–69 age cohort (Figure 4.21e). Yet while a higher proportion of women than men make between $60,000 and $80,000 a year, the proportion of women in their 60s who make less than $40,000 a year is substantially greater than in men (43 percent compared to 19 percent). Moreover, a full 23 percent of men in their 60s make over $80,000 per year, but there were no women respondents in this salary bracket. Among those in their 50s, 63 percent of the women make under $50,000 per year, while 89 percent of the men make $50,000 or more (Figure 4.21d). Nearly 50 percent of the women in their 40s make between $20,000 and $40,000 per year while 32 percent of women in this cohort make between $40,000 and $60,000 per year (Figure 4.21c). In contrast, 42 percent of the men make $40,000–$60,000 per year, while less than 40 percent are in the lower $20,000–$40,000 bracket. The mean salary levels for archaeologists in their 30s is the same, between $20,000 and $40,000 (Figure 4.21b). Yet 22 percent of these women make under $20,000 per year, compared to only 8 percent of the men. Among professional archaeologists in their 20s (Figure 4.21a), there is a significant tendency for women to make under $30,000 per year, and for men to make more than this amount ($\chi^2=4.511$, df=1, p=.034).

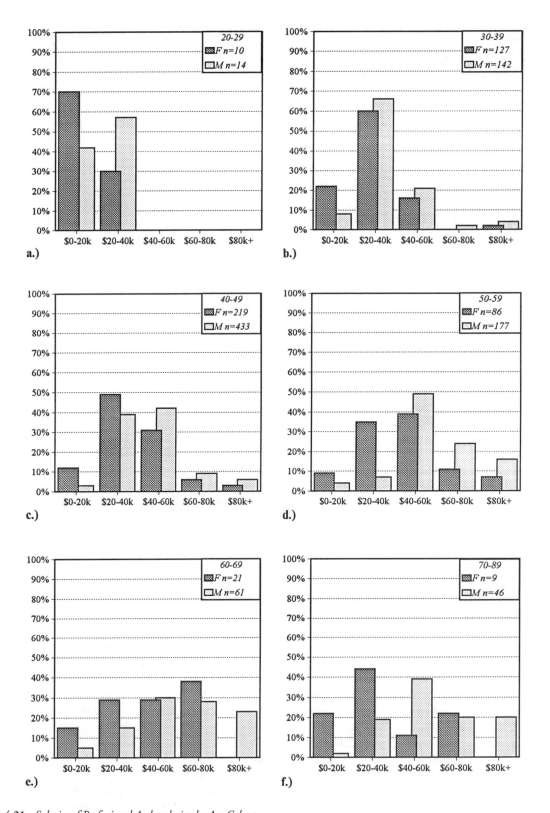

Fig. 4.21 *Salaries of Professional Archaeologists by Age Cohort*

a 20–29 age cohort (χ^2=1.731, df=1, p=.188)
c 40–49 age cohort (χ^2=32.055, df=4, p<.001)
e 60–69 age cohort (χ^2=9.497, df=4, p=.050)

b 30–39 age cohort (χ^2=11.886, df=4, p=.018)
d 50–59 age cohort (χ^2=40.140, df=4, p<.001)
f 70–89 age cohort (χ^2=11.016, df=4, p=.026)

Note the substantial salary gap between men and women in older cohorts, and the decrease of this difference in younger cohorts. Note, however, the persistent tendency for women to earn lower salaries and men to earn higher salaries in all cohorts.

Salaries by Gender and Seniority Since different people may begin their active careers at different ages, controlling for age does not necessarily control for seniority. Recognizing this problem, other studies have used the date of PhD award as the "0" hour on the seniority clock (Gifford-Gonzalez 1994). However, since roughly one-third of the Census respondents do not hold PhDs, this method of controlling for seniority was not appropriate here. A better way to partition these data would be by the number of years respondents have actually been practicing archaeology. Census respondents were asked to record the first year they received earnings for a professional-level position in archaeology (not including student assistantships and scholarships). And while we cannot control for breaks in active participation in the profession (time off to bear and rear children, for example), the number of years between the present (the Census occurred in 1994) and the year of first entry into the professional job market is the best means available for measuring the relative seniority of this broad and diverse respondent population. When we plot the mean number of years respondents have been in the profession against their age cohort (Figure 4.22), we see that there is indeed a major gap in the relative seniority of men and women in the older age cohorts. Male archaeologists in their 60s have been employed in archaeology for an average of 33 years, 11 years more than the average for women in their 60s. This gap narrows to about eight years among archaeologists in their 50s, and further to two years among archaeologists in their 40s. The fact that there is no gap in seniority between men and women in their 20s and 30s does *not* necessarily mean that there is now parity in the ages at which men and women enter professional archaeology. Late entries into the job market (both men and women) have yet to make their presence felt in these youngest cohorts. This conclusion would, however, seem to be a logical extension of the trend noted in older cohorts toward more parity in age of entry into the profession. Thus, to ensure better control over varying levels of seniority, data will be presented not by age cohort, but by decade of entry into professional archaeology as determined by the year in which respondents held their first professional job in archaeology. When examining salary levels by entry decade, it is important to keep in mind that these salaries reflect *current* earnings of people who entered the professional job market during a certain decade. They are not entry-level salaries earned during the first decade of employment.

Figure 4.23 displays the salary distributions of men and women by entry decade. Once again there appear to be fairly marked differences between the current salaries of older archaeologists who have been in the job market the longest (Figure 4.23a and b). At first glance the salary distributions of men and women who entered archaeology in the 1960s are quite similar (Figure 4.23c). On closer examination, however, it would appear that the current salaries of women who entered the job market in the

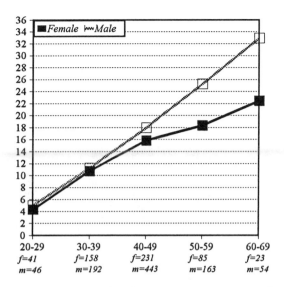

Fig. 4.22 *Average Number of Years Since Receiving First Professional Salary by Age and Gender*

Note the large disparity in the number of years during which older men and women have been actively engaged in professional careers in archaeology, and the decrease in this difference among younger archaeologists.

1960s more frequently fall in the lower salary brackets (less than $40,000 per year), while proportionately more men in this cohort earn upper-bracket salaries, especially in the highest bracket of salaries of greater than $80,000 a year. The gap between the current salaries of men and women who entered the job market in the 1970s is quite large and highly significant. The salaries of archaeologists who began their careers in the 1980s are more similar (Figure 4.23b). Yet even though the means of the salaries of men and women overlap in this cohort, there is still a clear and significant tendency for women to be better represented in lower salary brackets while proportionately more men make salaries higher than the general mean. The apparent differences between the salaries of the small population of archaeologists who entered the job market in the 1990s (Figure 4.23a) is not statistically significant when the chi-square statistic is computed using the five salary levels. However, there is a significant tendency for men in this cohort to make more than $40,000 per year and women to make less than this amount ($\chi^2 = 4.046$, df=1, p=.044).

Salaries by Gender and Employment Sector We noted earlier that the employment profiles of men and women in different age cohorts vary substantially. Thus, to make salaries of men and women in archaeology more comparable, we need to further partition the sample by employment sectors. Figure 4.24 presents aggregate salaries of men and women in different employment sectors. Salary distributions of men and women in three of the four sectors (academia, museums, and the private sector) are significantly different from one another. In academia there is

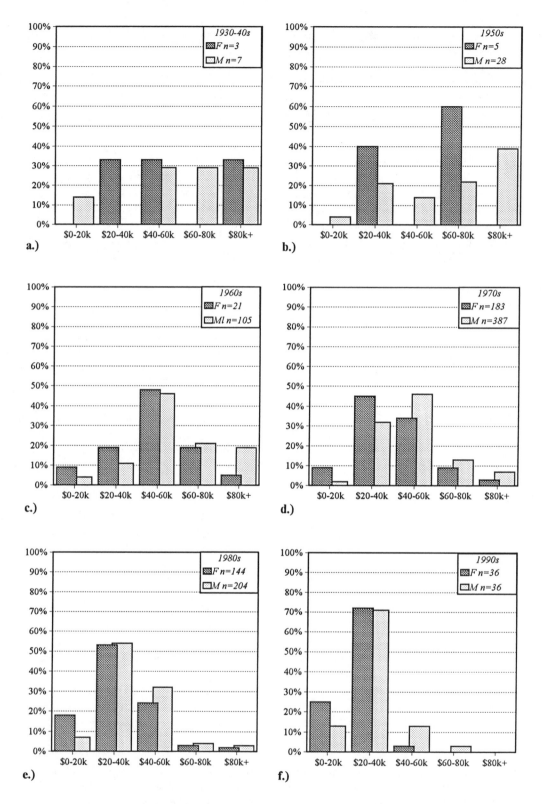

Fig. 4.23 *Salaries of Professional Archaeologists by Entry Decade*

a 1930s and 1940s entry decades (χ^2=3.651, df=4, p=.455)

b 1950s entry decade (χ^2=5.775, df=4, p=.217)

c 1960s entry decade (χ^2=4.256, df=4, p=.372)

d 1970s entry decade (χ^2=30.429, df=4, p<.001)

e 1980s entry decade (χ^2=16.438, df=4, p=.002)

f 1990s entry decade (χ^2=5.655, df=3, p=.130)

Note the substantial salary gap between men and women in earlier entry decades, and the decrease of this difference in more recent entry decades. Note, however, the persistent tendency for women to earn lower salaries and men to earn higher salaries in all cohorts.

a marked split between the salaries of men and women at the $40,000 level (Figure 4.24a). In museums the concentration of women making under $40,000 is plainly evident, as is the high proportion of men making over $80,000 a year (Figure 4.24b). Aggregate salaries of men and women in the private sector are closer, but women are still proportionally better represented in the lower salary brackets below $40,000 and men are better represented in the upper brackets (Figure 4.24d).

The salary distributions of men and women government archaeologists are, in contrast, very similar (Figure 4.24b). Although slightly more women fall into the $20,000–$40,000 bracket and men into the $40,000–$60,000 bracket, gender-based salary differences in government archaeology are not significant (despite the relatively large sample of government archaeologists). This is true

even when the proportions of men and women making more and less than $40,000 are compared. Another notable feature of government salaries is their more restricted range; 90 percent of both men and women in government archaeology make between $20,000 and $60,000 a year. In contrast, other employment sectors have a much wider spread in salaries, with proportionately more people making salaries in the upper brackets, and, especially, more people at the lowest salary levels. To some extent, then, the generally more restricted range of salaries in government may enhance the impression of greater gender parity.

While the limited size of the respondent groups in the four smaller employment categories makes it difficult to test the significance of gender-based salary differentials (Figure 4.25), there are clear differences in the salaries of men and women who fall into the mixed (Figure 4.25a),

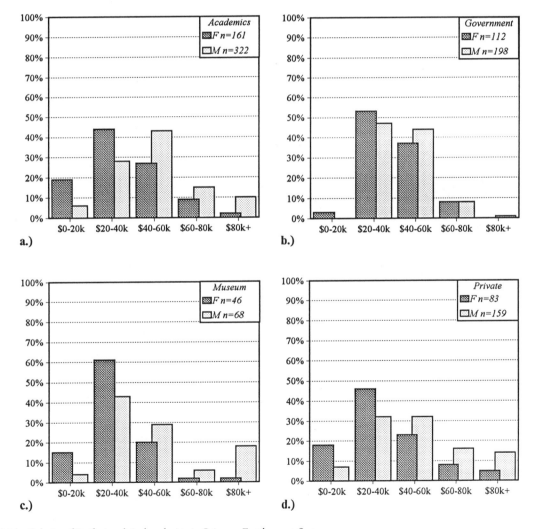

Fig. 4.24 *Salaries of Professional Archaeologists in Primary Employment Sectors*

a Academics (χ^2=46.266, df=4, p<.001)
c Museum professionals (χ^2=13.141, df=4, p=.011)

b Government archaeologists (χ^2=7.778, df=4, p=.100)
d Private sector archaeologists (χ^2=16.215, df=4, p=.003)

Note the large difference between the salaries of men and women in museum settings and academia. Note also the somewhat smaller difference in the private sector, and the similarity of the salaries of men and women in government.

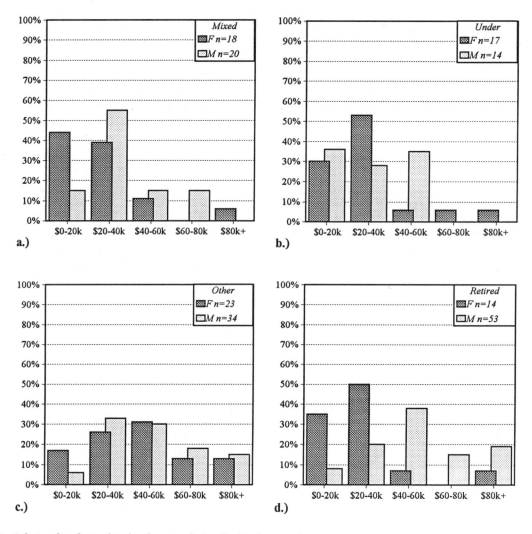

Fig. 4.25 *Salaries of Professional Archaeologists in the Smaller Employment Categories*

a Mixed settings (χ^2=7.277, df=4, p=.122)
c Other nonarchaeological employment settings (χ^2=2.123, df=4, p=.713)
b Underemployed archaeologists (χ^2= 6.359, df=4, p=.174)
d Retired archaeologists (χ^2=16.414, df=4, p=.003)

Note the substantial differences between the salaries of men and women in the mixed settings, underemployed, and retired categories, and the close match between salaries of respondents employed outside of archaeology.

the underemployed (Figure 4.25b), and, especially, the retired category (Figure 4.25d). In all cases, proportionately more women make less than $40,000 a year, while there are proportionately more men in the higher salary brackets. In contrast, there is virtual parity in the salaries of men and women employed outside of archaeology (Figure 4.25c).

Salaries by Gender, Employment Sector, and Seniority
The next four graphs break down the current salaries of men and women in each of the four major employment sectors by decade of entry into the professional workforce (Figures 4.26 through 4.29). These graphs show a persistence of patterns evident in the broader groupings of men and women with different levels of seniority (Figure 4.23), as well as those seen in comparisons of male and female

salaries within different work sectors (Figure 4.24). In each employment sector, there is increasing parity in the salaries of younger archaeologists just entering the archaeological job market. In every case the substantial gap between the current salaries of men and women who entered the job market in the 1960s and 1970s lessens among archaeologists who began their careers in the 1980s. This is true even among government archaeologists (Figure 4.27), where for all entry decades current salary differentials between men and women are less marked than in other employment sectors. However, all employment sectors still show a tendency for the most recent women entrants into the job market to be better represented at the low end of the salary scale and for proportionately more men to fall into the upper brackets. This pattern is quite clear among the

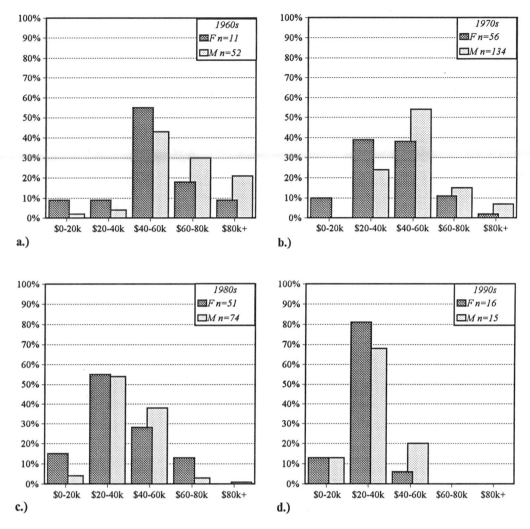

Fig. 4.26 *Academic Salaries by Entry Decade*

a 1960s entry decade (χ^2=3.497 df=4, p=.478)

c 1980s entry decade (χ^2=6.374, df=4, p=.173)

b 1970s entry decade (χ^2=22.234, df=4, p<.001)

d 1990s entry decade (χ^2=13.60, df=2, p=.506)

Note the decrease in the salary differentials between men and women in each more recent entry decade, but the persistent tendency for women to be better represented in lower salary brackets and men to be better represented in upper brackets.

larger pools of respondents with entry dates in the 1980s, though it is still apparent in the smaller groups of people who earned their first professional salaries in archaeology in the 1990s.

Differentials between the salaries of men and women are most marked in museum settings (Figure 4.28). Current salary levels of museum-based men and women who began their careers in the 1970s are starkly different (Figure 4.28b). Close to 80 percent of these women make less than $40,000 per year, while 55 percent of the men make more than $40,000 ($\chi^2$=6.571, df=1, p=.010). And while, as in all other employment sectors, the gap narrows between the current salaries of male and female museum professionals who entered the market in the 1980s, there is still a clear difference between these salaries. More than half of the women in museums who began their careers in

the 1980s currently make less than $30,000 per year, compared to only a little more than a third of the men (χ^2=2.795, df=1, p=.095).

The difference between the current salaries of men and women in academia, though less striking than among museum professionals, is still quite clear (Figure 4.26). This is especially true for academicians who entered the job market in the 1970s (Figure 4.26b). Among academics who entered the profession in the 1980s, the proportion of women making between $60,000 and $80,000 is higher than the proportion of men earning this amount (Figure 4.26c). However, there is still a significantly higher proportion of these women who earn less than $30,000 a year ($\chi^2$=6.025, df=1, p=.014). In the small group of academic archaeologists who entered the job market in the 1990s, there remains a tendency for men to be better represented

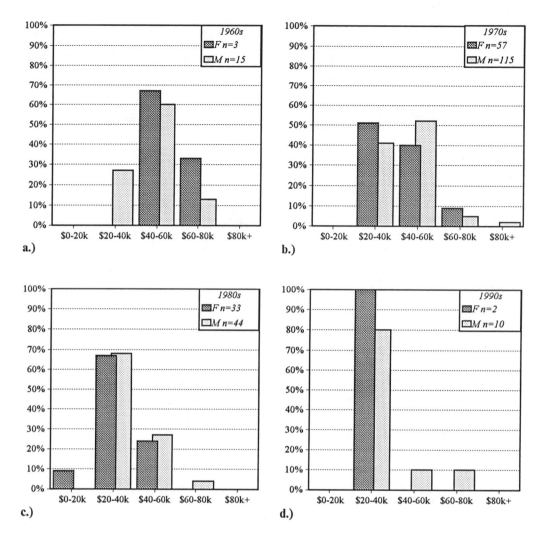

Fig. 4.27 *Government Salaries by Entry Decade*

a 1960s entry decade (χ^2=1.418, df=2, p=.492)　　　**b** 1970s entry decade (χ^2=3.712, df=3, p=.294)

c 1980s entry decade (χ^2=5.573, df=3, p=.134)　　　**d** 1990s entry decade (χ^2=0.480, df=2, p=.787)

Note that despite the generally greater overlap between the salaries of men and women in government, and the decrease in the salary differentials between men and women in each more recent entry decade, there is still some evidence that women in government work settings earn lower salaries than men.

in the higher end of the salary range; 20 percent of these men make between $40,000 and $60,000, compared to only 6 percent of the women.

As in the aggregate population of private sector consulting archaeologists (Figure 4.24d), there is a consistently closer match between the current salaries of men and women in every entry decade (Figure 4.29). Moreover, though women are still better represented in the lowest salary brackets among 1980s-entry-decade private sector archaeologists (Figure 4.29c), there is greater gender parity here in the upper brackets. There is no difference between the salaries of men and women in the small population of private sector archaeologists who began their careers in the 1990s (Figure 4.29d).

Salaries by Gender and Degree Yet it is not enough to simply compare salaries of men and women with similar years of seniority in similar employment sectors. As we have seen, there are substantial differences in types of degrees men and women hold, and the nature of these differences vary with age and employment sector. It is generally assumed that the higher the graduate degree, the higher one's earning potential. And while this assumption seems generally warranted, there are important differences in the extent to which degree status affects earnings.

Once again, when looking at aggregate data we notice significant differences between the salaries of men and women who hold the same highest degree (Figure 4.30), especially among PhDs. In the populations of nonstudents

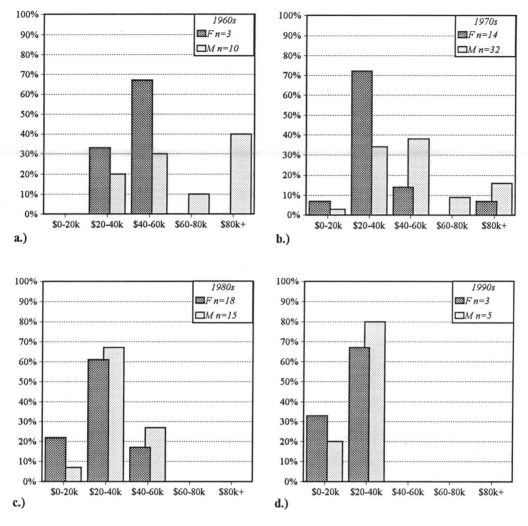

Fig. 4.28 *Museum Salaries by Entry Decade*

a 1960s entry decade (χ^2=2.484, df=3, p=.478)
c 1980s entry decade (χ^2=1.732, df=2, p=.421)

b 1970s entry decade (χ^2=6.865, df=4, p=.143)
d 1990s entry decade (χ^2=0.178, df=1, p=.673)

Note that while there is also a decrease in the salary differentials of museum men and women in more recent award decades, the difference between salaries of men and women in museums in all entry cohorts is larger than in other employment sectors.

with BAs and MAs (Figure 4.30a and b), a large group of both men and women fall into the $20,000–$40,000 bracket. Yet in each case there are proportionately more women who make below $20,000 a year, and more men who make over $40,000 a year. In the PhD population, a large number of women still fall into the $20,000–$40,000 bracket, whereas comparatively more male PhDs are found in the higher $40,000–$60,000 bracket (Figure 4.30c).

Salaries by Gender, Degree, and Seniority Partitioning the larger MA and PhD populations by entry decade (Figures 4.31 and 4.32) reduces, but does not eliminate, the salary differentials between men and women with similar degrees. In both the MA and the PhD populations, the differences between the current salaries of men and

women who entered the job market in the 1970s is statistically significant (Figures 4.31b and 4.32b). Among MA archaeologists who began their careers in the 1980s (Figure 4.31c), the tendency for women to make less than $30,000 a year and for men to make more than $30,000 is marginally significant at the .097 level of probability (χ^2=2.757, df=1). And while the population of MAs starting their careers in the 1990s is quite small (Figure 4.31d), the salary differentials between men and women are unmistakable. Among PhDs who entered the job market in the 1980s (Figure 4.32c), proportionately more women make less than $30,000, while men tend to make more than this amount (χ^2=51.783, df=1, p.<001). This is also the case among female PhDs who entered the profession in the 1990s (Figure 4.30d; χ^2=5.170 , df=1, p=.023).

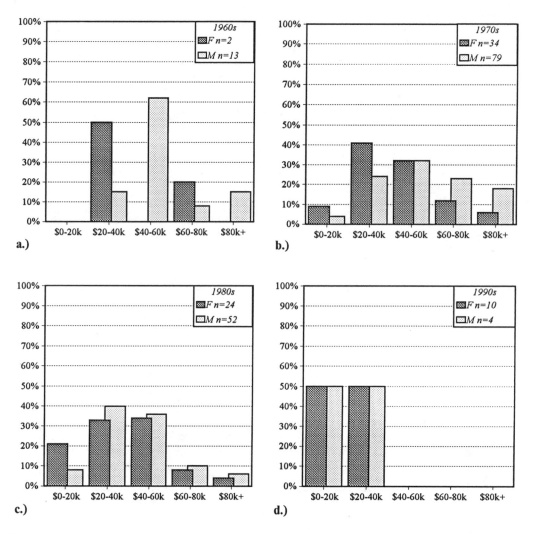

Fig. 4.29 *Private Sector Salaries by Entry Decade*

a 1960s entry decade (χ^2=4.904, df=3, p=.179) **b** 1970s entry decade (χ^2=7.358, df=4, p=.118)
c 1980s entry decade (χ^2=2.956, df=4, p=.565) **d** 1990s entry decade (χ^2=0.000, df=1, p=1.000)

Note that while a decrease in salary differentials is also found in the private sector, there is generally less difference between the salaries of men and women in the private sector than is the case for academia or museums.

Salaries by Gender, Employment, Seniority, and Degree
Without breaking the sample down to the level of specific positions (which we will do later in this chapter for academia and the private sector), the finest-grained partitioning possible is to compare the salaries of men and women employed in the same sectors of the workforce by degree status and by level of seniority (Figures 4.33 through 4.36). Because this fine-scale partitioning results in some very small groups, only the salaries of respondents entering the profession in the 1970 and 1980 entry decades are shown here. While doing this reduces some differences noted in the grosser groupings of these data, the basic patterns still remain. No matter how the data are partitioned, differentials between the current salaries of men and women decrease with each more recent entry decade. Yet in all cases there is still a tendency for women to be

better represented in the lower salary brackets and men in the upper. Once again, salary differentials are smaller among government archaeologists, where the spread of salaries is relatively focused on a fairly tightly defined middle range (Figure 4.34). Private sector salaries show the second smallest difference between the salaries of men and women with comparable training and seniority (Figure 4.36), followed by academic salaries (Figure 4.33). Gender-based differences seem the most marked among museum professionals, especially for those who began their careers in the 1970s (Figure 4.35).

Future Trends in the Salaries of Men and Women in Archaeology The data just presented have identified clear and significant trends in the salaries of men and women in archaeology. At the same time, however, they also raise

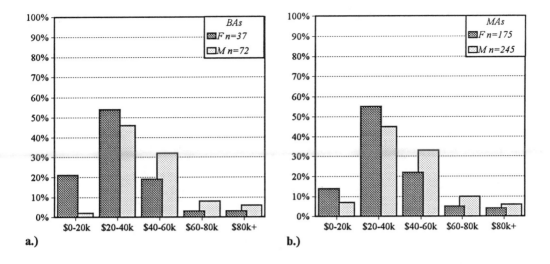

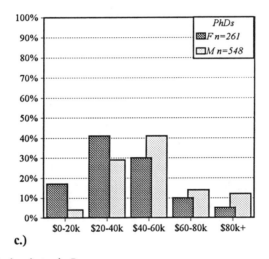

Fig. 4.30 *Salaries of Professional Archaeologists by Degree*
a BAs (χ^2=13.050, df=4, p=.011)   **b** MAs (χ^2=16.311, df=4, p=.003)
c PhDs (χ^2=65.702, df=4, p=.000)

Note the greater differential between the salaries of male and female PhDs than in the salaries of men and women with BAs and MAs.

several important, and as yet unresolved, questions about current and, especially, future trends in archaeological salaries. Do the salaries of women who entered the market in the 1970s lag so far behind those of men because these women have encountered the archaeological equivalent of the corporate glass ceiling (a "chipped stone" ceiling, perhaps), which has denied them access to higher-paying jobs? Or are there salary discrepancies among more senior archaeologists simply because these women started out in their careers at lower salary levels? Will the greater parity in salaries noted among younger archaeologists continue as they advance in their careers? Or will these younger women face similar impediments to promotion, as apparently seen among more senior women? There is no way to directly answer these questions with the data collected in the 1994 SAA Census. However, there are some ways to address them, at least obliquely.

First, we can examine entry-level salaries reported by Census respondents to see if the differential in the current salaries of more senior archaeologists is an artifact of disparities in entry-level salaries of men and women in past decades. Figure 4.37 displays the average entry-level salaries of men and women by entry decade. If the current salary differentials among more senior archaeologists is an artifact of past employment practices that brought women into the workforce at significantly lower salaries, then we would expect to see a major gap between male and female entry-level salaries among the most senior archaeologists, along with a decrease in this differential in progressively younger, less senior people. This is not what we find. Instead there is essentially no difference between the initial salaries of male and female archaeologists who embarked on their careers in the 1960s, the most senior group shown here. And while there is a gap between the entry-level salaries of men

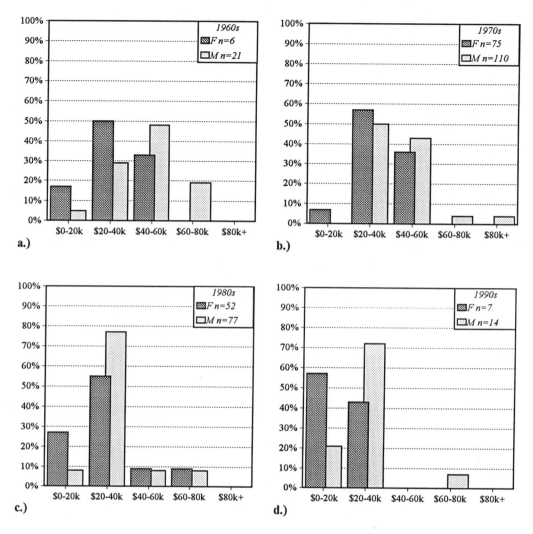

Fig. 4.31 *MA Salaries by Entry Decade*

a 1960s entry decade (χ^2=2.893, df=3, p=.408) **b** 1970s entry decade (χ^2=8.584, df=4, p=.072)
c 1980s entry decade (χ^2=6.361, df=4, p=.174) **d** 1990s entry decade (χ^2=2.321, df=1, p=.128)

Note the decrease in the salary differentials between men and women in each more recent entry decade, but the persistent tendency for women to earn lower salaries than men.

beginning their careers in the 1970s and 1980s, this difference is never more than $2,000—nowhere near the more than $10,000 gap in these individuals' current salaries. Nor does this differential in initial salaries decrease substantially over these two decades, as it must if differences in entry-level salaries were the root cause of the patterns noted here. Clearly, disparities in entry-level salaries among older archaeologists cannot account for these trends. This brings us back to the possibility that differentials in advancement potential are responsible for the disparity in the salaries of senior archaeologists.

We can get some measure of the salary growth by returning to Figures 4.33 through 4.36 and comparing the relative degree of difference between the current salaries of men and women who entered the workforce in the 1970

and 1980 entry decades. In every employment sector, and in each degree category, the current salaries of men who began their careers in the 1970s are distinctly higher than the current salaries of men who entered the workforce in the 1980s. In every case the salary distribution of these more senior men shows a major shift toward higher salary brackets when compared to more junior men. With some notable exceptions, this is usually not true for women. In museum settings and, for the most part, in academia there is essentially no difference in the salary distributions of most women with master's degrees regardless of seniority (Figures 4.33a and c and 4.35a and c). With the exception of two women who earn over $80,000 a year, the current salaries of museum women with PhDs who entered the profession in the 1970s are essentially the same as salaries

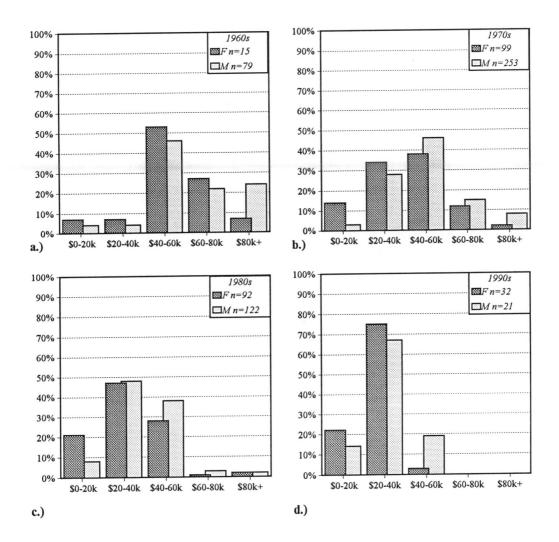

Fig. 4.32 *PhD Salaries by Entry Decade*

a 1960s entry decade (χ^2=2.522, df=4, p=.641) **b** 1970s entry decade (χ^2=22.451, df=4, p<.001)

c 1980s entry decade (χ^2=9.669, df=4, p=.046) **d** 1990s entry decade (χ^2=3.917, df=2, p=.141)

Note the decrease in the salary differentials between men and women in each more recent entry decade, but the persistent tendency for women to earn lower salaries than men.

of women who began their careers in the 1980s (Figure 4.35b and d). The situation is somewhat better among academic women with PhDs (Figure 4.33b and d), but even here there is much more overlap between the salaries of women with different levels of seniority than there is among academic men. A similar situation is seen among the bulk of private sector PhDs (Figure 4.35b and c).

In contrast, there is a distinct jump in the salaries of women consulting archaeologists with MAs between the 1970 and 1980 entry decades that is similar in degree and direction to that seen among MA men in the private sector (Figure 4.36a and c). This is also true for women with MAs in government settings (Figure 4.34a and c). Given the small size of the sample of PhDs in government settings, it is hard to evaluate patterns among PhD men and women

with different levels of seniority. There does, however, appear to be a clear and distinct shift toward higher salary levels among more senior women in government settings.

• At the very least, these data argue for an imbalance in advancement potential of more senior women in certain employment sectors. The advancement potential of women in museums seems to be particularly limited regardless of degree status, while that of women in academia seems only marginally better. The situation is somewhat different in the public and private sectors, especially among MAs, where the salary increases of women over this 10-year period are more comparable to those of men. And yet before we conclude that these data are the result of gender-based barriers in promotion potential, one additional factor

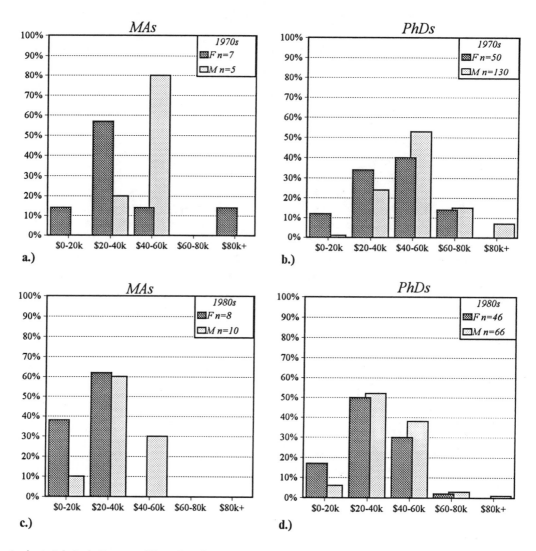

Fig. 4.33 *Academic Salaries by Degree and Entry Decade*

a 1970s-entry-decade MAs (χ^2=4.547, df=2, p=.103)
c 1980s-entry-decade MAs (χ^2=3.917, df=2, p=.141)
b 1970s-entry-decade PhDs (χ^2=17.600, df=2, p=.001)
d 1980s-entry-decade PhDs (χ^2=4.463, df=4, p=.347)

Note the persistence of patterns seen in broader groupings. Note also that for both MA and PhD academic males, there is a substantial difference between the current salaries of those who entered the workforce in the 1970s and those who began their careers in the 1980s. Among academic women with MAs and PhDs there is little difference between the current salaries of those entering the workforce in these two decades.

must be taken into consideration. Although it is the best available means of measuring seniority, the number of years since one first entered the profession is not necessarily the same as the amount of time one has been actively and primarily engaged in archaeology. If a higher proportion of older women work part time, or if a number of these women have recently reentered the job market after their children were grown or after divorce, then the seniority of men and women with the same entry date into the profession may not in fact be equivalent. The disparities in the salaries of older archaeologists may not be an artifact of barriers that prevent female archaeologists from realizing

the same salary growth as men with equivalent education and experience. Instead, these differences may reflect societal conditions that make women more likely to sacrifice career advancement for family commitments.

It is somewhat difficult to reconcile this latter scenario, however, with the apparent variation in the advancement potential of women in different employment sectors and degree categories. If the noted salary differentials stem solely from a tendency among women to work part time or to take time off from their careers, then this pattern should cut across all work sectors, or at least be more strongly expressed in employment sectors that are

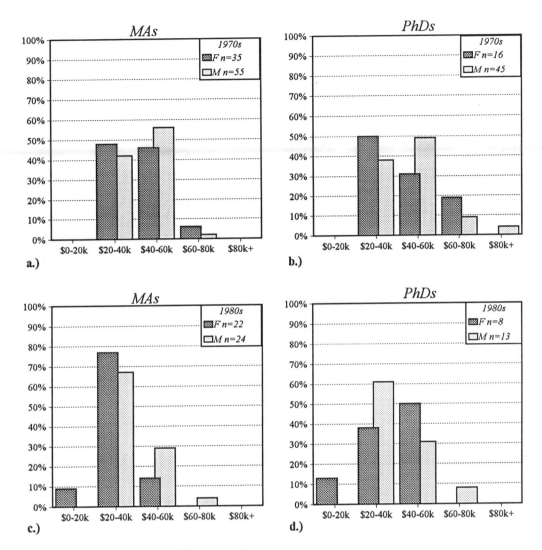

Fig. 4.34 *Government Salaries by Degree and Entry Decade*

a 1970s-entry-decade MAs (χ^2=1.658, df=2, p=.436)
c 1980s-entry-decade MAs (χ^2=3.610, df=2, p=.164)

b 1970s-entry-decade PhDs (χ^2=2.971, df=3, p=.396)
d 1980s-entry-decade PhDs (χ^2= 3.267, df=3, p=.352)

Note the persistence of earlier patterns seen in broader groupings. Note also the similarity in salary growth for both MA and PhD men and women in different entry decades.

more open to part-time employment or reentry into the workforce after a long hiatus—the private sector, in particular. Moreover, one might intuitively expect women with PhDs, who have invested more time and money in their training, to be less likely to make career sacrifices than women with MAs. And yet it is MA women in the public and private sectors who show the least discrepancy in salary growth when compared to men. Remember too that more than half of the women respondents over 50 are unmarried or not involved in a long-term partnership. Unless the low marriage rate among older women is entirely attributable to divorce, it would seem that many of these women have already opted for career over family. Without a follow-up survey aimed at directly measuring

the relationship between seniority and salaries, it remains an open question whether the gap between the salaries of older men and women is an artifact of active barriers to the advancement of women in archaeology, or of broader societal conditions that make women more likely to put family ahead of career.

We also cannot tell from the available data whether younger women will experience the same impediments to salary growth as they progress along their careers. The persistent tendency for even the youngest women in our sample to be disproportionately represented in the lower salary brackets may be an omen of greater salary disparities to come, especially since men and women currently enter the job market at the same salary levels (Figure 4.37). Without

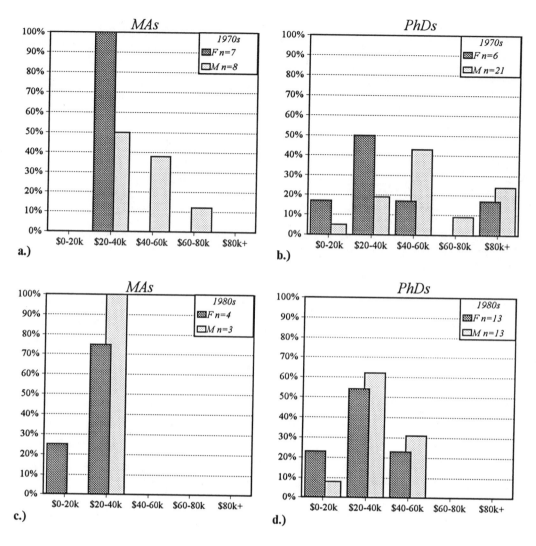

Fig. 4.35 *Museum Salaries by Degree and Entry Decade*

a 1970s-entry-decade MAs (χ^2=4.773, df=2, p=.092)

c 1980s-entry-decade MAs (χ^2=0.875, df=1, p=.350)

b 1970s-entry-decade PhDs (χ^2=4.160, df=4, p=.385)

d 1980s-entry-decade PhDs (χ^2= 1.210, df=2, p=.546)

Note the persistence of earlier patterns seen in broader groupings. Note also the large differential between the current salaries of both MA and PhD males in museums in the different entry decades, and the lack of salary growth among museum women beginning their careers in different entry decades.

the benefit of a crystal ball that would let us look into the future (or the results of a new census 10 years from now), we cannot know how these younger women will fare as they progress through their career trajectories. It may be that the sheer number of women among the ranks of younger archaeologists will prove an effective wedge for breaking through salary barriers that still block the advancement of older women in archaeology. Moreover, there may be better support systems available to younger women who wish to attempt the difficult task of having a family without sacrificing their ability to pursue an active, full-time career in archaeology. •

Potentials for Salary Growth in Different Employment Sectors Before we leave the subject of salaries in archaeology, we need to broaden our focus and take a look at the relative salary levels and potentials for salary growth in different sectors of archaeological employment. Figures 4.38 and 4.39 contrast the current salaries of the combined sample of men and women by employment sector, education, and seniority. Each of the four graphs displayed in these figures represents one of the four primary work sectors. The current salaries of respondents who entered the workforce in the 1970s are presented on the left of each graph, the current salaries of 1980s entrants on the

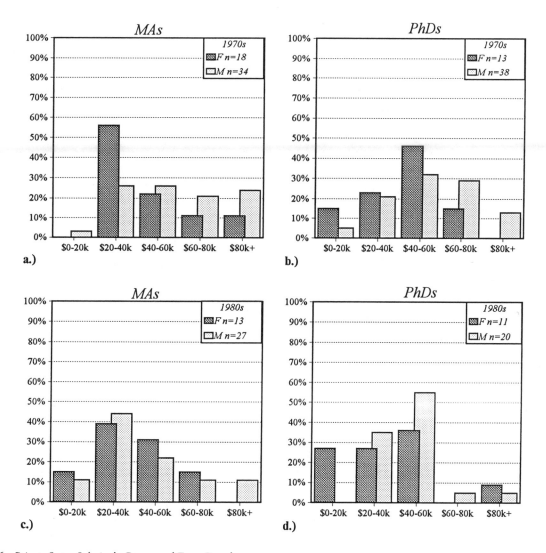

Fig. 4.36 *Private Sector Salaries by Degree and Entry Decade*

a 1970s-entry-decade MAs (χ^2=4.894, df=4, p=.298)

c 1980s-entry-decade MAs (χ^2= 2.031, df=4, p=.730)

b 1970s-entry-decade PhDs (χ^2= 4.276, df=4, p=.370)

d 1980s-entry-decade PhDs (χ^2=6.829, df=4, p=.145)

Note the persistence of earlier patterns seen in broader groupings. Note also the larger differential between the salaries of PhD males in the two entry decades when compared to PhD women in the private sector, but the more similar rate of salary increase among male and female MAs.

right. Figure 4.38 presents these data for people with MAs, while Figure 4.39 contrasts the salaries of PhDs.

Archaeologists with MAs have the best chance of earning more money more quickly if they join the private sector (Figure 4.38). Nearly 40 percent of the private sector archaeologists who entered the profession in the 1970s make more than $60,000 per year, and more than half of these individuals are making more than $80,000 (Figure 4.38d). No other work setting comes close to these salary levels. Perhaps even more impressive is the fact that nearly half of the private sector individuals with MAs who began their careers in the 1980s are making over $40,000 per year. Two of these individuals are making more than

$100,000 a year. In contrast, a little less than one-quarter of the MAs in government who entered the workforce in the 1980s make more than $40,000, compared to about 15 percent of the academic MAs and none of the MAs in museums. Next to the private sector, the second-highest salaries among MAs are seen in government settings (Figure 4.38b). With the exception of one individual from the 1970- entry decade who makes over $80,000, most MAs in academia do not seem to do as well as either private-sector or government MAs (Figure 4.38a). There are more academic MAs in the lowest salary bracket, in both the 1970s and 1980s entry cohorts, than in any other work setting. Overall, however, MAs in museums have the

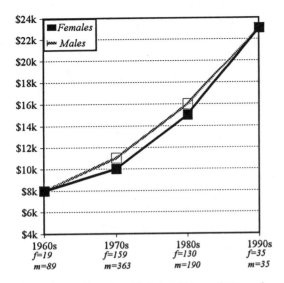

Fig. 4.37 *Average Entry-Level Salaries of Men and Women by Entry Decade*

Note the growth in entry-level salaries over time, and the relatively small difference between male and female entry-level salaries in all entry decades.

lowest salaries (Figure 4.38c). More than 70 percent of the museum professionals with MAs in both the 1980s and 1970s entry cohorts make between $20,000 and $40,000 a year.

Private sector salaries are also highly competitive among PhDs (Figure 4.39). In the cohort of people who entered the profession in the 1970s, there are more PhDs making over $60,000 in the private sector than in any other sector of archaeological employment (Figure 4.39d). The proportion of PhD consulting archaeologists making more than $40,000 in the 1980s entry cohort is also impressively large relative to other work sectors. Academic archaeologists with PhDs have the second-highest salary levels (Figure 4.39a), followed closely by PhDs in government (Figure 4.39b). With the exception of a group of museum professionals making over $80,000 per year in the 1970s entry cohort (consisting of six individuals, five of whom are male), salaries of museum professionals with PhDs, like those of MAs in museums, are somewhat depressed relative to other employment sectors (Figure 4.39c). This is especially true of museum professionals who began their careers in the 1980s (a larger proportion of whom are women).

The data for MAs and PhDs is combined in Figure 4.40, allowing us to more directly compare the relative advantage of different degrees in different employment sectors. Once again, the salaries of people who entered the profession in the 1970s are presented on the left, while the salaries of the 1980s entry cohort are displayed on the right. Clearly a PhD gives one the greatest earning potential in academia and, especially, in museums (Figure 4.40a and c). While PhDs seem to have more earning potential

in government employment settings, especially among more recent entrants into the job market, there is much more overlap between the salaries of MAs and PhDs in government work settings than is seen in either academia or in museums (Figure 4.40b). Degree status seems to make the least amount of difference in earning potential in the private sector (Figure 4.40d). Although PhDs are better represented in some of the higher salary brackets in the 1970s entry cohort of private sector archaeologists, there are still proportionately more MAs in this group who earn over $80,000. Nearly 20 percent of the 1970s-entry-decade MAs in the private sector earn more than $80,000 per year, compared to only 10 percent of the PhDs. In the 1980s entry cohort there are proportionately more MAs in both the $60,000–80,000 salary bracket and the highest $80,000+ bracket. In fact the salaries of MAs in the private sector are generally higher than the salaries of PhDs in each of the other three employment sectors, including academia. For the most part these data dovetail nicely with the relative proportions of individuals with different kinds of degrees in these different work sectors discussed earlier in the chapter. Employment sectors where PhDs have the greatest earning power (academia and museums) are dominated by PhDs. Employment sectors with higher proportions of MAs, like government and the private sector, seem to put less weight on degree status in setting salary levels and earning potential.

• It would seem that more people earn more money and advance up the salary scale more quickly in the private sector than in any other sector of archaeological employment. Earning potential also seems least affected by degree status in the private sector; indeed, MAs may even have some advantage here. And this is true both for men and for women. In fact, while salaries of PhD males in academia and museums come close to the salaries men attain in the private sector, a woman's earning potential is substantially higher in the private sector than in any other employment setting, regardless of degree. Academic PhDs (especially male PhDs) have the second-highest earning potential, followed by PhDs in government settings. Although they fall somewhat behind government PhDs, MAs in government still fare better than MAs in either academia or museums. Finally, with the exception of a few highly paid males, museum salaries for both MAs and PhDs are generally the lowest and slowest-growing of any of the primary employment sectors examined, particularly for women in museums. Thus, if a primary criterion in choosing a career trajectory in archaeology is to earn the most money as rapidly as possible, then the clear choice would be to obtain a master's degree and enter the private sector. Moreover, this choice would be the same for both men and women. In fact it would seem that women have even more to gain in terms of earning potential by entering the private sector. Salary considerations may be a factor in

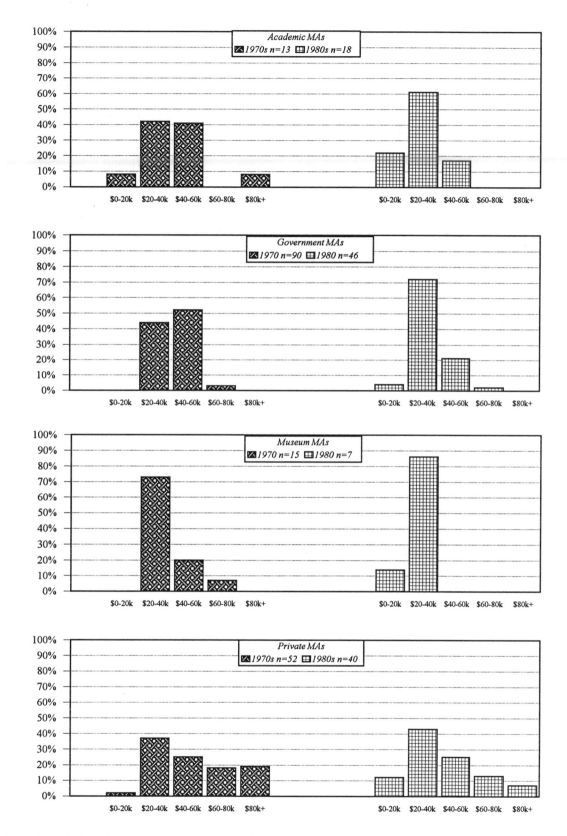

Fig. 4.38 *MA Salaries in Different Employment Sectors by Entry Decade*

a Academia

b Government

c Museums

d Private sector

Note the higher salaries of MAs in the private sector and government, and the lower salaries of MAs in academia and museums.

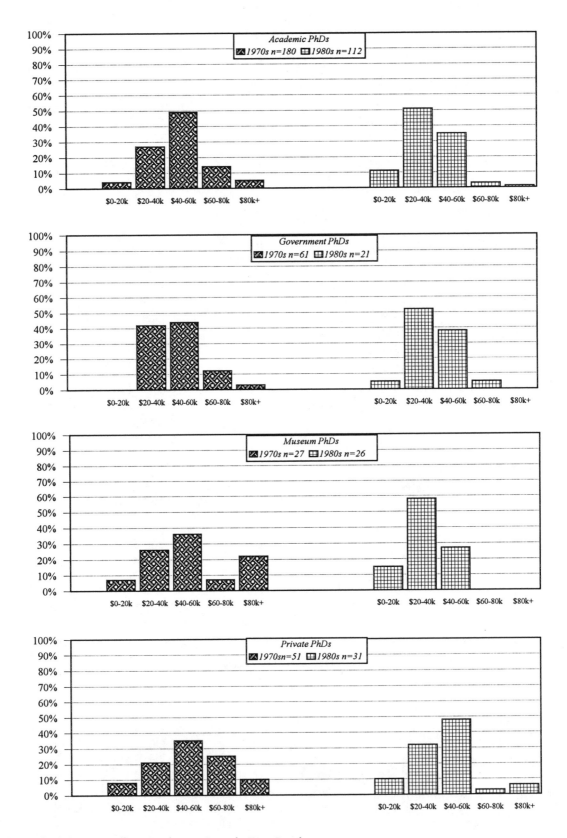

Fig. 4.39 *PhD Salaries in Different Employment Sectors by Entry Decade*

a Academia

b Government

c Museums

d Private sector

Note the higher salaries of PhDs in the private sector and academia, and the generally lower salaries of museum professionals with PhDs.

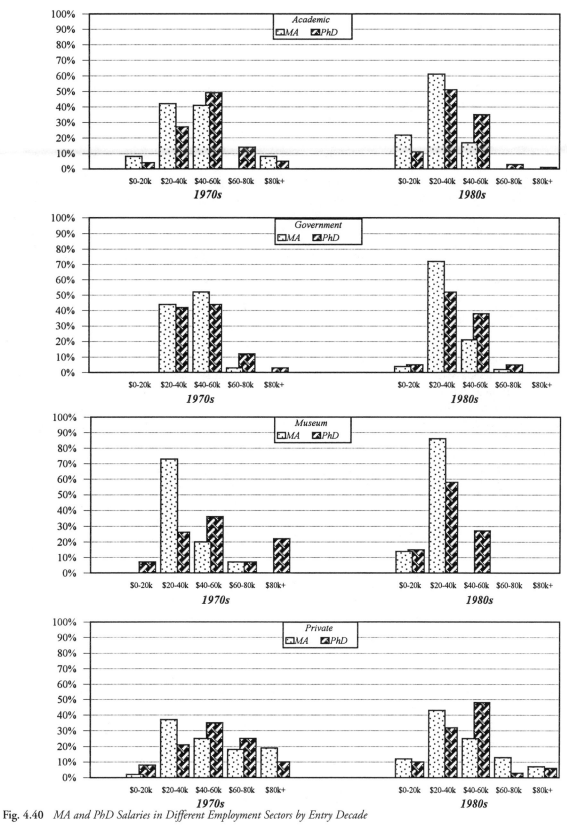

Fig. 4.40 *MA and PhD Salaries in Different Employment Sectors by Entry Decade*

a Academia
b Government

c Museums
d Private sector

Note that the salaries of MAs in the private sector are generally higher than salaries of other professional archaeologists regardless of degree or employment sector.

the increasing number of younger men who are concluding their education with master's degrees and entering the private sector. And yet while consulting archaeology is a growth area among younger women, women have not experienced anywhere near the scale of changes in education and career trajectories as that seen among men. Moreover, the financial advantages of a career in the private sector do not seem to play a major role in determining employment preferences that, for both men and women, clearly favor academic and museum settings. The stronger preference of women for employment in museums would seem particularly hard to reconcile with the marked differential in salaries and potential for growth between women and men in museums. Clearly, the factors that shape the educational and career choices of younger women and men are more complex than simply the promise of higher salaries and more rapid salary advancement. •

Sources of Income and Uncompensated Effort

The salaries discussed above are based on respondents' total yearly income from all sources, both inside and outside archaeology. This method of recording salary information made it easier to more directly compare the income of archaeologists whose salaries are set on a full 12-month cycle to that of those, like academics, whose primary salary may be gauged on shorter, 9- to 10-month cycles. It also provides a measure of the earnings of people who are actively engaged in archaeology (or at least maintain an active interest in the field), but whose primary income is derived from sources outside of the discipline. To capture

information on the sources of income, we asked respondents to list both the proportion of their current income that came from archaeology-related sources, as well as the proportion of their yearly income earned from sources not related to archaeology. To get a better picture of the relationship between levels of compensation and the total work effort in archaeology, respondents were also asked to estimate the proportion of volunteer work effort in archaeology they performed without financial compensation.

Charting the proportion of total income earned from sources outside of archaeology by gender and age (Figure 4.41a) produces a U-shaped curve with relatively high proportions of outside income in the older and younger cohorts, and a lower proportion of total income coming from outside of archaeology in the cohorts in the middle. The proportion of income earned from sources outside the discipline is relatively high among respondents in the 60–69 age cohort. This is especially true for men in their 60s, who, as we saw earlier in this chapter, tend to retire earlier than women. The proportion of income received from sources outside the field falls steadily for both men and women from the 50–59 age cohort to the 40–49 age cohort, where it is at its lowest point (16 percent for women and 12 percent for men). This figure rises again among respondents in their 30s, and in the youngest cohort of archaeologists, those in their 20s, it reaches levels similar to those of respondents in their 60s. With the exception of the 60–69 age cohort, the proportion of income from outside sources is consistently higher among women. However, the difference between men and women in all cohorts under 60 is very slight and never statistically significant.

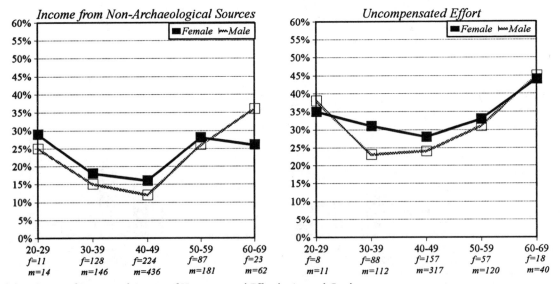

Fig. 4.41   *Sources of Income and Amount of Uncompensated Effort by Age and Gender*

a Proportion of salary from sources outside of archaeology   b Proportion of uncompensated effort

Note that both curves peak in the older and younger cohorts, and decline with archaeologists in their 30s and 40s. Note also the general similarity between males and females, except for the greater amount of uncompensated effort among women in their 30s.

The proportion of voluntary, nonreimbursed archaeological effort seems closely correlated with the proportion of income from outside sources (Figure 4.41b). From a high of about 45 percent in the 60–69 age cohort, the proportion of nonreimbursed archaeological effort dips sharply in younger cohorts to between 25–30 percent among respondents in their 40s, before rising again to close to 40 percent in respondents in their 20s. In most cohorts, the proportion of volunteer effort is similar for both men and women. In the 30–39 age cohort, however, there is a relatively large difference. Thirty-one percent of the work effort of women in their 30s receives no remuneration, compared to 23 percent of effort of men in this cohort.

The reason for the divergence between amount of uncompensated effort among archaeologists in their 30s becomes evident when we look at these data by work setting (Figure 4.42). Both men and women who work in academic or museum settings receive a higher proportion of their income from outside sources than people employed in government and the private sector. This pattern suggests that people with nine-month contracts or part-time positions in academia and museums supplement their incomes by working in jobs unrelated to archaeology. The low proportion of outside income among government archaeologists reflects the fact that most are employed full-time for 12 months of the year. While private sector archaeologists, especially more junior people in consulting archaeology, may work on a contractual basis for a variety of different employers during a single year, Census respondents working in the private sector apparently make a higher proportion of their income inside the profession than either academics or museum archaeologists.

The amount of volunteer, uncompensated effort among archaeologists in academia and museums is also quite high relative to that seen in public and private sector settings (Figure 4.42b). The amount of uncompensated effort by men and women is quite similar in most employment settings, with the possible exception of academia. Thirty-five percent of the archaeological effort of women in academia receives no financial reimbursement, compared to 28 percent of the archaeological effort of academic men. This difference may be an artifact of the increasingly higher proportion of women in visiting and adjunct positions in academia, discussed later in the chapter. In contrast, the level of volunteer, uncompensated effort is low for both men and women in the private sector and, especially, in government settings.

• Thus, the divergence in the proportion of uncompensated effort between men and women in their 30s needs to be viewed in the context of broader changes in the career trajectories of younger archaeologists. The lower levels of uncompensated effort among younger men can be tied directly to the growing number of younger men in public and private sector employment settings. The increase in amount of uncompensated effort among women can be linked to the larger number of younger women employed in museums, and, perhaps, to an increase in the amount of uncompensated effort among younger women in academia. •

Figure 4.43 presents information on sources of income and nonreimbursed effort for the four smaller employment categories. Not unexpectedly, the proportion of income earned from sources outside of archaeology and the amount of volunteer effort in archaeology are both quite high among retired archaeologists. In contrast, these figures seem surprising low among people in the other

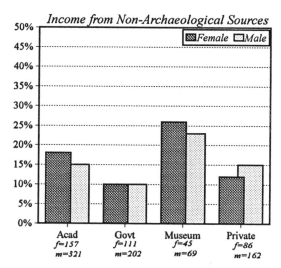

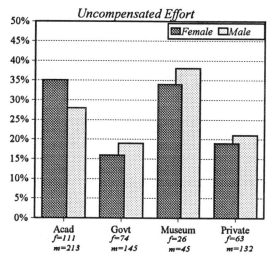

Fig. 4.42 *Sources of Income and Amount of Uncompensated Effort in the Four Primary Employment Sectors by Gender*

a Proportion of salary from sources outside of archaeology   **b** Proportion of uncompensated effort

Note the higher proportions of outside income and uncompensated effort in academia and museums, and the lower proportions in the private and public sectors.

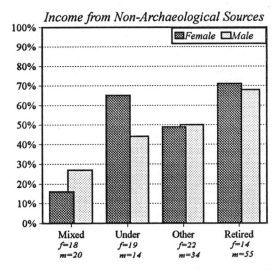

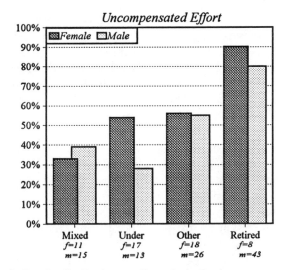

Fig. 4.43 *Sources of Income and Amounts of Uncompensated Effort in the Four Smaller Employment Categories by Gender*

a Proportion of salary from sources outside of archaeology   **b** Proportion of uncompensated effort

Note in particular the higher proportions of income from outside sources and uncompensated effort among underemployed females.

category who are employed in work settings only tangentially related to archaeology or outside the profession altogether. Clearly, a good deal of the work these individuals do, and get paid for, is closely related to archaeology. Of the group of people who spend less than half of their time in an archaeological work setting, women would seem to be more underemployed than men. A full 63 percent of the yearly income of these women comes from sources outside of the discipline, and more than half of their archaeological efforts receive no compensation. Although by definition people included in this category spend less than 50 percent of their time in an archaeological work setting, underemployed men still receive more than half of their total yearly income (which is generally higher than that of underemployed women, Figure 4.25b) from sources inside the discipline. Moreover, more than 70 percent of their total archaeological effort receives some form of compensation. People in the mixed employment category fall somewhere in between people in museum, academic, and private-sector settings in the proportion of outside income and voluntary effort.

Benefits

While major decisions about educational and career trajectories are probably not determined by whether or not a prospective employer is likely to offer a 401(k) retirement plan, the range of employee benefits available to archaeologists in different employment settings provides another useful way to examine archaeological employment. Respondents were asked to note whether they received any of four general categories of employee benefits in their current position: health, retirement, life insurance, and savings plans (Appendix). They were also asked to specify

other benefits they may receive. This is another question that, in retrospect, should have been framed in a different way. Instead of asking respondents to check various benefit categories received, they should have been asked to specify whether they received, *or did not receive,* a particular type of benefit. Without such a clear "yes" or "no" choice, we cannot be certain if respondents' failure to check any of the benefit categories means that they receive no benefits, or that they simply chose not to answer this question.

It seems unlikely that respondents would be more hesitant to supply information about employee benefits than they were about the seemingly much more sensitive subject of salaries, where the response rate was almost 100 percent. However, if for some reason respondents were reluctant to answer this question, I would not expect people in any one employment sector to be more shy about supplying this information than those in any other sector. Nor would I expect one gender to be more or less forthcoming on this topic. And yet there are strong and significant differences in the response rate to this question by both men and women, and among those in different employment sectors (Figure 4.44). In all but one employment setting, the proportion of women who responded to this question is smaller than the proportion of men. The difference between the response rate of men and women is significant at the .05 level of probability or better for each of the four main employment sectors (academia: χ^2=3.889, df=1, p=.049; government: χ^2=9.625, df=1, p=.002; museums: χ^2=4.878, df=1, p=.027; private sector: χ^2=24.435, df=1, p.001). There are also significant differences between men and women in most of the smaller employment categories (mixed: χ^2=8.827, df=1, p=.003; other: χ^2=4.739, df=1, p=.029; and retired: χ^2=3.109, df=1, p=.078). Only in the underemployed category was

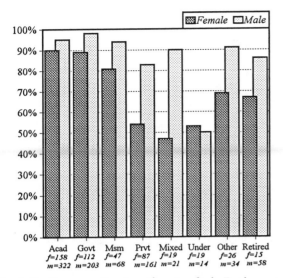

Fig. 4.44 *Response to Questions About Benefits by Employment Setting and Gender*

Note the differential response rate of men and women in almost all settings, and the generally lower response rate of private sector and underemployed archaeologists.

the response rate of men and women equally low (χ^2=.022, df=1, p=.881). There is also substantial variation in the response rate between general employment categories. People in government, academia, and museums all had a significantly higher response rate than those in the private sector. Those included in the underemployed category had the lowest response rates of all. These gender and employment setting differences, then, strongly suggest that the absence of a response to this question generally signifies a true lack of benefits.

These patterns become even clearer when the benefit rates of men and women in different employment sectors are broken down by benefit type (Figure 4.45). In each of the major employment sectors, health insurance is the most commonly held employee benefit, followed by retirement, life insurance, and savings plans. But within this general framework, there are significant variations in access to specific kinds of benefits. Overall, the most comprehensive and most widely available employee benefits are found in government settings (Figure 4.45b). Government archaeologists have better access to all four major types of benefits than employees in any other sector; this is true for both women and men. Even savings plans, the benefit with the lowest enrollment in government settings, have nearly 60 percent enrollment for both men and women. In comparison, less than 30 percent of the archaeologists employed in other sectors are enrolled in such plans. The more comprehensive benefit coverage among government archaeologists is undoubtedly due to a high proportion of full-time permanent staff positions, as well as the presence of state and federally mandated benefit packages.

Men in academia have the second-best access to employee benefits (Figure 4.45a), with 70 percent or more enrolled in employer-sponsored health, retirement, and life insurance plans. The proportion of women academics currently receiving various employee benefits, while lower than that of academic men, is still quite high. More than 60 percent of academic women receive benefits in the three most common benefit categories. The benefit profile of men in museums is almost identical to that of men in academia (Figure 4.45c), with an enrollment rate of more than 70 percent in employer-sponsored health, retirement, and life insurance plans. The picture is quite different for women in museums. Less than half of the professional women in museum have basic health benefits or retirement plans, and fewer still are enrolled in employer-sponsored life insurance or savings plans.

Benefit rates in the private sector for both men and women fall significantly below those in the other major sectors of archaeological employment (Figure 4.45d). This pattern is not surprising, given the number of private sector archaeologists who are independent consultants or are employed by small firms. What is surprising, however, is the major difference between the benefit profiles of men and women in the private sector. Roughly 75 percent of the men in the private sector have access to health benefits, compared to more than 90 percent of the men in academia, government, and museums. Less than half of these men receive retirement, life insurance, or savings plans through their employers. The access of private sector women to employee benefits is even poorer. Less than half of the women in the private sector receive health insurance from their employer. The enrollment of private sector women in employer-sponsored retirement, life insurance, and savings plans is even lower than that of men in the private sector, as well as that of women in museums. To some extent this difference may stem from the context rather than conditions of employment in the private sector. Close to 90 percent of the males in the private sector are employed by private firms, compared to less than 70 percent of the women. In contrast, the proportion of independent consultants is higher among women in the private sector than among men (32 percent for women compared to 23 percent for men). The likelihood that employees of private firms, especially larger firms, will have better access to employee benefits than independent consultants may, then, account for at least some of the differentials in access to benefits among men and women in the private sector.

Turning to the four smaller employment categories (Figure 4.46), there is also a marked difference in access to employee benefits between men and women who work in mixed settings (Figure 4.46a). Obviously the "mix" is not the same in all cases. Men who work in more than one employment sector are much more likely to receive basic benefits from one or more of their employers than are

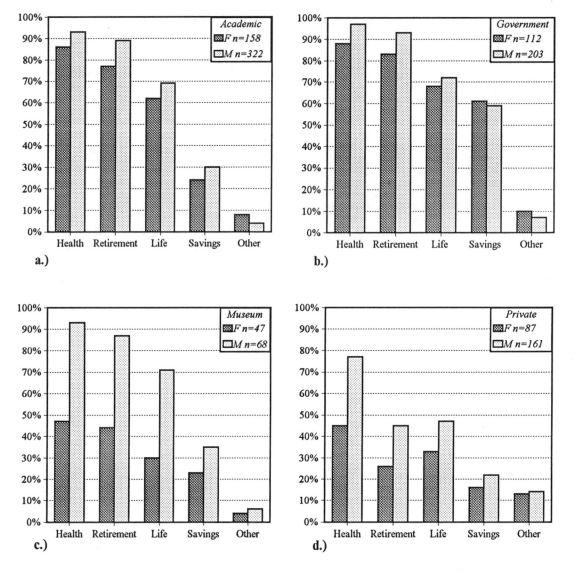

Fig. 4.45 *Proportions of Men and Women Receiving Different Benefits in the Four Primary Employment Settings*

a Academia   **b** Government

c Museums   **d** Private sector

Note the generally high benefit rates in government archaeology, the disparity between benefits received by men and women in museums, and the more restricted benefit access of private sector males, and, especially, private sector females.

women. Among retirees the high proportion of men with retirement plans (79 percent) compared to women (53 percent) is also noteworthy (Figure 4.46d). As mentioned earlier, the proportions of men and women in the underemployed category who have employee benefits are quite low (Figure 4.46b). The only major difference between men and women in this category is in the higher proportion of men who receive retirement benefits. It would seem that many of the men included in this category are, in fact, partially retired, but still engaged in some archaeological activities. This does not seem to be the case for underemployed women.

• Thus, the profile of employee benefits adds an important element to our broader understanding of financial compensation in American archaeology. We see that the solid mid-range salary levels of government archaeologists are accompanied by the broadest and most comprehensive employee benefit packages. Moreover, the general parity in the salaries of men and women in government is echoed by greater gender equity in access to employee benefits. Not only are men in academia paid relatively well, they also appear to have access to a wide range of benefits. Moreover, while there are fairly large disparities in male and female salaries among academics, women

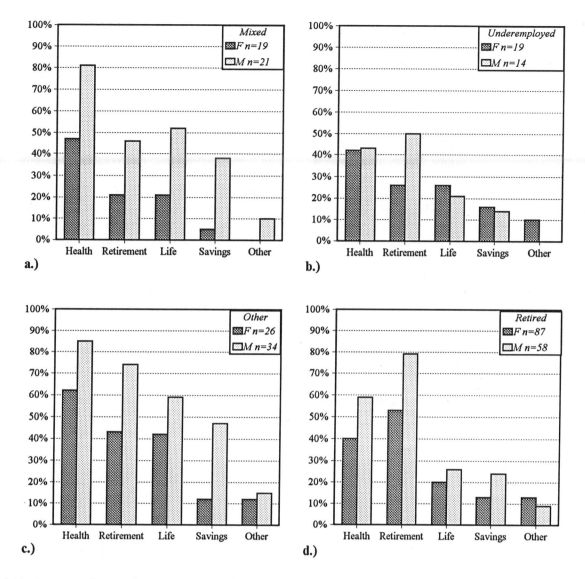

Fig. 4.46 *Proportions of Men and Women Receiving Different Benefits in the Four Smaller Employment Categories*

a Mixed settings

b Underemployed archaeologists

c Other nonarchaeological employment settings

d Retirees

Note the disparity in benefit access of males and females in mixed work settings, the high proportion of underemployed males receiving retirement benefits, and the disparity between retired males and females in access to retirement benefits.

academics still have generally good benefit coverage. This is not the case for women in museums. Not only do these women earn less and advance up the salary ladder more slowly than men, they are also much less likely to receive benefits than males in museums. Finally, while the private sector offers both men and women the greatest opportunities for higher salaries and faster salary growth, it has the poorest record in the proportion of people receiving all types of basic employee benefits. Moreover, though the salaries of women consulting archaeologists come closer to their male counterparts than in either academia or museums, and though many of these women make more than

women in the other employment sectors, these women fall significantly behind private sector men, as well as women in different sectors of archaeological employment, in their access to basic employee benefits. •

Academic and Private Sector Positions

Defining Positions Within Academic and Private Sector Archaeology

Thus far our examination of employment conditions within different sectors of American archaeology has remained on a fairly general level. While we have been able to partition our sample of respondents in the major employment sectors by gender, seniority, and academic credentials, we have not yet looked at the status of different jobs within these sectors. One of the Census questions asked respondents to list their current titles (Appendix). From these responses we were able to devise hierarchies of standard titles found in academia and the private sector that allow a more focused examination of conditions within these two major employment sectors. In this section we will examine the access of men and women to different positions within academia and the private sector, as well as the levels of compensation earned by the individuals who hold these titles. We will also fine-tune the resolution of our comparison of salary levels in academia and the private sector through a direct comparison of pay scales of different positions within each sector.

Devising a hierarchical classification of positions within academia was relatively easy, since most academic institutions use the same five-tier hierarchy of positions: visiting professors (including adjunct and lecturer positions), assistant professors, associate professors, full professors, and deans. It was a bit more difficult to do this for the private sector, but there was still enough commonality in private sector job titles to construct a similar five-tiered hierarchy. These positions are crew member, crew chief, field director, project manager, and president/CEO. Unfortunately, there was too much diversity in the titles of government and museum-based archaeologists to construct similar position hierarchies.

Not all respondents in the private sector, or even in academia, could be classified by title, however. A number

of people in the private sector listed their title as "consultant," and likewise a number in academia gave only the title of "professor," neither of which could be included in this framework. Because of this, the sample of people with titles that could be classified according to these schemes was fairly limited relative to the overall number of respondents from these two employment sectors. The number of academics included in this list was also limited by the exclusion of current students from the pool. Nevertheless there were still a total of 351 professional academics that could be thus classified and a total of 117 private sector respondents. In addition, another Census question collected information on the tenure status of academic respondents. A total of 555 academicians responded to this question.

Academia

Gender Trends in Access to Academic Positions When viewed in the aggregate there is a clear and highly significant difference between the distribution of academic titles among men and women (Figure 4.47a; χ^2=18.866, df=4, p=.001). Men predominate in upper-level academic positions, while women more commonly occupy lower-level positions. The high proportion of women in visiting professor positions relative to men is particularly striking, as is the proportion of men in full professor positions. Looking at the relative representation of men and women within each title (Figure 4.47b), there is a steady decline in the proportion of women in each progressively higher-ranked position. Women comprise 60 percent of the total pool of visiting professors; among assistant and associate

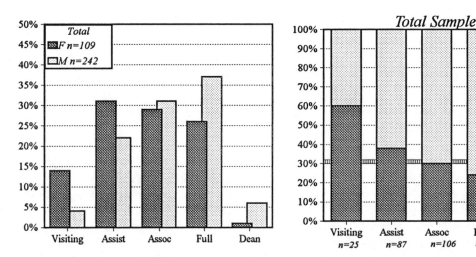

Fig. 4.47 *Academic Positions Among Professional Archaeologists by Gender*

a Distribution of academic positions among males and females

b Proportions of males and females in each academic position (hatched bar = proportion of professional women in academia)

Note the tendency of males to fill higher-level positions in academia and females to be employed in lower-level positions. Note, especially, the high proportion of women in visiting professor positions.

professors, the proportion of women is about the same as it is in the pool of academic professionals in general; but women make up only 24 percent of the full professors in our sample, and just 7 percent of the deans.

Much of this imbalance can be attributed to age and seniority differences between male and female academics, as we see when these data are broken down by decade of entry into the archaeological workforce (Figure 4.48). Although there is still a tendency in almost all entry decades for men to be disproportionately better represented in the higher-ranking titles, for the most part the distribution of titles within each gender is quite similar (Figure 4.48a, c, and e). Moreover, the proportion of women in each position is generally the same as the overall proportion of women in the academic workforce (Figure 4.48b, d, and f). However, there is still a persistent, and apparently increasing, tendency for women to hold the balance of visiting professor positions. In each entry decade, disproportionately more of the women who began their careers during that decade hold visiting professor positions than men. In each case the proportion of women among visiting professors is much greater than the proportion of women in the overall pool of academics in that entry decade.

Gender Trends in Tenure Status These patterns are echoed in the data on tenure status. In the aggregate there is a stark and highly significant difference in the tenure profile of male and female academics (Figure 4.49; χ^2=10.994, df=2, p=.004). Fifty-three percent of the academic males in our sample have tenure, compared to only 35 percent of the women. On the other hand, 48 percent of the women are in nontenure-track positions, compared to only 31 percent of the males. The proportions of men and women in tenure-track positions are essentially the same at about 16 percent each.

When these data are displayed by entry decade, this pattern not only persists but becomes increasingly more marked in each more recent decade (Figure 4.50). In both of the 1970s and 1980s entry decades a higher proportion of the men who entered the workforce in that decade hold tenured positions than is the case for the women who entered the profession at about the same time (Figure 4.50a and c). Men also numerically dominate in the ranks of tenured positions to a greater extent than they do in the population of academics as a whole (Figure 4.50b and d). Moreover, the tendency for men to hold tenured positions among the 1980s entry cohort is greater than in the 1970s cohort. In the cohort of people who entered the workforce in the 1990s, where there is only one tenured individual (a woman), men occupy a disproportionate share of the tenure-track positions (Figure 4.50e and f). Fifty-seven percent of men who entered the academic workforce in the 1990s hold tenure-track positions, compared to only 35 percent of the women.

One of the most striking patterns evident in Figure 4.50 is the increase in the proportion of people in nontenure-track positions in each more recent entry decade. To a certain extent this pattern may simply stem from the fact that junior academics are more likely to hold these kinds of noncareer positions than more senior people. However, this pattern may also signal a real increase in the overall proportion of nontenure-track academic jobs as part of a general trend within academic institutions to convert formerly tenured or tenure-track positions into short-term, untenured jobs. In each entry decade proportionately more of the women than men who entered the workforce in that decade hold nontenure-track jobs (Figure 4.50a, c, and e). In each decade the proportion of nontenure-track positions held by women is greater than the proportion of women in the general pool of academics who began their careers during that decade (Figure 4.50b, d, and f).

Moreover, over these three decades the tendency for women to occupy nontenure-track positions has increased. In the 1970s entry cohort, 39 percent of the women hold nontenure-track positions, compared to 28 percent of the men, a difference of 11 percentage points. In the 1980s entry cohort this difference has grown to 13 percentage points, with 58 percent of the women in nontenure-track positions compared to 45 percent of the men. The proportion of men in nontenure-track positions actually falls a bit in the 1990s entry cohort, to 43 percent, while the proportion of women in nontenure-track positions has increased to 61 percent. The differential between the proportions of men and women in nontenure-track positions is now 18 percent.

The Private Sector

Representation of Private Sector Positions The most obvious feature of the distribution of respondents in the five private sector positions is the low proportion of people in lower-level positions (Figure 4.51). People employed as crew members and crew chiefs (combined here into one category) and those who hold higher-level field director positions make up less than 20 percent of the private sector people represented in our sample. Clearly this is not representative of the actual proportion of these people in the private sector. In fact, I would suspect that crew members and their in-field supervisors make up the majority of people employed in the private sector. Instead the underrepresentation of private sector employees in these positions probably has more to do with the make-up of the SAA membership. It is quite likely that the private sector archaeologists employed in these lower-level jobs do not join the SAA because the membership dues are too high and the perceived benefits too low. However, as we will see when we compare the salaries of people in these positions to lower-level positions in academia (where SAA

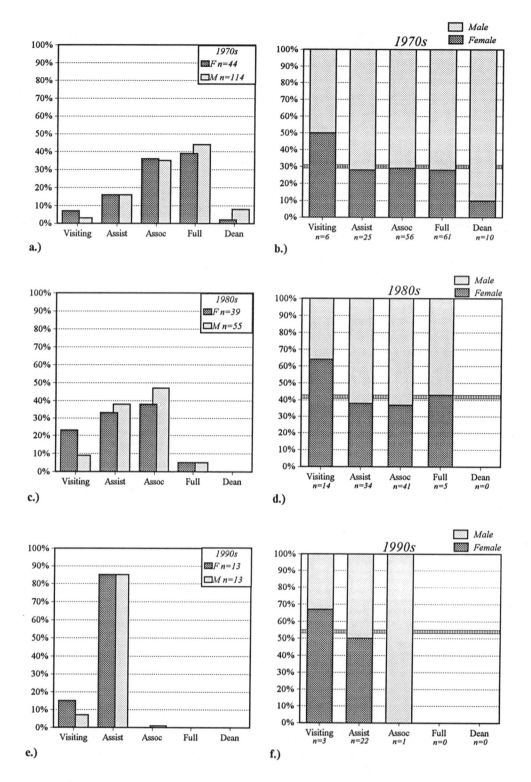

Fig. 4.48 *Academic Positions Among Professional Archaeologists by Entry Decade and Gender (hatched bar = proportion of professional women in academia in each entry decade)*

a Distribution of academic positions, 1970s entry decade
c Distribution of academic positions, 1980s entry decade
e Distribution of academic positions, 1990s entry decade

b Proportions of males and females, 1970s entry decade
d Proportions of males and females, 1980s entry decade
f Proportions of males and females, 1990s entry decade

Note the generally even distribution of positions among men and women in different entry decades. But also note the persistent tendency for men to fill higher-level positions, and, especially, the increasing proportion of women in visiting professor positions.

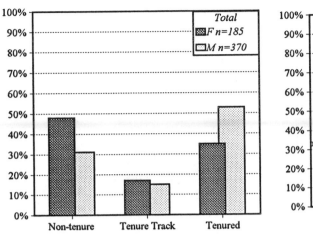 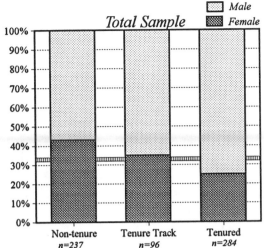

Fig. 4.49 *Tenure Status of Professional Archaeologists by Gender*

a Distribution of different tenure categories among males and females

b Proportions of males and females in each tenure category (hatched bar = proportion of professional women in academia)

Note the tendency of males to occupy tenured positions, and of females to occupy nontenure-track positions.

membership rates are apparently much higher), this is not the only reason these people fail to join the SAA. Instead, many of the people in these positions may decide not to join the SAA because they feel that SAA membership is less relevant to them. In contrast, it would seem that private sector archaeologists employed in higher-level positions both have a greater interest in SAA membership and can better afford to join the society. The depressed levels of private sector enrollment in the SAA relative to that seen in other societies like the SHA and SOPA (Figure 4.2) may, however, indicate that private sector archaeologists at all levels are less likely to join the SAA than archaeologists in other sectors of archaeological employment. These perceptions will be explored in more depth in Chapter 6, which examines respondent involvement in and attitudes about various professional organizations.

Gender Trends in Access to Private Sector Positions
However, even if private sector enrollment in the SAA is depressed relative to that of other archaeological employment sectors, it is unlikely that one gender would be less likely to join than another. General distribution patterns of men and women across this hierarchy of positions should, then, reflect real tendencies in private sector employment. Unlike academia, where there is a decided lack of gender parity in access to different positions, the similarity between the aggregate employment profiles of men and women in the private sector (Figure 4.51a) suggests that there is more equal access in the private sector to jobs at all levels (χ^2=0.438, df=3, p=.932). And while it is clear that there are fewer women than men in the private sector overall (Figure 4.51b), in no case is the proportion

of women in any private sector position significantly greater or less than the general proportion of women in the private sector pool.

The smaller sample of private sector respondents who could be classified by title makes it difficult to break these data down further into entry cohorts (Figure 4.51c, d, e, and f). This is especially true for the crew and fiel-director positions, which in both the 1970s and 1980s entry cohorts fall below 10 individuals apiece. It is also true for the category of "president" in the 1980s entry cohort. Judging from these data, especially that of the larger 1970s entry cohort, however, it would seem that there may be some tendency for women to be better represented in lower-ranked positions, while men are a little more likely to occupy upper-echelon positions. But again, given the restricted size of this sample, it is hard to evaluate the significance of these differences.

Salary Levels of Academic and Private Sector Positions

Gender Trends in Academic Salaries Figure 4.52 presents the salaries of men and women in different academic positions first for the sample as a whole (Figure 4.52a), and then by entry cohort for the 1970s, 1980s, and 1990s (Figure 4.52b, c, and d). Salaries compared include those of visiting, assistant, associate, and full professors. Since there is only one woman dean in our sample, these salaries are not shown here. We can note that the salaries reported by the deans in our sample overlap closely with those of male full professors, though there are proportionately more deans in the upper two salary brackets than is the case for full professors.

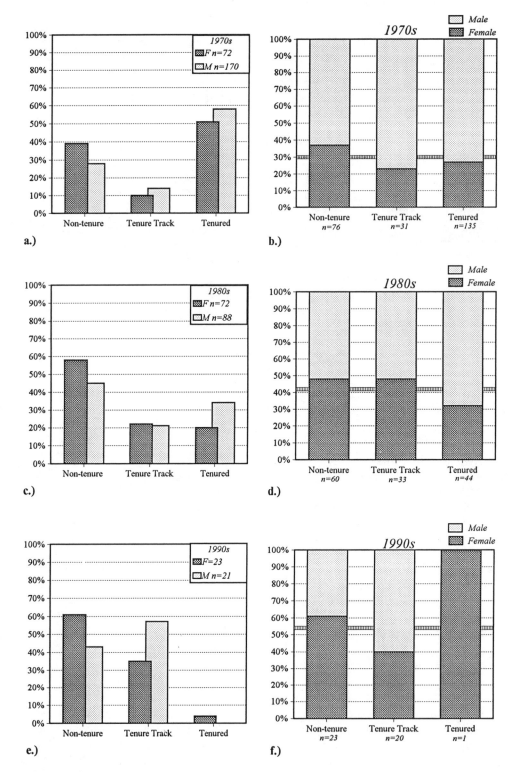

Fig. 4.50 *Tenure Status of Professional Archaeologists by Entry Decade and Gender (hatched bar = proportion of professional women in academia in each entry decade)*

a Distribution of tenure categories, 1970s entry decade
c Distribution of tenure categories, 1980s entry decade
e Distribution of tenure categories, 1990s entry decade

b Proportions of males and females, 1970s entry decade
d Proportions of males and females, 1980s entry decade
f Proportions of males and females, 1990s entry decade

Note the tendency for males to occupy tenured or tenure-track positions, and the increasing tendency for females to occupy nontenure-track positions. Note also the increased proportion of nontenure-track positions in each entry decade.

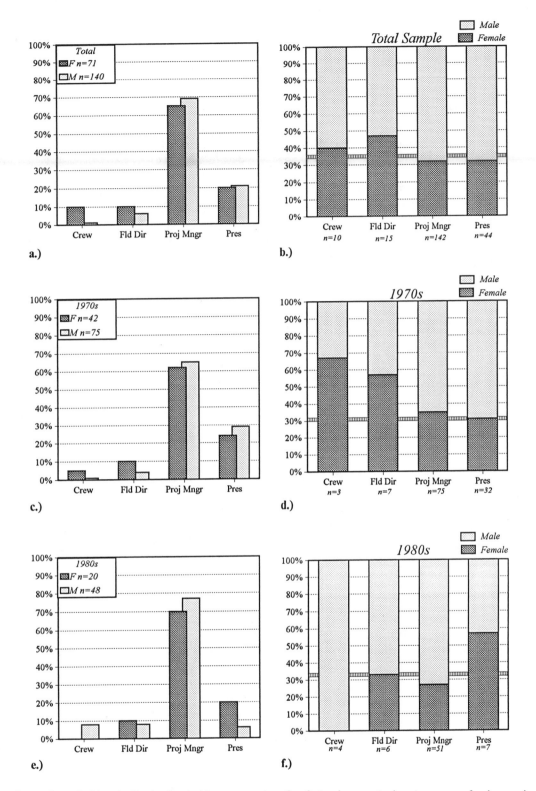

Fig. 4.51 *Private Sector Positions by Gender (hatched bar = proportion of professional women in the private sector of each entry decade)*

a Distribution of private sector positions, all entry decades
c Distribution of private sector positions, 1970s entry decade
e Distribution of private sector positions, 1980s entry decade

b Proportions of males and females, all entry decades
d Proportions of males and females, 1970s entry decade
f Proportions of males and females, 1980s entry decade

Note the small proportion of lower-level private sector positions in the Census sample. Note also the generally even distribution of private sector positions among men and women in the larger aggregate sample, but the tendency for men to hold higher-level positions and women to occupy lower-level positions in the smaller 1970s entry cohort.

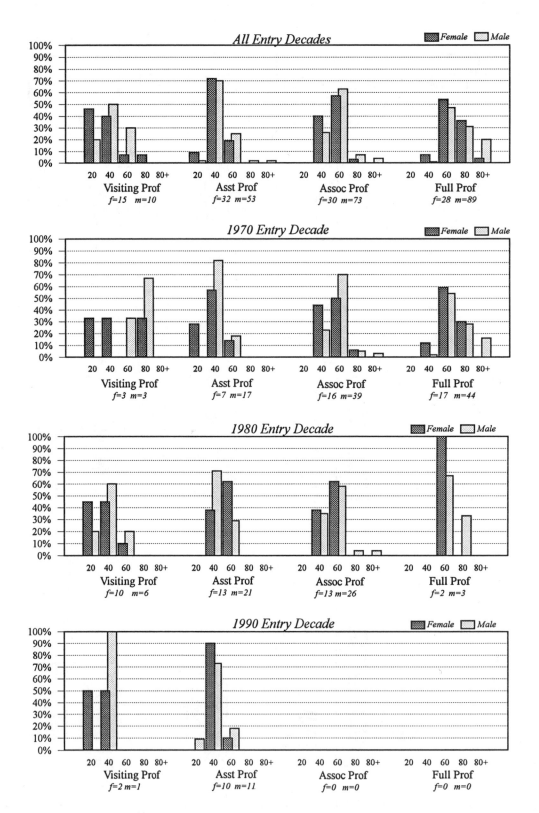

Fig. 4.52 *Salaries of Men and Women in Different Academic Positions*

a All entry decades

b 1970s entry decade

c 1980s entry decade

d 1990s entry decade

Note that even though salaries of men and women holding the same position are similar, there is still a tendency for women to be better represented in lower salary brackets and men to be better represented in higher salary brackets in essentially all academic positions, regardless of entry decade.

Mindful of the fact that it is difficult to evaluate the statistical validity of salary comparisons between such finely partitioned groups, one is struck here by the persistency of the salary trends seen in more broadly defined groups. Although there is a good deal of overlap between the salaries of men and women holding the same academic title, women in academia still tend to be better represented in the lower salary brackets, while men are better represented in the upper salary brackets. The only exception to this pattern is found in the comparison between the salaries of assistant professors who entered the workforce in the 1980s. In all other cases, regardless of position or seniority, there are more men in the upper salary brackets, while women are proportionately better represented in lower brackets.

Gender Trends in Private Sector Salaries The picture is somewhat different in the private sector (Figure 4.53). Given the small size of the sample of crew members and field directors, it is difficult to evaluate salary differentials between men and women, especially when these positions are broken down by entry decade. Census data suggest that male crew members and crew chiefs fare better than females, while women field directors may tend to earn more than their male counterparts. Larger samples are required, however, to accurately characterize salaries in these positions.

In the larger sample of project managers, salaries of males and females are very similar, both in the aggregate and in each entry cohort. There may be proportionally more women project managers in the lowest salary bracket, but in every case there are also more women in the highest salary bracket. The salaries of male and female project managers in the 1980s entry cohort are especially closely matched. This is not true for people who hold the title of president or CEO in the private sector. Here there is a clear and significant difference between the salaries of men and women (for the aggregate population in Figure 4.53a: χ^2=18.307, df=3, p<.001), with 51 percent of the males who hold the title of president making more than $60,000 per year, and 64 percent of the female presidents making under $40,000. In fact, there are more female project managers in high-end salaries than there are female presidents.

Comparison of Academic and Private Sector Salaries It is also instructive to compare the salaries of different positions in the academic and private sectors of archaeological employment. Figure 4.54 presents the aggregate data for men and women in these two sectors, first for all entry decades combined (Figure 4.54a), and then for the 1970s and 1980s entry cohorts (Figure 4.54b and c). The salaries of entry-level positions in each sector form the first point of comparison (visiting professors compared to private sector crew members and crew chiefs), and then each sub-

sequently higher position in each sector is compared, ending with a comparison of full-professor salaries to those of private sector presidents. Positions compared are somewhat mismatched in terms of academic credentials and the length of time required to obtain them. Virtually everyone in an academic position, from visiting professors to deans, has a PhD. In contrast, a large proportion of the people in the private sector, even in upper-echelon positions, have master's degrees. Crew members and crew chiefs may not even have earned their bachelor's degrees. It normally takes three to six years for an assistant professor to earn tenure and progress to the level of associate professor, and then several more years before being considered for promotion to the rank of full professor. Promotion in the private sector is not so highly structured, so that climbing the corporate ladder in the private sector may take substantially less time than it takes to progress along the tenure track in academia.

Despite these differences, the match between the salaries of academic and private sector people in these different positions is really quite close. While visiting professors, especially males, generally make more than private sector crew members and crew chiefs, there is still a good deal of overlap between the salary distributions of people who hold these entry-level positions, notably in the 1980s entry cohort. With the exception of a few highly paid, quite senior assistant professors, the salaries of assistant professors and field directors are even closer. Similarly, while there are more project managers in the lowest salary brackets, there are also more project managers making high-end salaries than associate professors. The salaries of private sector presidents and full professors are also quite similar, even with female presidents included in the pool. When the salaries of male full professors and private-firm presidents are compared, the private sector salaries are clearly higher. Only 7 percent of the male full professors and 14 percent of the deans in our sample make over $100,000 per year. In contrast, 27 percent of the males who head private sector firms make more than this amount.

• This more focused examination of positions within academia and the private sector has added important new insights to our understanding of recent employment trends in American archaeology. Earlier in the chapter we saw that the proportional representation of women in the academic workforce has grown over the last several decades to the point where essentially half of the new entries into the academic workforce are women. However, the data just presented indicate that these women have increasingly and disproportionately been channeled into academic positions that have little career potential. On the other hand, while the proportion of men in academia has been steadily decreasing, those men who do enter academia would seem to have a better chance of securing a tenure-track job. Moreover, the tendency for women in academia to earn somewhat less than male academics, seen when

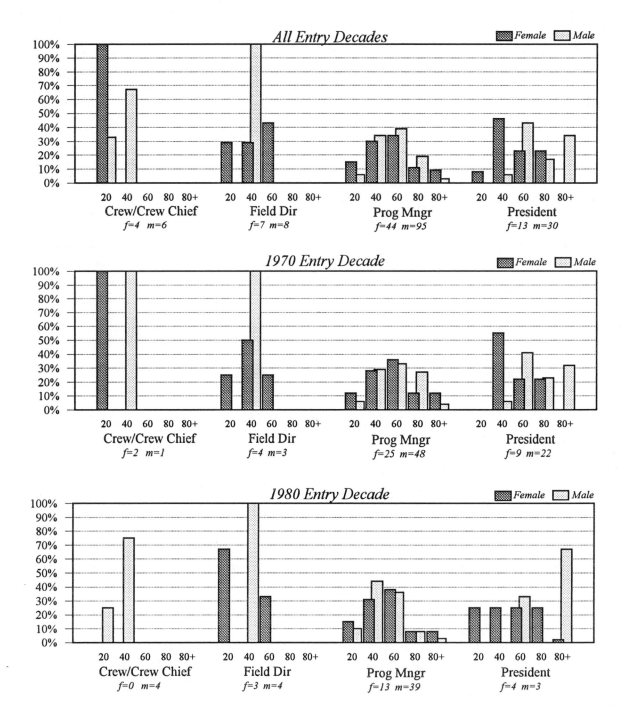

Fig. 4.53 *Salaries of Men and Women in Different Private Sector Positions*

a All entry decades
b 1970s entry decade

c 1980s entry decade

Note the similarity of salaries of men and women in most private sector positions, with the exception of the private sector presidents, where men make substantially more than women.

salary data were grouped by seniority and educational credentials, also holds true when specific titles within academia are compared. And there is little, if any, apparent movement toward correcting these salary imbalances among more recent entrants into the academic workforce.

In contrast, while proportionately fewer women enter the private sector, those women who do so have more equal access to higher-level positions and high-end salaries. This is especially true for women in project-manager positions. And yet, while the proportion of women who head consulting firms is about the same as that of men, there are

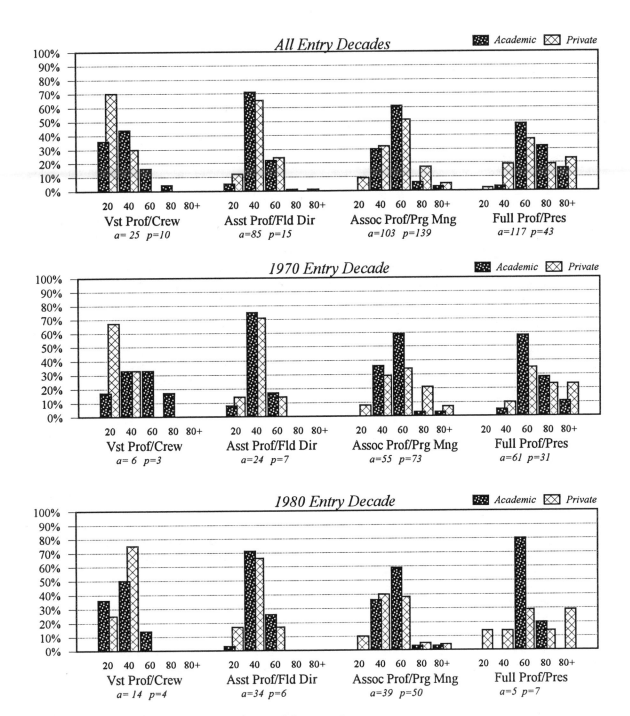

Fig. 4.54 *Salaries of Comparable Positions in Academia and the Private Sector*

a All entry decades
b 1970s entry decade
c 1980s entry decade

Note the similarity of salaries of academics and private sector individuals at different levels. Note also the higher salaries of private sector archaeologists in upper-level positions when compared to academics.

large differentials in the salaries paid to male and female CEOs in the private sector. This difference is more likely a reflection of the size of the firms headed by men and women than of gross differentials in the salaries of men and women who head firms of similar size. Earlier the possibility that women tend to work in smaller firms or as independent consultants was linked to the large discrepancies in access to benefits in the private sector. Differentials in the salaries of male and female CEOs complement these data, and suggest that male CEOs head larger firms capable of paying high-end salaries, while women CEOs direct much smaller operations.

Finally, a direct comparison of the salaries of different positions in academia and the private sector supports the earlier conclusion that the private sector offers the greatest opportunities for salary growth in archaeology. Private sector salaries at all levels are at least competitive with, if not higher than, salaries of positions of roughly comparable rank in academia. The greater potential for salary growth in the private sector is even more impressive when one considers the shorter length of time required to obtain qualifying degrees and the less structured path to promotion in the private sector. •

Satisfaction

To this point our examination of employment conditions in American archaeology has relied primarily on empirical measures of "how many?" or "how much?" We have measured how many people work in the public sector and how much money they earn, how many women are engaged in fieldwork and how much effort they devote to this kind of work, how many people in government receive health benefits. From these numbers, proportions, and percentages, we have been able to construct a fairly detailed picture of where American archaeologists work, what they do there, and how well they are compensated for this work. With the exception of the discussion of employment preferences, however, we have *not* looked at how respondents feel about the conditions of archaeological employment today. And yet it is the perceptions people hold about these conditions that may ultimately play more of a role in shaping employment trends than any of these drier facts and figures. Many of the long-term trends in archaeological employment may not be obvious to those currently making decisions about which degree to pursue or which area of employment to focus on. And even when they are, an individual's personal preferences and expectations may play more of a role in shaping major educational and career decisions than a general understanding of what is happening to other people pursuing careers in archaeology. We already have some indication that the educational and career choices made by younger archaeologists are only partially directed by actual prospects for employment and the potential for financial compensation. Here we will examine respondents' opinions about several key aspects of their employment in archaeology in some depth, and explore how well, or how poorly, these opinions correspond to some of the more empirical measures discussed earlier.

Measuring Levels of Satisfaction

Four questions in the SAA Census solicited respondents' opinions about their careers in archaeology (Appendix). The first asked respondents to rank their level of satisfaction with their current position, and to grade how well they thought their academic training prepared them

for their current position. In both cases respondents were to choose between four levels of satisfaction: highly satisfied, satisfied, marginally satisfied, and unsatisfied. Respondents were also asked whether their current position in archaeology is consistent with their projected career path, and whether they feel their current gross income meets their basic financial needs. Both of these last two questions requested a simple "yes" or "no" response.

It is important to note at the outset that *all* archaeologists, regardless of gender or employment setting, are generally content with their careers in archaeology. The number of archaeologists who are dissatisfied with current positions, training, direction of career, or salaries is quite low. Clearly archaeology is not just another way to make a living. Instead people are drawn to the field because they enjoy doing archaeology, and this positive outlook pervades the profession as a whole. Despite these generally high levels of satisfaction, there are important variations in respondent opinions about their careers that give us a deeper and richer understanding of current conditions of archaeological employment. In some cases these opinions are easily reconciled with the empirical data on education, employment, and levels of compensation. In others, the actual conditions of employment and people's opinions about these conditions differ considerably.

Gender Trends in Satisfaction

Trends in the Aggregate Data Figure 4.55 compares the responses of the aggregate sample of men and women to these four questions. Turning first to career satisfaction (Figure 4.55a), men and women differed significantly in their degree of satisfaction with their current careers (χ^2=11.643, df=2, p=.003). While a relatively high proportion of men said they were highly satisfied with their current positions, women were somewhat less enthusiastic about their current positions. Women instead seemed to be either simply satisfied or marginally satisfied (combined here as a single category) with these jobs. Moreover, though there was only a small proportion of both men and women who said they were unsatisfied with their current positions, the proportion of the women respondents who expressed dissatisfaction was slightly higher than male respondents. In contrast, men and women seem to have almost identical and statistically indistinguishable opinions about how well their training prepared them for their current careers (Figure 4.55b). About 30 percent of both men and women are highly satisfied with their training, a little over 60 percent profess to be satisfied that their training prepared them well for their current careers, and about 8 percent were unsatisfied with their training.

While more women than men feel that their current career is inconsistent with their career expectations (Figure 4.55c), this difference is not statistically significant (χ^2=2.621, df=1, p=.105). There is a significant difference,

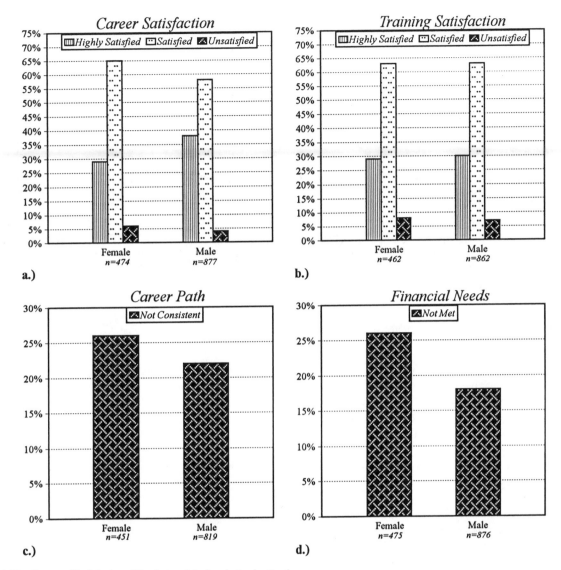

Fig. 4.55 *Degree of Satisfaction of Professional Archaeologists by Gender*

a Satisfaction with current position

b Satisfaction with training for current position

c Career path consistency with career expectations

d Sufficiency of income to meet basic financial needs

Note the generally lower levels of career satisfaction among women, and the higher proportion of women who feel that their careers are inconsistent with their original career expectations and that their current income fails to meet basic needs.

however, between the responses of men and women on the subject of income sufficiency (Figure 4.55d). About a quarter of the women polled felt that their current salaries did not adequately meet their basic needs, compared to only 18 percent of the men (χ^2=11.769, df=1, p=.001).

Age-Related Trends Once again these patterns become more complex, and more interesting, when the data are partitioned by age. Comparing career satisfaction of different age cohorts, there is a steady, and significant, decline in the proportion of people who claim to be highly satisfied with their current positions, and a corresponding increase in each younger cohort in the number who are either simply satisfied, or actually unsatisfied, with their

current careers in archaeology (Figure 4.56). This pattern is more strongly expressed among women, but is still quite evident among men (comparing the career satisfaction profiles of the 60–69 age cohort to the 30–39 age cohort for women: χ^2=7.635, df=2, p=.022; for men: χ^2=6.264, df=2, p=.044).

While the aggregate data on training satisfaction showed little difference between men and women, some interesting variations become evident when these data are displayed by age (Figure 4.57). In both men and women there is a dramatic drop between the 60–69 and 50–59 age cohorts in the proportion of people who are highly satisfied that their academic training in archaeology prepared them well for their current careers. Among younger

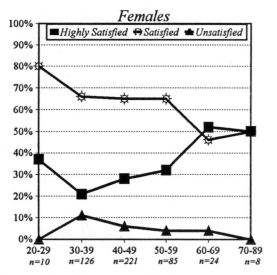

Fig. 4.56 *Career Satisfaction by Age and Gender*

a Females   b Males

Note the decline in career satisfaction of men and women in younger cohorts.

women there is a steady recovery in the proportion of people who are highly satisfied with their training. For men, on the other hand, the initial drop in highly satisfied individuals is not as steep as that seen among women. Yet instead of some improvement, there is a continued decline in the proportion of men who are highly satisfied with their training, which is accompanied by a steady increase in the proportion who are satisfied with their training, as well as some increase in the proportion of those who believe that their training did not prepare them well for their current careers in archaeology. As we will see below,

this trend is likely tied to changes in the employment context of younger men.

The impact of these broader employment changes is also evident in the opinions of respondents in different age cohorts about how well their current careers match their original career expectations (Figure 4.58a). While there is an increase in the proportion of women between the 60–69 age cohort and the 50–59 age cohorts who feel that their careers are inconsistent with their expectations, for the most part there is little change with age in the degree to which women's current careers meet their career

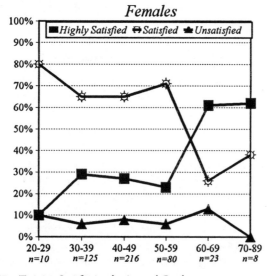

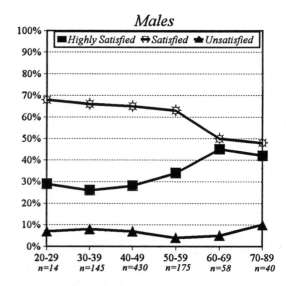

Fig. 4.57 *Training Satisfaction by Age and Gender*

a Females   b Males

Note the drop in both genders in training satisfaction between respondents in their 60s and 50s. Note also the slight increase in satisfaction with training among younger women, but the continued decline among younger men.

expectations. This congruity may well reflect the general lack of change in the employment profile of women in these different cohorts (see Figure 4.7a). Among men, however, there is a marked and significant increase in the number who feel that their career path is inconsistent with their expectations between the 60–69 and 40–49 year old cohorts (χ^2=3.936, df=2, p=.047). This pattern echoes the sharp increase in the proportion of younger men employed in the private and public sectors and the corresponding decline in the proportion of men in academia (Figure 4.7b), strongly implying that the employment trends of younger cohorts of males are increasingly out of sync with original career expectations. The slight drop in the proportion of men in their 30s who feel their current positions are inconsistent with expectations, despite the continued increase in the proportion of these men employed outside of academia, may signal some realignment of expectations in light of current employment trends.

Perhaps not unexpectedly, there is a marked increase in the proportion of younger people who feel that their current incomes do not meet their basic needs (Figure 4.58b). The lack of correspondence between respondents' perceptions about their financial circumstances and their actual earnings, however, is somewhat curious. The proportion of men in their 40s who feel that their income fails to meet their current needs is statistically indistinguishable from the proportion of women who find their income inadequate. Yet as we have seen, there are major, highly significant disparities in the incomes of men and women in their 40s (Figure 4.21c). Moreover, despite the decrease in the

salary gap between men and women in their 30s (Figure 4.21b), the difference between their perceptions about the adequacy of their salaries widens considerably in this cohort. Thirty-one percent of the women in their 30s felt that their income failed to meet basic needs, compared to only 20 percent of the men in their 30s, a difference that is statistically significant at the .027 level of probability (χ^2=4.867, df=1). In fact the proportion of men in their 30s who feel that their income is insufficient is slightly *lower* than that among men in their 40s, though the salaries of these older men in all work settings are, in actuality, significantly higher. Clearly the definition of what constitutes "basic needs" and the income required to meet these needs is not the same in all cases.

Satisfaction in Different Employment Settings

Aggregate Patterns by Employment Sector We see the greatest variation in respondent opinions when they are grouped by employment sector. Figure 4.59 presents responses to these four questions for the combined sample of men and women by employment sector. Looking first at career satisfaction (Figure 4.59a), a strikingly high 45 percent of museum professionals are highly satisfied with their current positions. No other employment sector comes close to museums in this index of respondent satisfaction. The second highest proportion of highly satisfied individuals is found in the private sector (35 percent), followed by an essentially identical proportion of academics (34 percent) who are highly satisfied with their current

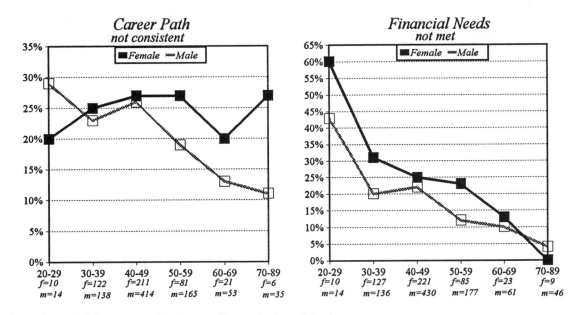

Fig. 4.58 *Career Path Consistency and Sufficiency of Income by Age and Gender*

a Career path consistency

b Financial sufficiency

Note the relatively constant opinions about consistency of career path among women, and the sharp increase in the proportion of younger men who feel their careers are inconsistent with their original expectations. Note also the increase of both younger men and women who feel that their incomes do not meet basic needs.

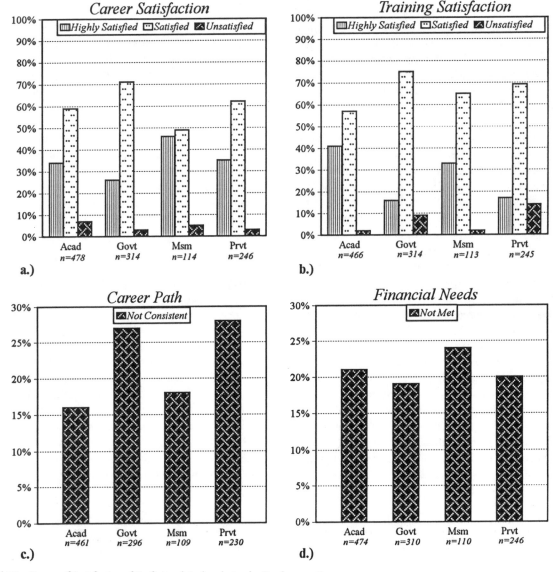

Fig. 4.59 *Degree of Satisfaction of Professional Archaeologists by Employment Sector*

a Satisfaction with current position

b Satisfaction with training for current position

c Career path consistency with career expectations

d Sufficiency of income to meet basic financial needs

Note the high level of career satisfaction among museum professionals, and the relatively higher proportion of individuals who are unsatisfied with their current positions in academia. Note also the higher levels of training satisfaction and lower levels of people who feel their current careers are inconsistent with expectations among academics and museum professionals, and the reverse pattern among government and private sector respondents. Note, finally, the higher proportion of museum professionals who feel their salaries are inadequate to meet basic needs, and the lower level of government archaeologists who feel that their incomes are inadequate.

careers in archaeology. Academia and the private sector differ, however, in the higher proportion of private sector respondents who say they are satisfied with their current positions, and the greater proportion of dissatisfied academics (χ^2=4.820, df=2, p=.090). Government archaeologists are distinguished from those working in the other three primary employment sectors by the relatively large number of people who are neither highly satisfied nor unsatisfied but simply satisfied with their current positions in archaeology (70 percent).

When we look at satisfaction with training by employment sector, we see some very marked differences (Figure 4.59b). More than a third of the respondents employed in academia and museums said they were highly satisfied that their academic training prepared them well for their current careers, and less than 5 percent are dissatisfied with their training. In contrast, relatively few government and private sector archaeologists claimed to be highly satisfied with their training, while the proportion of dissatisfied people is quite high. Almost 10 percent of the respondents in government settings and 14 percent of those in the private sector feel that their education did not prepare them well for their current careers. Opinions of academics and museum professionals on the subject of training differ from those of government and private sector archaeologists at better than a .001 level of probability, while the responses of those in academia and museums and those in government and the private sector are each statistically indistinguishable from one another. Similarly, government and private sector archaeologists are significantly more likely to feel that their current careers are inconsistent with their expectations than are those employed in academia and museums (Figure 4.59c).

Respondents' opinions about the sufficiency of their current incomes generally correspond to empirical data on salary levels. Almost a quarter of those employed in museums, where salary levels are generally lower than in other employment sectors, feel that their income fails to meet basic needs (Figure 4.59d). Although relatively large numbers of academics and private sector archaeologists are in the highest salary brackets, there are also a number of people in these employment sectors in the lowest brackets. These low-end salaries may, then, account for the around 20 percent of academic and private sector archaeologists who feel that their salaries do not provide a viable living wage. It is also possible that the wide range of salaries within these two sectors of archaeological employment has had an impact on perceptions of financial sufficiency. People may be more likely to feel that their salaries are insufficient when they know that other people employed in the same setting are making significantly more than they are. The small number of government archaeologists who feel that their salaries are insufficient suggests that the mid-range salaries of government archaeologists, coupled with

the comprehensive benefits available to government archaeologists, do a better job in meeting basic needs than do the salaries offered in any other sector of archaeological employment.

Trends by Employment Sector and Gender When we look at career satisfaction by work setting and gender (Figure 4.60), it is clear that lower levels of career satisfaction seen among women as a group cut across all employment sectors. In each employment sector the proportion of women who are highly satisfied with their current positions is less than that of men in that sector. It is interesting to note, however, that the proportion of women in each employment sector who are unsatisfied with their careers is not uniformly greater than it is among men. In both museum settings and the private sector, the proportion of men unsatisfied with their current positions is slightly greater than that of women.

Women in museums are the most satisfied with their current careers, followed by women in the private sector (Figure 4.60a). Women in government seem generally satisfied with their positions, with relatively few expressing strong satisfaction or dissatisfaction with their jobs. The proportion of academic women who are highly satisfied with their jobs is relatively depressed, compared to women in museums and the private sector. The proportion of dissatisfied women in academia, at almost 10 percent, is the highest seen in all employment settings, for either women or men.

Levels of career satisfaction among men follow the same general trends, but are much more marked (Figure 4.60b). Particularly noteworthy is the fact that more than half of the men in museums say they are highly satisfied with their current positions. But it is also interesting to

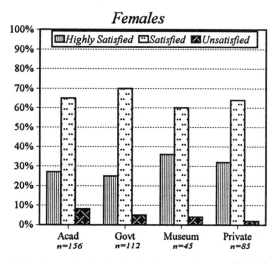

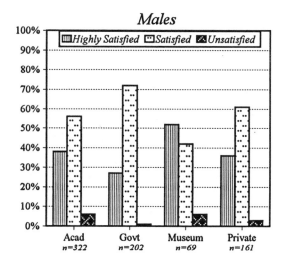

Fig. 4.60 *Career Satisfaction by Employment Sector and Gender*

a Females

b Males

Note the generally lower level of career satisfaction among women, and the higher proportions of highly satisfied individuals in museum settings of both men and women.

note that more men in museums are dissatisfied with their careers than in any other sector. Levels of satisfaction among men in the private sector and academia are fairly evenly matched, though proportionately more men in academia are unsatisfied with their careers than is the case for private sector men. The lowest proportion of both highly satisfied and dissatisfied men is found in government archaeology, where nearly 80 percent say they are satisfied with their current positions.

Once again the opinions of men and women on the subject of training are essentially identical (Figure 4.61). Both men and women in academia and museums show a high level of satisfaction with their academic training, while a much greater proportion of men and women in government and the private sector feel that this training failed to prepare them well for their current careers. Men and women in different employment sectors also seem in general agreement about how well their current careers mesh with their expectations (Figure 4.62a). For both, there seems to be a better match in academia and museums, and more of a disjunction in the government and private sectors. Among academics, however, there is a greater proportion of women than men who feel that their careers do not meet their original career expectations—a difference that is marginally significant at the .092 level of probability (χ^2=2.834, df=2). This pattern may correspond to the higher proportion of women who are unsatisfied with their current careers in academia (Figure 4.60a). It is also possible that both of these trends are linked to the apparent increasing proportion of women employed in nontenure-track positions in academia. More

men than women in the private sector feel that their careers differ from their original expectations, though this difference is not statistically significant.

For the most part, opinions of men in various employment sectors about the sufficiency of their incomes follow patterns seen in the aggregate population and correspond to real differentials in earning potential. Indeed it is the responses of men (who are numerically dominant in each employment sector) that are principally responsible for the above-noted correspondence between impressions about financial sufficiency and actual variations in earning power in different employment sectors (see Figure 4.59d). In contrast, the perceptions of women about financial sufficiency are often quite different from those of their male counterparts. They are also sometimes at odds with their actual earning power in these different sectors.

There is a major, and highly significant, difference between the proportions of men and women in academia who are satisfied that their current incomes meet their basic needs (χ^2=9.808, df=2, p=.002). Men in academia are more likely to feel that their income meets basic needs than are men in other employment sectors, including the private sector. Women in academia are more likely to feel that their salaries are insufficient than are women employed in nonacademic work settings. And yet, there are more academic women in upper salary brackets than in either government or in museums. Perhaps the number of academic women in the lowest salary brackets, plus the fairly marked disparity between the salaries of men and women in academia, as well as a greater feeling of job insecurity among women in nontenure-track visiting professor positions, all create a

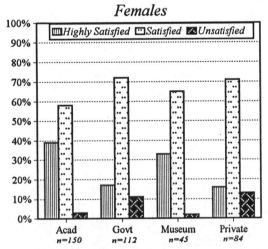

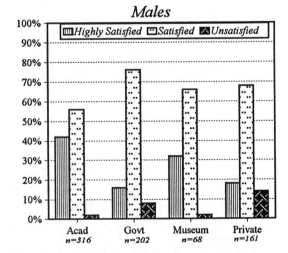

Fig. 4.61 *Training Satisfaction by Employment Sector and Gender*

a Females

b Males

Note the higher levels of training satisfaction among both male and female academics and museum professionals, and the greater dissatisfaction among both male and female private and public sector archaeologists.

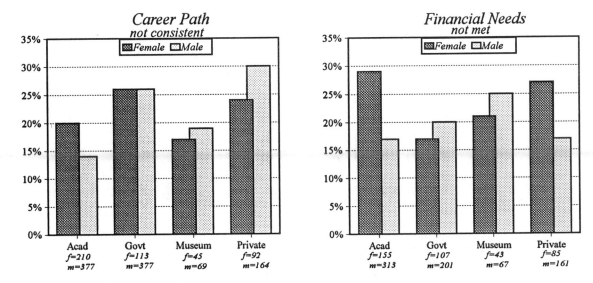

Fig. 4.62 *Career Path Consistency and Sufficiency of Income by Employment Sector and Gender*

a Career path consistency   **b** Financial sufficiency

Note the general agreement among men and women in different settings about career path consistency. But also note the lack of agreement between men and women about the adequacy of their incomes.

generally higher impression of financial insufficiency. In contrast, women in the private sector generally make more than women in any other employment sector, and the differential between the salaries of men and women in the private sector is not as great as it is in academia or, especially, in museums. Yet despite the empirical realities of female salaries in the private sector, the proportion of private sector women who feel that their salary fails to meet basic needs is unexpectedly high. In this case, the higher proportion of women working as independent consultants or as employees of smaller firms may boost the level of financial insecurity and hence elevate perceptions of salary insufficiency. The response of museum women to this question was the most puzzling of all. Although women in museums have generally lower salaries and less promotion potential than women in other employment sectors, and though there are marked disparities between the salaries of men and women in museums, the proportion of museum women who feel their salaries are insufficient is lower than in either academia or the private sector. General levels of salary satisfaction among women in government archaeology agree with patterns seen among men, and follow logically from the salary data that show women in government making solid, mid-range salaries that are only a little less than those paid to men with comparable educational credentials and seniority.

Looking briefly at the opinions of people in the four remaining employment categories (Figure 4.63), we see that opinions about career satisfaction among men and women who work in mixed employment sectors are strikingly similar to those found among male and female aca-

demics (Figure 4.63a and b compared to Figure 4.60). This is not surprising, since academia is almost always one of the employment settings in which these individuals work. As was the case for academics, considerably more of the men who work in mixed settings expressed a high degree of satisfaction with their current positions than did women in mixed employment settings. In fact, the proportion of both men and women in mixed settings who are highly satisfied with their careers is higher than it is among academics. Indeed, women in mixed settings are substantially less likely to express dissatisfaction with their current employment circumstances than are women employed primarily in academia. Levels of training satisfaction are also higher among these individuals than among academics, especially for women (Figure 4.63c and d compared to Figure 4.61). The relatively high proportions of both men and women in mixed settings who feel that their current positions are a departure from their original career expectations (Figure 4.63e) would suggest that despite the generally higher level of satisfaction with their careers, people who divide their time between two or more employment sectors probably expected to be employed in only a single work setting. There is also a major discrepancy among these men and women in their opinions about the adequacy of their incomes. A full 55 percent of the women in mixed settings feel that their salaries are insufficient, more than in any of the other seven employment categories examined here. However, the proportion of men in mixed settings who feel this way about their incomes is about the same as that seen in academic men (Figure 4.63b). These data would seem to agree with the large differentials in the

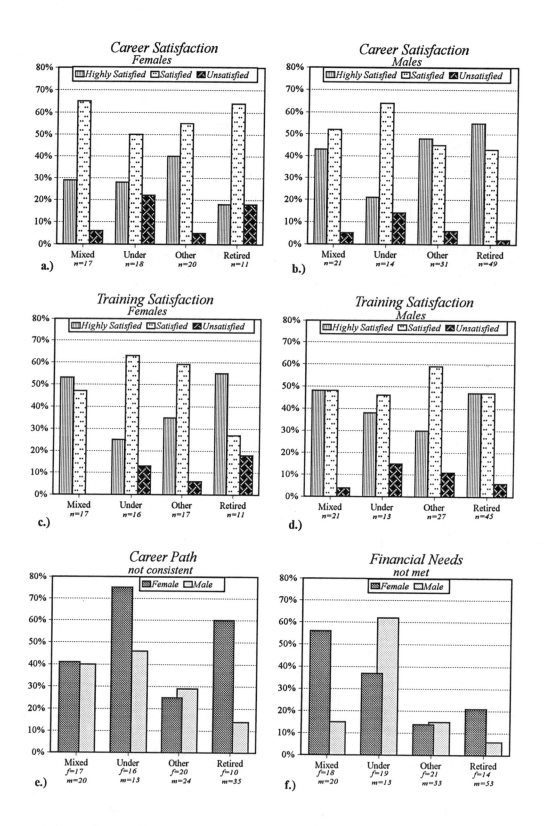

Fig. 4.63 *Degree of Satisfaction of Professional Archaeologists in the Four Smaller Employment Categories*

a Satisfaction with current position among females

c Satisfaction with training among females

e Career path consistency among females and males

b Satisfaction with current position among males

d Satisfaction with training among males

f Financial sufficiency among females and males

Note the similarity between the opinion profiles of men and women in mixed settings and those employed primarily in academic settings. Note also the low levels of satisfaction among underemployed individuals, but the unexpectedly low proportion of underemployed women who feel their incomes are inadequate. Note, finally, the very different opinion profiles of retired men and women.

salaries of men and women employed in mixed settings (Figure 4.25).

Not unexpectedly, underemployed individuals have the lowest levels of career satisfaction, and they are the most likely to feel that these circumstances are a significant departure from their original career expectations (Figure 4.63a, b, and e). This is especially true for underemployed women. Women with less than half-time employment in archaeology are also more likely than men to feel that their training ill prepared them for their current employment environment (Figure 4.63c and d). Yet while the proportion of people who are dissatisfied with their training is quite high among the underemployed, the proportions of men and women in this group who are highly satisfied with this training is still higher than it is among men and women in the private or public sectors. At 62 percent, the proportion of underemployed men who feel that their salaries do not meet basic needs is the highest in any employment category (Figure 4.63f). This is also not surprising, given the generally lower income of underemployed men when compared to men who have more full-time employment in archaeology (Figures 4.24 and 4.25). However, even though underemployed women tend to earn quite a bit less than underemployed men, the proportion of underemployed men who feel this income is inadequate is twice as large as the proportion of underemployed women who feel this way. It is interesting to note that 73 percent of the women in this employment category are married, the highest marriage rate among women in any employment category. In contrast, only about 63 percent of the women employed in the four primary employment sectors are married or engaged in long-term relationships, and the proportions of married women among those employed in mixed settings and among female retirees, at 55 percent and 31 percent respectively, are lower still. If the income of underemployed women is largely supplemental to those of their spouses or partners, then the proportion of these women who feel that their financial needs are not being met might be expected to be fairly low. Thus, it may be that while many of the underemployed men fall into this category because they are partially retired (as we surmised earlier from the high proportion of these men who receive retirement benefits), many of the underemployed women are working less than half time in archaeology because they have put family considerations ahead of their careers. Also of interest is the fact that 73 percent of these women hold PhDs, the second-highest proportion of PhD women in any employment category. Undoubtedly, these women went to the considerable effort and expense to obtain these degrees with the expectation that a PhD would help them pursue a career in archaeology—a factor that may explain why they are more likely to feel fairly dissatisfied with careers in archaeology that have failed to follow the trajectories originally expected.

Men and women employed outside of archaeology hold very similar opinions about their careers and are relatively satisfied with their current positions, their training, the consistency of their careers with their original expectations, and their incomes. As such, these people form an interesting point of comparison to archaeological employment categories where there are marked differences in the attitudes of men and women toward their careers.

The opinions of men and women retired archaeologists about their careers in archaeology are particularly distinctive. Retired men are among the most satisfied group of individuals in our sample. More than half of the male retirees are highly satisfied with their careers in archaeology; they feel that their training prepared them well for careers that were consistent with their expectations; and even in retirement they think their financial needs are being met. The outlook of retired women is quite different. Levels of career satisfaction among retired female archaeologists are very low, and more than half of them feel that their careers did not meet their original expectations. The proportion of retired women who feel that their retirement income is inadequate is also substantially higher than among retired men, as might be expected from the considerable gap between these incomes (Figure 4.25). It is not as high as might be expected, however, when compared to women in primary sectors of employment (especially academia and the private sector). Although women in these work settings are likely to make much more than retired women, they are also more likely to feel that their incomes fail to meet their needs.

• For the most part, levels of career satisfaction of archaeologists employed in work settings agree with data presented earlier on employment preferences. People seem to be generally satisfied with their current positions in archaeology, and, in fact, would prefer to work in their current employment sector over any other (Figure 4.15). Even government archaeologists, who work in what is seemingly the least-preferred work settings and perform the least-preferred activities, are generally satisfied with their current positions. Given the preference of essentially all archaeologists in every employment sector for work in a graduate university, and the fact that work in academia commonly involves more highly preferred activities and relatively few activities with low preference levels, it is surprising that levels of career satisfaction are not higher among academic archaeologists. Academia may be a preferred work setting in which people get to do preferred things, but the satisfaction levels of those within academia fall below those of people in other archaeological employment sectors. This is especially true for women in academia, who are generally less satisfied with their current positions than women in other employment sectors. Even among men, however, the proportion of those who are highly satisfied with their academic positions is still less than the proportion of highly satisfied men in museums. Moreover, the level of dissatisfaction among academic men is higher than in either the private or public sectors of archaeological employment.

Preference data also spotlighted museum settings as a generally preferred work setting. And here satisfaction levels seem to correspond to, if not exceed, preference levels. This is especially true for men who, though they expressed some preference for museums, did not seem to favor museum settings as much as women. And while museum women do not hold quite as high opinions about their current employment as men in museums, they are still generally more satisfied with their current positions than women in other work settings. Both the high preference levels and the generally positive attitudes toward current employment conditions of museum women belie their demonstrably lower salaries, poorer earning potential, and generally limited access to employee benefits. Clearly there are less tangible factors that make museum positions attractive to women. Indeed, the relatively high level of job satisfaction among museum women may elevate their level of satisfaction with their compensation, despite the fact that their incomes are decidedly lower than those of their male peers in museums, or even than those of their female peers in other work settings.

In fact, these dollars-and-cents issues seem generally poor predictors of preference and satisfaction. The relatively high earning potential and good benefit coverage available to academic men does not seem to elevate their somewhat depressed levels of career satisfaction. Nor do the generally lower salary levels of most men in museum settings preclude more than half of them from expressing a high degree of satisfaction with their jobs. At the same time, the comprehensive benefit package available to government archaeologists does not seem to have done much to boost the level of government archaeologists who are highly satisfied with their jobs, though the more generous government benefits may contribute to the generally positive attitude about government salaries. Nor does the poor benefit coverage in consulting archaeology seem to dampen the enthusiasm of private sector men and women for their current careers.

One of the most important findings here has been the close correspondence between the fulfillment of career expectations and the levels of satisfaction with academic training. In both academia and museums, people seem to be quite satisfied that their training prepared them for their current careers, and that these careers are generally consistent with the expectations held when they entered the profession. In contrast, more private and public sector archaeologists feel that their academic training did not give them the necessary tools for their current employment, and that this employment is inconsistent with their expectations. These opinions should *not* be read as an index of career satisfaction. As we have seen, satisfaction levels among academics are somewhat lower than might be expected; those among private sector archaeologists are relatively high. Rather, these data should be viewed as an indication that the archaeological training offered in academic institutions is geared toward traditional research and teaching positions found in academia and museums, but does not prepare people well for the kind of archaeology practiced in government and the private sector.

We have also seen that the range of activities practiced by archaeologists in the private and public sectors do indeed differ significantly from those practiced by academic and museum professionals. Some additional reinforcement for this position is provided in the following chapter, which examines the regions and topics studied by archaeologists, as well as the approaches and tools they use in these studies. Given these differences, it is easy to see how a graduate program that emphasizes the areas of knowledge and the skills needed to do well in an academic or museum-based job could be viewed as irrelevant to the practice of archaeology in the public and private sectors. Moreover, not only is this training more relevant to careers in academia and museums, it also seems to create, or at least reinforce, expectations among students that their careers will follow these more traditional lines. Such an inclination is strongly indicated in the employment and activity preferences of student respondents, which are clearly oriented toward careers in academia. Indeed, an increasing sense that a traditional academic education in archaeology is irrelevant to archaeological practice in government and private sector settings may be a major factor contributing to the decline in the proportion of younger men pursuing doctoral degrees, as well as the growth of MA programs more geared toward providing training for careers in these growing sectors of archaeological employment. •

5 Archaeological Research in the Americas

Introduction

Chapter Summary

In this chapter we turn our attention to the subject matter of American archaeology. What regions of the world are American archaeologists most interested in studying? What questions do they ask, and how do they frame these questions? What theoretical and methodological approaches do they use to address these questions? While we have seen that the education, the employment, and even the family lives of men and women archaeologists often follow very different trajectories, it would seem that gender plays only a limited role in shaping research interests. There is some tendency for women to focus on complex societies and historical periods, while men may be somewhat more drawn to the study of Paleolithic and early Neolithic cultures. There is also a tendency for women to subscribe to schools of archaeological practice that can be grouped under the rubric of "postprocessualism"—a recent paradigm of archaeological inquiry that draws from postmodern, relativistic approaches to the social science and the humanities. Gender studies in particular seem the almost exclusive domain of women archaeologists. Men, on the other hand, seem more drawn to "processual" approaches to archaeology grounded in a logical-positivist approach to scientific inquiry.

Yet there are other factors that seem to have greater impact on determining the kinds of questions archaeologists study and how they conduct their research. In particular, age is more important than gender in determining an archaeologist's allegiance to one or another paradigm of archaeological practice. Culture historical approaches to archaeology show a sharp decline among younger men and women archaeologists, as does, to a much lesser extent, the practice of archaeology grounded in cultural ecology. And while there are gender-based differences in the degree to which men and women follow processual and postprocessual paradigms, both approaches show a steady increase among younger men and women. There are also age-related trends in the analytical approaches archaeologists use in their pursuit of the past. In particular the proportion of younger archaeologists engaged in zooarchaeological research is considerably greater than in older cohorts, while the proportion of those engaged in ceramic and lithic analysis has decreased in younger

cohorts. Not surprisingly, there is also a close linkage between regional research interests and region of residence among archaeologists working in North America.

But by far the most important factor shaping archaeological research interests is one's work setting. Academics, in particular, stand apart from professional archaeologists in all other employment sectors in their regional, topical, theoretical, and analytical approaches to archaeology. The practice of archaeology in academia is most distinctively different from the archaeology practiced in the government and private sectors. And while museum archaeologists resemble academics in several respects, they too have a distinctive profile in terms of their interests and approaches to archaeological inquiry. These data echo previous patterns discussed in Chapter 4, which revealed distinctive differences in the kinds of activities in which academics commonly engage when compared to professional archaeologists in different employment sectors (see Figure 4.19).

Also noted in this earlier chapter was the close correspondence of the preferred activities of student archaeologists and the profile of activities performed by professional academics (Figures 4.18 and 4.19a). In this discussion of archaeological research interests we see that these archaeologists of tomorrow also pattern their research after their academic professors. In fact, in several respects student research interests differ even more sharply from those of archaeologists employed in government and private sector work settings. Yet, as we have seen, both the public and, especially, the private sector have been steadily increasing in their share of the archaeological job market. This disjunction between student research interests and the research conducted in these two employment sectors, then, adds to the impression that the academic training of tomorrow's archaeologists is out of step with the realities of today's job market.

Measuring Research Interests

Before turning to a consideration of the data on archaeological research interests, a word is needed about the how these data are presented. In each of the questions pertaining to research, respondents were asked to note their primary and secondary interests (Appendix). While many followed these instructions, noting either a "1" or "2" next to the two topics in a certain research domain that interested them most, others simply checked one, two, or sometimes several of the possible responses listed in a particular question. To report the responses of as broad a sample as possible, the data presented here will not distinguish between primary and secondary interests, but rather will give equal weight to all respondent choices. Moreover, data on research interests are presented in the form of percents based on the number of *responses* to a particular question, rather than on the number of *respondents* to a question (which was the method used to construct current and preferred employment and activity profiles in Chapter 4). Computing the relative distribution of respondent research interests in this way makes it possible to combine specific categories of interest into more general categories—specific regions in the United States and Canada into a general North American category, for example, or several schools of archaeology, like gender studies, Marxist approaches, and critical theory, into a single postprocessual category. If data were reported as the percentage of respondents rather than the percentage of all responses, popular aggregate categories (like North American archaeology) would receive confusing 100+ percent percentage scores.

Research Interests by Gender and Age

While there are some significant differences in the research interests of men and women archaeologists, the impact of gender is subtle and hard to isolate from other factors that may play a more significant role in defining the topics and tools of archaeological study. Data on research interests by age and gender are based on the entire sample of respondents, both professionals and students. Including students in the sample provides a more robust view of research trends among younger age cohorts, and gives some insight into future research trends.

Regional Interests

The general regional research interests of male and female archaeologists are virtually identical (Figure 5.1). Slightly over 60 percent of both men and women expressed an interest in the archaeology of North America, while about 18 percent of men and women expressed interest in the archaeology of Latin American countries (Mexico, Central and South America). An equivalent proportion of respondents expressed an interest in archaeology practiced outside the Americas—grouped here under the rubric of "Old World" archaeology.

The strong showing of interest in North American archaeology is not unexpected. After all, the respondent pool is comprised primarily of American archaeologists who belong to the Society for American Archaeology. While the regional focus of the SAA has broadened over the years, the society was expressly founded to represent the

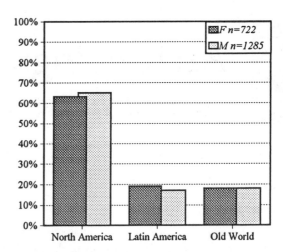

Fig. 5.1 *General Regional Research Interests by Gender*

Note the predominant interest in the archaeology of North America, but also the even representation of Latin American and Old World archaeology. Note also the similarity between male and female regional research interests.

archaeology of the Americas. Both the flagship journal of the SAA, *American Antiquity,* and its recently initiated sister journal, *Latin American Antiquity,* still primarily feature archaeology conducted in the Americas. Given this strong Americanist emphasis, it is surprising that the level of interest in Latin American archaeology is not considerably higher than the degree of interest in regions outside of the Americas. Since archaeologists practicing outside the Americas might be more likely to join other professional societies with a more international focus in their basic missions and in their journal outlets, it is likely that interest in the archaeology of regions outside the Western Hemisphere is even higher in the actual universe of American archaeologists than is evident among SAA Census respondents.

There is little change in general regional interests across the various age cohorts represented in the respondent pool (Figure 5.2). Some drop is evident in the level of interest expressed in North American archaeology among respondents in their 20s, and there is a concomitant increase in interest in Latin American and Old World archaeology. However, this trend is not indicative of a major restructuring of the regional research interests of tomorrow's archaeologists. Rather, it is more likely an artifact of the composition of the 20–29 year old cohort shown here, which is dominated by students. As we will see later, Latin American and Old World regional interests make a better showing among professional academics and students than among those in other employment sectors.

The regional research interests of men and women working in North America also strongly resemble each other (Figure 5.3). For both, interest in Southwestern archaeology is strongly dominant, with Southeastern archaeology the second best represented regional research interest.

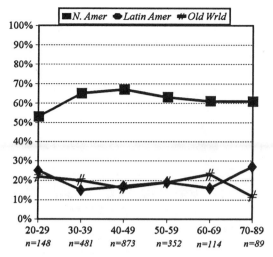

Fig. 5.2 *General Regional Research Interests by Age*

Note the constant general regional research interests across all age cohorts.

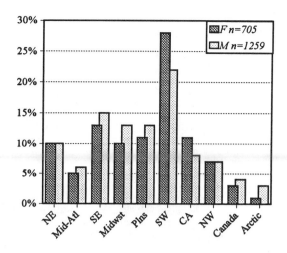

Fig. 5.3 *North American Regional Research Interests by Gender*

Note the high level of interest in the archaeology of the Southwestern United States among both men and women. Note also the slightly higher level of interest among men in the Southeast, Midwest, and Plains, and the higher level of interest among women in the Southwest and California.

However, there are significant differences in the regional profiles of men and women working in North America (χ^2=24.386, df=9, p=.004). Interest in the Southeast, Midwest, and Plains regions in particular is proportionately higher among male respondents, while interest in the archaeology of the Southwest and California is higher among women.

Figure 5.4 shows that the regional interests of North American archaeologists are strongly linked to their current region of residence. In each case, those residing in a certain region seem especially interested in the archaeology of that region. Each regional interest profile is significantly different from every other at better than the .001 level of probability. Thus, the differences in male and female regional research interests are most likely linked to regional differences in the distribution of male and female archaeologists, as noted in Chapter 2, with men somewhat better represented in the Southeast, the Midwest, and the Plains, while women, especially women students, are better represented in the Southwestern and Western United States.

Research interests of men and women in regions outside North America are essentially identical (Figure 5.5). The archaeology of Mexico and Central America is the dominant non–North American regional interest of men and women. The level of interest in European archaeology matches, and among men exceeds, the stated interest in the archaeology of South America. Again the strength of non-Americanist archaeology among the SAA respondent pool is noteworthy. There is some tendency for men to express an interest in the archaeology of Oceania, but this interest might be tied to the number of men in the private and public sectors of archaeological employment, who, as we shall see later, show a high level of interest in Oceanic archaeology. The tendency for proportionately more

women to express an interest in South American archaeology might be a function of the generally younger age of women archaeologists in the sample. The popularity of South American archaeology shows some increase among both younger men and women.

Topical Research Interests

Interest in different topics of archaeological study was measured in two separate questions that asked respondents to characterize topical interests along broadly defined arenas of archaeological inquiry (prehistoric archeology, historic archaeology, archaeological methods, archaeological history/philosophy/theory), as well as more specific topics of concentration (hunter-gatherers/Paleolithic societies, village farmers/Neolithic societies, complex societies/states, protohistoric/contact periods, colonial/historic periods, 19th–20th century urban archaeology). Census results showed little difference in the more general topical research interests of men and women. Specifically, the proportions of men and women who expressed an interest in prehistoric archaeology versus historic archaeology are very similar (Figure 5.6). In both cases, prehistoric archaeology is strongly dominant. There is, however, a slightly greater tendency among male respondents to express an interest in prehistoric archaeology, while women tend to show a slightly greater interest in historic archaeology. For both men and women there is a virtually identical 50–50 split in the respondents who expressed a primary interest in theoretical issues in archaeology and those who expressed a stronger interest in archaeological methods (Figure 5.7). There are no age-related trends in these broad topical interests.

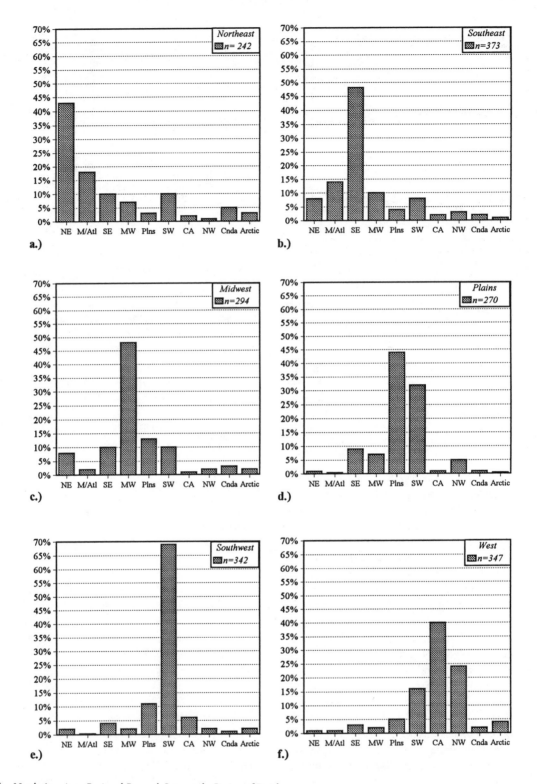

Fig. 5.4 *North American Regional Research Interests by Region of Residence*

a Northeast residents

c Midwest residents

e Southwest residents

b Southeast residents

d Plains residents

f West residents

Note the strong correlation between North American regional research interests and region of residence.

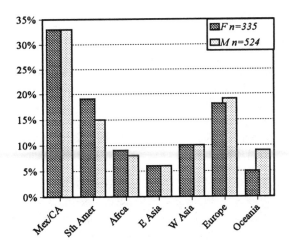

Fig. 5.5 *Non–North American Regional Research Interests by Gender*

Note the predominance of interest in Mexico and Central America and the high level of interest in European archaeology. Note also the similarity between the regional research interests of men and women.

The more specific topical interests of men and women also closely resemble each other (Figure 5.8). For both men and women there was more interest expressed in the study of Paleolithic and Neolithic societies. But while the general profile of topical interests of men and women is similar, they still vary significantly from one another (χ^2=18.686, df=5, p=.002). In particular the graph shown in Figure 5.8 brings into sharper relief the slight difference between men's and women's interest in prehistoric versus historic periods noted in Figure 5.6. Although an interest in Paleolithic and Neolithic periods of cultural development is dominant among both men and women, propor-

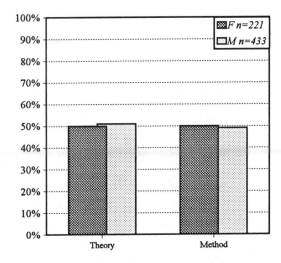

Fig. 5.7 *Interest in Theory Building Versus Methods Development by Gender*

Note the even split between interest in archaeological theory and methods, and the similarity between male and female interests.

tionately more men expressed an interest in the archaeology of these societies, while proportionately more women expressed interest in complex societies, protohistoric, historic, and urban/industrial archaeology. These gender-based differences are constant across all age cohorts, and there are no age-related changes in the primacy of various topical research interests.

Analytical Tools

Once again, while the general profile of analytical tools used by men and women in their research is roughly

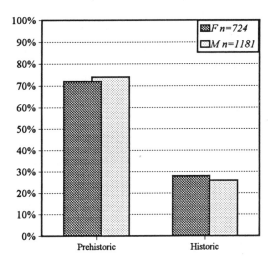

Fig. 5.6 *Interest in Prehistoric and Historic Archaeology by Gender*

Note the predominant interest in prehistoric archaeology, and the similarity between male and female interests.

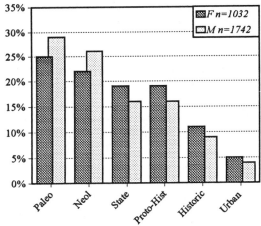

Fig. 5.8 *Topical Research Interests by Gender*

Note the predominance of interest in Paleolithic and Neolithic societies in both men and women. But also note that there is a higher level of interest among men in Paleolithic and Neolithic societies, and more interest among women in complex societies, protohistoric, and historic periods.

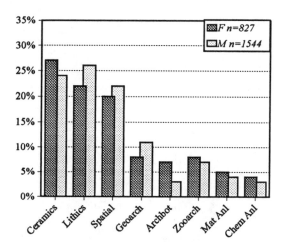

Fig. 5.9 *Analytical Tools by Gender*

Note the greater use of lithic and spatial analysis and geo-archaeological methods by men, and the greater use of ceramic analysis and archaeobotany among women.

similar (Figure 5.9), there are some significant differences worth noting (χ^2=28.496, df=7, p.<001). Proportionately more men utilize lithic, spatial, and geomorphological analysis, while proportionately more women employ ceramic analysis and archaeobotany in their archaeological research. Although women show a slightly greater tendency to use zooarchaeology, as well as material and chemical analytical methods, the proportion of men and women who use these analytical tools are quite close. To a certain extent, gender-based differences in the use of different analytical methods may stem from the above discussed differences in topical interests. Lithic analysis would seem of particular importance in the study of aceramic Paleolithic and early Neolithic societies. Spatial analysis of tool and settlement distribution might also be more frequently used in the study of these early stages of cultural development. Geomorphology is particularly useful in the reconstruction of paleoclimates, which is an important element of the archaeology of the Late Pleistocene and Early Holocene. In contrast, ceramic analysis is a primary analytical approach used to study questions of economy and social identity in state-level and historic societies. It is difficult to see how this difference in problem orientation can be linked to the relatively high proportion of women engaged in archaeobotanical analysis, however, especially when one considers the importance of archaeobotany in the study of agricultural origins so central to research conducted on Neolithic societies. It is interesting to note that the female dominance of archaeobotany is not matched in zooarchaeology, where men and women are proportionately more evenly represented.

When we look at the use of analytical methods by age, we see a marked decline in the primacy of ceramic and lithic analysis among younger cohorts and a corresponding increase in the proportion of archaeologists who count zooarchaeology as a primary analytical method (Figure 5.10). Comparing the 50–59 age cohort to the 20–29 age cohort, the increase in the proportion of archaeologists who use zooarchaeology as a primary research tool relative to those who focus on ceramic analysis is significant at the .010 level of probability (χ^2=6.637, df=1). Relative to those who use lithic analysis, the increase in zooarchaeologists in this youngest cohort is significant at the .006 level of probability (χ^2=7.419, df=1). This pattern is found in both men and women archaeologists. The use of other analytical tools examined in the Census remains relatively constant across age cohorts represented in the respondent pool.

Archaeological Paradigms

Over the past four decades there have been profound shifts in the underlying paradigms that define the questions American archaeologists ask of the past and the methods they use to answer these questions. The archaeology of the first half of the 20th century was largely driven by the need to establish baseline historical parameters of the past. This culture historical approach to archaeology held as its primary goals the delineation of distinct culture groups and the construction of clear spatial and temporal frameworks into which these groups could be placed (Willey and Phillips 1958). The publication of Julian Steward's influential book *Theory of Culture Change* in 1955 marks a growing appreciation of the importance of human interaction with the natural environment in shaping human cultural evolution—an appreciation that underlies the "cultural

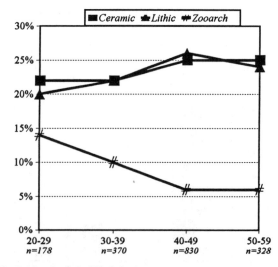

Fig. 5.10 *Analytical Tools by Age*

Note the increase in use of zooarchaeological methods in younger age cohorts, and the decrease in the use of ceramic and lithic analysis.

ecological" approach to the study of the human past. Cultural ecology, in turn, served as a springboard for the "new" archaeology of the mid to late 1960s that called for a focus on the processes of human interaction with the environment and with each other as the primary context of archaeological inquiry (Binford 1972). Also known as "processual" archaeology, this new paradigm sought to apply an "explicitly scientific" logical-positivist approach in addressing archaeological problems, with the ultimate goal of discovering underlying principles that govern human behavior (Flannery 1967; Fritz and Plog 1970; Schiffer 1976; Watson et al. 1971). Growing out of the postmodern intellectual movement in humanistic and social science disciplines of the 1980s (Arato and Gebhardt 1978), the most recent new perspective to emerge in American archaeology adopts a more relativistic approach to the study of the human past that is often framed within the context of current-day social and political concerns (Gero and Conkey 1991; Leone et al. 1987; McGuire and Paynter 1991; Patterson 1986). A number of different approaches to the past can be grouped under this general rubric of "postprocessual" archaeology, such as Marxist archaeology, critical theoretical approaches, and gender studies.

To track the prominence of these different paradigms or schools of archaeological thought within American archaeology, respondents were asked to characterize the archaeology they practice as it falls within one or more of these various approaches. While respondents were given eight different paradigms to choose from (Appendix), for our purposes these different choices are grouped under the four broader archaeological paradigms discussed above.

When we look at the distribution of respondent paradigm choices presented in Figure 5.11, we see that for both men and women processual archaeology is the dominant paradigm, followed closely by cultural ecology. Given the bulge in our sample in the 40 to 59 year old age groups, this is not unexpected. Archaeologists in these age groups were, after all, the vanguards of these movements in archaeological theory. However, the paradigm profiles of men and women vary significantly from one another (χ^2=32.640, df=3, p<.001). Specifically, proportionately more men are attracted to culture historical and processual approaches to archaeological inquiry, while women tend to be more drawn to postprocessual paradigms. Gender studies in particular are dominated by women. Of the 53 respondents who listed gender studies as a primary paradigm for their work, 46 (or 87 percent) were women. When we look at these data more closely, it becomes clear that the differences seen between the research paradigms of men and women archaeologists are shaped by a complex interplay of both age and gender.

Figure 5.12 compares the proportion of men and women who subscribe to each of the four general schools of archaeology by age cohort. Turning first to culture his-

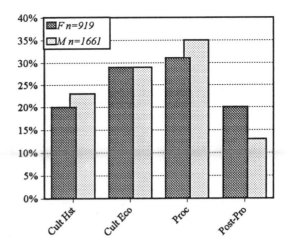

Fig. 5.11 *Archaeological Paradigms by Gender*

Note the predominance of processual and cultural ecological paradigms among both men and women. Note also, however, the greater proportion of men who subscribe to culture historical and processual approaches, and the greater tendency for women to use postprocessual approaches.

torical paradigms (Figure 5.12a), in all age cohorts the proportions of men and women who take this approach to archaeological inquiry are essentially identical. Moreover, for both men and women the proportion of archaeologists who operate within this framework sharply and progressively declines among archaeologists under 60. Thus, the higher proportion of men who subscribe to a culture historical approach is largely an artifact of the better representation of older age cohorts among the male respondents to the Census noted in Chapter 2.

The essentially even representation of male and female proponents of cultural ecology evident in the aggregate in Figure 5.11 cuts across all age cohorts (Figure 5.12b). Moreover, the proportion of men and women who subscribe to this school of archaeological practice is quite steady across the larger age cohorts. Some decline in practitioners of this approach may be indicated, however, beginning with archaeologists in their 30s and becoming even more marked among archaeologists in their 20s.

Turning to adherents of processual and postprocessual schools of research (Figure 5.12c and d), it is clear that the differential representation of these two paradigms among men and women seen in the aggregate is consistent in all age cohorts. The proportion of men who say they operate within a processual framework is greater in all but the small sample of 70 to 89 year olds. Likewise, the proportion of women who ascribe to postprocessual paradigms in their work is higher than the proportion of men who subscribe to these paradigms in almost every age class.

Interestingly, both schools show a more or less steady increase in the number of both male and female adherents in each younger age cohort. However, the stronger male

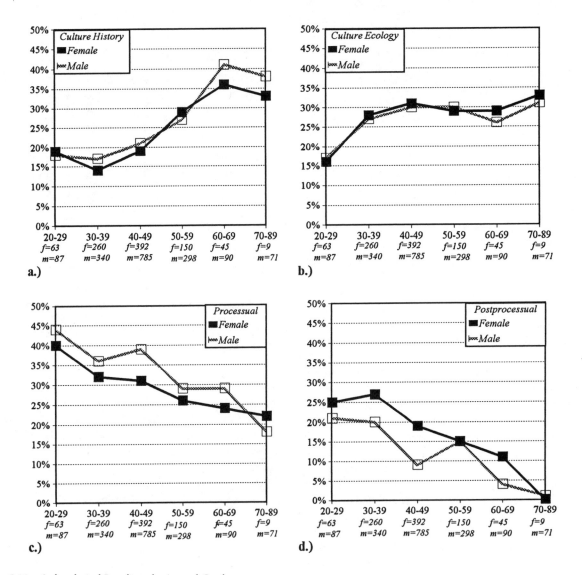

Fig. 5.12 *Archaeological Paradigms by Age and Gender*

a Culture history   **b** Cultural ecology

c Processual   **d** Postprocessual

Note the decline in culture historical approaches in younger cohorts, the fairly steady representation of cultural ecological approaches in all but the youngest cohorts, and the increase in adherence to processual and postprocessual paradigms among both men and women.

interest in processual archaeology is still apparent. Among male archaeologists in their 30s there is a 16 percentage point spread separating processual and postprocessual archaeologists. In contrast, the proportion of women in their 30s who say their work falls within a processual frame of reference is only 5 percent greater than the proportion of women in this cohort who subscribe to postprocessual approaches to archaeology, at least among members of the SAA. Finally, there is no evidence that processual archaeology (which, along with its founders, is now decidedly middle-aged) is about to be eclipsed by a nascent postprocessual paradigm. In fact, the growth rate of postprocessualism seems to flatten among male archaeolo-

gists in their 20s and even decline among women in this youngest age cohort. In contrast, processual approaches show a sharp increase among archaeologists in their 20s, especially among younger women.

Contributing Disciplines

Archaeologists draw on a number of related disciplines in the conduct of their research, not only more closely related subfields of anthropology (ethnology, physical anthropology, and linguistics), but also other less directly related fields of social, biological, and physical sciences. With the expansion of such interdisciplinary approaches to

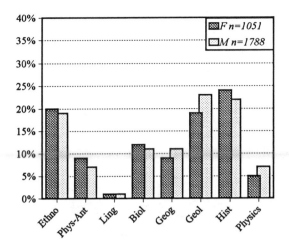

Fig. 5.13 *Importance of Nonarchaeological Disciplines by Gender*

Note the greater importance of geology and history, and the comparative lesser importance of subfields of anthropology. Note also the greater tendency for men to draw from geology in their research while women tend to draw more from history.

archaeological inquiry as archaeobotany, zooarchaeology, and archaeometry, these more distant disciplinary cousins can be expected to play even greater roles in framing the intellectual context in which archaeologists conduct their research. Respondents were asked to note the non-archaeological disciplines that have the greatest impact on their work, in an effort to let us monitor the contributions of various nonarchaeological disciplines to American archaeology.

As with other research parameters considered, the profile of nonarchaeological disciplines of greatest importance to male and female archaeologists are generally quite similar (Figure 5.13). Nonanthropological disciplines of history and geology seem to make the greatest contribution, especially to men, while ethnology is only of secondary or, in the case of men, of more tertiary value. Other anthropological subdisciplines fare even more poorly, with physical anthropology only the sixth most important nonarchaeological field, and linguistics the least important field of all eight disciplines considered.

While generally similar, there are some distinctive differences between male and female archaeologists in the nonarchaeological disciplines most important to their research (χ^2=24.762, df=7, p.<001). Geology, geography, and physical sciences make somewhat greater contributions to the research conducted by male archaeologists, while history, ethnology, biology, and physical anthropology seem to contribute more to the archaeological research conducted by women. Some of these differences may be attributable to the above-noted differences between men and women in the types of societies they tend to study and the tools they use to conduct their research. Geological

sciences might be expected to make an important contribution to the study of Paleolithic societies for which men show some preference, while history would be a major contributor to historical archaeology, in which a somewhat higher proportion of women seem to be interested. Some of these apparent gender-based differences may also be attributable to the context within which the work is conducted rather than to the gender of the researcher. For example, as we will see below, ethnology and physical anthropology are more important to academics and students than to archaeologists working in different employment sectors. The high proportion of women among students may then be the primary factor contributing to the slightly greater importance of these disciplines to the research conducted by women respondents.

Research Interests by Employment Sector

The greatest variation in archaeological research interests is seen when comparing professional archaeologists working in different employment sectors. In particular, academic archaeologists have the most distinctively different research profiles, though they share several interests in common with museum-based archaeologists. And while private and public sector professionals show some variation from one another, their research interests are generally much more similar than those of academic and museum archaeologists.

The next 10 figures (Figures 5.14 through 5.23) compare the research interests of professional archaeologists in the four primary employment sectors identified in Chapter 4: academia, government, museums, and the private sector. In addition, each figure contains a profile of student interests that will be discussed in the final section of this chapter. Results of chi-square statistical tests are also included with each figure in the form of a 5x5 matrix that compares the profiles of professionals in the four employment settings and students against each other. The chi-square values are presented in the bottom part of the matrix, and the significances of the comparisons are presented in the upper part. The degrees of freedom for the test are recorded in the upper left corner of the matrix.

Regional Research Interests

Turning first to regional interests, the proportions of archaeologists working outside of North America is clearly highest among academic archaeologists, with 20 percent of the academic archaeologists expressing an interest in Latin American archaeology, and 22 percent in the archaeology of regions outside of the Americas (Figure 5.14). Museum archaeologists have a similar profile in their general regional interests, but the emphasis on North America is stronger here. Not surprisingly, government and,

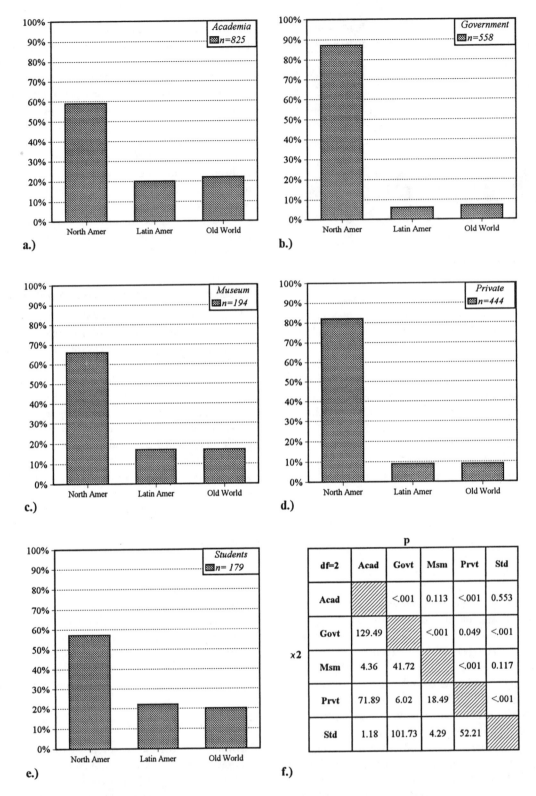

Fig. 5.14 *General Regional Research Interests by Employment Sector*

a Academia

c Museums

e Students

b Government

d Private sector

f Chi-square matrix

Note the greater interest in regions outside of North America among academics, museum professionals, and students, and the more exclusive focus on North America among government and private sector archaeologists.

especially, private sector archaeologists focus almost exclusively on North American archaeology.

Of those working within North America, academic and museum archaeologists tend to share similar regional research interests that are distinctly different from the interests of archaeologists working for the government and the private sector (Figure 5.15). While the Southwest is the dominant region of interest in all sectors, both academics and museum professionals expressed a stronger interest in the archaeology of regions east of the Mississippi. In contrast, the private and public sector archaeologists tend to have a stronger emphasis on regions from the Plains to the West Coast. These regional research interests within the United States follow residential patterns of archaeologists employed in these different work settings (discussed in Chapter 4), which showed more of a concentration of academics and museum professionals in the Eastern United States, and more government and private sector archaeologists in the West (Figure 4.12).

Interest in areas outside of the United States are more similar in the four primary work settings (Figure 5.16). Yet, as is consistently the case, the interests of academic and museum professionals resemble each other more than those of other professional archaeologists, while private and public sector archaeologists correspondingly seem to have more in common. The high levels of interest of private and public sector archaeologists in Oceania is remarkable, and are probably linked to American territories in the Pacific that employ federal and state archaeologists and that are subject to laws that mandate assessment of cultural resources in advance of development.

Topical Research Interests

In broadly defined topical interests, academics stand out in their heavy emphasis on prehistoric archaeology (Figure 5.17). Nearly 80 percent of the professional academics polled expressed a primary interest in prehistoric archaeology. Although museum archaeologists are more similar to academics, archaeologists in all three of the chief sectors differ significantly from academics in their stronger interest in historic archaeology. This is especially true for government archaeologists. The number of government archaeologists, at both the state and federal level, who monitor compliance with historic preservation laws is likely to elevate the prominence of historic archaeology among government archaeologists. Similarly, the number of projects aimed at assessing the impact of development on historic sites likely contributes to the stronger interest in historic periods among private sector archaeologists.

In contrast, academics are identical to government archaeologists in the split in interest in archaeological theory versus archaeological methods (Figure 5.18). For both groups, interest in theory building slightly exceeds an interest in development of archaeological methods. Conversely, in museums and, especially, in the private sector, interest in methodology dominates. This pattern is more easily understood for private sector archaeologists where the scope of the archaeological research conducted is dictated by law and contractual agreements, rather than by the problem orientation of the individual archaeologist. Interest in the methods employed in conducting the contracted work might then be expected to be greater in the private sector. But it is not clear why this pattern is seen among museum archaeologists, who resemble academic archaeologists in so many other aspects of their research.

In more specific topical research interests, however, academics and museum professionals show a stronger resemblance to one another, while private and public sector professionals are, once again, more similar (Figure 5.19). Museum and academic archaeologists show a higher interest in Neolithic and, especially, complex societies. Government and private sector archaeologists, on the other hand, share a stronger interest in Paleolithic and protohistoric/historic societies. This pattern can be linked to the broader international focus of the archaeological research in academia and museums. Agricultural origins and the emergence of social complexity figure more prominently in the archaeology of regions outside of North America, which, as we have seen, are more frequently studied by academics and museum-based archaeologists.

Analytical Tools

The same pattern is found when examining the analytical tools used by archaeologists in these different employment sectors (Figure 5.20). An emphasis on lithic analysis is particularly strong among government and private sector professionals, which is probably a reflection of the stronger interest in Paleolithic societies in these sectors of archaeological employment. Zooarchaeology is more frequently used in academic and museum settings than in either the private or public sectors. Academics and museum professionals differ only in the less frequent use of spatial analysis among museum-based archaeologists. Perhaps this difference can be attributed to a greater emphasis on collections-based research in museums, which would encourage the use of analytical techniques that focus on the objects themselves, rather than on the spatial relations of objects to one another.

Archaeological Paradigms

Academics are perhaps most distinctively different from other professional archaeologists in the archaeological paradigms within which their research is conducted (Figure 5.21). Particularly noteworthy is the very high proportion of academics who say they operate within a processual frame of reference (42 percent). Adherents of postprocessual approaches, who make up 17 percent of the

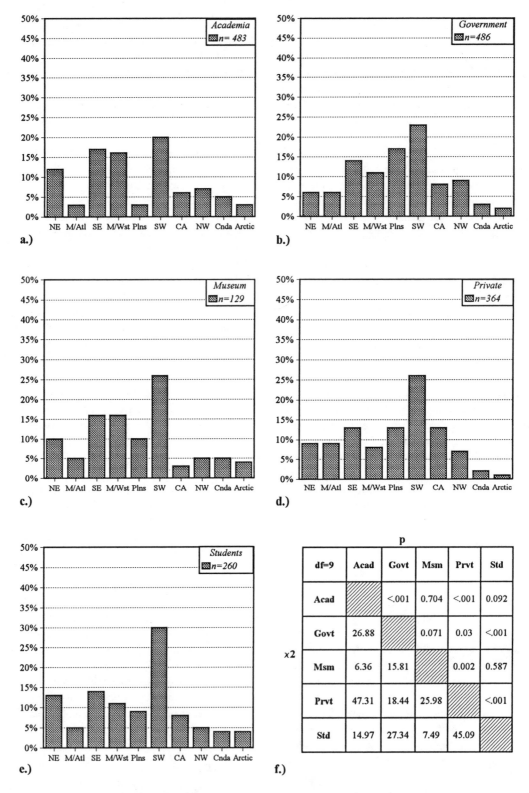

Fig. 5.15 *North American Regional Research Interests by Employment Sector*

a Academia

b Government

c Museum

d Private sector

e Students

f Chi-square matrix

Note the similarity between the regional research interests of academics, museum professionals, and students working in North America.
Note also the greater similarity of the North American regional interests of government and private sector archaeologists.

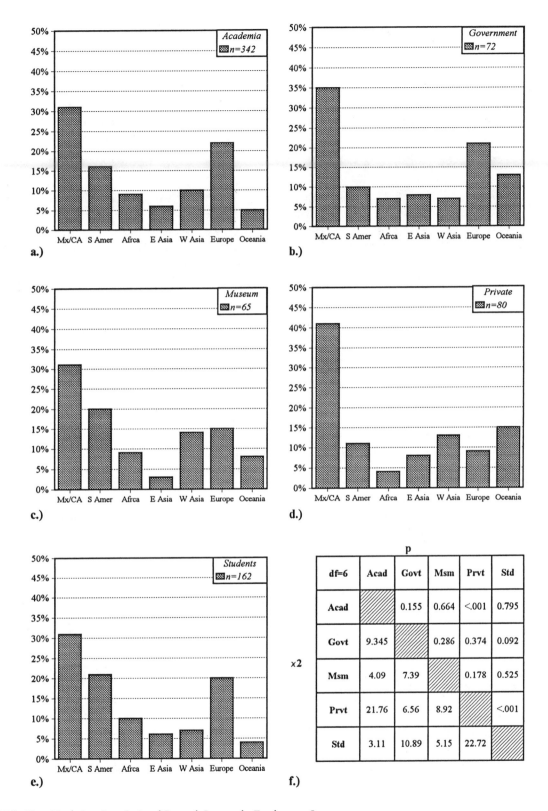

Fig. 5.16 *Non–North American Regional Research Interests by Employment Sector*

a Academia
c Museums
e Students

b Government
d Private sector
f Chi-square matrix

Note the similarity between the regional research interests of academics, museum professionals, and students, and the greater similarity of the interests of government and private sector archaeologists.

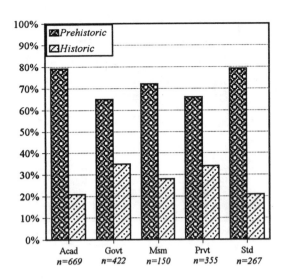

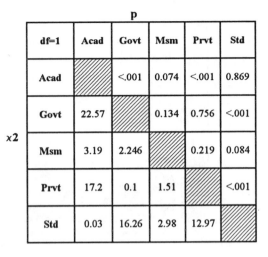

Fig. 5.17 *Interest in Prehistoric and Historic Archaeology by Employment Sector*

a Professionals in the four primary employment sectors and students

b Chi-square matrix

Note the greater interest in prehistoric archaeology of academic professionals and students, and the somewhat greater interest in historic archaeology of government archaeologists, museum professionals, and private sector archaeologists.

sample of academics, are also markedly more common in academic settings than in other archaeological employment sectors. In contrast, processual approaches are represented by only about 30 percent or less of the sample of archaeologists in the other three primary employment sectors, while postprocessual archaeologists comprise only a little over 10 percent of the respondents working in these

settings. Museum-based archaeologists differ sharply from academics in the smaller proportions of adherents to processual and postprocessual paradigms, and in the greater proportion of people who say they operate within a culture historical frame of reference. Government and private sector archaeologists differ from academic archaeologists in the higher proportions of adherents to cultural ecological

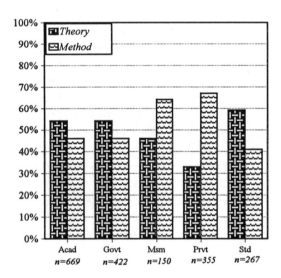

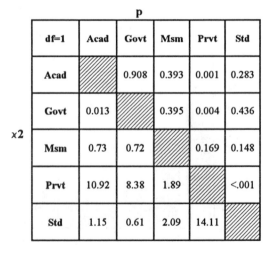

Fig. 5.18 *Interest in Theory Building Versus Methods Development by Employment Sector*

a Professionals in the four primary employment sectors, and students

b Chi-square matrix

Note the greater interest in theory building of academic and government professionals, and especially students. Note also the greater interest in methods development of museum professionals and private sector archaeologists.

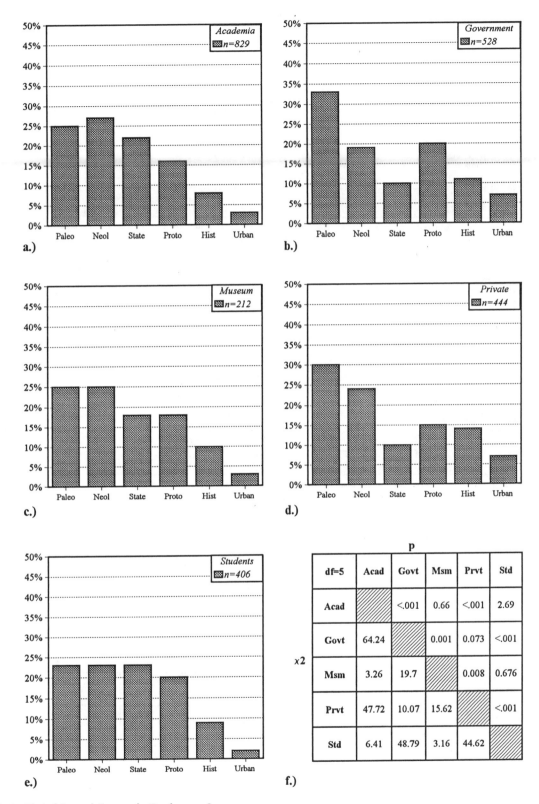

Fig. 5.19 *Topical Research Interests by Employment Sector*

a Academia
c Museums
e Students

b Government
d Private sector
f Chi-square matrix

Note the similarity of the topical research interests of academics, museum professionals, and students, and the greater similarity of the interests of government and private sector archaeologists.

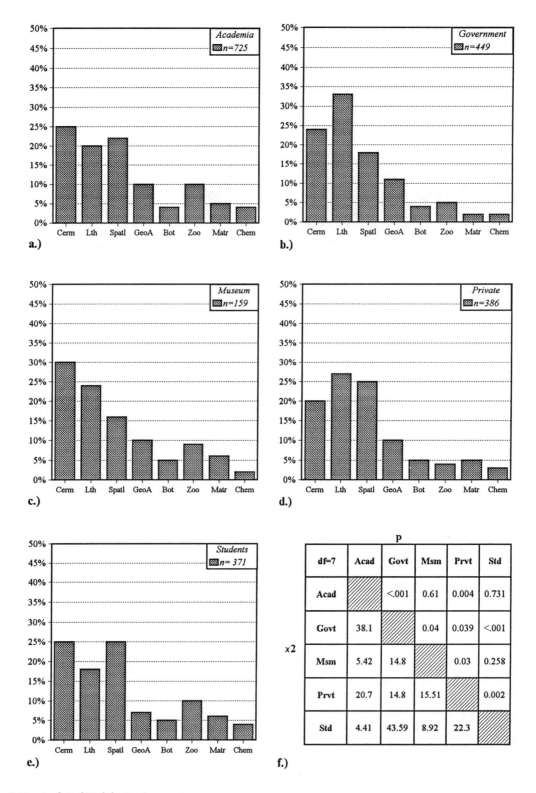

Fig. 5.20 *Analytical Tools by Employment Sector*

a Academia
c Museums
e Students

b Government
d Private sector
f Chi-square matrix

Note the similarity between the analytical tools used by academics, museum professionals, and students, and the greater similarity of the analytical tools used by government and private sector archaeologists. Note, in particular, the importance of lithic analysis among government and private sector archaeologists, and the much less frequent use of lithic analysis by students.

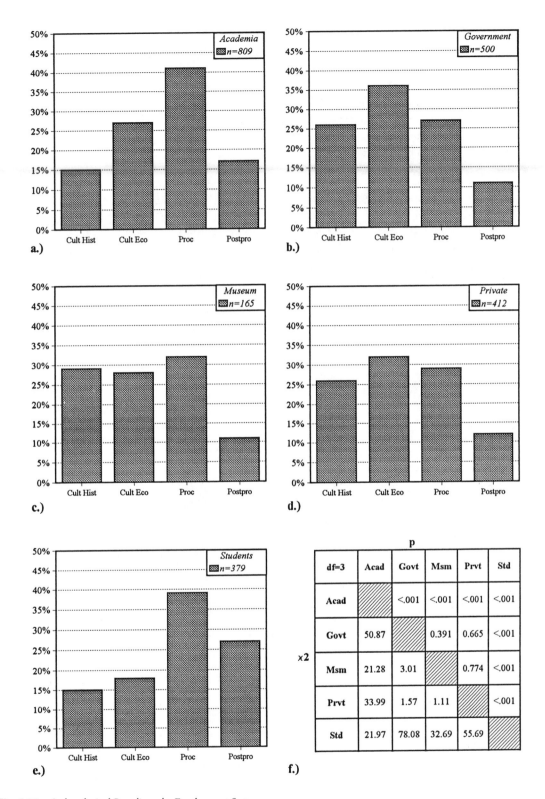

Fig. 5.21 *Archaeological Paradigms by Employment Sector*

a Academia

c Museums

e Students

b Government

d Private sector

f Chi-square matrix

Note the interest of academics in processual and postprocessual paradigms, and the greater importance of culture historical and cultural ecological approaches among government archaeologists, museum professionals, and private sector archaeologists. Note also the strong representation of postprocessual approaches among students.

and culture historical approaches. Proponents of cultural ecology are particularly well represented in government work settings.

When the paradigm profiles of different professional archaeologists are broken down by gender (Figure 5.22), several interesting patterns emerge. First, it is clear that women in all work settings are more drawn to postprocessual approaches. This is especially true of women in academia, 24 percent of whom operate within a postprocessual framework. In contrast, only about 15 percent of women in other employment sectors subscribe to postprocessual research paradigms. Academic men, however, also seem more drawn to postprocessual approaches than men in other employment sectors. Fourteen percent of male academics subscribe to postprocessual approaches to archaeological research compared to only about 10 percent or less of men in other work settings.

The high proportion of museum professionals who subscribe to culture historical approaches is largely attributable to a strong preference for this approach among males working in museums. Women in museums are drawn more to cultural ecological and processual approaches. This difference is in part a function of the ages of men and women museum professionals. Seventy-two percent of the female museum professionals are in their 30s and 40s, with 36 percent in the 30–39 age cohort alone. In contrast, only 12 percent of the males in museums are in their 30s, while over 80 percent are over 40. The high proportion of private sector women who subscribe to a culture historical approach cannot be as clearly linked to age differentials within private sector men and women. We have seen, however, that the rate of growth of the private sector among younger male professional archaeologists is higher than among women, perhaps contributing to the better representation of more recent archaeological paradigms among males in the private sector.

Contributing Disciplines

Finally, academics are distinctive in the profile of nonarchaeological disciplines that make the greatest contributions to their archaeological research (Figure 5.23). Specifically, sister anthropological disciplines of ethnology and physical anthropology make a much larger contribution to academic archaeology than to the archaeology practiced in other employment sectors, especially the public and private sectors. Clearly the four-field approach that serves as the unifying principle for many university anthropology programs is of less utility to professional archaeologists in nonacademic work settings than it is to academic archaeologists.

In contrast, archaeologists in the private and public sectors make much greater use of geological sciences and history in their archaeological research. The high proportion of government archaeologists who draw from history in their research corresponds to the greater importance of historical archaeology in this employment sector noted earlier. The greater emphasis on historical periods seen among museum-based professionals probably also contributes the greater importance of history in the archaeology conducted in museums.

Student Research Interests

Profiles of student research interests are included in each of the 10 figures displaying interests of professional archaeologists in different work settings. In each case, student interests are either essentially identical to, or at least most similar to, those of academic professionals. This is particularly true in the case of the general regional research interests of students (Figure 5.14), in student interest in regions outside of North America (Figure 5.16), in their emphasis on prehistoric archaeology versus historic archaeology (Figure 5.17), and in the nonarchaeological disciplines that contribute most to their research (Figure 5.23). Like those of academics, student research interests also share some similarities with the research interests of museum professionals. The similarities between museum archaeologists, academics, and students are likely attributable to the number of museum professionals in our sample who are based in university museums, and who therefore regularly engage in teaching and supervising students.

Some important differences between students and academics, however, should be noted. In some cases, this variation can be attributed to age, with students reflecting the most recent trends in archaeological research. For example, students differ from academic professionals in the greater emphasis on Southwestern archaeology among those working in North America (Figure 5.15), which is likely attributable to increasing predominance of universities in the Southwest in producing recent archaeology graduates, as noted in Chapter 3. In other instances, the variation between students and academics cannot easily be linked to age-related trends, but seems to reflect a general tendency for students to place even stronger emphasis on those aspects of research that distinguish academics from other professional archaeologists. For example, students show a stronger interest in theory building than professional archaeologists in all work settings (Figure 5.18). In this regard they stand in stark contrast to private sector professionals. Students also show even less emphasis on Paleolithic archaeology than academics, which again is quite different from private sector and government archaeologists (Figure 5.19). Lithic analysis is even less commonly used in student research than by academic professionals (Figure 5.20). On the other hand, lithic analysis is the analytical tool most frequently employed by government and private sector archaeologists.

But perhaps the most distinctive aspect of student research can be found in the paradigms to which students

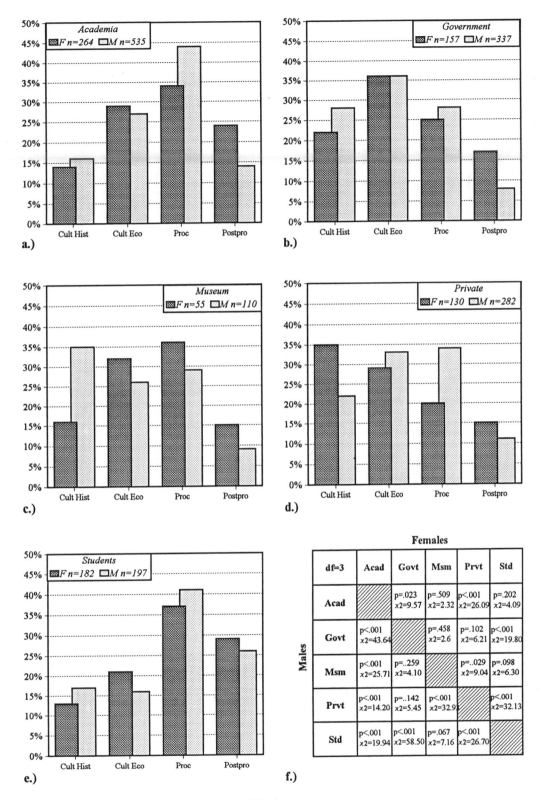

Fig. 5.22 *Archaeological Paradigms by Employment Sector and Gender*

a Academia

c Museums

e Students

b Government

d Private sector

f Chi-square matrix

Note the greater proportion of women in all employment sectors who operate within a postprocessual framework, and the greater interest in postprocessual approaches of both men and women academic professionals and students.

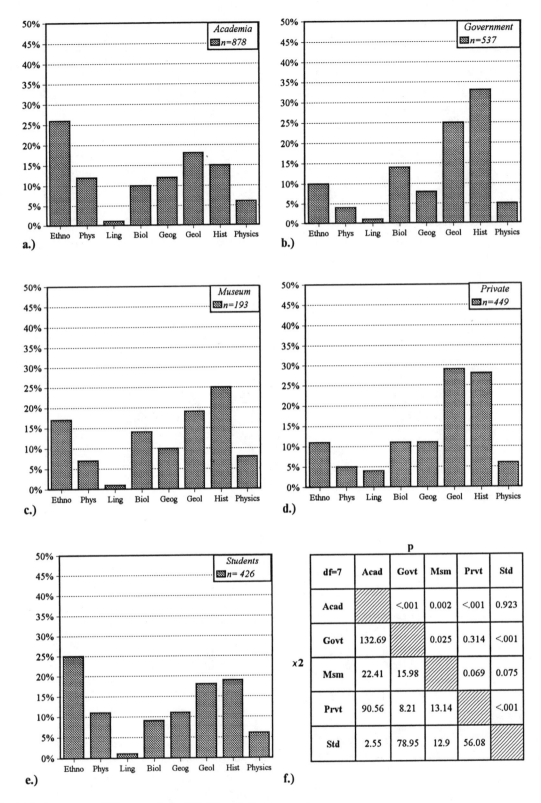

Fig. 5.23 *Importance of Nonarchaeological Disciplines by Employment Sector*

a Academia   b Government
c Museums   d Private sector
e Students   f Chi-square matrix

Note the greater importance of anthropological subfields among academic professionals and students, and the greater relevance of geology and history to the archaeological research conducted in government and the private sector.

subscribe (Figure 5.21). Twenty-seven percent of the students polled follow a postprocessual approach in their archaeological research, a full 10 percent more than seen among academics, and about 16 percent more than for professionals in other employment sectors. Moreover, the strong representation of postprocessual approaches among students is not an artifact of the high proportion of women among student respondents, but rather is a pattern found in both male and female students (Figure 5.22). Men and women students differ, however, in the types of postprocessual approaches they follow. The proportion of male students who say they follow Marxist analytical approaches is eight times greater than the proportion of female students who characterize their research in this way, while the number of female students who expressed a primary interest in gender studies is four times greater than the number of male students.

• It would seem that students closely pattern their research after that of professional academics, which itself differs from that of other professional archaeologists in almost every respect—from its regional focus and topical emphases, to its analytical approaches and intellectual context. In fact, students' research interests are even more markedly different than those of professionals in nonacademic employment sectors. This is particularly true when student research interests are compared to those of private sector archaeologists. But it is also true for research conducted in government work settings, and, to a lesser extent, in museums. The disjunction between academic and nonacademic research interests may help explain the higher level of dissatisfaction among government and private sector archaeologists with the adequacy of their academic training. It also probably contributes to a tendency of professionals in these employment sectors to feel that their current careers are not consistent with their original career expectations.

Most of the student respondents are advanced graduate students nearing completion of their doctoral studies. We already knew that these students show a strong predilection for the kinds of activities in which academics commonly engage, as well as a decided preference for employment in academia. We now see that these students are also drawn to the distinctive subject matter and research approaches of academic archaeologists. Given current employment trends that show a steady increase in the proportion of archaeologists employed in the private and public sectors, these data raise questions about how well students are being trained to meet the realities of the current archaeological job market. In fact, the mismatch between the research interests of the students and those of the professional archaeologists employed in the public and private sectors may be a reason why many younger archaeologists (especially young males) are apparently turning away from the traditional PhD-granting programs, and entering the job market with master's degrees more targeted at preparing students for careers in nonacademic archaeology. •

6 Publication and Professional Activities

Introduction

Chapter Summary

The practice of archaeology does not result in a tangible product that can be bought or sold, demanded or supplied. Nor do archaeologists provide vital services that enhance the daily lives of a consuming public. As a result, when attempting to measure the productivity of American archaeology, we cannot count the number of widgets produced or consumers served. Instead, archaeology's primary product comes in the form of the presentation of the results of archaeological investigation in either the written or spoken word. Both the mode of presentation and the target audience may vary. Oral presentation of the results of archaeological investigation may range from a brief report given at a meeting of a regional archaeological association, to an illustrated lecture presented at a public forum, to a segment on a television documentary broadcast nationally or even internationally. Publication of results may take the form of a short article in a professional journal, a booklet explaining the significance of an archaeological ruin to the visiting public, a monograph filed with a state's department of transportation, or a book aimed at a scholarly audience. Thus the number of presentations, the form they take, and their intended audiences all provide a gauge of the productivity of American archaeology, as well as an appreciation for the various means and objectives of archaeological presentation.

The efforts of archaeologists also have other, even less easily measured, products. Not only do archaeologists work at replicating themselves through training students, they also work to enact and enforce legislation that promotes the preservation of archaeological resources. They are involved in shaping and implementing public policy relating to complex issues of the ownership of the past. They work to build a better appreciation of the value of archaeological research among the general public, and coincidentally to help ensure broad public support for continued expenditure of tax-based funds for that pursuit. Many of these efforts are conducted as part of the day-to-day activities of the workplace. Thus their importance to American archaeology can be assessed, at least in part, by computing the proportion of the archaeological workforce employed in settings that focus on these issues and monitoring the types of activities in which archaeologists com-

monly engage within these different settings. For example, the increasing proportion of the archaeological workforce employed in the public and private sectors, and the amount of effort individuals in these different sectors devote to compliance oversight and contract review, noted in Chapter 4, can be linked to the increased involvement of the profession in the preservation and excavation of threatened sites. But there is another way to monitor the involvement of archaeologists in these areas, for, along with their role in the dissemination of archaeological information, professional societies also play an important part in helping formulate archaeological policy in areas like public education, site preservation, and archaeological ethics. Thus we can gain some understanding of this aspect of archaeological effort by examining the participation of archaeologists in various professional organizations.

Looking at gender-based differences in productivity, there is a consistent tendency for men to produce a higher volume of written and oral presentations than women, regardless of the format of these presentations. This is generally true for all age cohorts and for all employment sectors. There are also age-related trends in the types of publications archaeologists produce. In particular, the proportion of both men and women who write article-length publications decreases with age, while the proportion of people who write books increases. The proportion of people who are not actively publishing or presenting papers is quite low among archaeologists in their 30s and 40s, but rises among archaeologists in their 50s, 60s, and 70s, especially among women. The increasing proportion of younger men involved in writing cultural resource management (CRM) reports is likely tied to the strong representation of private sector employment among younger males.

Different sectors of the archaeological workforce also tend to vary in the formats and forums they typically use to present archaeological information. Academics are much more likely to publish books than are archaeologists in other employment sectors. Private sector archaeologists, not surprisingly, are the most likely to publish their work in the form of CRM reports, producing, on average, an impressive 44 CRM reports over a five-year period. But by no means is the production of CRM reports limited to the private sector. A significant proportion of professional archaeologists in all employment sectors is involved in writing CRM reports. Even in museums, where participation in writing CRM reports is the lowest, over one-third of the museum-based professionals who responded to the Census had produced one or more CRM reports over the past five years. Moreover, despite the apparent preference of students for careers in academia, and the disjunction between student research interests and those of professionals in the private sector, half of the student respondents had written CRM reports, producing an average of about two reports per year. In the area of oral presentations, government and museum-based archaeologists are more active in presenting archaeological research to the general public than are archaeologists in other employment sectors. On the other hand, academic and museum-based archaeologists are much more likely to present papers at SAA annual meetings than are either government or private sector archaeologists.

The greater involvement of academics in the Society for American Archaeology becomes even more apparent when we look at the participation of archaeologists in different professional organizations. The proportion of academic respondents who have been involved in SAA committee work or who have served on the SAA Executive Board is significantly higher than the overall proportion of academics in the respondent pool as a whole. Academics are also more likely to name the SAA as their preferred organization than are archaeologists employed in other work settings. In contrast, government and private sector archaeologists are more likely to join and actively participate in regional and state-level archaeological organizations. They also tend to feel these kinds of organizations better meet their needs and interests than other professional organizations, including the SAA. Once again these data echo earlier patterns that indicate a marked divergence in the activities, interests, and professional concerns of private and public sector archaeologists when contrasted to archaeologists in academia.

A sampling of respondent comments on policy issues highlights a high level of interest in promoting public education that cuts across both gender and workplace differences. There is some variation, however, in the emphasis different archaeologists place on other prominent policy issues like archaeological legislation, relations with Native American groups, archaeological preservation, the status of women and minorities, and archaeological ethics.

Publications and Oral Presentations

Measuring Productivity in Publications and Oral Presentations

Census respondents were asked to record the number of written and oral presentations they have completed in the last five years (Appendix). Publications were classified as either books, book chapters and journal articles, CRM reports, or "other" publications. Oral presentations were classified as papers presented at SAA or other professional meetings. Respondents were also asked to report the number of presentations they had given to the general public over the past five years.

These data are summarized in two different ways: as the relative number of people who have presented archaeological research in a certain way, and as the average number of books, articles, reports, or oral presentations produced over a five-year period. Proportional data are computed by dividing the number of respondents who have produced at least one example of a certain type of publication or oral presentation over five years by the total number of Census respondents in a certain constituent group. Thus when, in one of the graphs presented below, the bar labeled "Articles" reaches 80 percent, it means that 80 percent of the people in this group (for example, women, students, or academics) published one or more articles in a journal or in an edited volume over five years, *not* that 80 percent of the publications produced by this group were journal articles or book chapters. Since people engage in multiple formats of presentation, for any group examined the proportional data in the graphs below will usually total more than 100 percent.

Volume is measured by computing the average number of publications or oral presentations of a particular kind that have been completed by a group of archaeologists over a five-year period. Averages are based on the number of respondents who participated in a specific form of presentation, rather than on the total number of Census respondents in a specific category of people. Thus when it is reported that students published an average of 9.7 CRM reports over a five-year period, it means that those students who wrote CRM reports produced an average of 9.7 reports over five years, *not* that the pool of student respondents to the Census as a whole averaged 9.7 CRM reports during this period.

Finally, I have also included a category for those who did not report any publications or oral presentations. There is some ambiguity here. Failure to respond to this portion of the Census does not necessarily mean that an individual did not produce any written or oral presentations over the five years prior to the implementation of the Census in 1994. Instead, it may mean that the respondent did not want to take the time to count publications and presentations in this way. However, as we will see below, patterning in the data suggests that a significant proportion of the people who failed to respond to these questions did so because they had nothing to report. Thus while the actual proportion of people with no publications or oral presentations is likely lower than reported here, general patterning among nonresponders probably reflects real conditions.

Gender and Age Trends in Productivity

One of the more unexpected patterns found in the Census data, and one of the most difficult to explain, is the clear tendency for women to be less actively engaged than men in producing publications and oral presentations of archaeological research.

Publications Turning first to publications, even when we limit the pool of respondents to professional archaeologists, the publication record of women is significantly different from that of men (Figure 6.1a; χ^2=28.213, df=4, p<.001). Proportionately fewer women produced publications in each of the four different publication categories than men over the five years preceding the Census. The disparity between the publication records of men and women is especially great in the categories of books and articles, but is also clear in the publication of CRM reports, and, to a much lesser extent, in other publications. Moreover, nearly 15 percent of professional women respondents did not record any publications, compared to only 8 percent of the men. As discussed above, this figure does not necessarily indicate that a full 15 percent of women respondents had no publications over the five years that preceded the Census. However, the fact that consistently fewer women have published books, articles, CRM reports, and other publications than men, combined with a relatively high proportion of professional women with no recorded publications, suggests that women are significantly less active in archaeological publication than men.

There is more variability in the average number of publications produced by men and women (Figure 6.1b). Although men are more likely than women to write books, women who engage in this form of publication produce on average the same number of books as men. In contrast, not only do proportionately more men write journal articles and book chapters than women, they also seem to produce more articles per capita. Men who produced article-length publications averaged 7.5 articles over five years, compared to an average of 5.4 articles per female respondent. Although proportionately fewer women have written CRM reports over this period, those who have produced these reports tend to produce slightly more of them than men. Finally, men have produced a slightly higher volume of other publications than women.

Since women professionals tend to be somewhat younger than men, perhaps the discrepancy between the publication rates of men and women in the aggregate data is a function of age rather than gender-based differences in publication productivity. Yet looking at publication data by age and gender (Figure 6.2), the patterns noted in the aggregate population of professional archaeologists remain fairly constant across all age cohorts. The proportion of men who have written books is consistently higher than the proportion of women book authors in all age cohorts, but the large disparity between older male and female authors narrows considerably among archaeologists in their 20s and 30s (Figure 6.2a). The volume of books published by men and women is variable in different cohorts (Figure 6.2b). In all cohorts (except for the small group of nonstudents in their 20s) the proportion of male professionals who publish articles in journals and edited volumes is greater than that of women (Figure 6.2c). As with books, the gap between the proportion of men compared to women who have written articles decreases in

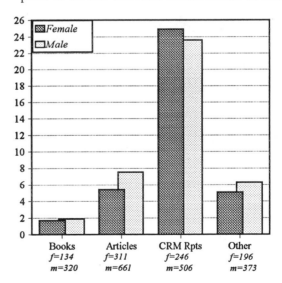

Fig. 6.1 *Publication Productivity by Gender*

a Proportions of men and women who have produced different types of publications, including proportions with no reported publications

b Average number of publications in each publication category for men and women with at least one publication in that category

Note the higher productivity of men in all categories in terms of both the proportions who publish and the volume of publications. Note also the higher proportion of women with no reported publications.

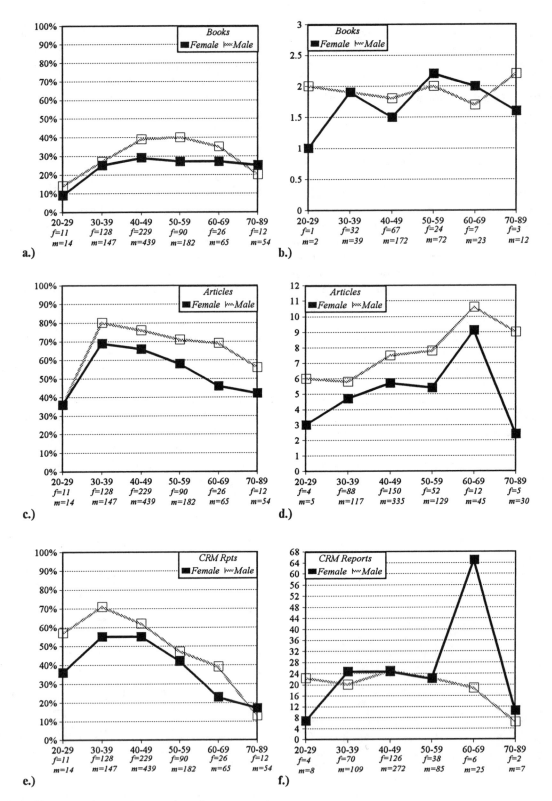

Fig. 6.2 *Publication Productivity by Age and Gender*

a Proportions publishing one or more books

b Average number of books published

c Proportions publishing one or more articles

d Average number of articles published

e Proportions publishing one or more CRM reports

f Average number of CRM reports published

Note that in general men have higher publishing productivity in all cohorts than women, especially in the publication of articles in journals and edited volumes. Note also the high proportion of younger men engaged in writing CRM reports.

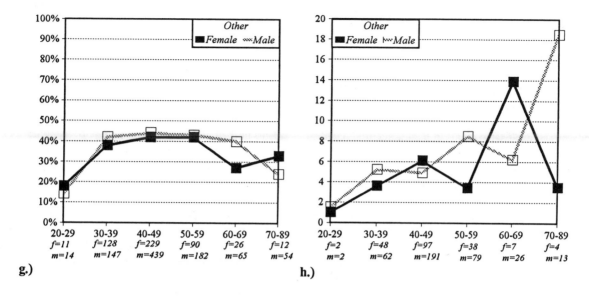

g.)   h.)

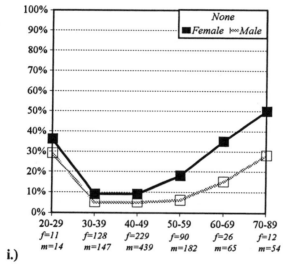

i.)

Fig. 6.2 *Publication Productivity by Age and Gender (continued)*
g Proportions publishing one or more other publications   **h** Average number of other publications published
i Proportions with no reported publications

younger cohorts. Even so, there is still a 10 percent difference between the proportions of men and women in their 30s who had written one or more articles in the five years preceding the Census. Moreover, the volume of articles published by men is also markedly higher in all cohorts (Figure 6.2d).

It is also interesting to note that the proportion of professional men and women engaged in writing article-length publications peaks in the 30–39 age cohort, and then falls steadily in each older age group, especially among women (Figure 6.2c). However, the number of articles per capita steadily increases among the smaller pool of older archaeologists who are still publishing journal articles and book chapters (Figure 6.2d). The proportion of archaeologists writing books peaks somewhat later, for women in the 40–49 year old cohort and for men in the 50–59 year old cohort, remaining fairly constant among older cohorts of women, and falling slightly among older men (Figure 6.2a). The average volume of books published among the larger, and thus statistically more reliable, cohorts peaks for both men and women in the 50–59 age cohort (Figure 6.2b).

It would seem, then, that younger professionals are more likely to write articles than are older archaeologists, while older archaeologists are more likely to write books than are younger archaeologists. And yet the productivity of both the men and women who are actively publishing books and articles increases with age. Moreover, there is no evidence to suggest that men and women reach peak productivity in publication at different stages of their careers—with younger men, for example, publishing a high volume of material as part of their quest for tenure, and women publishing more after early child-rearing years. Instead, it seems that while the productivity of women is always somewhat lower than that of men, men and women follow generally similar age-related trends in publishing productivity.

The tendency for more men to write CRM reports noted in the aggregate population is also consistent across all cohorts. Yet unlike age-related trends in the publication of books and articles, there is an increase in the disparity between the proportions of younger men and women who have written CRM reports (Figure 6.2e). This pattern can probably be attributed to the increasing proportions of younger men employed in the private sector noted in Chapter 4. With the exception of the high volume of CRM reports produced by the small cohort of women in their 60s (primarily attributable to two women who are CEOs of private firms), and the small output of the four women in their 20s, the volume of CRM reports produced by men and women is quite similar in most cohorts (Figure 6.2f).

Comparing the proportions of men in different cohorts engaged in publishing CRM reports to those engaged in more traditional forms of archaeological publishing helps to highlight the growing importance of this arena of archaeological activity. Seventy-four percent of the men in their 30s have participated in writing CRM reports over a five-year period, only 5 percent fewer than

the proportion of men in this cohort who have written journal articles or book chapters during this time. In contrast, only 46 percent of the men in their 50s have been involved in publishing CRM reports, a full 25 percent less than the proportion of men in their 50s who have recently written at least one or more articles. Similar patterns are seen among women respondents.

For both men and women, the proportion of respondents in their 30s and 40s with no reported publications is quite low, at about 10 percent for women and about 5 percent for men (Figure 6.2i). For both, the proportion without reported publications increases among older cohorts. But this increase is much more pronounced among women than men. Between the cohorts of women in their 40s and 50s, the proportion of women with no reported publications nearly doubles from 10 percent to just under 20 percent. It nearly doubles again to about 35 percent among women in their 60s. Half of the small cohort of women in their 70s and 80s had no reported publications. In contrast, while the proportion of the men who did not report any publications also increases in older cohorts, nearly 75 percent of the men in their 70s and 80s are still actively publishing.

Oral Presentations Data on oral presentations also show significant differences in the productivity of men and women (Figure 6.3; $\chi^2=18.785$, df=3, p<.001). With the exception of presentations given at SAA meetings (where there is greater similarity in the proportions of men and women giving papers and the numbers of papers they pres-

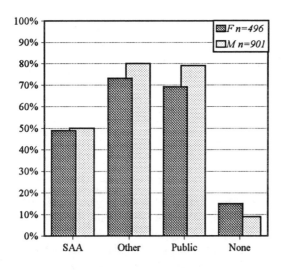
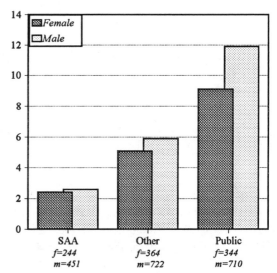

Fig. 6.3 *Productivity in Oral Presentations by Gender*

a Proportions of men and women with different types of oral presentations, including proportions with no reported oral presentations

b Average number of oral presentations in each category for men and women with at least one presentation in that category

Note the higher productivity of men in the presentation of papers at the meetings of non-SAA professional conferences and in public presentations, both in terms of the proportions of men who make oral presentations and the volume of presentations.

ent), proportionately more men than women presented papers at professional meetings of societies and also gave lectures to the general public. Moreover, the volume of oral presentations per capita is generally higher among men than among women, especially in the area of public presentations. As was the case for publications, the proportion of professional women who failed to report any oral presentations, at 15 percent, is considerably higher than the proportion of men with no reported presentations (9 percent).

Once again these patterns remain consistent when the data are examined by age (Figure 6.4). With the exception of the 50–59 year old cohort, both the proportions of men and women who have presented papers at SAA meetings and the average number of papers presented are similar in most of the larger cohorts (Figure 6.4a and b). In all cohorts, however, proportionately more men than women present papers at meetings of other professional societies, and they also generally average a higher number of presentations at these conferences (Figure 6.4c and d). In all of the larger cohorts, more men have given more public lectures than women (Figure 6.4e and f). Finally, the pattern of men and women with no reported oral presentations (Figure 6.4g) echoes that seen earlier for publications. For both men and women, the proportion of nonpresenters drops from about 35 percent of the professionals in their 20s, remains low among 30 and 40 year olds, and then rises among older archaeologists. Once again, the proportion of women with no apparent activity in this area is higher than the proportion of men, though these figures are closer in oral presentations than they are for publications. In terms of general age trends, delivering papers at SAA meetings seems to be particularly common among younger professionals, while proportionately more older archaeologists present papers in other professional settings. Presentation of public lectures is also more common among older archaeologists.

Trends in Productivity by Employment Setting

Archaeologists employed in different work settings differ markedly in the manner of presentation of archaeological research. As has consistently been the case, once again academics, museum professionals, and students share many similarities, while private and public sector archaeologists seem to resemble one another in presentation of research results. Moreover, the lower productivity of women in publication and oral presentation noted above is shown here to cut across all employment sectors.

Publications Publication profiles of archaeologists in academia and museums are statistically indistinguishable (Figure 6.5a, b, e, and f). Over 80 percent of the academic and museum archaeologists have produced at least one article in a five-year period, compared to only 62 percent

in the private sector, and 55 percent in government settings. At the same time proportionately fewer of these archaeologists have written CRM reports than is the case in the public and private sectors. About half of the people employed in academia and museums produce a variety of miscellaneous other publications, again a higher proportion than in either the public or private sectors of archaeological employment. There are some differences between the publication profiles of academics and museum-based archaeologists, however. Not only do proportionately more academics publish books, articles, and CRM reports than museum professionals, but also they tend to publish a higher volume of articles and CRM reports than archaeologists in museums. Moreover, proportionately more museum professionals than academics had no reported publications.

Publication profiles of government and private sector archaeologists are significantly different from those of academic and museum archaeologists at better than the .001 level of probability (academic versus government archaeologists: $\chi^2=89.836$, df=4; academic versus private sector: $\chi^2=101.023$, df=4; museum versus government: $\chi^2=31.428$, df=4; museum versus private sector: $\chi^2=46.222$, df=4). More people write CRM reports in government and, especially, in private sector settings than any other form of publication (Figure 6.5c, d, g, and h). The volume of CRM reports written by archaeologists in these employment sectors is remarkable. Government archaeologists produced an average of 23 CRM reports over five years, and private sector archaeologists an average of 45 reports during this same time. Although these archaeologists are less active in other forms of publication than academics and museum professionals, productivity in these areas is still quite high. A little over 20 percent of the respondents employed in these sectors have written one or more books over five years, and more than half have written articles (62 percent in the case of private sector archaeologists), producing an average of about two books and five articles over five years. Public and private sector archaeologists vary significantly from one another in the greater proportion of private sector archaeologists who have published CRM reports, articles, and books, and the higher proportion of government archaeologists with no reported publications ($\chi^2=18.164$, df=4, p=.001).

It is possible to relate the level of productivity evident in the private sector publication data to the high proportion of consulting archaeologists who regularly engage in writing, noted in Chapter 4 (Figure 4.19d). Just under 90 percent of the private sector archaeologists who responded to the Census write for publication, devoting an average of about one-third of their total work effort to writing. In comparison, only about 65 percent of academics are engaged in writing for publication, spending an average of a little less than one-quarter of their time writing.

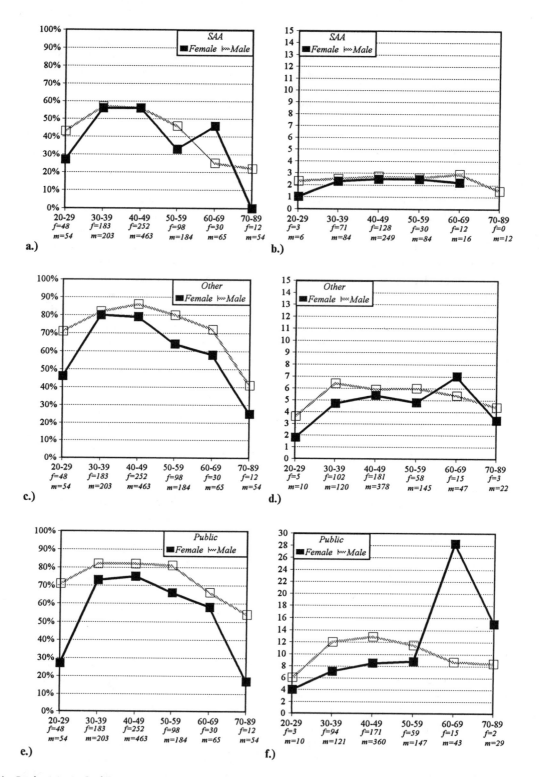

Fig. 6.4 *Productivity in Oral Presentations By Age and Gender*

a Proportions presenting one or more papers at a SAA meeting

b Average number of papers presented at SAA meetings

c Proportions presenting one or more papers at a meeting of another professional society

d Average number of papers presented at the meetings of other professional societies

e Proportions with one or more public presentation

f Average number of public presentations given

Note the persistent tendency for more males to present more papers at the meetings of other professional societies, regardless of age, as well as their higher productivity in public presentations. Note also the similarity in all cohorts in the proportions of men and women who present papers at SAA meetings, and in the volume of papers presented.

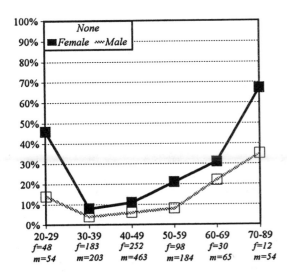

Fig. 6.4 *Productivity in Oral Presentations by Age and Gender (continued)*

g Proportions with no reported oral presentations

As was the case for academic and museum professionals, articles are the dominant form of publication among students (Figure 6.5i and j). However, proportionately more students write CRM reports than either academics or museum-based archaeologists. Half of the student respondents had written one or more CRM reports in five years, producing, on average, just under two reports a year. We saw in Chapter 4 that student respondents were quite focused on pursuing academic careers. And in Chapter 5 we saw that the basic research interests and approaches of students essentially mirrored those of academics, and were starkly different from those of private sector archaeologists. Yet despite these preferences and predilections, it would seem that students are quite actively engaged in consulting archaeology while they are pursuing their academic degrees. Moreover, while fewer professional academics and museum professionals have written CRM reports than is the case for government and private sector archaeologists, the proportion of people in these settings who have written one or more of these reports in the five years that preceded the Census is still quite high (43 percent of the academics and 35 percent of museum professionals). Clearly, active involvement in consulting archaeology and the production of CRM reports cuts across all work settings in American archaeology.

Breaking these data down by gender, it is clear that the lower productivity of women in archaeological publication is found in all employment sectors (Figure 6.6), especially in government and museum settings (Figure 6.6c and e). And while proportional data for men and women are closer in academia and the private sector, academic men are still more likely to publish books and articles than academic women (Figure 6.6a). Moreover, the proportion of private sector men who have recently published journal

articles and book chapters is almost 20 percent greater than the proportion of private sector women who published articles in the five years prior to the Census (Figure 6.6g). Even among students, men are more likely to publish books, articles, and CRM reports than women, while women are more likely to have no reported publications (Figure 6.6i). And though there is more variability in the volume of publications of men and women in different settings (in particular in the publication of CRM reports in government and museum settings), in all employment sectors men still tend to average a slightly higher volume of most publication formats.

Once again these data complement data collected on the activities of men and women employed in different work settings, which show that in all employment sectors proportionately more men are engaged in writing publications than women (Figure 6.7a). The similarity in the amount of work effort men and women devote to writing in these different settings (Figure 6.7b) may explain the greater similarity in the number of publications men and women produce. However, it does not seem to result in similar productivity in writing articles, where women consistently lag behind men in all professional settings.

• No matter how the data are partitioned, by age or by work setting, there is a consistent pattern of higher male productivity. The reasons for this difference are not clear. Even Oliver Stone would find it difficult to argue for the existence of a general conspiracy against the publication of manuscripts submitted by women hatched by a wide range of publishers, journal editors, and peer reviewers. It would be equally difficult to accept facile arguments that attribute this pattern to inherent gender-based differences in motivation, ability, and ambition. We do have some indication that men and women tend to occupy different levels of positions within different work settings. In academia a higher proportion of women are in nontenure track visiting or adjunct professor positions, and proportionately more women are assistant professors, while more men occupy full professor positions. In museums the marked salary differentials between men and women suggest that they occupy very different rungs of the museum career ladder. Moreover, activity data show that while 63 percent of male museum professionals write for publication, only 46 percent of museum women do so, the largest disparity between men and women seen in any employment setting. In fact, museum women are less likely to spend time writing for publication than any other group of archaeologists, including students. In government, where salaries of men and women are more equal, there is still some differential in pay scales that suggests that men and women occupy different types of positions. And while there is more gender parity in private sector positions than seen in academia (and while both men and women in the private sector are very active in producing CRM reports), the

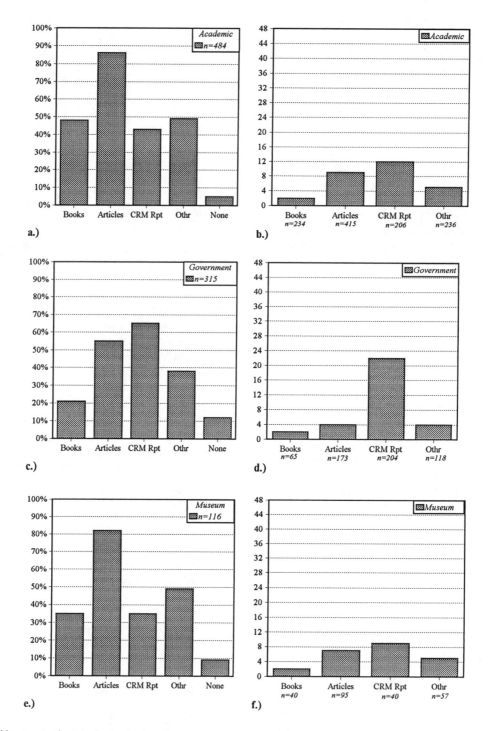

Fig. 6.5 *Publication Productivity by Employment Sector*

a Proportion of professional academics with different types of publications

c Proportion of government archaeologists with different types of publications

e Proportion of museum professionals with different types of publications

b Average number of publications of academics

d Average number of publications of government archaeologists

f Average number of publications of museum professionals

Note the high proportion of academics and museum professionals who publish articles in journals and edited volumes, and of academics who write books. Note also the high proportions of public and private sector archaeologists who write CRM reports, and the very high volume of reports produced, especially in the private sector. But also note that a significant number of archaeologists employed in other sectors, also produce a fairly high volume of CRM reports, especially students.

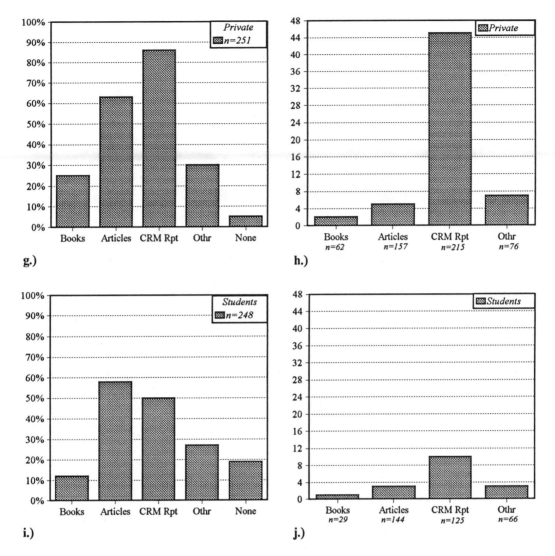

Fig. 6.5 *Publication Productivity by Employment Sector* (*continued*)

g Proportion of private sector archaeologists with different
   types of publications
i Proportion of students with different types of publications

h Average number of publications of private sector
   archaeologists
j Average number of publications of students

salary differentials between private sector men and women suggest some difference in the scope of positions that may afford private sector males more opportunity or responsibility to produce books and journal articles than private sector women. In the student population, the older average age of female students (Figure 2.2) and the slightly greater tendency for male students to spend the balance of their time in academic settings (Figure 4.14) may also mean that women students may be more likely to work outside of academia, and therefore have less time to write for publication. Thus it is possible that the general tendency for women to be less active then men in publication might, at least in part, be linked to a somewhat greater tendency for women in all settings to occupy positions

either that do not include a writing component or that allow less time for this activity. Clearly, a follow-up survey targeted at exploring the nature of these gender-based differences in publication productivity—and, in particular, at isolating their root causes—is needed to understand this clearly gender-based pattern. •

Oral Presentations The profile of oral presentations of archaeologists in different work sectors also shows a high degree of similarity between academics and museum professionals, on the one hand, and, on the other, a tendency for government and private sector archaeologists to resemble one another (Figure 6.8). In particular, both academics and museum professionals are much more likely to present

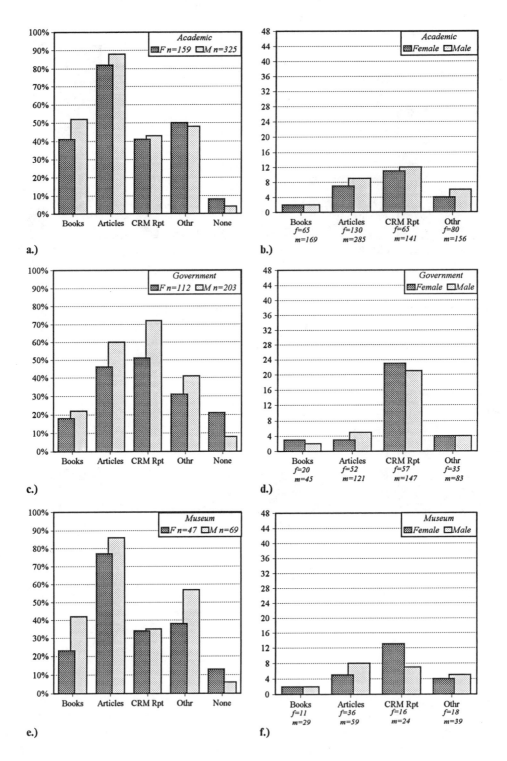

Fig. 6.6 *Publication Productivity by Employment Sector and Gender*

a Proportion of male and female professional academics with different types of publications

b Average number of publications of male and female professional academics

c Proportion of male and female government archaeologists with different types of publications

d Average number of publications of male and female government archaeologists

e Proportion of male and female museum professionals with different types of publications

f Average number of publications of male and female museum professionals

Note that males have higher publishing productivity in all employment categories, including students, but especially in government and museum settings. Note also that in all settings more men publish more articles than women.

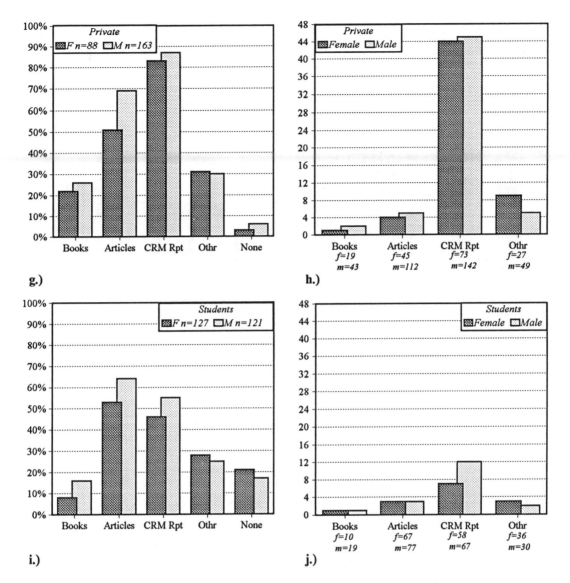

g.)

h.)

i.)

j.)

Fig. 6.6 *Publication Productivity by Employment Sector and Gender (continued)*

g Proportion of male and female private sector archaeologists with different types of publications

i Proportion of male and female students with different types of publications

h Average number of publications of male and female private sector archaeologists

j Average number of publications of male and female students

papers at SAA meetings than are either government or private sector archaeologists. Nearly 70 percent of academic professionals, and just under 60 percent of museum professionals, presented papers at SAA annual meetings, in both cases averaging just under three papers over a five-year period (Figure 6.8a, b, e, and f). In contrast, only 35 percent of both government and private sector archaeologists presented papers at SAA meetings over five years, with an average of two papers during this period (Figure 6.8c, d, g, and h). Academic and museum archaeologists are also more likely to present papers at the meetings of other professional societies; however, here the disparity between academic and museum archaeologists and archaeologists employed in the

public and private sectors is much less than it is for the presentation of papers at SAA meetings.

Also noteworthy is the high proportion of people who present public lectures in all four employment sectors: nearly 80 percent in academia, government, and museums, and just under 70 percent in the private sector. There is a great deal of variability, however, in the volume of public presentations given in different settings. Museum professionals have the highest volume of public presentations, followed by government archaeologists (Figure 6.8d and f). These results are not unexpected, because public education is a prominent component of the basic missions of both employment sectors. In contrast, the average

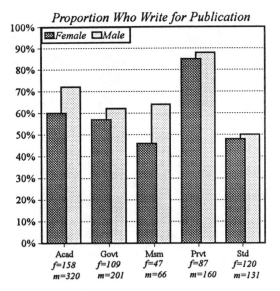

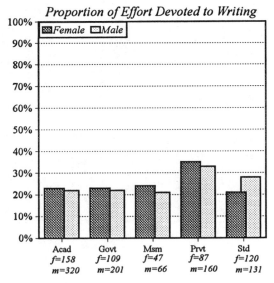

Fig. 6.7 *Involvement in Writing for Publication by Men and Women in Different Employment Sectors*

a Proportion of men and women who write for publication in various work settings

b Percentage of total effort spent writing for publication

Note that in all settings, but especially in academia and museums, proportionately more men regularly write for publication than women. Note also, however, that those women who do write devote about the same amount of their total effort to this activity as men.

number of public presentations given by academics and private sector archaeologists are, by comparison, both quite low (Figure 6.8b and h).

While the proportions of students involved in making oral presentations is lower than for professional archaeologists, the types of oral presentations that students commonly give are generally more similar to those of academics and museum professionals. Specifically, the proportion of students who have presented papers at SAA meetings, relative to the proportion who have read papers at meetings of other professional societies, is more similar to academics and museum professionals than to public and private sector archaeologists. The relatively depressed number of students who gave papers at annual meetings is a bit surprising, however, especially the low proportion of students who had presented a paper at an SAA meeting. Since the student respondents were generally nearing the end of their graduate studies, and since previewing one's work at an SAA meeting is a proven way to promote oneself in the academic job market, student participation in SAA meetings might have been expected to have been somewhat higher. In contrast, the participation of students in public presentations is somewhat higher than expected. More than half of the student respondents reported having made presentations to the public, averaging about one public presentation per year.

Turning briefly to the breakdown of oral presentations by gender (Figure 6.9), as was the case in publication, women in all sectors of archaeological employment tend to present fewer papers in all different venues than men. Once again, this pattern is most strongly expressed in gov-

ernment and museum settings (Figure 6.9c, d, e, f), but is also evident in academia (Figure 6.9a and b), in the private sector (Figure 6.9g and h), and even among students (Figure 6.9i and j).

Professional Activities

Measuring Professional Activities

The Census also contained a series of questions seeking information about participation in professional organizations (Appendix). Respondents were asked to record information about the different types of organizations to which they belonged, ranging from professional organizations with a national or international scope (such as SAA, American Anthropological Association, Society for Historical Archaeology, or the International Union of Prehistoric and Protohistoric Sciences), to regional organizations (Southeastern Archaeological Conference, Plains Conference, and the like), state and local organizations (for instance, state historical or archaeological societies), and nonarchaeological organizations (such as the Geological Society of America). They were also asked to name the one organization that they felt best represented their interests and needs. Participation in the governing bodies of different professional organizations was measured in a series of questions asking if respondents had served on committees or executive boards of various different types of organizations. Respondents were not explicitly queried about the various policy issues that professional organizations might focus on (for example, legislation, professional ethics, and so on), since a follow-up survey was planned that would

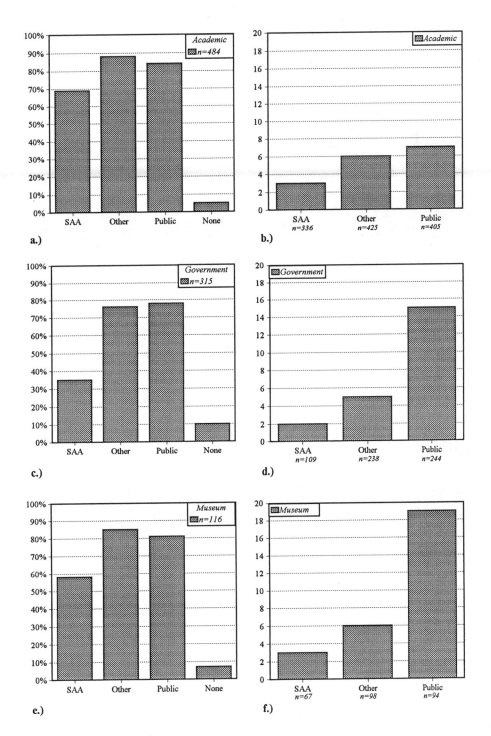

Fig. 6.8 *Productivity in Oral Presentations by Employment Sector*

a Proportion of professional academics with different types of oral presentations

c Proportion of government archaeologists with different types of oral presentations

e Proportion of museum professionals with different types of oral presentations

b Average number of oral presentations of professional academics

d Average number of oral presentations of government archaeologists

f Average number of oral presentations of museum professionals

Note the higher proportion of academics and museum professionals who present papers at SAA meetings, and the higher proportion of public and private sector archaeologists who present papers at the meetings of other professional societies. Note also the high proportion of archaeologists who give public presentations, and the especially high volume of public presentations given by museum and government archaeologists.

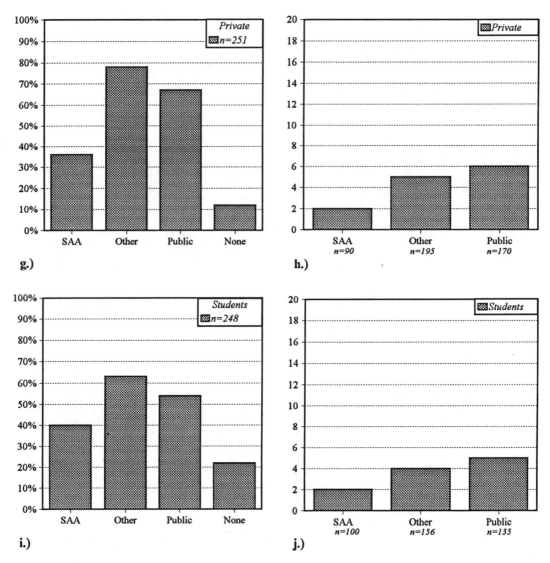

Fig. 6.8 *Productivity in Oral Presentations by Employment Sector (continued)*

g Proportion of private sector archaeologists with different types of oral presentations

i Proportion of students with different types of oral presentations

h Average number of oral presentations of private sector archaeologists

j Average number of oral presentations of students

focus on these types of issues. Respondents *were* asked, however, to comment on the issues they felt should be addressed in this follow-up survey. And while respondents were queried specifically about the policy issues they felt the SAA should concentrate on, their comments give us insight into the range of issues they feel should be addressed by professional organizations in general.

Involvement in Professional Organizations

Gender-Related Trends Men and women show little variation in their participation in professional organizations, as Figure 6.10 illustrates. Over 95 percent of both

men and women belong to at least one national or international professional organization—a result that is hardly surprising, since 90 percent of Census respondents were members of the SAA. State and local organizations are the next best represented among respondents; about 70 percent of all men and women are members of one or more state/local archaeological organizations. Men, however, are more likely to join these organizations than women. The level of participation of men and women in one or more regional archaeological organizations and nonarchaeological organizations is about the same, with around 50 percent of both men and women holding membership in one or more of these types of organizations. There is, however,

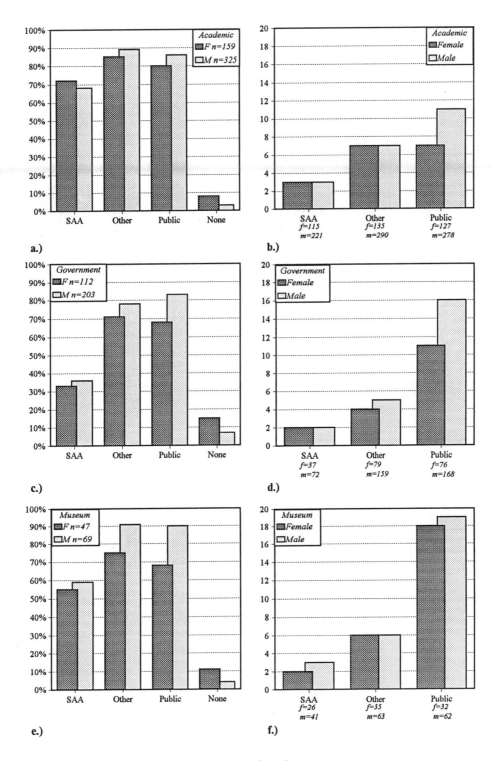

Fig. 6.9 *Productivity in Oral Presentations by Employment Sector and Gender*

a Proportion of male and female professional academics with different types of oral presentations

b Average number of oral presentations of male and female professional academics

c Proportion of male and female government archaeologists with different types of oral presentations

d Average number of oral presentations of male and female government archaeologists

e Proportion of male and female museum professionals with different types of oral presentations

f Average number of presentations of male and female museum professionals

Note that males are more active in presenting papers at professional meetings (including the SAA) and in giving public lectures regardless of work setting, including students, but that this pattern is most strongly expressed in government and museum settings.

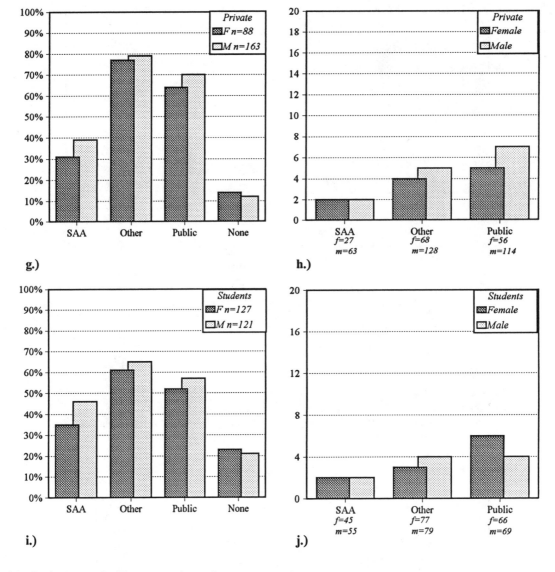

Fig. 6.9 *Productivity in Oral Presentations by Employment Sector and Gender (continued)*

g Proportion of male and female private sector archaeologists with different types of oral presentations

i Proportion of male and female students with different types of oral presentations

h Average number of oral presentations of male and female private sector archaeologists

j Average number of oral presentations of male and female students

a slightly greater tendency for men to join regional organizations than women.

Figure 6.11 displays compositional data on the proportions of men and women in the memberships (Figure 6.11a), committees (Figure 6.11b), and executive boards (Figure 6.11c) of various organizations. In each case the proportion of women in these different bodies is compared to the proportion of women in the Census respondent pool as a whole (the hatched line running through each graph). Since the majority of the respondents to the survey are SAA members, this bar most directly reflects the proportion of women in the membership of the SAA. However, the 38 percent representation of women in the

pool of student and professional respondents to the SAA Census is the same as the representation of women in other archaeological survey efforts (for example, women also comprised 38 percent of the respondents to the SHA survey) (Wall and Rothschild 1995: 24), and is, thus, probably a good estimate of the overall representation of women in American archaeology as a whole. Data on the gender composition of SAA executive boards over the past 25 years are presented in Figure 6.11d for comparison to Census data on SAA executive board composition.

The composition of the membership of different professional organizations is quite consistent and very close to the proportions of men and women in the Census

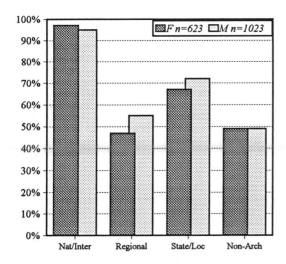

Fig. 6.10 *Proportions of Men and Women Who Belong to Different Types of Professional Organizations*

Note the general similarity in the types of organizations men and women join, but note that men seem to join regional and state organizations at a slightly higher rate than women.

respondent pool (Figure 6.11a). Only in regional organizations are women somewhat less well represented than they are in the general pool of Census respondents, but this difference is only weakly significant at the .075 level of probability (χ^2=3.181, df=1). Representation of women on the committees of various professional organizations is generally lower than their representation in the general respondent pool (Figure 6.11b), but only in the larger sample of respondents who have served on committees in regional and state organizations is this difference significant (χ^2=6.198, df=1, p=.013). The gender composition of executive boards of all organizations examined (apart from the SAA) shows little difference from the composition of committees, with women making up more than 33 percent of the boards of national, regional, and nonarchaeological professional organizations. Census data indicating that women have comprised less than 20 percent of SAA executive boards are misleading, and are not representative of the actual composition of SAA boards over the past 25 years (Figure 6.11d). Instead, data from SAA records indicate that the proportion of women on SAA boards from 1970 to 1995 is about 32 percent, essentially identical to Census data for other professional organizations. In fact, partitioning these data by decade, it would seem that over time the proportion of women on SAA executive boards has closely followed the proportion of women in the archaeological workforce (see Figure 2.4), especially in academic archaeology (Figure 4.6). Thus while the proportional representation of women in the governing bodies of professional organizations is a bit depressed relative to their representation in the membership of these organizations, the underrepresentation of

women in these areas is only very slight, and is consistent across essentially all professional organizations. Moreover, at least for the SAA, representation of women in the policy-setting and governing bodies in professional organizations has kept pace with the increasing proportion of women in the archaeological workforce.

Men and women *do* show significant differences in the organizations they believe best represent their interests and needs (Figure 6.12: χ^2=11.594, df=3, p=.009). While the SAA is the preferred choice of most men and women respondents, proportionally more men than women chose the SAA as their preferred organization. Moreover, proportionately more men than women named either a state or a regional organization as their preferred organization. Women, on the other hand, were more likely to name some other national or international organization as the one that best represented their interests and their needs.

Trends by Employment Setting There is more variation in the professional activities of archaeologists in different employment sectors. Once again, academics, museum-based archaeologists, and students show the greatest similarity, while government and private sector archaeologists seem more alike (Figure 6.13). National or international archaeological organizations are well represented within all employment sectors, again, at least in part, a reflection of the high proportion of SAA members in the respondent pool. However, state or local organizations are much better represented among government and private sector archaeologists (80 percent or more of whom belong to at least one state or local archaeological organization) than they are in other work settings. Moreover, the proportion of public and private sector archaeologists who hold memberships in state archaeological organizations is much higher than the proportion of these archaeologists who join regional organizations and nonarchaeological societies. In contrast, in other employment sectors the level of participation in these three categories of professional organizations (regional, state, and nonarchaeological) is more even, especially among academics.

We can also measure the professional activities of archaeologists in different employment sectors by computing the proportional representation of each sector in the membership, the committees, and the executive boards of various organizations (Figure 6.14). As was done when looking at gender-based trends in professional activities, compositional data for the membership, committees, and executive boards are compared to the proportional representation of the four primary work settings among Census respondents as a whole. In this case, comparative data are presented as the last bar labeled "Total" in each of the four graphs in this figure. Again, these comparative data should be taken first of all as a direct reflection of the employment composition of the SAA membership, and only less directly as a measure of the proportional representation of

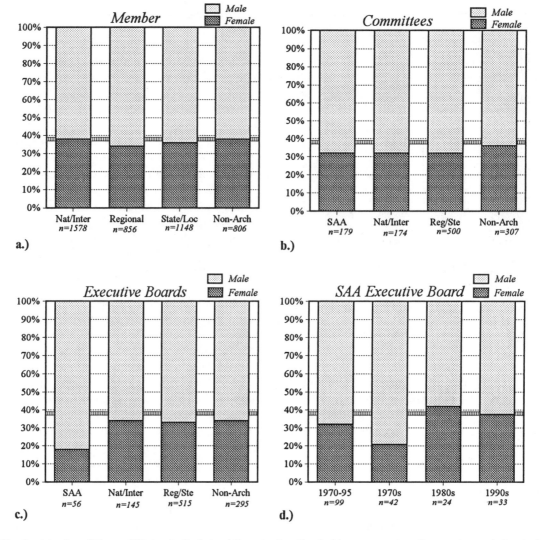

Fig. 6.11 *Participation of Men and Women in Professional Organizations (hatched bar = proportion of women in population, including students and professionals)*

a Proportional representation of men and women in the memberships of various professional organizations

b Proportional representation of men and women on committees in various professional organizations

c Proportional representation of men and women on the executive boards of various professional organizations

d Proportional representation of men and women on SAA executive boards over the past 25 years

Note that the proportional representation of women in the membership, committees, and boards of various organizations (with the exception of Census data for the SAA) is similar to one another, and that the representation of women on committees and boards is only slightly depressed relative to the proportion of women among Census respondents. Note also that actual data on SAA executive board composition shows that the proportion of women on SAA boards over the past 25 years is essentially the same as their representation on the boards of other organizations, and that the representation of women has increased in more recent SAA boards.

archaeologists employed in these different work settings in American archaeology as a whole. As discussed in Chapter 4, academics are probably somewhat overrepresented in the Census respondent pool, while government and private sector archaeologists are likely somewhat underrepresented relative to their actual numbers among American archaeologists. Data on the professional composition of SAA executive boards taken from the roster of

SAA board members for the past 25 years are also included for comparison with Census data (Figure 6.14d).

As might be expected from the profiles of respondent participation in various professional organizations discussed above, only the composition of state and local archaeological organizations varies significantly from the overall composition of Census respondents (Figure 6.14a; χ^2=12.645, df=3, p=.005). Specifically, government and

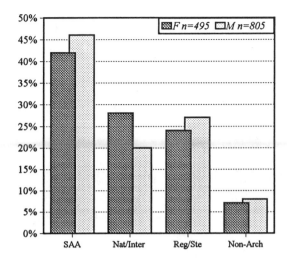

Fig. 6.12 *Preferred Organizations of Men and Women*

Note that proportionately more men name the SAA and various regional or state organizations as the organization that best meets their interests and needs, while women show a greater preference for other national or international organizations

private sector archaeologists are somewhat overrepresented in the membership of these organizations, relative to their representation among Census respondents, while academics are somewhat underrepresented. When we look at the composition of committees (Figure 6.14b), we see that academics tend to be overrepresented in the SAA and other national and international organizations, which in the case of the SAA is significant at the .003 level of probability (χ^2=14.229, df=3). In contrast, the composition of committees in regional and state/local organizations varies significantly from the composition of Census respondents in the strong representation of government archaeologists and in the depressed representation of academics (χ^2=13.619, df=3, p=.003).

These patterns become even more marked when looking at the composition of executive boards (Figure 6.14c). Academics are even better represented in the SAA and other national/international organization boards relative to the Census respondent pool (for the SAA board: χ^2=14.599, df=3, p=.002; for national organizations' boards: χ^2=6.427, df=3, p=.093) than they were in either the general membership or in the standing committees of these organizations. In contrast, government archaeologists are markedly better represented on the executive boards of regional and state/local organizations than they are in the Census respondent pool (χ^2=12.568, df=3, p=.006).

Data collected on composition of SAA executive boards over the past 25 years indicate an even stronger bias toward academics than is evident in the Census data (SAA 1970–95 versus Census respondents: χ^2=27.154, df=3, p<.001). Sixty-seven percent of the members on SAA executive boards from 1970 to 1995 came from academic settings. In contrast, academics make up only 46 percent of the Census

respondent pool. Museum professionals are also overrepresented in the SAA executive boards of the past 25 years relative to their representation in the respondent pool. Private sector, and especially government archaeologists, are noticeably underrepresented. When one considers that academics are likely somewhat overrepresented in the Census respondent pool compared to the actual universe of American archaeology, the bias in favor of academics in past SAA executive boards becomes even more remarkable. Over time, however, the composition of SAA executive boards has changed. Nearly 80 percent of SAA executive board members of the 1970s were academics. In contrast, academics comprise only 58 percent of SAA board members in the 1980s and 1990s. In particular, the representation of government and private sector archaeologists has increased quite a bit in the SAA executive boards of the 1990s when compared to earlier decades.

When asked to name the organization that best represented their interests and needs, more than 50 percent of both professional academics and students named the SAA (Figure 6.15a and e). While museum professionals also show a strong preference for the SAA as their primary professional organization, they also cited nonarchaeological organizations more frequently than did professionals in other employment sectors (Figure 6.14b). In contrast, government archaeologists were more likely to name either a regional or a state/local organization as their preferred organization (Figure 6.14b). Among private sector archaeologists the SAA holds only a slight margin over regional and state/local organizations (Figure 6.14d). It is important to remember here that the majority of government and private sector archaeologists who responded to the Census were SAA members and that there is some reason to believe that a large number of private and public sector archaeologists do not belong to the SAA. Thus it seems likely that preference for the SAA is even lower in the actual universe of private and public sector archaeologists.

• Clearly, there are conspicuous differences between archaeologists in different employment sectors in their levels of participation and in their allegiance to different types of professional organizations. In particular, the SAA seems to play a much more important role in the professional activities of academics and museum-based archaeologists than it does for government and private sector archaeologists. Private and public sector archaeologists, on the other hand, are more likely to participate in other professional organizations, both in the presentation of scholarly papers and in their level of participation in the professional activities of these organizations. Organizations with a more focused regional or topical mission, especially state and local archaeological societies, seem to be of greater salience to people in these employment sectors than the SAA or other national or internal professional organizations.

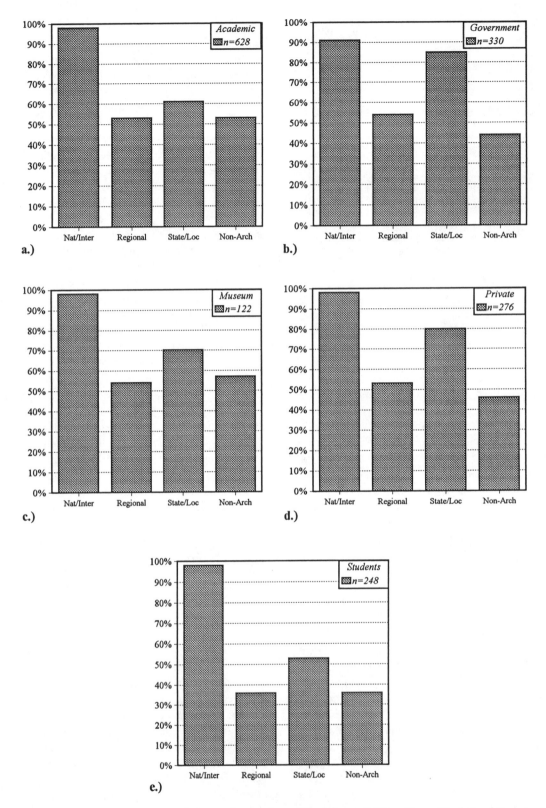

Fig. 6.13 *Proportions of Archaeologists in Different Employment Sectors Who Belong to Different Types of Professional Organizations*

a Academia
b Government
c Museums
d Private sector
e Students

Note the higher proportion of public and private sector archaeologists who join state or local organizations.

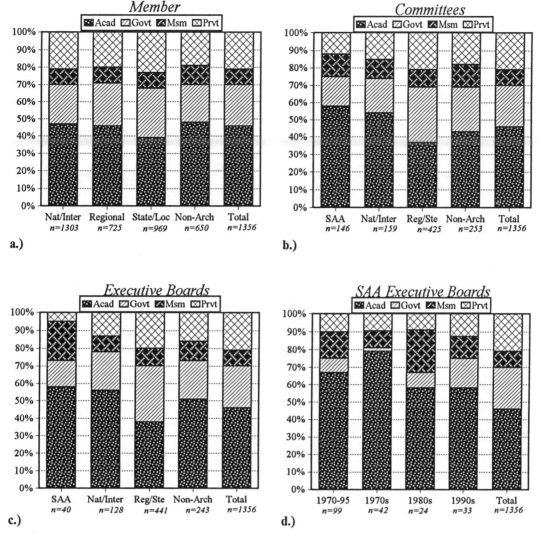

Fig. 6.14 *Participation of Different Employment Sectors in Professional Organizations (final "Total" bar = representation of different employment sectors in the Census population)*

a Proportional representation of different employment sectors in the memberships of various professional organizations

b Proportional representation of different employment sectors on committees in various professional organizations

c Proportional representation of different employment sectors on the executive boards of various professional organizations

d Proportional representation of different employment sectors on SAA executive boards over the past 25 years (taken from SAA records)

Note that academics are overrepresented on the committees and executive boards of the SAA and other national archaeological organizations when compared to the composition of the Census respondent pool, while public and private sector archaeologists are better represented on the committees and boards of regional and state organizations. Note also that SAA records show an even higher representation of academics than Census data, but that over time (and especially in the 1990s) the representation of public and private sector archaeologists on SAA boards has increased.

Respondent comments appended to the Census underscore the depth of feeling of many archaeologists in these two employment sectors about the division between academic versus nonacademic archaeology. About one-third of the respondents in all employment sectors, including students, wrote comments, which ranged from specific remarks about the Census or about the SAA, to concerns about archaeological employment and funding, to policy issues in American archaeology, to general impressions of the current status of American archaeology. Sixty-three percent of the private sector archaeologists who wrote comments expressed their concern over a disjunction between academic archaeology and what many termed "real world" archaeology. Sometimes this concern was expressed in comments that maintained that the SAA represented the interests of academic archaeologists over those of public and

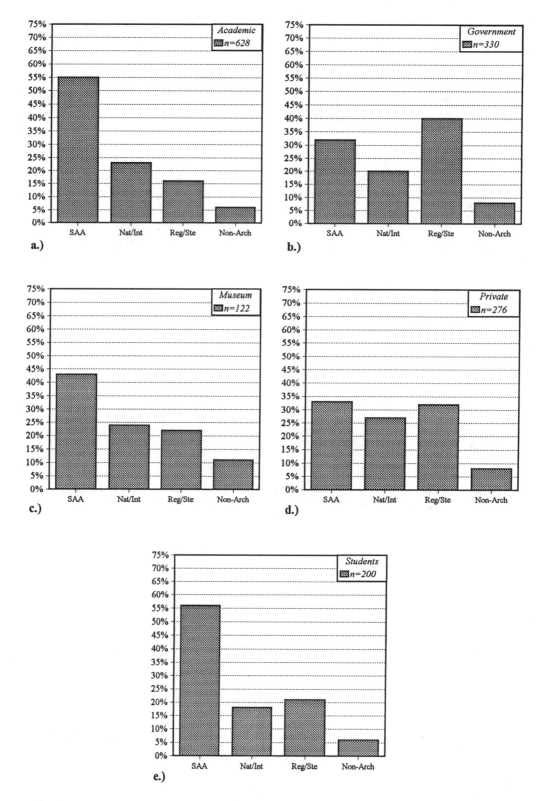

Fig. 6.15 *Preferred Organizations of Different Employment Sectors*

a Academia   b Government
c Museums   d Private sector
e Students

Note that proportionately more academics, museum professionals, and students name the SAA as the organization that best meets their interests and needs, while public and private sector archaeologists show a greater preference for other regional and state organizations.

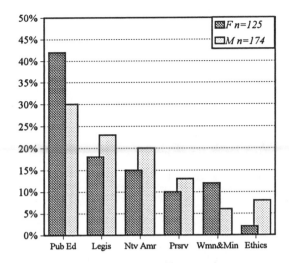

Fig. 6.16 *Policy Issues of Greatest Concern to Men and Women*

Note the high proportion of both men and women who commented on public education in archaeology. Note also, however, that proportionately more women than men commented on public education and on the status of women and minorities, while men seemed more concerned about issues pertaining to archaeological legislation, Native American relations, archaeological preservations, and archaeological ethics.

private sector archaeologists, or that the Census was aimed explicitly at academics and did not "fit" the kind of archaeology they practiced. At other times these respondents wrote more generally about a growing schism between academic archaeology and the archaeology practiced outside of academia. Nearly half of the government archaeologists who responded to this part of the Census voiced similar concerns. In contrast, only 25 percent of academic archaeologists, 23 percent of students, and 32 percent of museum professionals commented on these issues. •

Policy Issues in American Archaeology

Measuring Interest in Policy Issues Respondent comments also provided a window on the policy issues of greatest concern to archaeologists today. Policy concerns raised by respondents consistently centered on six general topics: public education, government legislation affecting archaeology, Native American relations (including repatriation), preservation of archaeological and historic sites and artifacts, the status of women and minorities in archaeology, and archaeological ethics. The frequency with which different groups of archaeologists commented on various policy issues can be taken as a rough measure of the relative importance of these issues among different constituencies.

Gender Trends in Policy Issues For the most part, the policy concerns of men and women respondents are quite

similar (Figure 6.16). For both, public education was the area of greatest concern, followed by legislation, and then relations with Native Americans. However, proportionately more women commented on public education in archaeology, while men were more likely to mention archaeological legislation, Native American relations, and archaeological preservation. Women were more likely than men to comment on the status of women and minorities in archaeology. Men were more likely to comment on archaeological ethics.

Policy Issues by Employment Sector The need for better or more active involvement in public education is also the dominant policy issue when these data are partitioned by employment setting (Figure 6.17). But beyond this generally high level of interest in public education, archaeologists in different work settings placed different emphases on the other five general policy areas. Government archaeologists, predictably, emphasized legislative issues. Comments of private sector archaeologists also frequently focused on archaeological legislation, again perhaps predictably given the link between private sector archaeology and federal and state laws mandating the management of cultural resources. Comments of government archaeologists also frequently raised issues pertaining to Native American relations and the repatriation of Native American skeletal remains and artifacts, as did museum-based professionals. Again this interest is understandable, since archaeologists working in government and museum settings tend to be on the forefront of crafting, implementing, and monitoring federal- and state- mandated repatriation activities (see also Figure 4.19b and c, which indicates a higher degree of participation in repatriation-related activities in these two employment sectors). Museum archaeologists commented more frequently on archaeological preservation than did archaeologists in other employment sectors, though both government and private sector archaeologists tended to raise preservation issues more frequently than academics. Academics, on the other hand, commented more frequently about the status of women and minorities in archaeology than any other group. Finally, archaeological ethics seemed to be more of a concern among private sector archaeologists than archaeologists in other employment sectors. Clearly, these results are only impressionistic and do not represent a scientific polling of the opinions of different archaeological constituencies on these issues. They do, however, help underscore the different perspectives, audiences, and methods of expression of archaeologists in different employment settings that have been evident throughout this discussion of the scholarly productivity and professional activities of American archaeologists today.

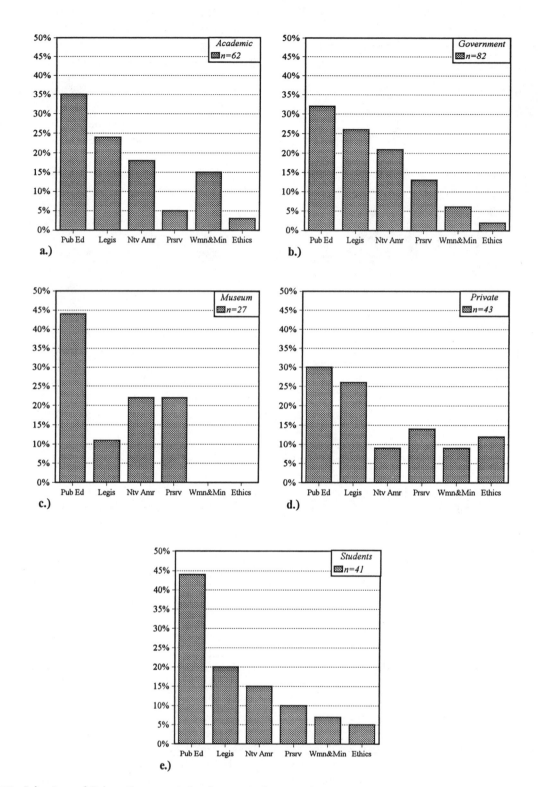

Fig. 6.17 *Policy Issues of Greatest Concern to Archaeologists in Different Employment Sectors*

a Academia   b Government
c Museums   d Private sector
e Students

Note the high level of interest in public education expressed by archaeologists in all settings, including students. Note also the higher interest in legislative issues of government and private sector archaeologists, the interest in Native American relations and repatriation on the part of government archaeologists and museum professionals, the interest in issues relating to the status of women and minorities among academics, and the higher level of interest in archaeological ethics among private sector archaeologists.

7 Paying for American Archaeology

Introduction

Chapter Summary

Archaeology is an expensive undertaking. It takes a lot of money to mount a field operation, pay for field crews, purchase equipment, and support travel to and from the field. With the application of more advanced technology to archaeological research, the costs of archaeological laboratory analysis have also skyrocketed. The specialized studies of archaeological materials responsible for many of the most impressive advances in recent years require highly trained researchers who expect reasonable compensation for their work. Moreover, archaeology is not a self-sustaining business; the products of the profession do not generate the capital required to conduct more archaeology. Although home institutions may underwrite salary support while researchers are engaged in field or laboratory work, and perhaps some of the costs of the archaeological research itself, the primary funding for archaeology must come from external sources. The competition for these funds has become more intense in recent years as the numbers of archaeologists have grown and the sophistication of their methods of analysis has increased. But by far the biggest change in the funding of American archaeology in the last three decades has resulted from the implementation of state and federal legislation mandating the assessment, if not the preservation, of cultural resources affected by development. Compliance with these cultural resource protection laws has fostered an entire new industry of archaeological practice and opened up new sources of both government and private funding that support archaeology on a vastly, perhaps even exponentially, larger scale. Analysis of the sources and allocation of funds that support archaeology, then, gives insight into the lifeline of American archaeology and a better understanding of major trends shaping the profession.

This chapter explores archaeological funding, examining the sources and process of funding, and the allocation of funds to support more traditional archaeological research (termed here non-CRM funding), as well as the funding directed to support the assessment and preservation of cultural resources (CRM, or cultural resource management, funding). As in preceding chapters, variation in funding is examined by both gender and employment sector, bringing our analysis of primary themes in American archaeology to a conclusion with this most critical aspect of the conduct of archaeology in America today. Data presented here show that the proportions of men and women who apply for various sources of funding, the numbers of applications they submit, and their award rates are very comparable to one another, and, at least for non-CRM funding, closely follow the actual proportions of men and women in the archaeological workforce. While the proportion of women who are active in seeking funds for CRM-related activities is depressed relative to their overall representation in the workforce, the success rate of women in this arena is generally somewhat higher than that of the men who apply for these funds.

There is, however, a dramatic imbalance in the proportion of actual funds allocated to men and women from both non-CRM and, especially, from CRM-related sources. In the case of funds directed toward the support of CRM activities, this imbalance is most strongly expressed in the private sector, where, as noted in earlier chapters, the larger firms (which compete for larger projects) are more likely to be directed by men. The causes for the imbalance in the allocation of funds to women in non-CRM-related funding are harder to discern, yet this imbalance can be found in practically all sources of funding, in all age groups, and in most work settings. The disparity between the levels of CRM funding received by men and women is particularly great in academic and museum settings, and, to a lesser extent, in the private sector. Only in government archaeology, which is a relatively small player in the competition for funding, is there equity in the amounts of money men and women receive in support of non-CRM archaeology. Thus, while the proportion of women who apply for non-CRM funds is representative of the proportion of women in the field, and while women are generally just as likely to be successful in their application for funds as men, the amount of funding they receive is substantially, and significantly, less. Until more targeted surveys of archaeological funding are conducted, it will be difficult to tell whether women receive a disproportionately smaller share of archaeological funding for non-CRM activities because they tend to ask for less funds then men at the outset, or whether granting panels tend to favor the smaller requests for funds submitted by women.

Examining funding by employment sector reveals that, not surprisingly, academics and museum-based archaeologists are more active and more successful in the competition for sources of non-CRM funding than government or private sector archaeologists. It is also not unexpected that archaeologists employed in the private sector write more applications for CRM-related funding, have higher success rates, and receive, by far, the lion's share of funds allocated in support of archaeological preservation. However, what may be surprising to many is the extent to which archaeologists in all employment sectors initially enter into the competition for CRM funding. Although private sector archaeologists produce the largest volume of applications per applicant, the proportion of archaeologists from different employment sectors who have sought CRM funding in the past five years directly reflects their representation in the archaeological workforce. And this is true for almost all sources of CRM funding. Thus, while private sector archaeologists may play harder and for higher stakes in the competition for funds to support CRM activities, and while they are vastly more successful in this arena, *all* archaeologists in *all* employment sectors are active players in the game.

The reason for this becomes clear when we look at the amount of money available from these two different pools of archaeological funding. Over a five-year period the 650 respondents to this portion of the Society for American Archaeology Census garnered just over $62 million in support of non-CRM-related archaeology. In contrast, over the same five-year period 302 Census respondents were awarded over $300 million in support of CRM archaeology. Moreover, though they receive the largest share, the private sector is not the sole beneficiary of this huge CRM funding pool. In fact, in all employment sectors the amount of money received in support of CRM-related archaeology is greater that the amount received to support more traditional kinds of non-CRM archaeological research. This is true even in academia, where over the past five years 390 academics reported that they received almost $40 million in non-CRM-related research funds, while 127 academics reported $69 million in support of CRM-related activities.

This chapter also presents data on the types of activities supported by archaeological funding. When comparing the activities for which men and women have received outside funding support, we find no apparent difference between men and women in the proportions who received support for fieldwork, laboratory analysis, or other archaeological activities from either the non-CRM or CRM funding arena. Funding for CRM-related activities tends to be directed toward collections development and archival research more than non-CRM funding, but in general the profiles of activities supported by non-CRM and CRM funding are quite similar. In fact, the types of activities supported by outside funding seem to vary more by

employment sector than by the funding source. Within each of the four different employment sectors (academia, government, museums, and the private sector), both CRM and non-CRM funding supports a characteristic profile of activities, which is distinctive from the profile of activities supported by outside funding in the other three employment sectors. Funding in academia seems to be directed primarily to field and laboratory work, while collections development is better represented in museum funding, and archival research better represented in the funding of work conducted by private and pubic sector archaeologists.

Archaeologists employed in different sectors are also likely to vary in the types of activities that receive home-base institutional support. A uniformly high proportion of archaeologists in all work settings receive institutional support for attending professional meetings. Academic men and women are about equally likely to receive some institutional support for fieldwork and laboratory analysis, while in museums there is a large disparity between men and women in their access to funds to support these activities. Government archaeologists, who tend not to be very active in seeking outside funding, are more likely to receive some institutional support for field and laboratory activities than are archaeologists in other employment sectors. In contrast, private sector archaeologists, who tend to be very active in the pursuit of outside funding, are the least likely to receive corporate support for basic field and laboratory activities.

Measuring Archaeological Funding

Before exploring these patterns in archaeological funding in more depth, however, it is necessary to consider how information on funding was recovered and how it will be presented. The final section of the Census consisted of a series of questions about archaeological funding (Appendix). Respondents were asked to supply information on funding for projects unrelated to cultural resource management (non-CRM archaeology), and for projects that were specifically directed toward the assessment or preservation of cultural resources (CRM archaeology). A number of sources of funding were listed for these two funding arenas. For non-CRM funding, respondents were asked to report information pertaining to predoctoral National Science Foundation (NSF) grants, NSF senior grants, all National Endowment for the Humanities (NEH) grants as a single category, non-CRM support from other federal sources, from state and local funding sources, from university funding pools, from private sources, and from other sources not specified on the list. Categories listed for CRM funding included federal, state, and local sources, as well as funds solicited from universities, from private sources, and from other sources. For each funding source respondents were asked to itemize the number of applications they had submitted over the five years preceding the

Census (1989–1993), the number of awards they received, the number of awards on which they served as primary investigator (PI), and the total amount of money received from this source over five years.

This was the most time-consuming and complex part of the Census, and it was expected that a number of people would skip this section altogether. However, when designing the Census we felt that even if the response rate were low, this level of specificity was needed to draw a meaningful picture of archaeological funding. As it happened, the response rate to these funding questions was higher than expected; 55 percent of the total number of respondents to the Census took the time to provide the detailed information requested here. The response rate of men and women was similar, with 53 percent of the total of 613 female Census respondents replying to this section of the Census and 56 percent of the 1,013 men. As has been the case with other sections of the Census, it is not clear whether failure to respond to this section of the Census indicates a lack of activity in applying for and receiving outside funds, or whether it simply reflects a lack of time or lack of records readily at hand to fill out this lengthy portion of the Census. Accordingly, when proportions of applicants are presented here, they are based on the pool of respondents who provided any information on either CRM or non-CRM funding, *not* on the basis of the overall number of Census respondents.

A note is also needed about how amounts of money received from various sources were reported. Respondents were asked to record the total dollars they received from a source over a five-year period. Since we know the number of awards granted over this period and the total amount received, it was possible to compute the average dollar amount per award. However, the actual amount granted per award was not recorded, thus limiting the level of statistical treatment possible. For example, only the mean amount of awards granted from a single source can be computed, not the median amount, nor the standard deviation of the dollars granted per award. More can be done, however, with the total amount garnered by a particular group of respondents from a source over this five-year period. But even here, the data are also of limited use in some respects. In an attempt to more accurately track the amounts of money individual archaeologists received in support of their archaeological endeavors, respondents were asked to report only the amount of money they received for their own use. In retrospect this was not the best way to elicit this information, and there was some confusion over how to respond to questions about the amounts of funding received. Moreover, there is no guarantee that the same award was not reported by multiple co-PIs, as well as by subcontractors included on larger grants. Therefore, information on the amounts of funding received are examined on a fairly low level of resolution, comparing overall amounts of money received, mean

award amounts, and mean and median amounts received by various respondent groups over a five-year period. No attempt is made, however, to conduct a more rigorous statistical treatment of these data.

The observant reader will notice a disparity between the number of awards reported in graphs comparing relative success rates, and the number of awards cited in graphs reporting amounts of funds allocated per award. This is because around 10 percent of the individuals who provided information on the number of applications submitted and awarded did not provide information on the amounts of money received. Thus while these individuals are included in tabulations of applicants, applications, awards, and PIs, they are excluded from presentations of the amounts of funds received. The reader might also notice that the sums of dollars awarded by individual funding sources within the CRM and non-CRM funding pools are considerably less than the total amounts reported for each of these pools as a whole. For example, the sum of the dollars reported for the nine different sources of non-CRM funding comes to about $49 million, while the total for non-CRM funds reported here equals $59 million. The overall figure for CRM support reported by Census respondents comes to around $300 million, while the sum of dollars reported for individual CRM sources totals $200 million. This is because totals derived from individual funding sources are based only the responses of those who filled in the detailed funding grid. Totals reported for each funding area as a whole represent not only these responses, but also the responses of those who supplied the total amount of funds garnered over this time for various non-CRM and CRM-related activities, without itemizing these awards by funding source.

Gender Trends in Archaeological Funding

Non-CRM Funding Compared to CRM Funding

Figure 7.1 compares funding data for men and women in both the non-CRM and CRM arenas of funding. Looking first at data on the applicants to these two funding pools (Figure 7.1a), it is immediately apparent that many more respondents applied for non-CRM-related funds in the five years preceding the Census than sought funds to support CRM-related activities. It is also clear that the proportions of men and women who applied for non-CRM funding are essentially the same (with women slightly more likely than men to apply for these funds), while men are more likely than women to apply for CRM-related funding. When the average number of applications submitted by men and women to these two general pools of archaeological funding are compared (Figure 7.1b), we see that even though fewer respondents sought CRM-related funding, those who did had a much higher rate of applications per applicant than those who sought funding to support non-CRM-related activities. On average, both

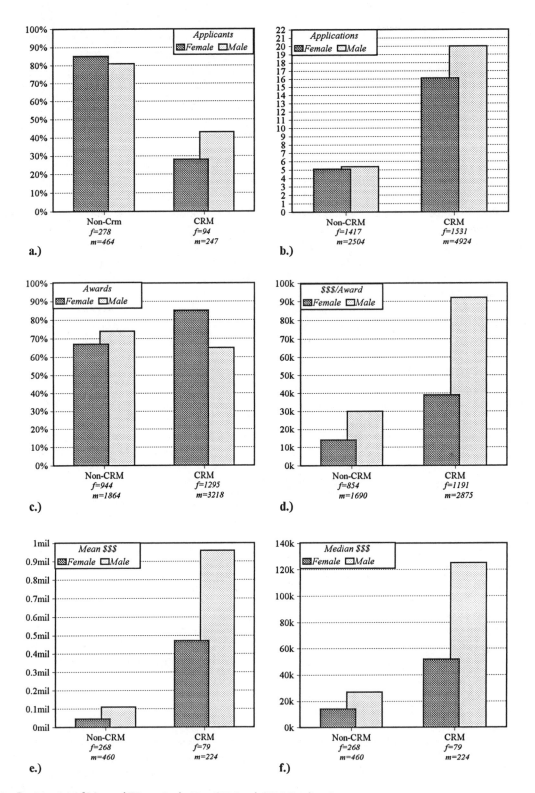

Fig. 7.1 *Participation of Men and Women in the Non-CRM and CRM Funding Arenas*

a Proportion of applicants for non-CRM and CRM funding
c Proportion of applications awarded funding
e Mean dollars awarded

b Applications submitted per applicant
d Average dollars per award
f Median dollars awarded

Note the high proportion of respondents who apply for non-CRM funding, the large number of applications per applicant in the CRM funding arena, and the different success rates of men and women in the two funding arenas. Note, above all, the large disparity in money allocated to men and women in both the non-CRM and CRM funding arenas.

men and women who applied for non-CRM funding over the five years preceding the Census submitted slightly over 5 applications for non-CRM funding (1 per year). In contrast, women applying for CRM funding averaged around 16 applications over this same period, while men averaged around 20 applications per applicant (5 per year). Turning to the proportions of successful submissions (Figure 7.1c), we see that the success of men and women applying for non-CRM funding is quite similar (though men have a slightly higher overall success rate), while in the CRM funding arena the success of applications submitted by women is substantially higher than that of men.

But it is in the allocation of funds that there are the most marked and significant differences between men and women. The final three graphs in Figure 7.1 compare the amount of funds allocated to men and women from these different funding pools. Figure 7.1d presents these data as the average dollars granted per award, Figure 7.1e reports the mean dollars awarded over five years to successful applicants, and Figure 7.1e shows the median dollars awarded to men and women from these two funding pools. Clearly, there is a dramatic difference in the scale of funding received from non-CRM and CRM sources. The average award received by men from CRM sources ($90,000) is three times greater than the average award received by men from non-CRM sources ($30,000). These graphs also highlight large differentials in the levels of funding received by men and women. This is especially the case for CRM funding, where the average successful male

applicant received nearly $1 million over the past five years, while the average woman garnered only half that much.

These data can also be used to track the funding process by comparing the proportions of men and women represented in the applicant pool, in the number of applications submitted, in the awards granted, and in the relative share of the dollars allocated to men and women (Figure 7.2). This comparison allows us to identify places in the funding process where the proportional representation of men and women varies from their representation in the preceding stage of the funding process. For example, a rise in the proportion of women among the pool of successful applications compared to the representation of women in the applicant pool might highlight some preference in the selection of applications that are awarded funding. Comparing these proportions to the overall proportions of men and women in the Census respondent pool (represented by the hatched line running through the figure) also allows us to gauge the level of participation of men and women in various stages of the funding process. If the proportion of men in the applicant pool is lower than the proportion of men in the Census respondent pool, for example, it may signal a lower level of participation of men in the competition for these funds.

When this is done for the non-CRM funding (Figure 7.2a), we see that the proportions of men and women in the applicant pool and in the number of applications submitted resemble one another, and they are both virtually

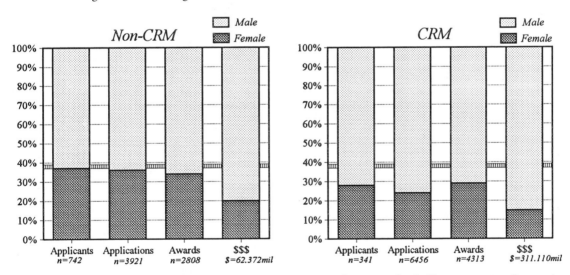

Fig. 7.2 *Funding Process for Men and Women in the Non-CRM and CRM Funding Arenas (hatched bar = proportion of women in population, including students and professionals)*

a Proportions of men and women in the applicant pools, number of applications submitted, awards granted, and money allocated in the non-CRM funding arena

b Proportions of men and women in the applicant pools, number of applications submitted, awards granted, and money allocated in the CRM funding arena

Note that the proportion of women among applicants, applications, and awards is roughly the same as men, but women receive a much lower proportion of the money allocated in both funding arenas. Note also that the proportion of women applying for non-CRM funding is the same as the proportion of women among respondents to this section of the Census, but the representation of women in the CRM funding arena is somewhat depressed.

identical to the proportional representation of men and women among Census respondents. The proportional representation of women in the pool of successful applications is slightly depressed relative to their representation among the applicants and applications, a difference that is significant at the .033 level of probability (χ^2=4.564, df=1). Yet the major disparity comes in share of the total dollar amount awarded to women, which is significantly different from the representation of women among Census respondents—at better than a .001 level of probability (χ^2=316.258, df=1). Women received 34 percent of the 2,808 awards of non-CRM funds reported, but only 20 percent of the total $62 million allocated.

The proportion of women entering the CRM funding arena is significantly lower than the overall proportion of women among Census respondents (Figure 7.2b; χ^2=13.070, df=1, p.<001). Yet women's share of the total number of applications for CRM funds is close to their representation within the CRM applicant pool, and their share of the awards granted is higher than their share of the applications submitted (χ^2=34.476, df=1, p<.001). Again, however, received funds reported by women are markedly depressed relative to their share of the number of awards. Funds reported by women account only for 15 percent of the overall $300 million in CRM funding garnered by Census respondents in the five years preceding the implementation of the Census, compared to their nearly 30 percent share of the awards granted in this funding arena (χ^2=680.739, df=1, p.<001).

Sources of Non-CRM Funding

We can also look more closely at trends within individual sources of non-CRM funding (Figure 7.3). For the most part the proportions of men and women who applied for funds from various sources of non-CRM funding are similar to one another (Figure 7.3a). The major exception to this pattern is seen in the NSF senior archaeology program, to which men seem more likely to apply than women. These results compare well to data supplied by John Yellen, Program Director for Anthropology at the NSF, who reports that over the years 1989 to 1993, 25 percent of the applications for NSF senior grants were submitted by women (Yellen, personal communication, October 1996). Census results indicate that women comprised 27 percent of the applicant pool for NSF senior grants during this same period (see Figure 7.5b). The similarity between the submission rate of men and women for non-CRM funding, seen in the aggregate data (Figure 7.1b), would seem to cut across all sources for non-CRM funding (Figure 7.3b). There is no real difference between men and women in the number of applications they submit to these various sources.

Before we explore trends in the proportions of successful applications submitted by men and women (Figure

7.3c), a note is needed about the reliability of success rates derived from Census data. Data supplied from NSF records suggest that, at least for this source of non-CRM funding, success rates provided by Census data are somewhat high. NSF data for the years 1993 to 1995 report a success rate of 48 percent for predoctoral submissions, somewhat lower than the 55 percent success rate for this category of funding reported by Census respondents. For the senior grants, the difference between success rates reported by NSF data and those of Census respondents is even greater. Over the years 1989 to 1993, NSF data record a success rate of 26 percent for NSF senior grants, while the success rate computed on the basis of Census data over this same period was considerably higher at 42 percent. The reason for the higher Census success rates is not entirely clear. I do not believe this is the result of inaccurate or incomplete recording by Census respondents (that is, that respondents reported only successful attempts to solicit funds and not unfunded applications). A close review of individual responses to this section of the Census indicates that respondents were remarkably thorough in reporting the number of all applications for funding, both successful and unsuccessful. It is possible that Census success rates are higher because successful applicants were more likely to respond to this section of the Census. Or perhaps respondents to the Census in general tended to be more successful in the competition for funds. Whatever the reason, though the proportion of funded submissions reported here is likely somewhat elevated, the comparative success rates of different groups of archaeologists within and between various sources are probably reasonably accurate reflections of real trends.

Success rates of the applications submitted by men and women to various funding sources appear similar, though there is some tendency for the success rates of women to be somewhat lower than those of men in several of the different categories of non-CRM funding (Figure 7.3c). Men and women are essentially equally successful in obtaining NSF senior grants (a trend supported by NSF data), as well as in competing for funds from other federal sources, from local governments, and from universities. In contrast, men seem more likely to be successful in their application for NSF dissertation improvement grants, perhaps owing to the number of male professors who served as the PI of dissertation improvement grants awarded to their student advisees. However, it is interesting to note that NSF data for the years 1993 to 1996 also indicate that male doctoral candidates are more successful in securing dissertation improvement grants (men have a 53 percent acceptance rate over this time compared to a 42 percent rate among women applicants). The apparently greater success of men in securing funds from the NEH is primarily attributable to the high success rate of museum-based male archaeologists, which is 16 percent higher than that of museum women. In comparison, there is only a 7

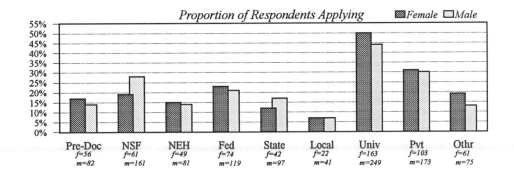

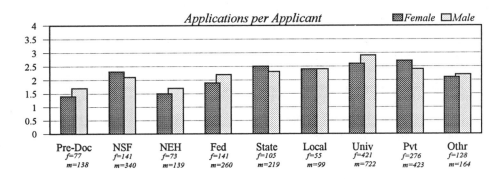

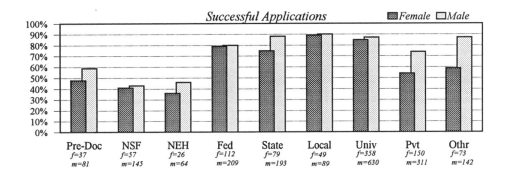

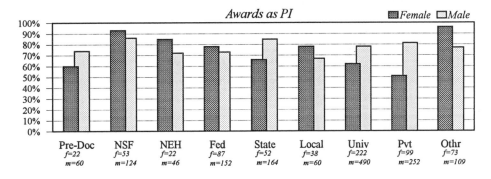

Fig. 7.3 *Participation of Men and Women in the Competition for Various Sources of Non-CRM Funding*

a Proportion of applicants for different sources of non-CRM funding

b Applications submitted per applicant

c Proportion of applications awarded funding

d Proportion of successful applications for which the recipient served as principal investigator (PI)

Note the general similarity between men and women in the application for and award of funds from most sources of non-CRM funding. Note, however, the slight depression in the proportion of female applicants for NSF senior grants, and the somewhat lower rates of success of female applications for funding for NSF dissertation improvement grants and NEH grants, and in applications for funding from state government, private, and other sources.

percent differential in the success of applications submitted to NEH by men and women in academia. The reasons for the higher success rates of men in receiving funds from state governments, private, and other sources are not clear.

For the most part the proportions of men and women who were listed as PIs on successful applications are quite similar, with women a bit more likely than men to serve as PIs on successful NSF senior grants, NEH awards, and awards from other federal and local government sources, as well as from other miscellaneous sources (Figure 7.3d). The higher proportion of male PIs among NSF predoctoral grants is again at least partially attributable to the number of male professors who served as PIs on dissertation improvement grants. Men are also more likely to serve as PIs on grants that receive funds from state, university, and private sources.

The earlier-noted tendency for men to receive more money for non-CRM activities cuts across almost all sources of non-CRM-related funding (Figure 7.4). Given the larger number of male respondents, the total dollar amounts granted to men by various sources over this five-year period are naturally greater than the total amounts allocated to women (Figure 7.4a). Yet the average awards granted to men from most sources are also larger than those awarded to women (Figure 7.4b), and both the mean and the median amounts of money reported by men over this five-year period are, in almost all cases, substantially higher than those reported by women (Figure 7.4c and d).

The large disparity in the amount of NEH funds awarded to men and women is attributable to a few very large awards granted to men in museums, probably as museum improvement grants awarded to (male) museum directors and curators. This imbalance is not seen in NEH awards to academics, where, according to Census data, awards to men and women averaged about $50,000. These data agree with those supplied by Bonnie Magness-Gardiner, former Archaeology Program Director for the NEH, who reports that over the 10-year period from 1985 to 1990, outright awards from the NEH for archaeological research (not counting matching funds or grants to museums) averaged an equivalent $42,000 for both men and women (Magness-Gardiner, personal communication, September 1996).

In contrast, the difference in the size of awards reported by men and women who received NSF senior grants is most pronounced in academia, where, according to Census data, the average amount of money received per award was $66,000 for men, compared to $36,000 for women. While NSF data on the average size of awards granted were not available, data on the average amount *requested* by male and female applicants *were*. For fiscal years 1995 and 1996 the size of the average requests of men and women was essentially equivalent, at about

$150,000 each. The difference in the average $150,000 requested per award reported in the NSF data and the much smaller average NSF awards reported by Census respondents is likely primarily because Census data included not only the funds received by PIs (who probably listed the total amount of dollars granted), but also the much smaller allocations received by individuals included on larger grants. The reasons are less clear, however, for the difference between the Census data, which show a large discrepancy between the size of the average awards reported by men and women respondents, and NSF data, which indicate that the average requests of men and women for NSF funding are essentially equivalent. This disparity does not come about because women are more likely to serve as subcontractors on larger awards. As we have already seen, female respondents were actually more likely than males to serve as PIs on successful NSF senior grant proposals (Figure 7.3d). We also know that there is no difference in the success rates of male and female submissions to NSF (Figure 7.3c), though success rate should have no impact on the observed differential in the sizes of awards men and women receive. Moreover, Yellen reports that NSF rarely cuts the budgets of funded grants much below the level of the original request, and never enough to account for the large disparity in the average NSF awards reported by male and female Census respondents.

It is possible that this discrepancy is due to sampling error. However, it is interesting to note that the total $9 million that Census respondents received from NSF senior archaeology grants over the five years from 1989 to 1993 is not too much less than the $12 million that NSF actually spent on this program over the five fiscal years from 1992 to 1996. Moreover, the NSF senior funds accumulated by Census respondents from 1989 to 1993 represent an average of $1.8 million per year. This is remarkably close to the actual dollar amounts allocated for NSF senior archaeology grants in 1992 and 1993, at $2.04 million and $2.16 million respectively. It seems, then, that the Census captured funding information from a large sample of the successful NSF applicants, and that the patterns seen in the Census data are generally fairly accurate.

If we can rule out differentials in the size of initial requests, success rates, tendency to serve as PIs on grants, postaward budget cuts, and sampling error as factors that contribute to the discrepancy in the size of NSF awards allocated to men and women, we are left with the possibility that there is some systematic differential in the success rates of varying sizes of requests submitted by men and women. Thus, while the dollar amounts initially requested from the NSF by men and women are equivalent, and the share of the total number of awards granted to men and women is proportional to the numbers of proposals they submit, these data suggest that successful proposals

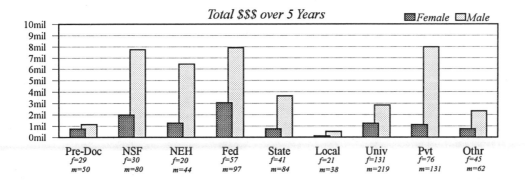

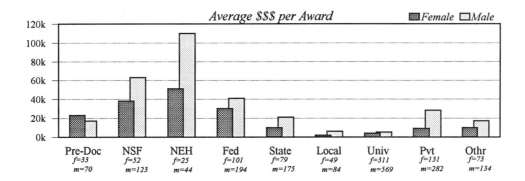

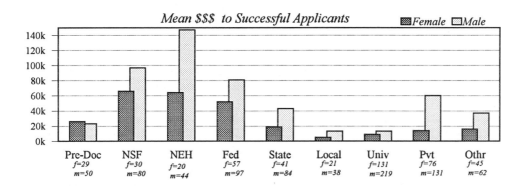

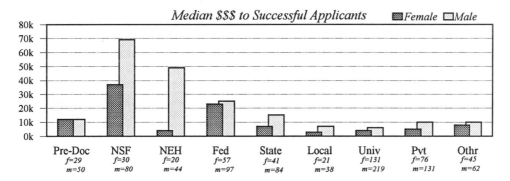

Fig. 7.4 *Comparison of the Funds Allocated to Men and Women from Various Sources of Non-CRM Funding*

a Total dollars awarded by various sources, 1989–1993
b Average value of awards allocated
c Mean amount of money allocated
d Median amount of money allocated

Note that a substantial disparity between the money allocated to men and women is seen in most sources of non-CRM funding, especially NSF senior grants, NEH grants, money from federal and state governments, and private and other sources of non-CRM funding. Note also that median amounts of funding for federal, state, private, and other sources are more similar, signaling that the presence of a few large grants to men in each category raised average allocation values.

submitted by women tend to be those requesting smaller amounts of money, while larger requests submitted by men stand a better chance of receiving funding.

In the case of some of the other sources where there are apparently large differences in the average awards made to men and women and the mean amounts accumulated over five years, the median figures show substantially less difference between men and women (that is, coming from federal, private, and other sources). The difference between mean and median data here reflects the presence of a few exceptionally large awards that have pulled up the average amounts reported. However, that these few larger grants seem to be awarded primarily to men is noteworthy.

Tracking the funding process within various sources of non-CRM support (Figure 7.5) shows that aggregate patterns for non-CRM funding (Figure 7.2a) affect virtually all of the individual sources of these funds. In most cases, women apply for and are awarded grants in direct proportion to their representation within the archaeological workforce (for example, federal funding, local government sources, and university sources; Figure 7.5d, f, and g). In NSF senior grants and grants from state sources, where the female submission rate is somewhat depressed relative to their representation in the workforce, the proportions of awards received by women are close to the representation of women in the applicant pool and among applications submitted (Figure 7.5b and e). Even when women's share in the total number of awards is depressed relative to their share of the applications, as in NSF dissertation improvement grants, NEH grants, and grants from private and other sources (Figure 7.5a, c, h, and i), the difference is only statistically significant for non-CRM funds granted from other sources (χ^2=5.365, df=1, p=.021)

Yet in almost all different non-CRM funding sources, except for NSF dissertation improvement grants, the difference between the proportion of awards granted to women and their share of the total number of dollars is highly significant at better than a .005 level of probability. This is even true of non-CRM funds granted by universities, where the proportion of dollars allocated to women appears more similar to their share of the number of the awards granted (χ^2=11.329, df=1, p=.001).

Sources of CRM Funding

Turning to the sources of funds granted in support of CRM-related activities, the greater tendency for men to apply for CRM funds seen in the aggregate data (Figure 7.1a) is also seen in almost every different source of CRM funding (Figure 7.6a). However, even though in the aggregate CRM data men submitted more applications per applicant (Figure 7.1b), we see here that women tend to have a higher application-to-applicant ratio for most of the primary sources of these funds (Figure 7.6b). The average number of applications per applicant submitted by males

only exceeds that of women in the case of funding from private sources. But since there were more applications submitted to private sources than to any other of the sources of CRM funds (nearly 3,000 applications), the very high activity of men in this arena effectively boosts their overall applications-per-applicant average. The higher success rate of women in the CRM arena evidenced in the aggregate data (Figure 7.1b) is seen here to cut across all sources of CRM funding (Figure 7.6c). Yet, unlike non-CRM grants, where women are generally just as likely as men to serve as PIs, men are listed as PIs on the majority of successful CRM applications in almost all cases (Figure 7.6d). The proportion of grants awarded to women PIs is only equal to that of men in the case of CRM awards from local government sources and from other sources.

But once again it is in the actual allocation of CRM funding that we see the most striking differentials between men and women (Figure 7.7). Men receive a disproportionately large share of the funds allocated by every funding source that supports CRM activities. And this is true whether the data are displayed as the average amount per award, or as the mean or median amount of money garnered over a five-year period. In fact, for most of the bigger funding sources, the disparity between the CRM funds allocated to men and women is even greater when we look at the median data than it is when comparing mean amounts awarded. This indicates that the tendency for men to receive more of the money awarded to CRM-related work, and for women to receive less, applies throughout the population of respondents, and is not simply an artifact of the award of a few exceptionally large grants to a handful of men.

Tracing the funding process within the various sources of CRM funding makes these trends even more apparent (Figure 7.8). While the proportion of women in the applicant pool for virtually all of the different sources of CRM funding is lower than the representation of women in the respondent pool, the representation of women among applications submitted and awards granted is consistent with their level of participation in the application for funds from this source. Indeed, with the exception of private sources of CRM funding, in all other cases the proportion of women among applications and awards shows a substantial increase, indicating a higher level of activity and success in this area of funding. However, in every source of CRM funding the proportional share of the CRM dollars awarded to women is substantially, and highly significantly, less than their share of the total number of successful applications, at better than a .001 level of probability. For example, though women claim an impressive 50+ percent share of the applications and awards for CRM funds granted by universities (Figure 7.8d), they still only received 13 percent of the $3 million awarded by universities for CRM work (χ^2=160.793, df=1, p<.001). Moreover, even in the category of other sources, where

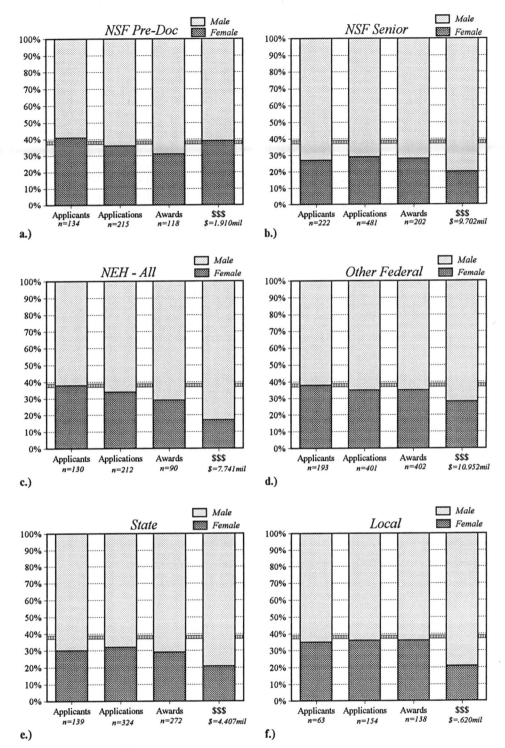

Fig. 7.5 *Funding Process for Men and Women Within Various Sources of Non-CRM Funding (hatched bar = proportion of women in population, including students and professionals)*

a NSF dissertation improvement grants

b NSF senior grants

c NEH grants

d Other federal sources

e State government sources

f Local government sources

Note the general similarity between the representation of women among applicants, applications, and awards, and the generally close match between these proportions and the representation of women among Census respondents. But also note that for all sources, except NSF dissertation improvement grants, the share of the money allocated to women is dramatically less than their share of the total number of awards, as well as their representation among Census respondents as a whole.

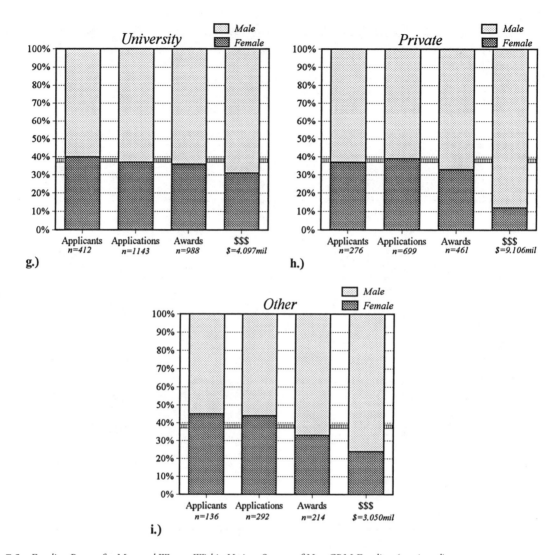

Fig. 7.5 *Funding Process for Men and Women Within Various Sources of Non-CRM Funding (continued)*
g University sources   **h** Private sources
i Other sources

there appears to be less of a disparity between the proportion of the dollars allocated to women and their share of the number of awards, this difference is still statistically highly significant (χ^2=12.713, df=1, p<.001).

The Impact of Age on Gender Trends in Funding

Throughout this study we have seen that age has an important impact on a wide variety of gender trends in American archaeology today. Thus when considering the possible causes for the remarkable disparity between the levels of funding from CRM and non-CRM arenas reported by men and women, the question naturally arises whether these patterns cut across all age cohorts, or whether there is a trend toward increasing equity in funding levels among progressively younger cohorts, similar to

that seen in many other aspects of archaeology today. We can address this question by tracking the non-CRM and CRM funding processes for the four primary age cohorts as it proceeds from applicants to applications, awards, and funding (Figures 7.9 and 7.10). In the case of non-CRM funding, all cohorts show a close match between women's representation in the numbers of applicants, applications, and awards. Among archaeologists in all age cohorts the proportions of women in the funding process closely matches the overall proportion of women in the cohort. However, only in the 50–59 year old cohort is the level of funding women receive consistent with the proportion of awards they are granted. In every other cohort the proportion of non-CRM-related funds allocated to women is significantly less than their share of the number of awards, at a probability level of .001 or better. This imbalance is

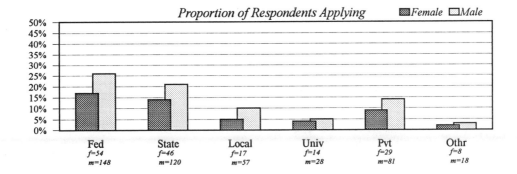

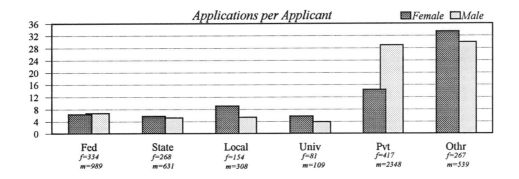

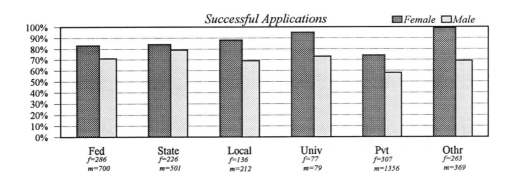

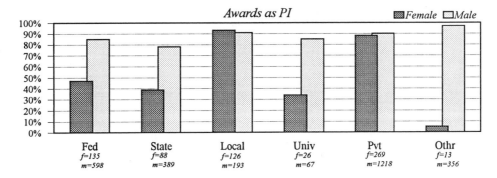

Fig. 7.6 *Participation of Men and Women in the Competition for Various Sources of CRM Funding*

a Proportion of applicants for different sources of CRM funding

b Applications submitted per applicant

c Proportion of applications awarded funding

d Proportion of successful applications for which the recipient served as principal investigator (PI)

Note that men are more likely to apply for all sources of CRM funding, but women submit more applications per applicant in all cases except private sources. Note also that female success rates are higher in all cases, but women are less likely to serve as the PI of successful applications granted by almost all sources of CRM funding.

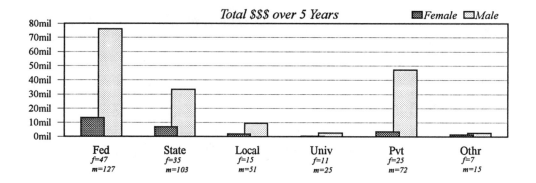

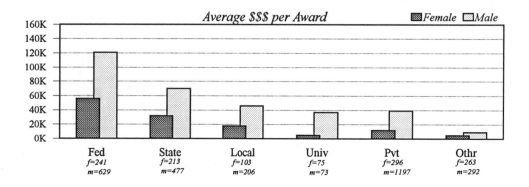

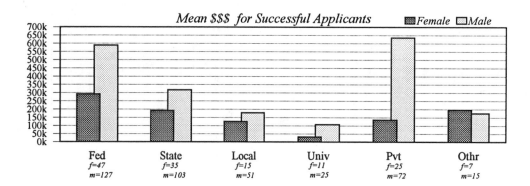

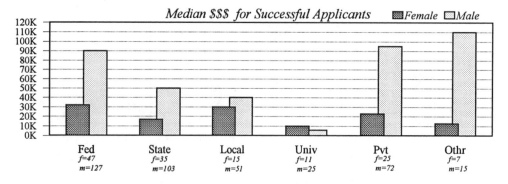

Fig. 7.7 *Comparison of the Funds Allocated to Men and Women from Various Sources of CRM Funding*

a Total dollars awarded by various sources, 1989–1993

b Average awards allocated

c Mean amount of money allocated

d Median amount of money allocated

Note that there is a substantial disparity between the money allocated to men and women in almost every source of CRM funding. Note also that differences between the median amounts of funding allocated to men and women from most sources are at least as imbalanced as the average awards and mean amounts of money allocated.

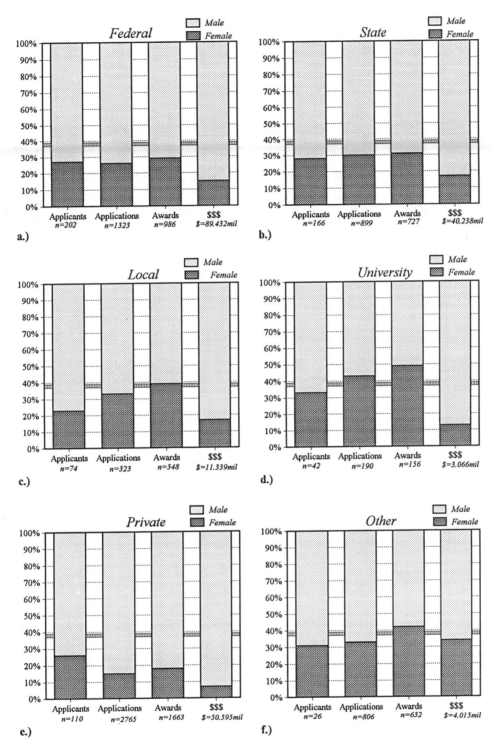

Fig. 7.8 *Funding Process for Men and Women Within Various Sources of CRM Funding (hatched bar = proportion of women in each age cohort)*

a Federal sources
c Local government sources
e Private sources

b State government sources
d University sources
f Other sources

Note the increase in the proportion of awards granted to women over their representation in the applicant pools, and in the applications submitted to several sources of CRM funding. Note, however, that for almost all sources the share of the money allocated to women is dramatically smaller than their share of the total number of awards. Finally, note the generally depressed participation of women in the competition for most sources of CRM funding relative to their representation among Census respondents.

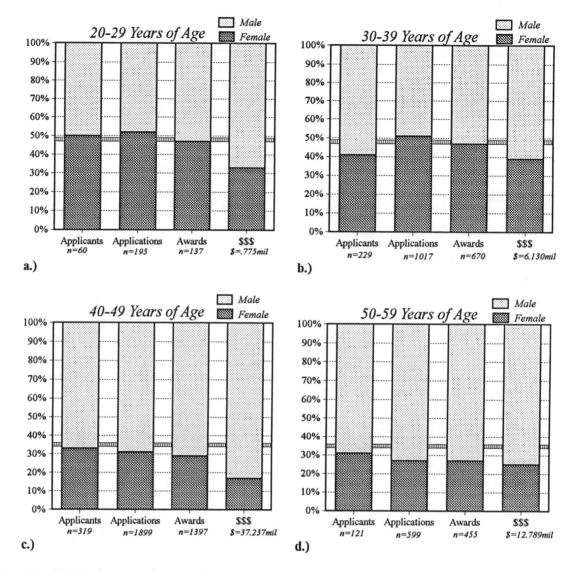

Fig. 7.9 *Non-CRM Funding Process for Men and Women by Age (hatched bar = proportion of women in each age cohort)*

a 20–29 age cohort

c 40–49 age cohort

b 30–39 age cohort

d 50–59 age cohort

Note that, with the exception of the 50–59 age cohort, the share of non-CRM funds allocated to women is depressed relative to their representation among applicants, applications, and awards. Note also that participation of women in their 20s and 30s in the competition for non-CRM funding closely matches their overall representation within these cohorts, while the representation of women in their 40s and 50s in this funding arena is somewhat depressed relative to their overall numbers in these cohorts.

particularly acute among archaeologists in their 40s, though it is also evident among younger archaeologists in their 20s and 30s as well. It would seem that only in the 50–59 year old cohort (where women's representation in the competition for non-CRM funding is the lowest, relative to their actual numbers in the archaeological workforce) is the share of the funding dollars granted to women consistent with their share of the total number of successful proposals. In all other cohorts the tendency for women to receive less, both per award and per successful applicant, is still quite strongly expressed. While the participation of younger women in the funding process has increased,

there is no trend toward greater equity in the allocation of non-CRM funding in younger cohorts.

We see similar patterns when we look at the CRM data for different age cohorts (Figure 7.10). The group of archaeologists in their 20s who had applied for CRM funds is too small to be considered representative, but the older cohorts contain larger, more reliable samples. Among archaeologists in their 40s and 50s the proportions of women competing for CRM funding, the numbers of applications they submit, and the number of awards they receive are all quite consistent with one another (Figure 7.10c and d). In fact, applications for CRM funds

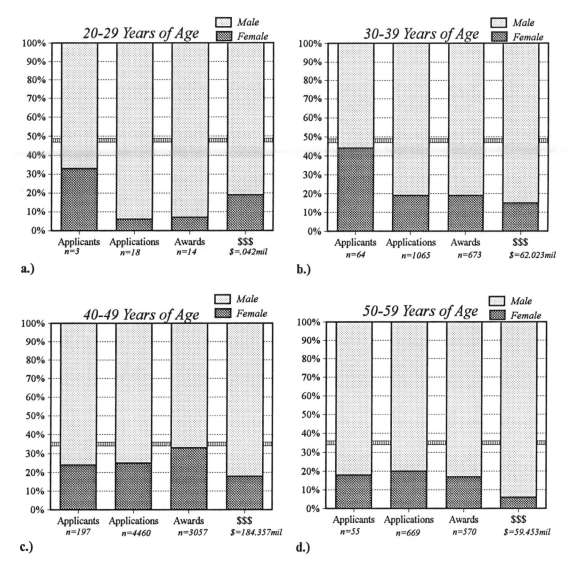

Fig. 7.10 *CRM Funding Process for Men and Women by Age (hatched bar = proportion of women in each age cohort)*

a 20–29 age cohort
b 40–49 age cohort
c 30–39 age cohort
d 50–59 age cohort

Note that, with the exception of the 30–39 age cohort and the very small 20–29 age cohort, the share of CRM funds allocated to women is depressed relative to their representation among applicants, applications, and awards. Note also the increase in women's share of the CRM awards allocated to archaeologists in their 40s relative to their representation among applicants and applications. Note finally that 30–39 year old women enter into the competition for CRM funding in direct proportion to their numbers among Census respondents in their 30s, but that their representation in later stages of the CRM funding process is quite depressed.

submitted by women in their 40s are particularly successful. However, women claimed a disproportionately smaller share of the impressive amounts of CRM funding reported by these cohorts. This is particularly true in the 50–59 year old cohort where the funds reported by women account for less than 10 percent of the total $60 million reported by this cohort. Among archaeologists in their 40s, CRM funds awarded to women account for only 18 percent of the total $184 million reported by this archaeologists in this cohort, even though women received 33 percent of the

total number of CRM awards granted to this cohort (χ^2=488.670, df=1, p<.001).

Archaeologists in their 30s who have applied for CRM funding deviate from this pattern (Figure 7.10b). Here the proportion of men and women applicants closely resembles the actual representation of men and women within this younger cohort, implying a greater degree of participation by younger women in the CRM funding process. However, the proportional share of the applications submitted by women in their 30s is dramatically less. This pattern probably relates to the higher proportion of younger men in the private sector, who, as we will see below, are particularly active in submitting proposals for CRM-related funding. The proportional share of CRM dollars awarded to women archaeologists in their 30s is only slightly depressed relative to the proportion of successful applications they submit. However, the similarity between the representation of women among CRM awards and their share of the CRM funds allocated to this cohort probably says more about the lower level of participation of younger women in this funding arena than its does about the level of funding they receive. Women in their 30s still only receive a minimal 15 percent share of the $62 million reported by this cohort, a figure similar to the share of women in the CRM funding pool in other age cohorts.

Thus, it is safe to conclude that in neither funding arena is there any evidence of an amelioration in the imbalance of the allocation of archaeological funding among younger cohorts. In fact, in some ways the different demographics of male and female archaeologists might actually exacerbate this imbalance. We know from data presented in Chapter 2 that women archaeologists tend to be somewhat younger than males. It is possible, then, that the higher proportion of younger women in the female applicant pool plays some role in the smaller share of funding received by women in general. Some measure of the impact of these different demographic patterns is gained by comparing the proportional share of each cohort in the total number of

awards to the size of the average awards made to individuals in each cohort (Figures 7.11 and 7.12).

Turning first to the non-CRM funding arena (Figure 7.11), there is a strong tendency in both men and women for the size of the average award to increase with age. This is especially true for women, where the 50–59 year old cohort received the highest average award of any female age cohort ($29,000). Among men, 40–49 year olds reported the highest average award ($35,000), though the size of the average award granted to men in their 50s is only slightly less ($33,000). For both men and women the average awards granted to 30–39 year olds, at $8,000 and $11,000 respectively, is quite a bit less than those found in older cohorts. When we look at the allocation of awards across these different cohorts, we find that 53 percent of the awards allocated to men were granted to those in the highest-earning 40–49 year old cohort. In contrast, 33 percent of the awards to women were granted to those in their 30s, where the average number of dollars per award is quite low. In sum, a larger share of the female awards went to a cohort where the average award size is comparatively small, while the bulk of the awards granted to men went to the cohort that received the largest average award of any group examined. Thus it is evident that the different age profiles of men and women archaeologists contributed to the disparities in male and female non-CRM funding seen in the aggregate population. But this is certainly not the only, or even the major, contributor to this

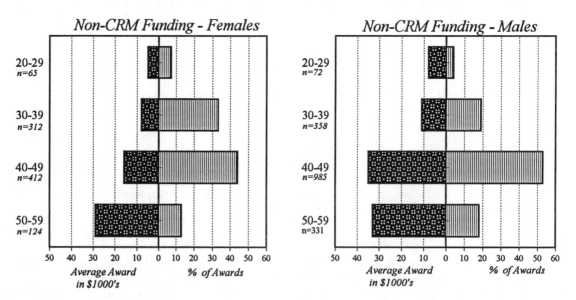

Fig. 7.11 *Distribution of Non-CRM Awards Across Four Age Cohorts and the Size of the Average Non-CRM Awards Allocated to Each Cohort*

a Females   **b** Males

Note that a larger share of the non-CRM awards granted to women are received by women in their 30s, for whom the size of the average non-CRM award is quite small. Note, however, that a much higher proportion of awards are allocated to men in their 40s, who have the largest average awards. Note finally that for all cohorts, but especially for the 40–49 year old cohort, the size of the average award allocated to men is substantially greater than that of women in the same cohort.

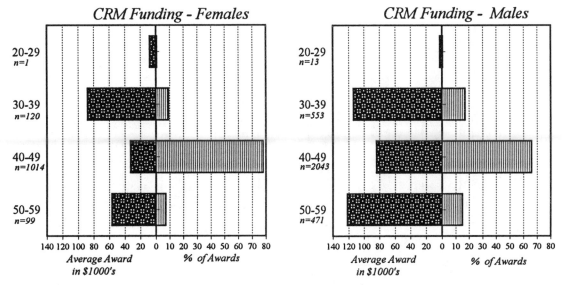

Fig. 7.12 *Distribution of CRM Awards Across Four Age Cohorts and the Size of the Average CRM Awards Allocated to Each Cohort*

a Females   b Males

Note that the largest share of CRM awards granted to women are received by women in their 40s, who have the smallest average awards of any cohort. Note also the higher proportion of awards claimed by men in their 30s, where the average award is quite large. Note, again, that for all cohorts the size of the average CRM award allocated to men is greater than that granted to women in the same cohort.

pattern. Far more significant is the fact that the average awards allocated to men in all cohorts are substantially higher than those allocated to women. This is especially the case among archaeologists in their 40s (the largest single group of award recipients for both genders), where the average award granted to women is $16,000 while that granted to men is $35,000. The mean dollars awarded to men in their 40s, at $163,000, is almost $100,000 greater than that of women in this cohort ($64,000).

The pattern for CRM funding is quite different (Figure 7.12). Here the proportion of awards reported by men and women in their 40s dominate, but more so among women than men. The proportions of awards reported by men in their 30s and 50s are both higher here than for women. Moreover, in sharp contrast to non-CRM funding, the average CRM awards made to both men and women in their 30s are substantially higher than the average awards to men and women in their 40s. In the case of non-CRM funding, the high proportion of younger female award recipients effectively lowered the level of funding of women as a group. In the CRM funding arena the higher representation of younger men helped boost the overall funding levels of men. Yet once again the most significant contributor to the imbalance between the levels of CRM funding received by men and women is the fact that the average awards granted to men in all cohorts are almost double those reported by women. Moreover, both the higher proportion of awards reported by men in their 30s, as well as the very high levels of funding they report, are likely attributable to the higher proportion of younger

men employed in the private sector in this cohort, which, in turn, suggests that employment sector plays the most significant factor shaping CRM funding.

Gender Trends Within Different Employment Sectors

This brings us to the question of the role of employment sector in shaping gender-based trends in archaeological funding. Specifically, we can ask whether all of the primary sectors of archaeological employment show the same patterns, or whether these trends are more marked in some employment sectors than others. For the non-CRM funding arena (Figure 7.13), it would seem that patterns evident in the aggregate data are more strongly expressed in academia and museums than they are in the private or, especially, the public sectors of archaeological employment. Data on the proportion of applicants applying for these different funds (Figure 7.13a) and the numbers of applications submitted (Figure 7.13b) both indicate a higher level of participation in this funding arena by academics and museum-based archaeologists. However, while academic women are as likely as men to apply for these funds, it would seem that museum-based women are much less likely than museum men to apply for non-CRM funding. In fact, women employed in government settings are more likely to apply for these funds than are women in museums. When we look at success rates by employment setting and gender (Figure 7.13c), we see that applications submitted by women in academia and museums are less likely to receive funding than those submitted by men in

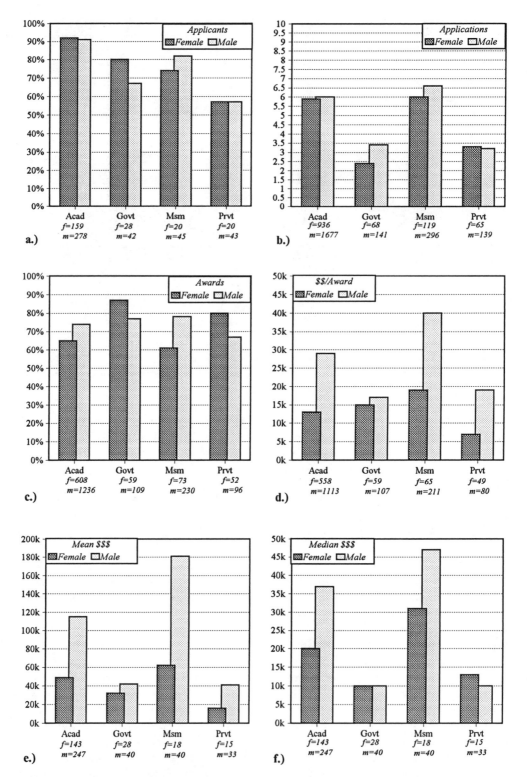

Fig. 7.13 *Participation of Men and Women in the Non-CRM Funding Arena by Employment Sector*

a Proportion of applicants in each employment sector
c Proportion of applications awarded funding
e Mean dollars awarded

b Applications submitted per applicant
d Average dollars per award
f Median dollars awarded

Note the lower success rates of women in academia and museums compared to men in these employment settings, and the higher success rates of women in government and private sector settings. Note, especially, the large disparity in the average award, mean amount, and median amount of money allocated to women in academia and museums when compared to men.

these employment sectors. This is especially true for women in museums. In contrast, a substantially higher proportion of the applications for non-CRM funding submitted by women employed in government and the private sector are awarded funding than is the case for men.

But it is in the allocation of funds that the differentials between men and women in academia and museums are most strongly expressed. Whether we look at the average amount per award, the mean, or the median amount of money received by successful applicants (Figure 7.13d, e, and f), there is a major disparity between the amount of non-CRM funding received by men and women in both academia and museums. In contrast, non-CRM funding levels for men and women in government are quite similar. And while there is some indication of a disparity between men and women in the private sector, this difference is not as pronounced as it is in academia and museums, and it is not evident at all in the median dollars reported. In fact, the median non-CRM funding garnered by women in the private sector is greater than that of private sector men.

While academics and museum professionals are more likely to apply for non-CRM funding, government and private sector archaeologists are more likely to apply for funds from the CRM arena (Figure 7.14a). In all sectors, men are more likely than women to apply for these funds, but this is especially the case in government and academic settings (Figure 7.14b). The number of applications submitted per applicant is similar in academia, government, and museums, with men somewhat more active in the number of submissions in government and museums, while women in academia seem to average slightly more applications per applicant than men. But by far the most active employment setting in the submission of proposals for CRM funding is the private sector. The average number of applications submitted by private sector men and women is far greater than in other employment sectors. This is especially the case for private sector men who average an impressive 53 proposals per applicant over a five-year period, while private sector women average 33 applications per applicant. Yet, though women in government and private sector archaeology submit fewer proposals for CRM funding than men, the proposals they submit tend to have a higher success rate than those submitted by men (Figure 7.14c). As in non-CRM funding, the success rate of women in academia and museums, however, is somewhat less than that of their male colleagues.

Looking at the allocation of CRM funds across the different employment sectors (Figure 7.14d, e, and f), it becomes clear that the private sector is the primary source of the disparity in the levels of CRM funding reported by men and women. CRM funding levels for men and women in academia and government are similar in terms of the size of the average award, as well as in the mean and the median dollars awarded to men and women. In museums there is a huge disparity between the size of the aver-

age awards of CRM funding granted to men and women. However, the similar median level of CRM funding of men and women museum archaeologists highlights the fact that the high average awards of CRM funding of museum males is attributable to a few men who received high levels of CRM funding.

In contrast, all measures of funding show an extraordinary difference between the amounts of money garnered by men and women in the private sector. The average CRM award reported by private sector males is $130,000, compared to only $34,000 for females (Figure 7.14d). In fact, the size of the average award reported by private sector women is substantially less than the average CRM awards reported by women in academia ($53,000) and government ($74,000). The mean amount of money earned by private sector men who responded to the Census is $2,771,000, compared to $846,000 for private sector women (Figure 7.14e). But the dramatic differential between CRM funding levels of private sector men and women is perhaps most impressive when viewed as median amounts (Figure 7.14f). The median CRM funding reported by private sector women, at $170,000, is higher than the median of CRM funds garnered by men and women in other employment sectors, which are all under $100,000. But all these figures are dwarfed by the median level of CRM funding reported by private sector men of $2,173,000.

- It would seem that in both funding arenas the gender-based difference in funding can be traced to imbalances in specific employment sectors—academia and museums for non-CRM funding and the private sector for CRM funding. The dominance of private sector men in the CRM funding arena might well be linked to the earlier noted tendency for men to head larger private sector firms. In Chapter 4, salary differentials between men and women CEOs of private sector firms pointed to a tendency for larger firms to be headed primarily by men, while women CEOs tend to head smaller consulting firms. We also found support for this conclusion in Chapter 6, where the remarkable productivity of private sector men in producing CRM reports could be traced to the heads of large firms reporting the high output of reports their firms produce. Here the high levels of CRM funding reported by private sector men can be linked to the male CEOs of larger firms that have the wherewithal to both compete for and, if successful, conduct larger, more expensive projects. This argument is bolstered by the fact that not only is the average number of applications submitted by men in the private sector extremely high, men are also listed as the PIs of 94 percent of the successful private sector proposals for CRM funding (compared to 75 percent in academia, which is close to the representation of academic men in the CRM applicant pool). Yet while the male CEOs of large companies may claim the largest share of the funds allocated for

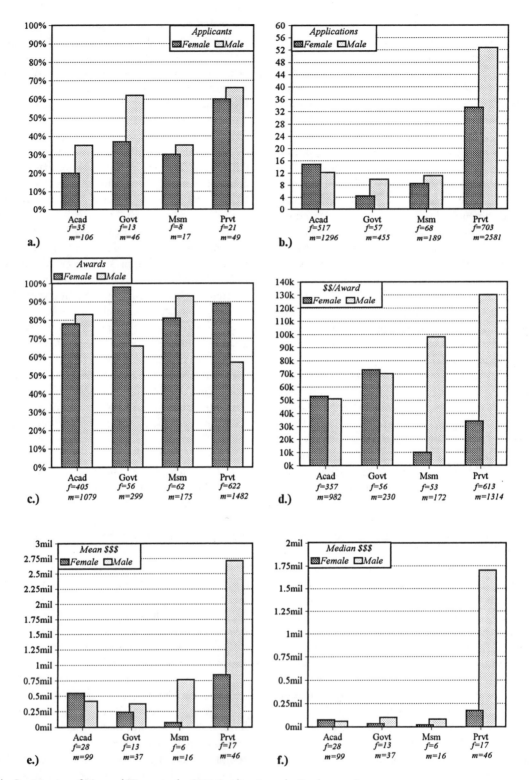

Fig. 7.14 *Participation of Men and Women in the CRM Funding Arena by Employment Sector*

a Proportion of applicants in each employment sector
c Proportion of applications awarded funding
e Mean dollars awarded

b Applications submitted per applicant
d Average dollars per award
f Median dollars awarded

Note the higher rates of government and private sector women in the proportion of successful applications, and the reverse pattern in academia and museum settings. Note, in particular, that the imbalance in the allocation of funds from CRM sources is confined almost exclusively to the private sector.

CRM activities, these funds undoubtedly support the activities of a large number of employees and subcontractors, both male and female, who actually implement the contracted projects awarded to these firms. Thus, the high levels of CRM funding reported by private sector men is likely an artifact of a corporate accounting system that attributes the funds received to support the activities of large number of people to the CEOs of the firms. The imbalance, then, lies more in the private sector corporate structure, where males seem more likely to head large firms than women, rather than in the CRM funding process itself.

The causes for the imbalance between non-CRM funding levels of male and female academics and museum archaeologists are less clear. As we will see, academics and museum archaeologists make up nearly 70 percent of the applicant pool for non-CRM funding, and they claim 84 percent of the funds allocated for this purpose. Thus it would seem that the imbalance evidenced in non-CRM funding affects all the major players in this arena. While the somewhat depressed success rates of women in academia and museums probably contributes to the imbalance in the allocation of non-CRM funds, this small discrepancy alone cannot account for the major differentials in the amounts of money allocated to men and women. The lower success rate of female applications for non-CRM funding has no bearing on the lower average awards allocated to women. Moreover, women in academia and museums are just as likely to serve as the PIs of successful grants as men in these employment sectors. We are left, then, with two possible explanations: (1) that women tend to ask for smaller amounts of money in the first place, or (2) that awards tend to favor the smaller requests for funds submitted by women. The data supplied by the NSF suggest that there is little difference in the levels of funding requested by men and women, implying that the latter factor played some role in the different levels of NSF funding reported by men and women Census respondents. Whether this pattern is found in other sources of non-CRM funding is not known. Unfortunately, Census respondents were not asked to report the amounts of money requested from various sources. Nor was the information on awards collected in such a way as to allow a more in-depth exploration of this question. Clearly, more investigation is needed to discover the root causes of the apparently endemic gender-based imbalance in the funding of archaeology conducted outside the cultural resource management arena. •

Trends in Archaeological Funding by Employment Sector

Non-CRM Funding Compared to CRM Funding

Having established that employment sector is the most significant factor affecting gender-based patterns in archaeological funding, it is useful to make a more general comparison of the participation of the various sectors of archaeological employment in these two different arenas of archaeological funding. As suggested earlier in the discussion of gender-related trends in various employment settings, it is clear that academic and museum archaeologists are much more likely to apply for non-CRM funding than are archaeologists employed in government and private sector settings (Figure 7.15a). In the five years that preceded the Census, more than 90 percent of the academics and 86 percent of the museum archaeologists who responded to this section of the Census sought funding for non-CRM archaeological activities. In contrast, only about 60 percent of both public and private sector archaeologists sought funding for non-CRM archaeology. Not unexpectedly, a higher proportion of archaeologists in public and private sector archaeology competed for CRM-related funds than was the case for academic and museum archaeologists. Between 50 and 60 percent of private and public sector archaeologists applied for CRM funding, compared to only 30 percent of the academic and museum-based Census respondents. The proportion of people in the other employment category, displayed in the last bar of the graph in Figure 7.15a, who applied for either source of funding is quite low. Since this group consists of people who split their time between multiple employment settings, or who either were employed less than half time in archaeology or worked outside the field altogether, or who are retired, their lower level of involvement in the competition for funding is not surprising. What is somewhat surprising, however, is that the number of private and public sector archaeologists who applied for non-CRM funding is quite similar to the number of these archaeologists who applied for CRM funding. In fact, government archaeologists are more likely to apply for funds to support non-CRM-related activities than for archaeology related to cultural resource management. Among private sector archaeologists, the proportion of individuals seeking CRM funding is only slightly greater than the proportion of people in private sector settings who apply for funds to support activities that lie outside of cultural resource management.

However, though the number of the private sector respondents who sought funding to support CRM-related activities is somewhat lower than expected, those who did apply for these funds seem to have been extremely active in their pursuit of CRM funding (Figure 7.15b). Over a five-year period, private sector archaeologists submitted an average of 45 applications for CRM funding per applicant, more than five times as many applications per applicant than in any other employment sector. The remarkable productivity in the number of applications submitted by private sector archaeologists masks another, perhaps equally important, trend in these data, and that is the relatively high level of activity of archaeologists outside of the private sector in the application for CRM-related funds. Only in

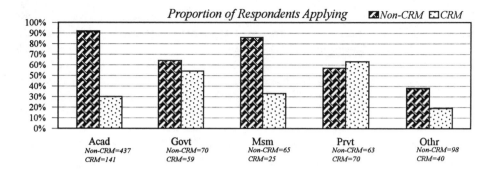

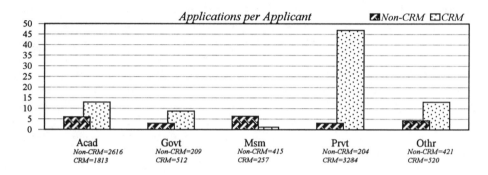

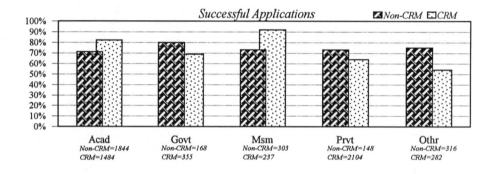

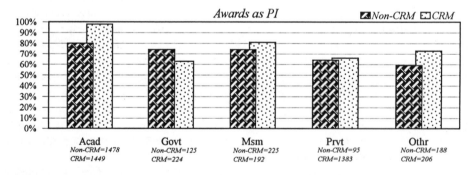

Fig. 7.15 *Participation of Different Employment Sectors in the Non-CRM and CRM Funding Arenas*

a Proportions of applicants for non-CRM and CRM funding in different employment sectors

b Applications submitted per applicant

c Proportion of applications awarded funding

d Proportion of successful applications for which the recipient served as principal investigator (PI)

Note that academics and museum archaeologists are more likely to apply for non-CRM funding than government and private sector archaeologists, while the reverse is true in the CRM funding arena. Note also the exceptionally high number of applications per applicant for private sector CRM submissions, but that the number of applications per applicant is also higher for CRM submissions in academia, government, and other employment settings. Note, finally, that academics are much more likely to serve as PIs on successful CRM proposals than are private sector archaeologists.

museums is the average number of applications per applicant for non-CRM funding greater than it is for CRM funding. In all other employment settings, archaeologists produce more applications per applicant for CRM funds than they do for non-CRM funds. This tendency is particularly strongly expressed among academics, where applicants for CRM funding submitted twice as many applications over a five-year period as did applicants for non-CRM-related funding. The high level of applications per applicant among archaeologists in the other employment category is probably attributable to the archaeologists in this group who are employed part time in both academia (or museums) and the private sector.

Success rates for non-CRM funding are roughly the same for all employment groups (Figure 7.15c). In contrast, applications submitted for CRM-related funding by academics and museum archaeologists seem to have a somewhat higher success rate than those submitted by government or private sector archaeologists. Archaeologists employed in academia, government, and museums are all about equally likely to serve as the PIs of successful applications for non-CRM funding (Figure 7.15d), while private sectors archaeologists and, especially, archaeologists in the various other settings are less likely to serve as PIs of successful applications for non-CRM funding. This pattern probably reflects the greater tendency of these individuals (particularly those in the other employment group) to serve as subcontractors for grants submitted by archaeologists in one of the three other primary employment sectors.

Turning to the primary investigator status of CRM proposals, both academics and museum-based archaeologists are more likely than private and public sector archaeologists to serve as the PIs of successful CRM funding applications (Figure 7.15d). The lower PI rate seen among private sector archaeologists is likely a reflection of the tendency for CEOs of firms to serve as the PI of proposals for funding prepared by the firm they represent. This pattern, in turn, is indicative of a more specialized approach to seeking funds, in which large numbers of proposals, prepared by a relatively small segment of the private sector workforce, place the chief executive officer of the firm in the role of principle investigator. If the proposal is successful, the CEO is then responsible for channeling funds received to various employees and subcontractors who perform the contracted work. In contrast, the high proportion of academics who serve as PIs on successful CRM proposals is indicative of a more decentralized way of operating within this funding arena.

Looking at the total number of CRM and non-CRM dollars reported by archaeologists in these different work settings (Fig 7.16a), one is immediately struck by the remarkable amount of money acquired by private sector archaeologists for CRM-related archaeology. Over five years, 63 private sector Census respondents garnered nearly $200 million in support of their cultural resource management projects. In contrast, over this same period of time, five times as many academic respondents (390) received only one-sixth this amount ($40 million) in support of their non-CRM-related work. The amount of CRM-related funds received per award is also substantially higher in the private sector than in other work settings, as are both the mean and the median amounts of funding reported by private sector archaeologists compared to archaeologists in other work settings (Figure 7.16b, c, and d). Figure 7.16 also makes clear, however, that archaeologists in all sectors of archaeological employment, including academia and museums, received more funding to support cultural resource management activities than they received to support more traditional kinds of archaeological research. Moreover, the average awards, the mean awards, and the median awards received for CRM archaeology by archaeologists in other employment sectors are higher, in all cases, than comparable figures for non-CRM funding.

Figure 7.17 helps summarize these patterns, bringing into sharper focus the comparison of non-CRM and CRM funding within each of the four primary employment sectors. The four graphs presented in this figure compare the proportions of applicants, applications, awards, and dollars generated by non-CRM and CRM funding appeals for each major sector of archaeological employment. They show that, at the outset of the funding process, the number of applicants for non-CRM funding in each sector is quite high relative to the number of applicants to sources of CRM funding. However, the proportional representation of the CRM funding arena increases at every subsequent step of the funding process, so that by the time we arrive at the allocation of dollars, in every employment sector the money acquired for CRM activities is greater than the funding received for non-CRM archaeological research. In the private sector, not unexpectedly, funds received in support of cultural resource management come to 99 percent of the total dollars reported by consulting archaeologists. Again not surprisingly, CRM-related funds comprise 88 percent of the total dollars reported by government archaeologists. But what may be surprising to some is that, even though applicants for CRM funding make up less than 30 percent of the applicant pool for archaeological funding in academia and museums, the dollar amounts received in support of CRM activities constitute 64 percent of the total funds accumulated in support of archaeological activities in both employment sectors.

It is also possible to track the success rates of each employment sector within each funding arena in way similar to that done when looking at gender-based trends in the funding process. Figure 7.18 compares the proportional representation of each employment sector at every stage of the funding process for both non-CRM and CRM funding. Just as was the case when examining gender-based patterns, if there is no difference in how well or how

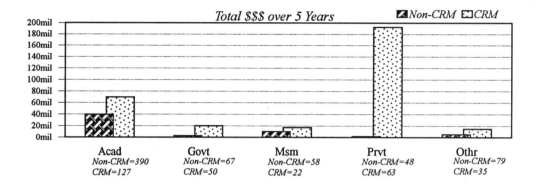

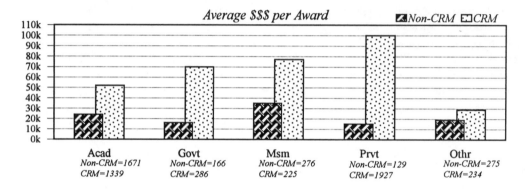

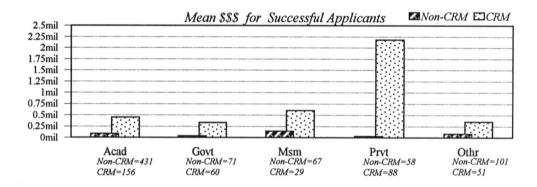

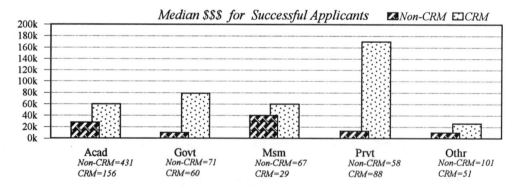

Fig. 7.16 *Comparison of the Funds Allocated to Different Employment Sectors from Non-CRM and CRM Sources*

a Total dollars awarded, 1989–1993   **c** Mean amount of money allocated
b Average awards allocated   **d** Median amount of money allocated

Note the very large amounts of CRM funds allocated to private sector archaeologists. Note also that all employment sectors receive more funding in support of CRM-related activities than they receive in support of non-CRM archaeology.

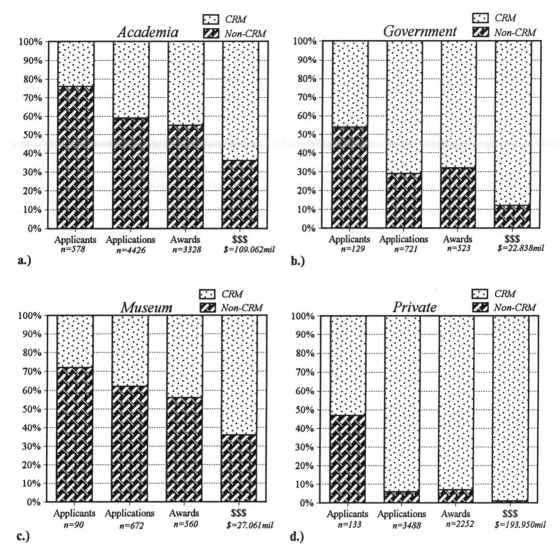

Fig. 7.17 *Representation of Non-CRM and CRM Funding Arenas in Various Stages of the Funding Process by Employment Sector*

a Academia

b Government

c Museums

d Private sector

Note that while applicants for non-CRM funding make up about half or more of the applicant pool in each employment sector, the proportional representation of the CRM arena increases at every stage of the funding process. In every employment sector the CRM funding arena supplied the majority of funds received.

poorly archaeologists in different sectors fare at any stage in the funding process, then the proportional representation of each sector in the applicant pool, the applications submitted, the awards granted, and the dollars allocated should all remain constant. Levels of participation in the process can be measured by comparing the representation of an employment sector at a certain stage against its representation in the Census respondent pool as a whole (the last bar of each graph, labeled "Total").

In the non-CRM funding arena (Figure 7.18a), it is clear that academics and museum-based archaeologists are disproportionately well represented throughout the non-CRM funding process. At every stage, from the number of

applicants, number of applications submitted, and number of awards granted, to the share of the funds allocated, academics and museum-based archaeologists dominate the non-CRM funding process.

In contrast, the proportions of archaeologists from different employment sectors who apply for CRM-related funds (Figure 7.18b) is quite similar to the proportions of these archaeologists in the respondent pool. This means that archaeologists in all work settings are entering into the competition for CRM funds in numbers that are roughly proportional to their representation in the archaeological workforce. Private sector archaeologists, however, first begin to dominate the CRM funding process in their share

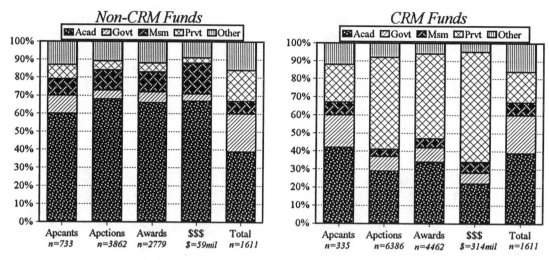

Fig. 7.18 *Funding Process for Different Employment Sectors in the Non-CRM and CRM Funding Arenas (final "Total" bar = representation of different employment sectors in the Census population)*

a Proportions of different employment sectors in the applicant pool, number of applications submitted, awards granted, and money allocated in the non-CRM funding arena

b Proportions of different employment sectors in the applicant pool, number of applications submitted, awards granted, and money allocated in the CRM funding arena

Note that academics and museum archaeologists dominate all stages of the non-CRM funding process. Note, however, that all sectors enter the CRM funding process in roughly similar proportions to their representation within the Census respondent pool, while the private sector dominates the CRM funding process in their share of the applications submitted, awards granted, and total dollars acquired.

of the total number of applications for CRM funds submitted, which, at 51 percent, is substantially greater than either the representation of private sector archaeologists among Census respondents (17 percent) or their representation within the applicant pool (21 percent). The decline in the private sector share in the proportion of CRM awards to 47 percent is indicative of the lower success rate of CRM proposals submitted by private sector archaeologists that we saw in Figure 7.15c. However, the lower success rate of private sector proposals does not seem to affect their overall share of the CRM dollars, which, at 61 percent, is even greater than their share of the total number of applications submitted, and is markedly disproportional to the representation of private sector archaeologists in the Census respondent pool (χ^2=1737.857, df=1, p<.001). Thus, the dominance of private sector archaeologists in securing CRM funding is primarily attributable to the greater level of activity of private sector archaeologists in seeking these funds, as well as to the greater likelihood that the projects they compete for are larger and more expensive than those for which other employment sectors compete.

It is also interesting to note that the participation of government archaeologists in both the CRM and the non-CRM funding arenas is significantly less than their overall representation among Census respondents. These data support indications from Census data discussed in earlier chapters that government archaeologists are more likely to be involved in awarding and

monitoring funds than they are in the process of applying for and spending these funds.

Sources of Non-CRM and CRM Funding

The tendency of academics and museum archaeologists to dominate the non-CRM funding arena is evident in essentially all of the individual sources of non-CRM funding examined here (Figure 7.19). Academics do especially well in the competition for National Science Foundation senior grants (Figure 7.19b), and, not surprisingly, grants awarded by universities in support of non-CRM archaeology (Figure 7.19g). Museum archaeologists fare well in National Endowment for the Humanities funding (again, an artifact of the NEH support of museum development), but are also especially successful in securing non-CRM funding from state and local governments, as well as from private and othr funding sources (Figure 7.19c, e, f, and h).

Turning to the various sources of CRM funding, not unexpectedly, private sector archaeologists are disproportionately well represented in the pursuit of CRM funding from all the various sources examined. However, they seem to do particularly well in securing funds from federal sources (Figure 7.20a) and, especially, from private sources (Figure 7.20e). This later pool probably reflects funds secured from private corporations, engineering firms, and development firms that are directed toward the archaeological assessment of areas slated for development.

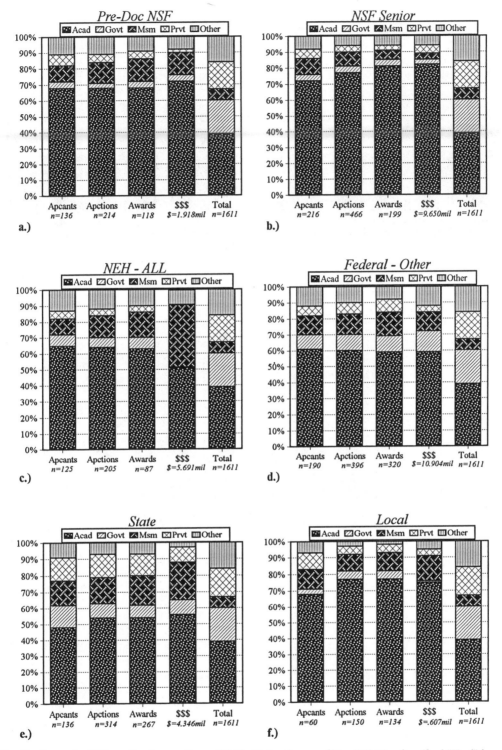

Fig. 7.19 *Funding Process for Different Employment Sectors Within Various Sources of Non-CRM Funding (final "Total" bar = representation of different employment sectors in the Census population)*

a NSF dissertation improvement grants

c NEH grants

e State government sources

b NSF senior grants

d Other federal sources

f Local government sources

Note that academics and museum archaeologists dominate the funding process for all sources of non-CRM funding. Academics are particularly well represented in NSF dissertation improvement and senior grants and in non-CRM funding from universities, while museum archaeologists seem to fare particularly well securing funds from NEH, state and local governments, private, and other sources.

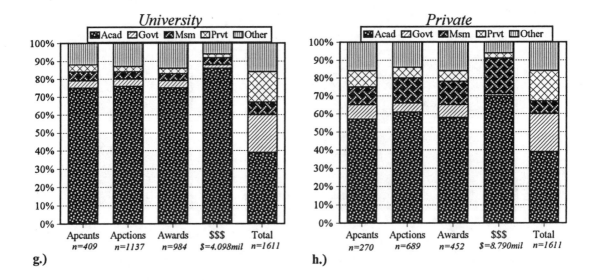

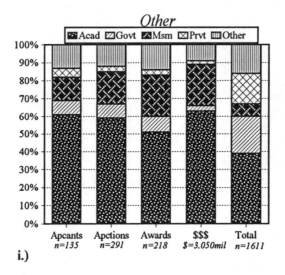

Fig. 7.19 *Funding Process for Different Employment Sectors Within Various Sources of Non-CRM Funding (continued)*

g University sources **h** Private sources

i Other sources

As was the case for non-CRM funding, both the level of participation and the amount of CRM funds secured by museum archaeologists from state and local governments far exceed the representation of museum archaeologists in the Census respondent pool (Figure 7.20b and c). It is also interesting to note that while academics are well represented among applicants for CRM-related funding available from universities, their representation in this funding pool steadily shrinks when we move from applicants, to applications, to awards, to the allocation of funds granted by universities in support of CRM activities (Figure 7.20d). The large share of the amount of funds allocated by universities for CRM archaeology reported by the other employment category is attributable to a single retired academic, now serving as a private consultant, who reported receiving a number of exceptionally high awards from university sources for CRM-related work.

• Perhaps the most significant finding here is that, regardless of the ultimate success of archaeologists from various sectors of employment in the competition for CRM funding, the proportions of archaeologists from these different sectors who apply for CRM funding from all potential sources is generally quite similar to their representation in the Census respondent pool. It would seem that all archaeologists in all employment sectors are actively pursuing funding to support CRM-related archaeology from all available sources. This is especially true for academics, who are well represented in the applicant pool for all of the various CRM funding sources. Coupling

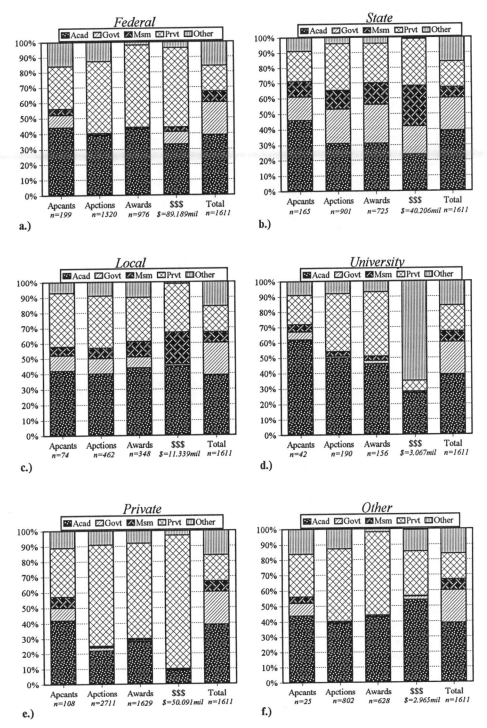

Fig. 7.20 *Funding Process for Different Employment Sectors Within Various Sources of CRM Funding (final "Total" bar = representation of different employment sectors in the Census population)*

a Federal sources

c Local government sources

e Private sources

b State government sources

d University sources

f Other sources

Note that private sector archaeologists are disproportionately well represented in the funds allocated by all sources of CRM funding, but seem to fare particularly well in securing funds from federal government and private sources. Museum archaeologists are well represented in the allocation of funds from state and local governments, while government archaeologists are underrepresented in all stages of the funding process for all sources. Note, however, that the numbers of archaeologists in all employment sectors who apply for each source of CRM funding are roughly proportional to their numbers among Census respondents, and that academics are often even better represented among applicants for CRM funds than they are in the Census respondent pool.

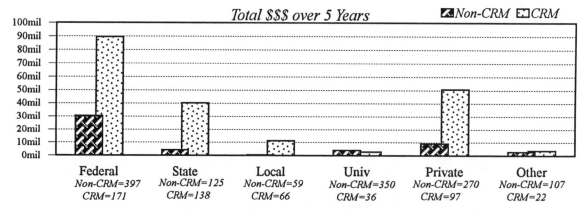

Fig. 7.21 *Total Dollars Allocated for Non-CRM and CRM Archaeology from the Same Sources*

Note the greater amounts of money allocated for CRM archaeology by almost all sources of archaeological funding, but especially from federal, state, and local government sources and from private sources. Note also the comparatively small number of people who generated the CRM funds acquired.

these data with the high proportion of students involved in producing CRM reports, noted in Chapter 6, one infers that a significant proportion of CRM funds garnered by academic institutions is directed toward student support.

The reason for the high level of involvement in the competition for CRM funding by archaeologists in all employment sectors is perhaps made most clear when we compare the amounts of non-CRM and CRM-related funding generated by the same general funding sources (Figure 7.21). With the exception of universities and other miscellaneous sources, both of which are fairly small players in archaeological funding, the amount of money received in support of CRM-related work from every source is vastly greater than the amount of funds generated by these sources for non-CRM-related research. This is especially the case for funds secured from various federal agencies. Census respondents report having received a little over $30 million in support of non-CRM archaeology from federal sources (shown here as the combined total of funds received from NSF, NEH, and other various federal sources), substantially more than from any other source in support of non-CRM-related activities. However, the levels of funding awarded by the federal government to support cultural resource management activities, at $90 million, is three times greater. The difference between levels of funding generated by these two different arenas is all the more remarkable when one considers that the number of people who received CRM-related funding is roughly one-third as large as the number of people who received funding to support non-CRM archaeology. It is also important to remember that the bulk of the more than $300 million received by Census respondents for cultural resource management was secured by a small group of private sector archaeologists (63 individuals), and that the funds reported here cover only a five-year period. If we extrapolate from these figures the levels of funding secured

for cultural resource management by the private sector as a whole over the past two decades, the implications for funding in American archaeology are staggering. •

Activities Supported by Archaeological Funding

Outside Sources of Support

But what is all this money *used* for? Are there differences in the types of activities supported by funds derived from these two different funding arenas? Do archaeologists in different employment sectors use these funds in different ways? And is there any support for the frequently cited contention that there are significant gender-based differ-

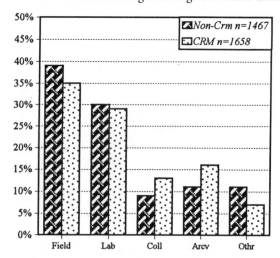

Fig. 7.22 *Activities Supported by Non-CRM and CRM Funding*

Note that, other than the greater representation of collections development and archival research among the activities supported by CRM funding, the profiles of activities supported by non-CRM and CRM funding are quite similar.

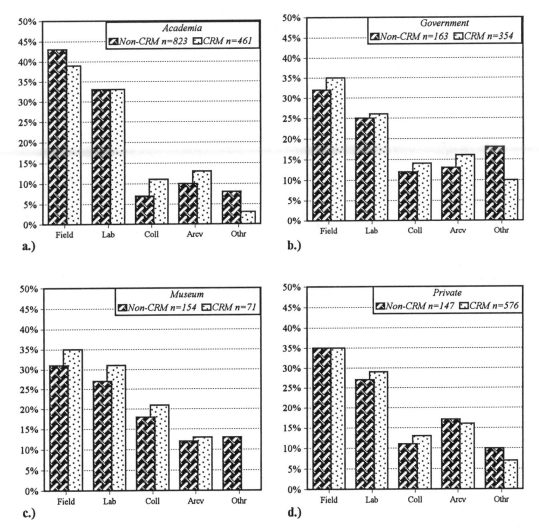

Fig. 7.23 *Activities Supported by Non-CRM and CRM Funding in Each Employment Sector*

a Academia
c Museums

b Government
d Private sector

Note that the profile of activities supported by non-CRM and CRM funding is similar in each employment sector, but that the profiles of funded activities in each sector differ substantially from those of other sectors.

ences in the types of activities supported by archaeological funding (Gero 1994: 41)? To answer these questions, the Census also collected information on the types of activities for which respondents had received support from outside sources over the five years preceding 1994. These activities included fieldwork, laboratory analysis, collections development, archival research, and other activities not included under these general categories (for example, public education or outreach). Respondents were also asked to distinguish between CRM and non-CRM funding received in support of various activities.

Figure 7.22 compares the profile of activities supported by non-CRM funding to that supported by CRM funds. These two profiles differ primarily in the greater representation of collections development and archival

research among the activities supported by CRM funding. Yet, while the difference between the activities supported by these sources of funding is statistically significant (χ^2=35.708, df=4, p<.001), these profiles are still strikingly similar. In both, field work dominates (though more so in non-CRM funding), followed by funds directed to the support of laboratory work, with collections development, archival research, and other activities being more poorly represented among the activities that have received outside support.

The profiles of activities supported by CRM and non-CRM-related funds are also quite similar when these data are presented by employment sector (Figure 7.23). In fact, there is greater variation between employment sectors than there is between sources of funding. As has been the case in other aspects of American archaeology, academia has the most distinctively, and significantly, different profile of activities supported by outside funding. Activities supported by both CRM and non-CRM funding in academia consist almost exclusively of field and laboratory work (Figure 7.23a). This pattern corresponds well to the profile of activities in which academics commonly engage, discussed in Chapter 4, in which field and laboratory work were also prominently featured (Figure 4.19). Collections development is especially well represented in the profiles of activities supported by both CRM and non-CRM funds granted to museum archaeologists (Figure 7.23c). The strong representation of other activities in the non-CRM funding received by museum archaeologists probably relates to funds devoted to exhibit development and other forms of public outreach. Support of public education is probably responsible for the elevated representation of this other category in the profile of funded activities in government archaeology (Figure 7.23b). Archival work is also well represented in government settings, as it is in the profile of activities supported by CRM and non-CRM funds in the private sector (Figure 7.23d). This support probably reflects the stronger representation of historic archaeology in these two employment sectors, as noted in Chapter 5. The prevalence of support for archival research in the private sector can also be tied to the importance of documenting the past ownership and use of areas slated for development.

Breaking the activity profiles for non-CRM and CRM work down by gender (Figure 7.24) reveals no significant differences in activities for which men and women have received support from either funding arena. There is a slightly, though not significantly, greater tendency for

CRM funding secured by men to be directed toward the support of fieldwork. However, there is no indication of major, gender-based disparities in the funding of field and laboratory work in either major funding arena.

Institutional Support

Finally, recognizing that not all archaeological support is secured from outside sources, respondents were asked about the kinds of support available from their home institutions. As was the intention in the examination of activities supported by outside sources, the goal here was to see if there were any distinctive differences in the types of institutional support provided in different employment sectors, as well as in the levels of support enjoyed by men and women employed in these different sectors. The types of activities listed were fieldwork, laboratory analysis and archival research, attendance of professional meetings, and, once again, other activities.

Looking at these data by both employment sector and gender (Figure 7.25), it is clear that in all employment settings, for both men and women, support for attendance of conferences is uniformly high, close to 90 percent in all settings. In academia a little more than half of both males and females receive some institutional support for field and laboratory analysis (Figure 7.25a), with the proportion of men who received this kind of support slightly, though not significantly, greater than women. In contrast, the proportion of male archaeologists in museums who received institutional support for field and laboratory activities is substantially greater than the proportion of museum women who received this support (Figure 7.25c). This pattern parallels other Census results that suggest that

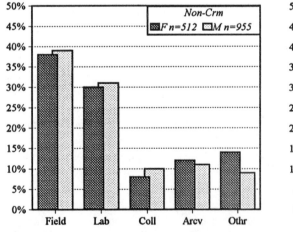 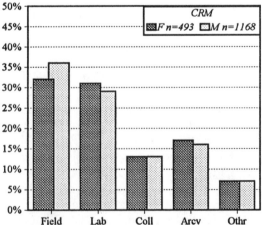

Fig. 7.24 *Activities Supported by Non-CRM and CRM Funding by Gender*

a Activities supported by non-CRM funding   **b** Activities supported by CRM funding

Note that there is essentially no difference between men and women in the profile of activities supported by funds from either non-CRM or CRM sources.

males employed in museums have jobs more similar to those of academics, while women in museums are more likely to serve in a support capacity.

Institutional support for field and laboratory work in the private sector, for both men and women, is quite low (Figure 7.25d). Given the nature of private sector work, which is funded almost entirely by grants and contracts secured from outside sources, these results are not surprising. The flip side of this pattern is evident in government archaeology, where the level of institutional support for field and laboratory work is the highest of any employment sector (Figure 7.25c). It would seem that the lower participation of government archaeologists in the pursuit of outside sources of CRM and non-CRM funding is compensated for, to some extent, by a higher level of institutional support for the archaeology conducted by government archaeologists.

● We see that the cross-cutting currents of gender and, most especially, workplace shape even the ways in which institutional support is granted, just as they shape almost every other aspect of American archaeology. But as has been consistently the case, the directions in which these currents take the profession are never easily predicted or explained, but are always part of the much larger story of the practice of archaeology in American today. ●

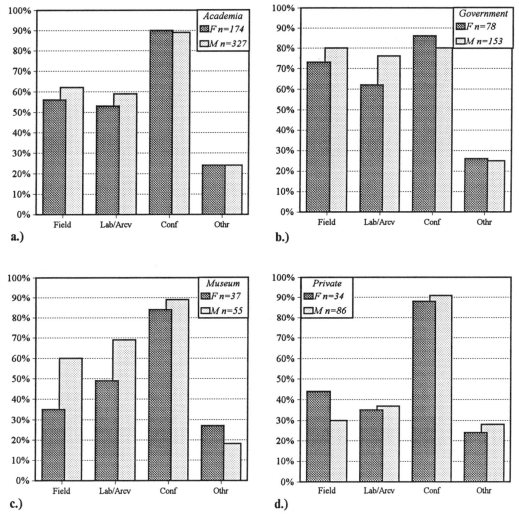

Fig. 7.25 *Activities Supported by Funds from the Home Institutions of Men and Women in Different Employment Sectors*

a Academia   b Government
c Museums   d Private sector

Note the high proportion of men and women in all settings who receive institutional support to attend conferences. Note also the disparity between the proportion of museum men and women who receive institutional support for fieldwork, laboratory analysis, and archival research. Note, finally, the low proportion of private sector archaeologists and the high proportion of government archaeologists who receive institutional support for these activities.

8   What's Next?

Introduction

Results of the 1994 Society for American Archaeology Census have provided the basis for a comprehensive and richly detailed study of the status of American archaeology at the end of the 20th century. Using the data generated by the Census we have been able to take an in-depth, empirically grounded look at central issues in American archaeology. We have built a basic demographic profile of archaeologists in the Americas. We have examined trends in archaeological education. We have made an intensive survey of the changing employment environment in American archaeology. We have tracked trends in research and have monitored the productivity of archaeologists today. And we have explored the sources of funding that are the lifeline of archaeological practice in the Americas. At different points throughout this narrative, an effort has been made to step back from the densely packed presentation of facts and figures, and to summarize primary findings and prevalent themes as they emerge from the analysis of this remarkable corpus of information about our profession. This has been done principally in the introduction to every chapter, which provides an overview of the major findings presented therein. Specially highlighted summary passages that occur throughout the text also present syntheses and major themes or trends that can be deduced from various aspects of the Census data.

There will, then, be no attempt to restate these findings in this final chapter. Instead I would like in these concluding remarks to touch on some of the ongoing trends and open questions raised by the Census that we were not able to resolve with Census data. In some cases, answering these open questions will require taking surveys more targeted at collecting specific kinds of information that lay outside of the scope of the SAA Census. In most cases, however, the resolution of these open issues will become apparent only with time, as the trends that have been identified play out in the profession over several decades to come.

Two principal ongoing trends in American archaeology will, as they have done in preceding chapters, provide the framework for this final discussion. The first is the increase in the representation of women in American archaeology, and the second is the impact of the growth of private sector archaeology on the profession as a whole. As we have seen, each of these trends has already had a pro-

found impact on almost all aspects on the practice of archaeology in America today. But as significant as these impacts have already been, by no means can it be concluded that the full ramifications of either of these major longitudinal trends have already been felt. Both of these ongoing trends are better viewed as forces of change, only now gathering momentum, that will ultimately transform our profession into something quite different from what it is in these final years of the 20th century.

Mixed Messages on the Movement Toward Gender Equity in American Archaeology

One of the strongest trends identified by the SAA Census has been the increase in the representation of women in the profession among younger cohorts. Over the past 20 years the proportion of women in archaeology has risen from less than 20 percent of the professional workforce to half of the youngest cadres of archaeologists entering the profession. Women now comprise more than half of the body of recent PhDs. They are no longer employed in more marginal positions in archaeology, but instead make up an increasing component of all the primary sectors of archaeological employment. In fact, the majority of the youngest cohort of postgraduate academicians and museum archaeologists are women. Women are also increasingly better represented in the competition for primary sources of archaeological funding.

Accompanying these trends we have also seen some evidence of amelioration in imbalances in gender equity faced by older generations of female archaeologists in their professional and personal lives. One of the most important of these is the narrowing of the substantial salary gap between older men and women with equivalent training and seniority holding equivalent positions. Yet we have no way of knowing, with the data at hand, whether the greater similarity in the salaries of younger men and women employed in similar jobs will accompany these archaeologists as they progress in their careers, or whether younger women will face similar impediments to career, and salary, advancement as those already faced by older women in the field. There are some ominous suggestions that this latter scenario is a real possibility. For despite the greater similarity in salaries, there is still a persistent tendency (no matter how finely the data are partitioned to control for training, experience, or responsibilities) for young women to be better represented in the lower salary brackets, while younger men are better represented among higher-end salaries. There is a disturbing, and apparently increasing, tendency for women to be hired in nontenure-track positions in academia, while men, despite their declining representation in academia, fill a disproportionate number of the available tenure-track jobs. There are still fairly pronounced imbalances evident in the salaries of junior men and women in museums. None of these trends augur well for future gender equity in career advancement in archaeology. However, we will only know the outcome of these age-related trends in male and female salaries when, 10 to 20 years from now, the question of salaries in American archaeology is revisited.

Census data also provided some indication that younger women may be less likely to sacrifice marriage and family life for a career in archaeology than were women in the past. However, as with the data on salaries, there is no way of knowing now whether the greater parity in marriage rates among younger archaeologists represents a trend toward more balance in the personal demands a career in archaeology makes on men and women, or whether these younger women will, in their late 40s and 50s, have high rates of divorce without remarriage, similar to those apparently experienced by older women in our sample. Here a more targeted survey looking at questions of marriage, divorce, and child rearing would help answer some of the issues that lay beyond the scope of the SAA Census. Ultimately, however, resolution of this issue, as well, must await the passage of time.

Another puzzle discovered, but not solved, by the Census was the apparently chronic lower productivity among women archaeologists in the publication and presentation of archaeological investigations. While there was less disparity in the productivity of younger men and women, there were still persistent imbalances among younger archaeologists that were apparent in all employment sectors, even among students. Some linkage was hypothesized between this pattern and the conditions of employment of women in these various settings. However, this linkage is admittedly tenuous, and there is a clear need for follow-up studies aimed at discovering the causes of this difference in the productivity of male and female archaeologists.

An equally perplexing pattern, with even greater significance for the understanding of the changing role of women in archaeology, was evident in persistently low levels of archaeological funding allocated to women despite their steadily improving representation among competitors for funds. An attempt was made to marshal a variety of different types of Census data to trace the roots of this pattern in both the cultural resource management and non-CRM funding arenas. For the CRM arena, the pattern was traced to the private sector, where the evident primacy of males holding positions as CEOs of larger firms was offered as a possible cause for this imbalance. For non-CRM funding the differences in funding levels that cut across all age groups of men and women was traced to academic and museum sectors of employment, which are the dominant players in the competition for these funds. After ruling out factors such as lower or less active participation in the competition for funds, differentials in the success rates of funding proposals, and gender differences in the PI status of successful grants, we were left with two alternative explanations for this pattern: (1) that grants submitted by women tended to ask for less funds than those submitted by men, or (2) that smaller requests submitted by women were more likely to be awarded funding. Although there was some evidence in the data supplied by one funding agency that lent support to the latter explanation, there is no way to resolve this very important issue with the data at hand. Surveys targeted at collecting more specific information from participants in the funding process are needed, as well as more robust data from the funding sources themselves.

The Census also revealed several instances where there was a disjunction between preference and satisfaction levels of women archaeologists employed in certain settings and the apparent realities of the conditions of employment women face in those settings. The most striking example of this was seen among women in museums. In general, all women (those employed in museums, as well as those in other settings, including students) showed a particularly strong preference for employment in museum settings. Moreover, women in museums also expressed relatively high levels of satisfaction with their careers in these settings, as well as with the sufficiency of the compensation they receive. And yet, museum women have the lowest salary levels of any of the primary employment settings, the largest gap between their salaries and the salaries of men with similar training and seniority, the slowest salary growth, and the most limited access to employee benefits. Museum women are much less likely to engage in preferred activities like fieldwork or writing for publication than museum men, or, for that matter, than women in other employment sectors. Not coincidentally, perhaps, they have the poorest publication records, the most limited success in securing funding from outside sources, and the most restricted access to funding support from their home institutions. One can understand that employment in a museum may, for a variety of reasons, hold a certain allure for women employed outside a museum setting. However, the strong preferences and high levels of satisfaction of women already employed in museums, where there appears to be the least gender equity in employment conditions of any employment sector, are hard to understand. In addition, it is interesting to note that while women also express a preference for working in academia, it would seem that some of the realities of employment in this setting have colored the satisfaction levels of women employed there, which are comparatively low. It is highly unlikely that museum women are not aware, at least at some level, of the existence of these inequities. Instead there must be other, perhaps more intangible, aspects of the careers of these women, not measured by the Census, that are responsible for their generally positive attitudes and outlooks.

We can also wonder why female preferences for employment in the private sector, as well the actual numbers of women in consulting archaeology, are not higher. While there appears to be some imbalance in a woman's access to the position of CEO in larger consulting firms, of all employment settings, the private sector presents women with the most opportunities for salary and career advancement. Yet what we see is that women are setting a course in their training and in their research interests for careers in more traditional, perhaps shrinking, employment sectors of academia and museums, where they are more likely to experience impediments to career advancement. Instead, it is younger men who are structuring their education and tailoring their career trajectories to pursue jobs in this growing sector of archaeological employment.

The Professionalization of American Archaeology: Impacts of the Growth of the Private Sector

For that matter, we can wonder why preference levels of both men and women for private sector employment are not higher. The private sector is perhaps the only growing area of archaeological employment. Archaeologists employed here generally earn higher salaries, and earn them more quickly, than archaeologists employed in other settings. Moreover, while a PhD seems a critical credential for employment and advancement in academia and museums, in the private sector those with a master's degree seem to fare as well as those with PhDs, perhaps better. Considering that it now takes, on average, 13 years after the receipt of a BA to obtain a PhD, compared to only 8 years to obtain an MA as a final degree in archaeology, the private sector would seem, at least based on these criteria, to be an obvious preferred career path.

As in the private sector, those with master's degrees also fare well in government archaeology, where a high proportion of people (both men and women) earn solidly middle-range salaries and have the best access to employee benefits of any archaeological employment sector. These aspects of government employment may account for the higher feeling of financial security of government archaeologists. However, the prominence of some of the least-preferred activities in government jobs (for example, administration, compliance and contract review, and repatriation) may contribute to the somewhat lower degree of

preference for careers in government archaeology seen among Census respondents, as well as the lower proportion of government archaeologists who are highly satisfied with their current careers. In contrast, activities in which private sector archaeologists commonly engage (such as fieldwork, laboratory analysis, and writing for publication) are among those most preferred by archaeologists in all employment settings—another factor that would seem to make the private sector a more preferred employment sector among Census respondents than it apparently is. And while levels of career satisfaction are comparatively high among private sector archaeologists when compared to academics, and while private sector archaeologists state some preference for employment in this arena, academia and museums still figure prominently among the preferred employment settings of consulting archaeologists, as they do for archaeologists employed in all sectors of the archaeological workforce.

Other less tangible aspects of employment in these various settings probably play the major role in coloring people's attitudes about employment in these settings. In particular, the greater freedom of academic and museum archaeologists to choose the research topics they pursue, to have more independence in framing the methods and scheduling of their research, and to tailor the publication of the results of this work to suit their own personal interests may well be primary, as yet unmeasured, elements in shaping both employment preferences and career expectations.

Yet regardless of what archaeologists might prefer or even expect to do in their careers, the fact remains that private sector archaeology has, over the last 10 to 20 years, become a major force in American archaeology. Private sector archaeology employs an increasingly large proportion of the archaeological workforce, it is the source of an enormous volume of archaeological literature, and it draws an exponentially larger amount of outside funding for its support than that applied to the support of more traditional kinds of archaeological research. Moreover, though the private sector does the lion's share of the cultural resource management work conducted in America, we have seen that all employment sectors are increasingly engaged in this kind of work. In all sectors there are a substantial number of people who are producing a large number of CRM reports. In addition, all sectors draw more funds in support of cultural resource management activities than they acquire in support of traditional archaeological research.

The pervasive impact of cultural resource management archaeology raises questions about future directions in archaeological research. There is a substantial amount of variation between the regions, topics, tools, and paradigms that direct the archaeology practiced in different employment sectors. These differences are particularly strong between archaeological research conducted in academia (and, to a lesser extent, museums) and that conducted by both public and private sector archaeologists. One wonders, then, how the growing number of practicing archaeologists employed in private sector settings, and the large amounts of funding available for the kinds of work they do, will affect the focus of future research in American archaeology. Will we see an ever more parochial focus on North American archaeology, greater attention to hunter-gatherer studies and historic archaeology, an abandonment of postmodern approaches to archaeological inquiry? Or will we simply see a sharpening of the already fairly sharply drawn lines between archaeological practice in academia and that practiced by the rest of the profession?

These different research trajectories also raise questions about the kinds of archaeology supported by current archaeological funding. Specifically, we know from the SAA Census data that the profile of activities supported by CRM funds differs little from the activities supported by non-CRM funding. However, the Census did not explore the research focus of the various projects supported by the CRM and non-CRM funding arenas. Given the dominance of academia in the non-CRM funding arena, one can safely posit that these funds are directed to the distinctive kinds of research conducted by academic archaeologists. In particular it is likely that a significant proportion of projects supported by non-CRM funding are conducted outside of North America, either elsewhere in the Americas or in the Old World. It is also likely that the kinds of research questions addressed and the overarching conceptual framework in which these questions are embedded are those more prominently figuring in the research profiles of academic archaeologists. On the other hand, CRM funding is likely to support very different kinds of work, both in terms of region and temporal focus, as well as methods and objectives of the work. Follow-up studies would certainly contribute to our understanding of the impact of the growth of cultural resource management archaeology and funding on the nature of archaeological research in America.

Counterpoising divergent research interests and approaches to archaeological practice brings us to what is perhaps the core defining issue in American archaeology today—the apparently deepening division between the archaeology practiced in academia and museums and that of archaeologists in the private and public sectors. Throughout this book we have seen evidence of a strong divergence between the interests, attitudes, and objectives of archaeology as an academic pursuit and archaeology as a business. As just discussed, the research interests of academic and museum archaeologists are distinctly different from those of public and private sector archaeologists. We have also seen that the day-to-day activities of archaeologists employed in these different settings are quite distinctive from one another. (It is interesting to note, however, that all archaeologists show strong preferences for certain types of activities, and also share a common set of activities

that they would prefer not to do.) The modes of publication and presentation of the results of work conducted in these different settings are also distinctive from one another. And there are differences among archaeologists in these various employment sectors in the degree of participation in and preference for different kinds of professional organizations. Moreover, while all archaeologists share certain concerns, archaeologists in different work settings apparently also differ in their levels of interest in various archaeological policy issues. The comments expressed by Census respondents underscored strong and growing tensions in American archaeology. Most often these tensions were expressed by private and public sector archaeologists as a belief that academic archaeology, and the organizations that represent it, is becoming less and less relevant to the kinds of archaeology that will soon dominate the field. Academics, in turn, expressed concern about the standards of archaeology conducted in the private sector and also about the ability to apply the results of CRM-oriented archaeology to more traditional kinds of archaeological scholarship.

Nowhere was this disjunction more keenly expressed than in private and public sector levels of dissatisfaction with the adequacy of archaeologists' academic training as a preparation for their current careers, as well as in the tendency among these individuals to feel that their current careers do not match the original career expectations they held when entering the profession. Clearly, many of these people feel strongly that the traditional academic training in archaeology is seriously out of step with the realities of archaeological practice in America today. Profiling student preferences and research interests gives special credence to the contention that academics are training future archaeologists primarily for careers in academia. In all cases, the interests and preferences of the students closely resemble those of professional academics, and to a lesser extent museum-based archaeologists. And in all cases, student interests and career preferences are significantly mismatched with those of private and public sector archaeologists. Plainly, these students about to embark on their careers have patterned their research interests and professional expectations after their academic professors. These patterns are all the more interesting, given the apparently high degree of involvement of students in the conduct of CRM archaeology as a means of supporting themselves while they earn their academic degrees.

But perhaps the most tangible manifestation of the growing disconnect between current academic training and the archaeology of the private and public sectors is seen in the educational trajectories of younger men. The steady drop in the proportion of younger men who receive PhDs, and the corresponding increase in the proportion who end their studies at the master's degree level, plus the shifts in the degree-granting institutions, all argue that these men are opting *not* to pursue the traditional graduate education targeted at the receipt of a PhD and a job in academia. Instead, they are consciously preparing themselves for careers outside of the traditional academic and museum settings that dominated the field until quite recently.

Our understanding of these issues would be significantly enhanced by follow-up studies that specifically track both the educational trajectories of students today, as well as their subsequent fortunes as they enter the archaeological workforce. Also needed is a comprehensive review of the curricula of doctoral and master's degree programs to assess how well the academic training of students prepares them for various careers in archaeology. It would also be useful to conduct a more in-depth polling of archaeologists in various professions to discover their attitudes about their training and its relevance to their current careers.

However, as was the case with the impact of the increasing representation of women in archaeology, only with time can we reach a fuller understanding of where the growth of an archaeology centered on the management of cultural resources will take the profession. Over the past century, archaeology in the Americas has grown from an antiquarian pursuit to a major, legitimate social science, making significant contributions to understanding of human society past and present. In the last 20 years a growing public concern with the preservation of natural and cultural resources has built an industry that has vastly increased the scope of archaeology conducted in this country, bringing with it a massive infusion of funding that promises to radically reshape archaeological practice in America. The potential is tremendous for using this opportunity to further broaden our already much-expanded understanding of the human past. So too are the dangers that an increase in the tensions evident in Census data will result in the marginalization of academic archaeology into an arcane pursuit of increasingly abstruse questions about the past, and the divorce of the growing business of archaeology from its scholarly underpinnings.

The SAA Census has provided the empirical basis for documenting the direction and magnitude of major trends in American archaeology. But just as Census data cannot forecast the precise trajectory of where these trends will take the profession, they also are of little utility in predicting the response of the archaeological community to the clear challenges to American archaeology highlighted here. The next decade will be a pivotal time for academics to reassess their role in training tomorrow's archaeologists, as it will be for private sector archaeologists to find ways to reconcile the often conflicting demands of business and scholarship. It will also be an opportunity for organizations, like the Society for American Archaeology, to embrace the challenge of moving from an organization that represents a discipline to one that represents a *profession,* serving as a bridge between a multifaceted membership with diverse interests and objectives. What the SAA Census has accomplished above all is to capture a profile of a profession undergoing a transformation in its composition, it orientation, its aims, its objectives. The trends we have identified and explored here will play an ongoing role, shaping the profile of American archaeology and presenting significant new challenges and opportunities to those who study the past as they move into the next millennium.

Bibliography

Arato, A., and E. Gebhardt. 1978. *The Essential Frankfurt School Reader.* Oxford: Blackwell.

Binford, L. R.1972. *An Archaeological Perspective.* New York: Seminar Press.

Bradley, C., and U. Dahl. 1993. Gender Differences in Careers. In *American Anthropological Association Newsletter* 34(7):34.

Brush, S. 1991. Women in Sciences and Engineering. *American Scientist* 79:404–419.

Claassen, C., ed. 1994. *Women in Archaeology.* Philadelphia: University of Pennsylvania Press.

Davidson, G., and L. C. Skidmore, eds. 1993. *Organizations Encouraging Women in Science and Engineering.* Washington, D.C.: National Research Council.

Evans, J. J. 1988. Management Study of the Short Range and Long Range Needs for Organization and Operation. A report for the Society for American Archaeology prepared by Fairbanks Associates, Alamo, Calif. On file with the Society for American Archaeology.

Flannery, K. V. 1967. Culture History v. Culture Process: A Debate in American Archaeology. *Scientific American* 217:119–122.

Fritz, J. M., and F. Plog. 1970. The Nature of Archaeological Explanation. *American Antiquity* 35:405–412.

Gero, J. 1985. Socio-Politics and the Woman-at-Home Ideology. *American Antiquity* 50:342–350.

———. 1994. Excavation Bias and the Woman-at-Home Ideology. In *Equity Issues for Women in Archaeology.* M. C. Nelson, S. M. Nelson, and A. Wylie, eds. Pp. 37–42. Archaeological Papers of the American Anthropological Association, no. 5.

Gero, J., and M. W. Conkey, eds. 1991. *Engendering Archaeology: Women in Prehistory.* Oxford: Basil Blackwell.

Gifford-Gonzalez, D. 1994. Women in Zooarchaeology. In *Equity Issues for Women in Archaeology.* M. C. Nelson, S. M. Nelson, and A. Wylie, eds. Pp. 157–171. Archaeological Papers of the American Anthropological Association, no. 5.

Hamel, E. A. 1993. Gender and Jobs: The Academic Market in Anthropology 1954–1987. Working Papers of the Program in Population Research, Institute of International Studies, University of California, Berkeley, no. 35.

Kelley, J., and W. Hill. 1994. Relationships Between Graduate Training and Placement. In *Equity Issues for Women in Archaeology.* M. C. Nelson, S. M. Nelson, and A. Wylie, eds. Pp. 47–52. Archaeological Papers of the American Anthropological Association, no. 5.

Kramer, C., and M. Stark. 1994. The Status of Women in Archaeology. In *Equity Issues for Women in Archaeology.* M. C. Nelson, S. M. Nelson, and A. Wylie, eds. Pp. 17–22. Archaeological Papers of the American Anthropological Association, no. 5.

Lees, W. B. 1991. Results of the Membership Survey, Society for Professional Archaeologists. Report on file with the Society for Professional Archaeologists.

Leone, M. P., P. B. Potter, and P. A. Schackel. 1987. Toward a Critical Archaeology. *Current Anthropology* 28:283–302.

Matyas, M. L., and L. S. Dix, eds. 1992. *Science and Engineering Programs: On Target for Women?* National Research Council, Washington, D.C.: National Academy Press.

McGuire, R. H., and R. Paynter, eds. 1991. *The Archaeology of Inequality.* Oxford: Basil Blackwell.

Meltzer, D. J., D. D. Fowler, and J. A. Sabloff. 1986. *American Archaeology Past and Future: A Celebration of the Society for American Archaeology, 1935–1985.* Washington, D.C.: Smithsonian Institution Press.

Nelson, M. C., S. M. Nelson, and A. Wylie, eds. 1994. *Equity Issues for Women in Archaeology.* Archaeological Papers of the American Anthropological Association, no. 5.

Noble, V. E. 1992. A Report on Two Direct Mail Surveys of the Archaeological Profession. Report on file with the Society for Professional Archaeologists.

Ogilvie, M. B. 1986. *Women in Science: Antiquity Through the Nineteenth Century. A Biographical Dictionary with Annotated Bibliography.* Cambridge, Mass.: MIT Press.

Patterson, T. 1986. The Last Sixty Years: Toward a Social History of Americanist Archaeology. *American Anthropologist* 88:7–26.

Plog, S., and D. Rice. 1993. PhD Programs in Archaeology: Results of an SAA Bulletin Survey. *SAA Bulletin* 11(1):8–11.

Rossiter, M. 1982. *Women Scientists in America: Struggles and Strategies to 1940.* Baltimore, Md.: Johns Hopkins Press.

———. 1995. *Women Scientists in America: Before Affirmative Action, 1940.* Baltimore, Md.: Johns Hopkins Press.

Schiffer, M. B. 1980. *Behavioral Archeology.* San Francisco: Academic Press.

Sonnert, G. (with the assistance of G. Holton). 1995a. *Gender Differences in Science Careers: The Project Access Study.* New Brunswick, N.J.: Rutgers University Press.

———. 1995b. *Who Succeeds in Science? The Gender Dimension.* New Brunswick, N.J.: Rutgers University Press.

Sonnert, G., and G. Holton. 1996. Career Patterns of Women and Men in the Sciences. *American Scientist* 84:63–71.

Steward, J. H. 1955. *Theory of Culture Change: The Methodology of Multilinear Evolution.* Urbana: University of Illinois Press.

Thomas, D. H. 1986. *Refiguring Anthropology: First Principles of Probability and Statistics.* Prospect Heights, Ill.: Waveland Press, Inc.

Thomas, D. H., ed. 1989. *Columbian Consequences: Volume 1. Archaeological and Historical Perspectives on the Spanish Borderlands West.* Washington, D.C.: Smithsonian Institution Press.

———. 1990. *Columbian Consequences: Volume 2. Archaeological and Historical Perspectives on the Spanish Borderlands East.* Washington, D.C.: Smithsonian Institution Press.

———. 1991. *Columbian Consequences: Volume 3. The Spanish Borderlands in Pan-American Perspective.* Washington, D.C.: Smithsonian Institution Press.

Wall, D., and N. A. Rothschild. 1995. Report on the Membership Questionnaire, Society for Historical Archaeology. *SHA Newsletter* 28(4):24–31.

Watson, P. J., S. A. LeBlanc, and C. L. Redman. 1971. *Explanation in Archaeology: An Explicitly Scientific Approach.* New York: Columbia University Press.

Webster, C. M., and M. L. Burton. 1992. Summary report on the Academic Employment of Women in Anthropology. *Anthropology Newsletters* 33(2):1, 21, 23. Washington, D.C.: American Anthropological Association.

Willey, G. R., and P. Phillips. 1958. *Method and Theory in American Archaeology.* London: Thames and Hudson.

Wylie, A. 1994. The Trouble with Numbers: Workplace Climate Issues in Archaeology. In *Equity Issues for Women in Archaeology.* M. C. Nelson, S. M. Nelson, and A. Wylie, eds. Pp. 65–71. Archaeological Papers of the American Anthropological Association, no. 5.

Zeder, M. A. 1997a. The American Archaeologist: Results of the 1994 SAA Census. *SAA Bulletin* 15(2):12–17.

———. 1997b. The American Archaeologist: Results of the 1994 SAA Census (Redux). *SAA Bulletin* 15(4): 26–31.

Appendix

Society for American Archaeology Census

SOCIETY FOR AMERICAN ARCHAEOLOGY
CENSUS

Please write number that appears on the top line of your mailing address. .... _____

A. *Membership Status*

1. If currently a member of the SAA, what is the status of your membership?

   Regular .... [ ]   International .... [ ]
   Student .... [ ]   Life .... [ ]
   Joint .... [ ]   Avocational .... [ ]
   Retired .... [ ]   Associate .... [ ]

2. If not currently a member, have you ever been a member of the SAA? .... YES [ ] NO [ ]
3. If a former member, how many years were you a member? .... _____
4. When did you terminate your membership in the SAA? .... 19____

B. *Demographic Information*

1. What year were you born? .... _____
2. What is your gender?

   Female .... [ ]
   Male .... [ ]

3. What is your family status?

   Single/Divorced/Widowed .... [ ]
   Married/Ongoing Partnership .... [ ]
   Number of Dependents .... _____

4. If you are married or in an ongoing partnership, is your partner also pursuing a career in
   archaeology? .... YES [ ] NO [ ]

5. How would you characterize your ethnic heritage? (Check one that applies.)

   African American .... [ ]   Hispanic American .... [ ]
   Asian American .... [ ]   Native American .... [ ]
   European American .... [ ]   Other (Please specify) ..... _____ [ ]

6. How would you characterize the socio-economic context in which you grew up? (Check one that applies.)

   Upper Class .... [ ]   Lower Middle Class .... [ ]
   Upper Middle Class .... [ ]   Lower Class .... [ ]
   Middle Class .... [ ]   Other (Please specify) ..... _____ [ ]

7. In what Country/State or Province do you currently reside? (Use state codes when applicable, e.g. CT,ON,JAL)

   Country .... _____   State/Province .... _____

C. *Training and Employment*

1. What is your current status in archaeology? (Check all that apply.)

   Professional Archaeologist .... [ ]
   Student .... [ ]
   Amateur/Avocational .... [ ]
   Other (Please specify)_____ .... [ ]

2. List the year, field, and degree granting institution for the degrees you hold.

   BA/BS .... 19__ Field: _____ School: _____
   MA/MS .... 19__ Field: _____ School: _____
   PhD .... 19__ Field: _____ School: _____
   Other (Specify) _____ 19__ Field: _____ School: _____

1

3. For each of the past 5 years, please check your work settings. (Use % of time devoted to each setting if more than one apply. At a minimum please answer for 1993.)

	1993	1992	1991	1990	1989
Private Foundation	___%	___%	___%	___%	___%
Private Consulting Firm	___%	___%	___%	___%	___%
Independent Consultant/Contractor	___%	___%	___%	___%	___%
Museum - Federal/State/Local	___%	___%	___%	___%	___%
Museum - University	___%	___%	___%	___%	___%
Museum - Private	___%	___%	___%	___%	___%
Federal Agency (Please Name)_____	___%	___%	___%	___%	___%
State Agency (Please Name) _____	___%	___%	___%	___%	___%
County/City Agency (Name) _____	___%	___%	___%	___%	___%
Community College	___%	___%	___%	___%	___%
University Based CRM	___%	___%	___%	___%	___%
University (Undergraduate Only)	___%	___%	___%	___%	___%
University (Including Graduate)	___%	___%	___%	___%	___%
Retired	___%	___%	___%	___%	___%
Other (Please Specify)_____	___%	___%	___%	___%	___%

4. For each of the past 5 years, what have been your general responsibilities? (Use % if more than one apply. At a minimum please answer for 1993.)

	1993	1992	1991	1990	1989
Administration	___%	___%	___%	___%	___%
Archival/Library/Museum Research	___%	___%	___%	___%	___%
Collections Documentation	___%	___%	___%	___%	___%
Collections Management	___%	___%	___%	___%	___%
Compliance Review	___%	___%	___%	___%	___%
Contract Oversight	___%	___%	___%	___%	___%
Course Work	___%	___%	___%	___%	___%
Exhibition	___%	___%	___%	___%	___%
Field Work	___%	___%	___%	___%	___%
Laboratory Work	___%	___%	___%	___%	___%
Public Education/Interpretation	___%	___%	___%	___%	___%
Repatriation Related Activities	___%	___%	___%	___%	___%
Teaching	___%	___%	___%	___%	___%
Writing Proposals	___%	___%	___%	___%	___%
Writing Reports/Publications	___%	___%	___%	___%	___%
Other (Please Specify)_____	___%	___%	___%	___%	___%

5. What is your current position in archaeology (e.g. Professor, Curator, Consultant)? .... _____
6. How many years have your been in this position? .... _____
7. What is your current title (e.g. Asst. Prof., Lab Tech., Crew Chief)? .... _____
8. How many years have you held this title? .... _____
9. How would you characterize your level of satisfaction with your current position? (Check only one.)

Highly Satisfied .... [ ]   Marginally Satisfied .... [ ]
Satisfied .... [ ]   Unsatisfied .... [ ]

10. Are you satisfied that your undergraduate and graduate training prepared you adequately for your present position in archaeology? (Check only one.)

Highly Satisfied .... [ ]   Marginally Satisfied .... [ ]
Satisfied .... [ ]   Unsatisfied .... [ ]

11. Is your present position consistent with your projected career path? .... YES [ ] NO [ ]

12. What is your preferred work setting? (Use % if more than one apply.)
     Private Foundation .... ____%
     Private Consulting Firm .... ____%
     Independent Consultant/Contractor .... ____%
     Museum - Federal/State/Local .... ____%
     Museum - University .... ____%
     Museum - Private .... ____%
     Federal Agency (Please Name)_____ ...... ____%
     State Agency (Please Name)_____ ...... ____%
     County/City Agency (Please Name) _____ .... ____%
     Community College .... ____%
     University Based CRM .... ____%
     University (Undergraduate Only) .... ____%
     University (Including Graduate) .... ____%
     Retired .... ____%
     Other (Please Specify)_____ ...... ____%

13. What is your preference of general responsibilities? (Use % if more than one apply.)
     Administration .... ____%
     Archival/Library/Museum Research .... ____%
     Collections Documentation .... ____%
     Collections Management .... ____%
     Compliance Review .... ____%
     Contract Oversight .... ____%
     Course Work .... ____%
     Exhibition .... ____%
     Field Work .... ____%
     Laboratory Work .... ____%
     Public Education/Interpretation .... ____%
     Repatriation Related Activities .... ____%
     Teaching .... ____%
     Writing Proposals .... ____%
     Writing Reports/Publications .... ____%
     Other (Please Specify)_____ ...... ____%

14. To the nearest $10,000, what is your current gross income from all sources, both archaeology related and non-archaeological?

$0-10	$10-20	$20-30	$30-40	$40-50	$50-60	$60-70	$70-80	$80-90	$90-100	$100+
[ ]	[ ]	[ ]	[ ]	[ ]	[ ]	[ ]	[ ]	[ ]	[ ]	[ ]

15. What % of your current income, as reported above, comes from archaeology related sources? .... ____%

16. What % of your current income comes from non-archaeology related sources? .... ____%
     Type of Employment .... _____

17. What % of your total work effort in archaeology receives no financial compensation? .... ____%

18. Does your current gross income meet your basic financial needs? .... YES [ ] NO [ ]

3

19. How many different positions have you held over the past 5 years, either sequentially or simultaneously? (Excluding promotions within the same job; e.g. asst. prof. to assoc. prof. in the same institution.)

In Archaeology . . . . _____

Outside of Archaeology . . . . _____

20. Do you currently receive job benefits?

Health benefits (Self only)	[ ]	Life Insurance	[ ]
Health benefits (Family)	[ ]	Savings Plan	[ ]
Retirement benefits	[ ]	Other (Please specify)_____	[ ]

21. How many years have you been earning income from archaeology related work? . . . . _____

22. What was your yearly income in your first professional position in archaeology?

Salary (To the nearest $10,000) . . . .$_____

Year Earned . . . . .19_____

Type of Employment . . . . _____

23. If employed by a university, is your position:

Non-tenure track	[ ]	Tenured	[ ]
Tenure track	[ ]	Other	[ ]

24. If engaged in teaching, how many courses do you teach in an academic year? . . . . _____
25. On average, how many students are enrolled in your largest class? . . . . _____
26. On average, how many students are enrolled in your smallest class? . . . . _____

27. What type of department are you employed or, if a student, are you enrolled in?

Anthropology	[ ]	Sociology/Anthropology	[ ]
Archaeology	[ ]	Other (Please specify)_____	[ ]

28. How many thesis committees do you serve on as either chair or a committee member?

Senior Honors (Chair)	___	Masters Thesis (Member)	___
Senior Honors (Member)	___	PhD Dissertation (Chair)	___
Masters Thesis (Chair)	___	PhD Dissertation (Member)	___

D. Archaeological Research Interests

1. What is your primary geographical area of interest? (Select no more than two. Please rank areal interests with 1 for your primary interest and 2 for your secondary interest.)

North America - Northeast	[ ]	Arctic	[ ]
North America - Mid-Atlantic	[ ]	Mexico/Central America	[ ]
North America - Southeast	[ ]	South America	[ ]
North America - Midwest	[ ]	Europe	[ ]
North America - Plains	[ ]	Africa	[ ]
North America - Southwest	[ ]	West Asia	[ ]
North America - California	[ ]	East/South Asia	[ ]
North America - Northwest Coast/Alaska	[ ]	Oceania	[ ]
North America - Canada	[ ]	Not Applicable	[ ]

2. What are the temporal spans and/or general time periods of primary interest to you? (No more than two. Please specify if using B.C/A.D or B.P. when listing dates. Avoid specific regional phase names.)

B.C./A.D or B.P. Dates _____to_____   _____to_____

General Phase Name (e.g. Paleolithic) _____   _____

4

3. Which of the following best characterizes your general interest in archaeology (Select no more than two. Please rank interests with 1 for your primary interest and 2 for your secondary interest.)

Prehistoric Archaeology .... [ ]   Archaeological History/Philosophy/Theory .. [ ]
Historical Archaeology .... [ ]   Archaeological Methods .... [ ]
Ethnoarchaeology .... [ ]   Other (Specify) . _____ [ ]
Experimental Archaeology .... [ ]   Other (Specify) .. _____ [ ]

4. Which of the following best characterizes your more specific interest in archaeology (Select no more than two. Please rank interests with 1 for your primary interest and 2 for your secondary interest.)

Hunter-Gatherers/Paleolithic-Mesolithic . [ ]   Colonial/Historic Period .... [ ]
Village Farmers/Neolithic .... [ ]   19th/20th Century Urban Archaeology ..... [ ]
Complex Societies/States .... [ ]   Other (Specify) . _____ [ ]
Protohistoric-Contact Period .... [ ]   Other (Specify) . _____ [ ]

5. What are your primary research tools? (Select no more than two. Please rank with 1 for your first choice and 2 for your second choice.)

Ceramic Analysis .... [ ]   Zooarchaeology .... [ ]
Lithic Analysis .... [ ]   Material Analysis (Petrography etc.) .... [ ]
Spatial Analysis .... [ ]   Organic/Inorganic Chemical Analysis ...... [ ]
Geoarchaeology .... [ ]   Other (Specify) . _____ [ ]
Archaeobotany .... [ ]   Other (Specify) . _____ [ ]

6. Recognizing that the categories below are not mutually exclusive, if you were asked to label the type of archaeology that you practice, or the "school" of archaeology to which you belong, what label would you adopt? (Select no more than two. Please rank with 1 for your first choice and a 2 for your second choice.)

Culture History .... [ ]   Marxist Archaeology .... [ ]
Cultural Ecology .... [ ]   Critical Theory .... [ ]
Evolutionary Archaeology .... [ ]   Gender Studies in Archaeology .... [ ]
Processual Archaeology .... [ ]   Other (Specify) . _____ [ ]
Post-Processual Archaeology .... [ ]   Other (Specify) . _____ [ ]

7. With which of the following non-archaeological disciplines do you have the most interaction? (Select no more than two. Please rank with 1 for your first choice and 2 for your second choice.)

Social Anthropology .... [ ]   Geological Sciences .... [ ]
Biological Anthropology .... [ ]   History .... [ ]
Linguistics .... [ ]   Physics/Chemistry/ Material Sciences ...... [ ]
Biological Sciences .... [ ]   Other (Specify) . _____ [ ]
Geography .... [ ]   Other (Specify) . _____ [ ]

E. Publication and Public Presentations

1. How many publications have you had in the last 5 years?

CRM Reports/Monographs .... ____
Books/Monographs .... ____
Book Chapters & Journal Articles .... ____
Other Publications .... ____

2. How many papers have you presented at archaeological meetings in the last 5 years?

SAA Meetings .... ____
Other Conferences .... ____

3. How many papers have you presented to the general public in the last 5 years? .... ____

F. Participation in Professional Organizations

1. How many archaeological organizations are you a member of?
   Number of national/international organizations (e.g. SAA, AAA, SOPA, UISPP) . . . . ____
   Number of regional organizations (e.g. SEAC, Plains) . . . . ____
   Number of state/local organizations (e.g. Iowa Arch. Soc., Narragansett A. S.) . . . . ____

2. How many non-archaeological professional organizations are you a member of? (e.g. GSA) . . . . ____

3. Please list the national/international organizations to which you belong. (No more than 4)

   _____   _____

   _____   _____

4. Please list the regional organizations to which you belong. (No more than 4)

   _____   _____

   _____   _____

5. Please list the state/local organizations to which you belong. (No more than 4)

   _____   _____

   _____   _____

6. Please list the non-archaeological professional organizations to which you belong. (No more than 4)

   _____   _____

   _____   _____

7. Of all the organizations to which you belong (archaeological and non-archaeological), which do you feel best represents
   your interests and needs. (List only one.) . . . .   _____

8. Are you certified by the Society of Professional Archaeologists? . . . . .YES [ ] NO [ ]

9. Have you ever been, or are you now, a member of the governing bodies of national, regional, state, or local associations?
   (Check all that apply.)
   SAA Executive Board . . . . [ ]
   Any SAA Committee . . . . [ ]
   Other Archaeological National/International Organizations' Executive Board . . . . [ ]
   Other Archaeological National/International Organizations' Committees . . . . [ ]
   Regional/State/Local Archaeological Organizations' Executive Board . . . . [ ]
   Regional/State/Local Archaeological Organizations' Committees . . . . [ ]
   Non-archaeological Organizations' Executive Board . . . . [ ]
   Non-archaeological Organizations' Committees . . . . [ ]

G. Funding History

1. To how many sources have you applied and how much funding have you received over the last 5 years for archaeological work that is not contract or preservation related? (To the nearest $1,000) .... $_____

Source	# Grants Applied For	# Grants Awarded	# Awarded As P.I.*	Amount Received**
NSF - Pre-Doctoral***				
NSF				
NEH				
Other Federal (Specify)				
State				
Local				
University				
Private				
Other (Specify)				

* - Number of successful grant applications in which you served as principal investigator or co-P.I.
** - Total amount received for your own work
*** - Graduate Studies support and dissertation improvement grants

2. To how many sources have you applied and how much funding have you received over the last 5 years for contract or preservation related funding for your work? (To the nearest $1,000) .... $_____

Source	# Grants Applied For	# Grants Awarded	# Awarded As P.I.*	Amount Received**
Federal Agency				
State Agency				
Local Agency				
University				
Private Development				
Other (Specify)				

* - Number of successful grant applications in which you served as principal investigator or co-P.I.
** - Total amount received for your own work

3. What kinds of archaeological work have you received funding for in the last 5 years? (Check all that apply.)

CRM-Related Field Work .... [ ]   Non-CRM Field Work .... [ ]
CRM-Related Laboratory Work .... [ ]   Non-CRM Laboratory Work .... [ ]
CRM-Related Collections Curation .... [ ]   Non-CRM Collections Curation .... [ ]
CRM-Related Archival Work .... [ ]   Non-CRM Archival Work .... [ ]
Other CRM Related Work (Specify) . _____ [ ]   Other Non-CRM (Specify) . _____ [ ]

4. What kinds of internal funding are available to you from your home institution?

Funding for Field Work .... [ ]   Funding for Conference Attendance .... [ ]
Funding for Laboratory/Archival Work .... [ ]   Other Funding (Please Specify) . _____ [ ]

H. Help us draft the next SAA survey.

Next year we will be distributing a second survey asking for your opinion on how well the SAA currently serves your interests and your needs, and where you think the Society should focus its energies in the future. We are currently in the process of drafting that survey and would like your input on the kind of issues you would like to see addressed. Are you concerned about the involvement of the SAA in education or legislation? Do you have concerns about SAA publications that you think should be included in the survey? Are there issues about the basic mission and scope of the SAA that should be put before archaeologists in this survey instrument? If so, please let us know in the space provided below. (Use an additional sheet of paper if necessary.)

I. Is there anything else?

Please make any other comments and observations you would like to make about this census form or this survey project below. (Use an additional sheet of paper if necessary.)

8

THANK YOU!

For taking this time to respond to this census.

Your input is critical in forming a full, balanced picture of our profession.

Please return this form no later than:

March 15, 1994

To:

SAA CENSUS
900 Second Street, NE, Suite 12
Washington, D.C. 20002

Please be sure to record the number that appears on the top line of your mailing address in the space provided on the first page of your census form.